Worlds of Consumption

Series Editors
Hartmut Berghoff
Institute for Economic and Social History
University of Göttingen
Göttingen, Germany

Uwe Spiekermann
University of Göttingen
Göttingen, Germany

Published in association with the German Historical Institute, Washington, DC, USA. This series brings together historical research on consumption and consumerism in the modern era, especially the twentieth century, and with a particular focus on comparative and transnational studies. It aims to make research available in English from an increasingly internationalized and interdisciplinary field. The history of consumption offers a vital link among diverse fields of history and other social sciences, because modern societies are consumer societies whose political, cultural, social, and economic structures and practices are bound up with the history of consumption. *Worlds of Consumption* highlights and explores these linkages, which deserve wide attention, since they shape who we are as individuals and societies.

More information about this series at
http://www.palgrave.com/gp/series/14382

Jan Logemann · Gary Cross ·
Ingo Köhler
Editors

Consumer Engineering, 1920s–1970s

Marketing between Expert Planning and Consumer Responsiveness

Editors
Jan Logemann
Institute for Economic and Social History
University of Göttingen
Göttingen, Germany

Gary Cross
Department of History
Pennsylvania State University
University Park, PA, USA

Ingo Köhler
Institute for Economic and Social History
University of Göttingen
Göttingen, Germany

Worlds of Consumption
ISBN 978-3-030-14566-8 ISBN 978-3-030-14564-4 (eBook)
https://doi.org/10.1007/978-3-030-14564-4

Library of Congress Control Number: 2019933871

Cover illustration: Roy Scott/Alamy Stock Photo

This Palgrave Macmillan imprint is published by the registered company Springer Nature Switzerland AG
The registered company address is: Gewerbestrasse 11, 6330 Cham, Switzerland

Contents

List of Contributors

Karin Carlsson Department of History, Stockholm University, Stockholm, Sweden

Gary Cross Department of History, Pennsylvania State University, University Park, PA, USA

Sabine Effosse Department of History, University of Paris Nanterre, Nanterre, France

Bernard Gallagher Independent Historian, Laurel, MD, USA

Andrew Godley Henley Business School, University of Reading, Reading, UK

Keith Heron Henley Business School, University of Reading, Reading, UK

Orsi Husz Department of Economic History, Uppsala University, Uppsala, Sweden

Ingo Köhler Institute for Economic and Social History, University of Göttingen, Göttingen, Germany

Jan Logemann Institute for Economic and Social History, University of Göttingen, Göttingen, Germany

Joseph Malherek George Washington University, Washington, DC, USA

Giselle Nath De Standaard, Groot-Bijgaarden, Belgium

Kevin Rick EWE AG, Oldenburg, Germany

Uwe Spiekermann University of Göttingen, Göttingen, Germany

Thomas Turner Independent Historian, London, UK

List of Figures

List of Tables

CHAPTER 1

Beyond the Mad Men: Consumer Engineering and the Rise of Marketing Management, 1920s–1970s

Jan Logemann, Gary Cross, and Ingo Köhler

By the middle of the twentieth century, corporate marketing had become a growing professional field and marketing experts increasingly shaped the way in which American companies understood their customers. No longer focused solely on sales and advertising, professional marketing increasingly entailed a broad array of business functions from product development and design to pricing and distribution. Marketing departments grew in number and size, and they increasingly relied on systematic market research to develop merchandise that fit changing consumer tastes. An entire new group of professional experts had appeared, offering their services as advertising consultants, market analysts, and market prognosticators to the consumer goods industry. As a "social technology," marketing now aimed not only at understanding consumers and analyzing their needs but also at shaping their desires. Especially since the economic crisis of the 1930s, marketers traded on the promise that they could socially "engineer" consumers and their behavior.[1]

The ascendancy of the "mad men" in mid-twentieth-century America—made famous more recently by the popular television series—has already received attention from historians.[2] Throughout the postwar boom years, the advertising industry on Madison Avenue developed novel ways of appealing to segments of the populace—from youths to African Americans—that had

J. Logemann (✉) · I. Köhler
Institute for Economic and Social History, University of Göttingen, Göttingen, Germany

G. Cross
Department of History, Pennsylvania State University, University Park, PA, USA

J. Logemann et al. (eds.), *Consumer Engineering, 1920s–1970s*,
Worlds of Consumption, https://doi.org/10.1007/978-3-030-14564-4_1

not previously been specifically targeted as consumers. Advertisers attempted to probe ever more deeply and consciously into the minds and psychological motivations of consumers.[3] Already in the 1920s, the rise of professional U.S. advertising agencies had a transatlantic dimension, and historians of European business have discussed the American agencies as spearheads of an "Americanization" of European marketing.[4] Yet these (m)ad men on Madison Avenue were but the tip of the iceberg for a broader shift in modern marketing on both sides of the Atlantic, which saw professionalized and increasingly creative approaches in areas ranging from market research and industrial design to corporate sales strategies and retail presentation. Looking beyond the (m)ad men employed by advertising agencies, we can find a broad array of expert professionals who as commercial designers, consumer psychologists, sales managers, or market researchers contributed to the rise of new systematic and creative forms of consumer-oriented marketing. These experts confidently saw themselves as "consumer engineers," selling their services and an enticing world of goods to consumers and corporations alike.

Marketing increasingly dissociated itself from older notions of educating people on how to make use of new products. Advertising gradually turned away from pure technical instructions and simple accentuations of a good's quality and benefits. Increasingly, marketing tried to touch the consumer emotionally, stressing the added values of social distinction, aesthetic appeal, and satisfaction of desires. The attempt to reach consumers at the level of their unconscious wishes and inner motivations required a new toolbox of social research methods and psychological analysis. The basic intention of consumer research, gathering information to better understand consumer behavior, was at times superseded by attempts at manipulating consumers. The rise of innovative research and the roots of marketing professionalization in part intersected with an overblown belief in the power of psychological methods to direct and control consumer behavior. The disparate nature of this transitional phase in the history of marketing has often been noted in the literature, but never systematically analyzed. The intention of this book is to give more concrete contours to this period of "consumer engineering."

We locate its beginnings within the interwar era with its crises and technocratic reform responses on both sides of the Atlantic. *Consumer Engineering: A New Technology for Prosperity* was the title of a 1932 book by two prominent U.S. marketing experts, Roy Sheldon and Egmont Arens.[5] As commercial designers and advertising men, the authors urged American businesses to overcome the Great Depression by creating consumer demand with concerted marketing efforts, for example, by consciously integrating industrial design or state-of-the-art psychological research into marketing strategies. The streamlined shapes of 1930s industrial goods reflected their agenda as much as the motivation research or the subliminal psychology of advertising appeals did in subsequent decades. Consumer engineering, to its cheerleaders, promised to increase sales and usher in a period of abundance and "adjusted life" in newfound affluence. Increasingly intricate market research and the exploration of consumer psychology aimed directly at "making goods desirable" and at inducing change in taste and "obsolescence."[6] Consumer engineering claimed to put "the consumer" and his or her wishes ever more directly at the center of corporate marketing strategies by offering a wider range of products, pricing, and carefully tailored advertising. This understanding advanced a paradigm shift from narrowly conceived production-led strategies toward more consumer-oriented marketing management that—for the first time—took consumer needs and desires seriously as an important market factor.

Consumer engineering's cautious beginnings in the interwar years ushered in a period of self-assured marketing expansion after World War II. To their postwar critics, the consumer engineers were nothing more than "hidden persuaders" who manipulated consumers into a rat race of unending consumption through accelerated product cycles and "planned obsolescence."[7] Mid-century merchandising, however, did not simply amount to corporate brainwashing but instead reflected a newfound belief in the power of professional marketing. Marketers now claimed they possessed the tools to avert market saturation and other forms of crisis. Sophisticated professional methods, consumer engineers claimed, would allow them to predict and even shape consumer behavior almost at will. With expanding full-service advertising agencies, new design studios, and market research laboratories and marketing departments emerging at consumer goods corporations, the decades from the 1930s to the 1960s came to represent a kind of "golden age" of self-confident modern marketing that ultimately reached beyond the United States to affect the entire Atlantic World.

The object of this volume is to transcend the familiar, but increasingly barren debate between proponents of advertising and mass consumption, who saw a vehicle for democratic capitalism, and detractors of the new marketing practices, who saw nothing more than consumer manipulation.[8] Instead, we ask more broadly about how and to what degree modern marketing managed to shape consumption practices and the culture of mass consumption, and in what ways marketing was merely a response to wider social and cultural dynamics. Simply put, did marketing shape the market or did the social dynamics of the market shape the marketing concepts? We seek to reassess the history of consumer engineering in a comparative and transnational framework that views the rise of marketing as part of a broader mid-century era of "high modernity," or what might be called the "age of engineers," which spans from the interwar decades to the 1960s.[9] At a time when experts and technocrats were engaged in schemes to manage and change politics, society, and the economy based on an optimistic belief in the power of sciences and social sciences, marketing professionals were but one group among many engaged in attempts to "engineer" social relations. We still do not know much about their motives, methods, and professional self-perceptions, however. We therefore need to put the key economic actors and professions firmly at the center of historical research.

Exploring the work of store and product designers or the strategies of fashion or automobile companies, a more ambiguous picture of consumer engineering emerges. What critics saw as marketing manipulation can also be seen as part of a mid-century celebration of the potential of the sciences and the call for economic predictability through the steering of aggregate and individual demand. Corporate market making, Andrew Godley and Keith Heron suggest in their chapter, entailed genuine attempts to establish trust and goodwill between consumers and corporations in order to make consumer markets function. Thus, we transcend both the focus on advertising prevalent in earlier studies of corporate marketing and the narrow issue of whether merchandisers meet or manipulate demand.[10] Instead, we look at the specific goals of innovators, at the challenges and problems faced by consumer product firms as they engaged increasingly stratified and fragmented consumer markets, and at the complex efforts of consumer movements to respond to marketing innovations.

Consumer Engineering as a Phase in Marketing in the United States and Europe

Mid-century consumer engineering emerges as a distinct phase of acceleration and professionalization in a longer history of consumer marketing and an increasingly "fast capitalism" since the late nineteenth century. Looking at developed consumer societies in North America and Europe, especially at mid-century, the essays in this volume address four interrelated sets of issues pertaining to the scope, periodization, and character of consumer engineering, as well to its broader implications for business and social history in the transatlantic world.

First, we examine how changing notions of "the consumer" among marketing professionals impacted marketing developments in particular and modern consumer culture more generally. Tracing the history of efforts to engineer consumers and looking at the proponents and detractors of this work sheds new light on the development of mass consumption in the transatlantic world during the crucial period between the Great Depression of the 1930s and the multiple crises of the 1970s. Wedged between these two dramatic downturns in economic development were both the global catastrophe of World War II and the "miraculous" postwar boom years, which both in their own way contributed to an unparalleled expansion of mass consumption across the Atlantic World.[11]

This book emphasizes the important linkages between interwar and postwar marketing developments. It identifies a longer, mid-century period of "high modernity" in marketing, which was characterized by a sustained belief in the powers of science, technology, and planning to bring about widespread improvements in living conditions, an abundance of material goods, and continuously new and improved consumer products. Such notions coalesced with a specific Fordist mode of consumption based on household rationalization and mass-produced durable goods. This model of high modernist mass consumption, many economists and policy makers hoped at the time, would be the engine of perpetual growth, and marketing would thus provide a valuable social service.[12] This was the world in which consumer engineers rose to prominence. While historians have long focused on mass production as a central pillar of the mass consumption economy, new approaches to mass marketing from product merchandising to retailing and financing were equally important. What impact did the professionalization of market research, industrial design, and other aspects of modern marketing have on mid-century mass consumption? And what role was attributed to "the consumer" within a broader framework of technocratic high modernity?

Second, the emergence of consumer engineering and the professionalization of marketing were not particular to American consumer capitalism, as is so often assumed in works that posit marketing as a central facet of "Americanization."[13] These trends need to be placed in a transatlantic context instead, so we ask about transnational transfers of marketing ideas and practices between Europe and the United States and vice versa. What impact, for example, did new consumer engineering practices have on European economies at a time when American consumer culture was making cross-Atlantic inroads in the context of the Cold War? Only a few studies have thus far traced the transatlantic diffusion of marketing practices and know-how at the company level. Postwar marketing has only recently attracted the attention of European business history. The present volume significantly adds to this literature by studying both the multidirectional transfers of marketing ideas and their concrete, practical application.[14] Who were the principal actors involved in relaying marketing innovations? How did expert discourses translate into marketing practices at the company level?

Third, understood as a distinct phase of transatlantic marketing history, consumer engineering represented a shift toward "scientific marketing" and "marketing management" in both the United States and Europe.[15] Reassessing existing periodization in marketing history, which currently directs particular attention either to the decades around 1900 or to the 1960s and 1970s, the present volume asks when the corporate operationalization and institutionalization of consumer-oriented strategies truly emerged, that is, when the influence of marketing experts on corporate decision-making processes made itself felt. We try to trace the adaption and implementation of modern marketing in business practice. When did these experts consciously begin to carve out and define their roles in everyday business processes, laying claim to specific expertise in understanding and analyzing consumers? Professional advertising had seen growing influence since the late 1800s,[16] but the methodological tool kit of marketing vastly expanded in the time period under consideration, with dramatic leaps, for example, in consumer psychology, motivation research, and survey statistics. Following the Great Depression, marketing experts increasingly strove to impact decision-making not only in sales and distribution but also in pricing and styling as well as in engineering and product development.

By the later 1960s, as marketers increasingly claimed to serve individual consumer needs and desires, the overly boastful claims of consumer engineering receded, especially its confidence in being able to anticipate and manipulate consumer needs. New historiographical thinking about the question of manipulating or accommodating consumers has to recognize this change. Now, marketing management intended to create, engineer, and market goods with the consumer in mind and to arrange management processes in a way that put consumer demand front and center. But was the consumer truly in charge? To some degree, the contributions assembled here suggest that companies had to work hard to gain consumer trust and confidence, which were key to successful market making. For producers, understanding and engineering markets were instrumental in managing risk, especially as competition rose in increasingly saturated markets. Thus, on the one hand, "fashion intermediaries" such as department store buyers and magazine art directors kept producers in touch with changing consumer tastes.[17] On the other hand, consumer engineering promoted the rise of "consumer experts" who claimed to speak and act on behalf of consumers, whether as part of a firm, as a consumer organization, or as consumption scholars and state regulators.[18] The rise of marketing management did not necessarily mean that consumers substantially gained in agency in the marketplace, but the broader analytic framework of this book takes us beyond the old dichotomy of agency versus manipulation in productive ways.

Fourth, the tension between expert control and consumer agency brings us back to broader questions regarding the interrelation between economic and social change. Historians of consumer culture can interpret the era of consumer engineering with its marketing-driven product innovations and frequent style changes as one stage in a longer trend toward increased acceleration in the turnover of ever new consumer goods or as a new form of "fast capitalism," as Gary Cross suggests in this volume. The roots of this development may be traced to early intuitive, but still unsystematic forms of product engineering and novelty marketing. These date back to the late nineteenth century and include such developments as extensive and continuously updated catalogs of recordings, the early "software" accompanying rapidly changing phonograph players. In other words, many trends that characterize consumer engineering did not actually originate during the middle decades of the twentieth century but instead became ever more dynamic and prevalent then.[19]

To what degree corporate marketing practices were responsible for this process of social and cultural acceleration or to what degree consumers themselves also had a collective and active hand in it remains contested.

Public policy certainly set the parameters for the expansion of mass consumption, as Lizabeth Cohen has shown for America's "consumers' republic."[20] Consumer practices and tastes had their own autonomous cultural dynamics as well. Marketers and advertisers could try to influence or co-opt consumers, targeting specific segments such as youth, but rarely could they manipulate consumers at will.[21] Department store buyers, audience scouts, and other fashion intermediaries had long engaged in tracking the pulse of shifting consumer tastes for business. Still, the advocates of consumer engineering were more convinced than preceding and subsequent generations of marketing experts that they could influence consumer behavior or "engineer consent" and goodwill for their goods and messages, as the public relations pioneer Edward Bernays put it in 1955.[22] The validity of their "scientific methods" and of the social benefits of their mission hinged on an overt belief in the malleability of consumers and in the possibility of "producing" them.

Marketing as Social Engineering?

Moving from changes in marketing to broader historical developments, we finally ask to what degree consumer engineering was a subset of more general social engineering efforts in fields such as architecture, urban development, state planning, and social reform. In many ways, our consumer engineers appear as one variant of the social engineers—those champions of high modernity—who firmly believed in the capacity of science and engineering to rationalize, modernize, and more generally reshape individuals and entire societies. Cutting across national and ideological boundaries, these experts and technocrats were at the height of their influence during the middle decades of the twentieth century.

Social engineering has emerged as an important historical paradigm for understanding and interpreting the mid-century era in transatlantic history, a paradigm which marketing historians can use as well.[23] Like the wayward youths or working-class tenants that social engineers sought to influence, consumers could be regarded as a social group in need of expert guidance in order to attain a happier, more fulfilled life. In 1930s America, this expertise could come from consumer engineers, who promised to improve the lot of consumers, corporations, and society as a whole. In interwar Germany, too, advertising experts such as Hans Domizlaff had begun to recognize marketing as a "*Markentechnik*" or "branding technology"—in Hartmut Berghoff's terminology, a "social technology" capable of shaping and manipulating individual and group behavior for commercial and political purposes.[24]

Many mid-century consumer engineers were actually hesitant to accept consumer desires at face value as a guiding force for social development. Consumers, they believed, lacked foresight and innovative imagination, and they did not really know what they wanted. Experts—engineers, designers, marketers—were more likely to advance the cause of what they viewed as modern consumer civilization. Artists and academics, businessmen and administrators would be the architects of a rationally organized, yet also creative consumer modernity that would improve the masses' standard of living and uplift them, to use the parlance of the time. Much like urban planners, economists, and social workers, then, consumer engineers saw themselves as social engineers or technocrats harnessing the social sciences to create a better world. They legitimized their "education" of consumers and their "engineering" of consumer desires and behaviors by characterizing their practices as efforts to enable "democratic" access to the abundance of goods and experiences available in Western consumer capitalism.

Whether working within corporations or for advertising agencies or more specialized consultancies, consumer engineers often genuinely believed that their work was improving the standard of living for millions of consumers and advancing modern civilization by making it both more efficient and enjoyable. Their goals were thus quite different from the proverbial "manipulative advertiser" focused on growing markets for corporate profits. Especially in the postwar years, consumer engineering was also a highly political endeavor. By the 1940s and 1950s, it became heavily intertwined with what historians today call the "Cold War social sciences" and the "cultural Cold War," a war fought as much with consumption statistics and kitchen exhibits as with nuclear deterrence.[25] Not until the 1960s did the seemingly manifest superiority of material affluence and designed obsolescence begin to appear less self-evident. Across Western societies in that decade, new social movements began to offer a grassroots critique of technocratic elitism in government and business alike.

The marketing mind-set represented by consumer engineering now faced challenges on several fronts. By the late 1960s, the era of unbridled confidence came to a close, and the prominent return of crises cast renewed doubt on the power of the consumer engineers. Few marketing experts were still inclined to make grandiose claims, becoming somewhat more humble and sober in their self-assessments. In part, this was a response to a consumer movement that made it less socially acceptable to talk openly about manufacturing obsolescence and manipulating consumers.[26] This movement challenged the "waste makers" and alerted consumers to marketing fraud and deception, most prominently perhaps in the scare over subliminal advertising. Consumer advocates admonished producers to keep consumer needs in mind, and political consumerism called for educated and informed consumers to exercise control over their own decisions. At the same time, marketing science itself had become too sophisticated to maintain the fiction of outright expert manipulation. Media and communications scholars as well as behavioral economists stressed the social embeddedness of mass communication, the role of opinion leaders, and the place of audience participation in shaping the meanings of messages, experiences, and aspirations.[27] To be sure, marketing experts during the 1960s and beyond remained engaged in efforts to influence consumers, for example, by creating and altering brand images or by defining and targeting new consumer segments. But they were now less likely to perceive such work as outright manipulation. Many even succumbed to their own rhetoric, believing that they were merely interpreting and fulfilling latent consumer wishes.

Again, the rise of social engineering in the first half of the twentieth century and the revolt against expert rule since the 1960s were shared, transatlantic phenomena. Thus, to historians of transatlantic social relations, the history of consumer engineering offers a fresh perspective on postwar economic transfers and debates over "Americanization."[28] In engaging these broad sets of issues, this volume thus seeks to explore the societal context of modern marketing both in Europe and the United States between the 1920s and the 1970s. By focusing on individual careers and on the transatlantic emergence of broad concepts and their practical implementation, the studies in this book show how new marketing approaches spread through companies and advertising agencies across the Atlantic World.

Marketing Innovation in the Context of Consumer and Business History

The first section of the book situates the concept of consumer engineering within the development of marketing and mass consumption during the twentieth century. It weighs the aspirations of marketing experts to reshape consumption against the limits that their work encountered in practice. Jan Logemann's chapter traces the concept of "consumer engineering" and the emergence of professional marketing in the United States from the interwar years. Many mid-century marketing experts—several of them transatlantic émigrés—viewed consumers as malleable objects and encouraged companies to devise new strategies and methods to engineer the tastes of newly defined groups of consumers. The rise of market and consumer research was central to this development. Focusing on the impact of transatlantic émigrés in consumer research, such as Alfred Politz and Ernest Dichter, the chapter also stresses the transnational dimension of marketing exchanges and the impact of European developments on those in the United States from the 1930s into the postwar decades.[29]

Looking at the larger trajectory of marketing innovations, the first section of this book also considers costs and benefits by contrasting the challenges faced by consumers with those faced by entrepreneurs. Both groups had very distinct perspectives on the meaning of marketing innovation and on the social and economic impacts of consumer engineering. The notion of a broader cultural acceleration of marketing as an outgrowth of "fast capitalism" stands at the center of Gary Cross' chapter. Taking the example of fashion goods and the music industry, Cross stresses that the phonograph and music records reflected an early acceleration of the process of commodification, creating shorter product life cycles, rising expectations for novelty among consumers, as well as the creation of a specific "teenage culture" in the United States. He notes that many of the themes of consumer engineering—from novelty and social segmentation to continuous improvement and ideas of obsolescence—had already emerged in American consumer culture by the early twentieth century. Arguing from the perspective of a social and cultural historian, he emphasizes the costs and benefits involved for consumers.

Andrew Godley and Keith Heron's chapter, by contrast, notes the costs for businesses and entrepreneurs involved in market-making innovations. Using institutional economics and transaction cost theory, Godley and Heron stress the importance of interaction between companies, marketing professionals, and the consumer. Marketing communication, they argue, was essential in forging relationships of trust to overcome information asymmetries between the two parties of producer and consumer. Without market making, that is, without articulating what a given product innovation could do for the consumer, potential markets could—and often did—easily fail. In this sense, proactive marketing was integral for innovation, with advantages not only for businesses but also for consumers, who stood to benefit from innovation. Overall, the first section of this book underscores that marketing innovation was both a precondition for and a consequence of the dynamics of accelerated consumer capitalism. While this process saw a clear intensification in mid-twentieth-century America, it was part of a longer trajectory of consumer capitalism since the late nineteenth century.

Consumer Engineers and Transatlantic Exchanges at Mid-Century

These changes in marketing and consumption were not just an American phenomenon. A new group of professional marketing experts was emerging on both sides of the Atlantic during the interwar years. The chapters in the second section of this book provide examples of individual consumer engineers and explore their respective roles in transatlantic exchanges. Their careers reveal a variety of professional self-perceptions, ranging from the aesthetic pioneer who created consumerist dreamscapes to designers who understood themselves as interpreters of consumer preferences to the rational expert who sought to turn sales and consumption into a science.

Taking the case of Victor Gruen, a Jewish architect and designer with a background in the socialist milieu of Vienna, Joseph Malherek provides an example of the influence of European émigrés on the conception of new places of consumption in mid-century America. Gruen promoted the idea of "engineering" the shopping experience, and he imagined shopping malls both as places set aside purely for consumption and as communal spaces for newly built suburbs. Here, consumer engineering entailed creating new physical spaces and environments for consumption. Bernard Gallagher's chapter focuses on the émigré Walter Landor, from Germany, a packaging designer who worked for large American corporations in industries ranging from food and beverages to airlines and financial institutions. Landor's work, Gallagher argues, hinged on the integration of systematic consumer research in his design work. His firm exemplified the growing importance of corporate image and product personality in mid-century marketing, connecting consumers to a brand. Responding to the rise of supermarkets and an increasingly visual consumer culture, Landor's packaging and graphic designs accentuated the fine line between integrating consumer tastes and preferences, on the one hand, and creating emotional appeals that guide and direct our buying behavior, on the other.

Despite their emphasis on aesthetics and emotions, retail architects such as Gruen and packaging engineers such as Landor saw marketing and design as efforts to make consumer behavior more predictable and "rational," a need that had resonated on both sides of the Atlantic since the interwar years. Uwe Spiekermann's chapter stresses the importance of business journals such as the German *Verkaufspraxis* for increasingly transnational connections in marketing. Such trade journals frequently propagated "American" methods of rationalization in production and sales. At the same time, though, American ideas were significantly transformed and adapted to German business practices. In light of such observations, we need to refrain from overly generalizing narratives of consumer engineering as "Americanization." In different forms, then, trends toward rationalization in distribution and more systematic marketing could be found in Europe as well as in the United States during the interwar period.

The Company Level: Changing Marketing Practices in Postwar Europe

Shifting the focus from individual marketing experts to corporate marketing practices in postwar Europe more broadly, the next three chapters illustrate the vibrant and multidirectional transatlantic exchanges that shaped the field of marketing. European companies employed many of the same marketing techniques long associated with "American-style" consumer engineering. The section begins with a contribution by Sabine Effosse on the widespread introduction of consumer credit in France after World War II. Price marketing and sales financing became important to fostering demand in postwar France as well. Here, the electronics sales financing company Cetelem was particularly influential in popularizing credit as a marketing tool. Effosse's chapter pays especially close attention to marketing efforts directed at women, a previously neglected target group among French credit experts.

To consumer engineers, then, creating markets entailed more than mere advertising. Next to offering financial incentives, the development and styling of new products and brand images became crucial for the business success of consumer goods producers. Even smaller, tradition-oriented German manufacturers, such as the shoe company Adidas, embraced new marketing techniques and paid heed to transatlantic trends, as Thomas Turner shows. The shoe manufacturer reacted to increasingly differentiated markets and in turn accelerated this trend by widening the range and selection of shoes on offer to include a variety of athletic and leisure shoes for numerous target groups. Such targeted marketing was combined with lifestyle marketing by the 1970s, contributing to the transatlantic success of this German family firm. Still, Turner argues, Adidas focused on technological innovation rather than merely engineered styling. He emphasizes the role of the product as a communicative icon and central intermediary between consumers and business. Far from being a story of straightforward consumer engineering, Adidas' rise from niche market to mainstream consumer product was about marketing following broader trends in leisure culture, not the other way around.

Few industries relied on the professional tools of consumer engineering, from market research to industrial design, as much as large automobile producers. They repeatedly turned to new marketing strategies, especially when faced with crisis situations. Ingo Köhler's chapter discusses the emergence of professional and scientific market research as a central force behind the emergence of modern, consumer-oriented product strategies in the automobile industry. He demonstrates that manufacturer competition in Germany increased as markets reached saturation in the late 1950s and 1960s. This prompted firms to engage in research on consumers to create brand loyalty. However, the carmakers' power to "engineer the consumer" also proved limited. As marketing attempted to appeal to an expanded notion of consumer lifestyles, different strategies stressed both emotion and rationality in brands and models. Similarly to Turner, Köhler emphasizes the transition toward a strategy of marketing management by the early 1970s that was more subdued in tone, but even more encompassing in its scientific approach—a significant caesura in the development of modern marketing. At least in part, we can argue, this shift in company marketing practice was also a response to broader societal shifts in buying behavior and consumer attitudes. A pluralization of consumer habits increased the uncertainty of corporate decision-making and called the confident claims of some consumer engineers into question.

Creating Rational Consumers? Consumer Engineering and the Consumer Movement

The ideas of consumer engineering were both challenged and advanced by consumer movements, which had interwar roots but gained traction during the 1960s. The conflicted relationship of consumer activists with ideas of consumer engineering stands at the center of the final section. Taking examples from Sweden, West Germany, and Belgium, these chapters analyze the often contradictory images of the consumer's role in the marketplace that came out of the emerging consumer advocacy movements. Empowering consumers through knowledge or institutional frameworks was seen as one way to protect them from the manipulative reach of "hidden persuaders." Many consumer activists, however, very much engaged in engineering consumer behavior themselves, efforts with roots in the same reform agenda of quality, rationalization, and efficiency that had given rise to consumer engineering in the interwar period.

Social actors from the state and civil society brought their own ideas about rational, engineered consumption to the table. In countries with relatively strong traditions of consumer policy, their ideas could significantly influence mass marketing and mass production. Orsi Husz and Karin Carlsson's chapter analyzes the changing conception behind IKEA kitchens. They show that the firm's emphasis on functionality in its marketing and design was not only a response to mass consumer capitalism in the United States but was instead also influenced by social welfare policies rooted in the interwar Swedish rationalization movement and ideas of progressive social engineering. The "classless IKEA kitchen" marketed globally since the 1970s can thus be interpreted as the outcome of a sociopolitical and commercial vision—the manifestation of a particularly Swedish form of consumer engineering.

This tension between embrace and rejection of new forms of mass marketing extended well beyond the Scandinavian model of social capitalism. Consumer movements elsewhere in Europe sought to curb the perceived manipulation of consumer engineers while also pursuing their own strategies to forge informed and rational consumers. Kevin Rick traces the rise of German consumer advice centers (*Verbraucherzentrale*) in the 1950s and their efforts to organize collective consumer action and to train consumers to behave in an informed way, for example, by educating them on strategies for comparison shopping. Established to promote growth by enabling individual, rational choice, these government-sponsored centers exemplify the involvement of states as actors in shaping consumption regimes and in influencing consumer behavior.

In the book's final chapter, Giselle Nath presents the example of two competing Belgian consumer organizations—one liberal, the other social-democratic—and their product testing efforts. She shows the importance of consumer movements as a counterweight to corporate consumer engineering. Although testing products was in many ways a rather technocratic process, both consumer movements also became engaged in politics as they attempted to "educate the consumer." In their efforts to formulate their own ideas about consumer interests, however, consumer organizations, too, pursued strategies of consumer engineering.

***

By the 1970s, at the end of the period under investigation in this volume, a more differentiated conception of modern consumer societies on the part of consumer goods companies converged with more complex understandings of consumer psychology in the marketing profession to challenge overt consumer engineering approaches. At the same time, state regulators and social protest from the environmental to the consumers' movement also contributed to the demise of an overly optimistic view of professional marketing's capacity to stimulate "insatiable demand." Marketing management continued to become more influential in subsequent decades, but the era of the consumer engineers had passed, as Ingo Köhler shows. How do we account for this shift? Did demand manipulation become less important as production became more flexible and targeted?[30] The empowered consumer as an active participant in the marketing process certainly became the new prevailing fiction of marketing thought. Yet, did the 1970s truly mark the end of manipulative consumer engineering schemes or did they simply live on in different guises? After all, some advertisers today still very much like to entertain the idea that they have the power to shape the desires and actions of millions of consumers, and some of their critics are similarly inclined to indulge such fantasies.[31] While the 1970s may have shattered high modernist optimism for social engineering schemes and belief in the power of consumer experts, the crises of that decade also encouraged a search for new marketing methods and, to recall Arens and Sheldon's 1932 phrase, new "techniques for prosperity."

***

This book originated in workshop entitled "'Consumer Engineering'—Mid-Century Mass Consumption between Planning Euphoria and the Limits of Growth, 1930s—1970," which was held at the University of Göttingen in March 2015 with support from the German Historical Institute Washington. We would like to thank both the GHI and the Institute for Social and Economic History in Göttingen for supporting this workshop and this volume. We would also like to thank all the workshop participants for their contributions and stimulating discussions. Finally, we are grateful for the comments and suggestions of an anonymous reviewer for Palgrave Macmillan and to Mark Stoneman (GHI) for his extensive editorial efforts and revisions.

Notes

1. On the longer history of marketing and market research, see, for example, Hartmut Berghoff, Philip Scranton, and Uwe Spiekermann, eds., *The Rise of Marketing and Market Research* (New York, 2012). The idea of marketing as a social technology is developed in Hartmut Berghoff, ed., *Marketinggeschichte: Die Genese einer modernen Sozialtechnik* (Frankfurt a.M., 2007).

2. See, for example, Thomas Frank, *The Conquest of Cool: Business Culture, Counterculture, and the Rise of Hip Consumerism* (Chicago, IL, 1997); and Dawn Spring, *Advertising in the Age of Persuasion: Building Brand America 1941–1961* (New York, 2011).
3. See, for example, Jason Chambers, *Madison Avenue and the Color Line: African Americans in the Advertising Industry* (Philadelphia, PA, 2008); and Lawrence Samuel, *Freud on Madison Avenue: Motivation Research and Subliminal Advertising in America* (Philadelphia, PA, 2010).
4. See Harm Schröter, *Americanization of the European Economy: A Compact Survey of American Economic Influence in Europe since the 1880s* (Dordrecht, 2005). Early developments in Germany: Alexander Schug, "Wegbereiter der modernen Absatzwerbung in Deutschland: Advertising Agencies und die Amerikanisierung der deutschen Werbebranche in der Zwischenkriegszeit," *Werkstatt Geschichte* 12 (2003): 29–52.
5. Roy Sheldon and Egmont Arens, *Consumer Engineering: A New Technique for Prosperity* (New York, 1932).
6. Sheldon and Arens embraced the notion of obsolescence, sharing in a wider discourse around that concept during the early 1930s. See, for example, Bernard London, *Ending the Depression through Planned Obsolescence* (New York, 1932). See also Giles Slade, *Made to Break: Technology and Obsolescence in America* (Cambridge, MA, 2009).
7. Most prominently: Vance Packard, *The Hidden Persuaders* (New York, 1957), and *The Waste Makers* (New York, 1960). Accounts of consumer engineering in interwar America include Jeffrey Meikle, *Twentieth Century Limited: Industrial Design in America, 1925–1939* (Philadelphia, PA, 1979); and Charles McGovern, *Sold American: Consumption and Citizenship, 1890–1945* (Chapel Hill, NC, 2006).
8. The classic critique is Stuart Ewen, *Captains of Consciousness: Advertising and the Social Roots of the Consumer Culture* (New York, 1976). For a sophisticated intellectual history of the debates over mass consumption, see Daniel Horowitz, *The Anxieties of Affluence: Critiques of American Consumer Culture, 1939–1979* (Amherst, MA, 2004).
9. On the concept of high modernity, see, for example, James C. Scott, *Seeing Like a State: How Certain Schemes to Improve the Human Condition Have Failed* (New Haven, CT, 1999). For the European context, see also Ulrich Herbert, "Europe in High Modernity: Reflections on a Theory of the 20th Century," *Journal of Modern European History* 5, no. 1 (2007): 5–21; and Lutz Raphael, "Ordnungsmuster der 'Hochmoderne'? Die Theorie der Moderne und die Geschichte der europäischen Gesellschaften im 20. Jahrhundert," in *Dimensionen der Moderne*, ed. Lutz Raphael and Ute Schneider (Frankfurt a.M., 2008), 73–92.
10. See, for example, Roland Marchand, *Advertising the American Dream: Making Way for Modernity, 1920–1940* (Berkeley, CA, 2008); or Spring, *Advertising in the Age of Persuasion.*
11. On the transnational dimension of consumption during World War II, see Hartmut Berghoff, Jan Logemann, and Felix Römer, eds., *The Consumer on the Home Front: Second World War Civilian Consumption in Transnational Perspective* (Oxford, UK, 2016).

12. For the United States, see Robert Collins, *More: The Politics of Economic Growth in Postwar America* (Oxford, UK, 2000); and Robert J. Gordon, *Rise and Fall of American Growth* (Princeton, NJ, 2016).
13. See, for example, Victoria de Grazia, *Irresistible Empire: America's Advance Through Twentieth-Century Europe* (Cambridge, MA, 2005).
14. On transatlantic exchanges in marketing, see especially Christian Kleinschmidt, *Der produktive Blick: Wahrnehmung amerikanischer und japanischer Management- und Produktionsmethoden durch deutsche Unternehmer 1950–1985* (Berlin, 2002); and Ingo Köhler, "Overcoming Stagflation: Innovative Product Policy and Marketing in the German Automobile Industry of the 1970s," *Business History Review* 84 (2010): 53–78. See also Harm Schröter, "Zur Geschichte der Marktforschung in Europa im 20. Jahrhundert," in *Geschichte des Konsums*, ed. Heinz Gerhard Haupt, Claudius Torp, and Rolf Walter (Wiesbaden, 2004), 319–36; Ursula Hansen and Matthias Bode, *Marketing und Konsum: Theorie und Praxis von der Industrialisierung bis ins 21. Jahrhundert* (Munich, 1999); and Peter Borscheid, "Agenten des Konsums: Werbung und Marketing" in *Die Konsumgesellschaft in Deutschland: Ein Handbuch*, ed. Heinz Gerhard Haupt and Claudius Torp (Frankfurt a.M., 2009), 79–96.
15. On the history of marketing in a comparative perspective, see Roy Church and Andrew Godley, eds., *The Emergence of Modern Marketing* (London, 2003); and Berghoff et al., eds., *Rise of Marketing*.
16. See, for example, Roland Marchand, *Advertising the American Dream: Making Way for Modernity, 1920–1940* (Berkeley, CA, 1985).
17. Regina Blaszczyk, ed., *Producing Fashion: Commerce, Culture, and Consumers* (Philadelphia, PA, 2008).
18. Alain Chatriot, Marie-Emmanuelle Chessel, and Matthew Hilton, eds., *The Expert Consumer: Associations and Professionals in Consumer Society* (Aldershot, 2006).
19. On the prehistory of consumer engineering, see, for example, Gary Cross and Robert Proctor, *Packaged Pleasures: How Technology and Marketing Revolutionized Desire* (Chicago, IL, 2014). See also Roman Rossfeld, "Unternehmensgeschichte als Marketinggeschichte: Zur Erweiterung traditioneller Ansätze in der Unternehmensgeschichtsschreibung," in *Marketing: Historische Aspekte der Wettbewerbs- und Absatzpolitik*, ed. Christian Kleinschmidt and Florian Triebel (Essen, 2004), 17–42.
20. Lizabeth Cohen, *A Consumers' Republic: The Politics of Mass Consumption in Postwar America* (New York, 2003).
21. For the 1960s, see, for example, Frank, *Conquest of Cool*.
22. Edward Bernays, *The Engineering of Consent* (Oklahoma City, OK, 1955).
23. On the concept of social engineering, see, for example, Kerstin Brückweh et al., eds., *Engineering Society: The Role of the Human and Social Sciences in Modern Societies, 1880–1980* (Basingstoke, 2012).
24. See Berghoff, ed., *Marketinggeschichte*.
25. Mark Solovey and Hamilton Cravens, eds., *Cold War Social Science Knowledge Production, Liberal Democracy, and Human Nature* (New York, 2012); and Greg Castillo, *Cold War on the Home Front: The Soft Power of Midcentury Design* (Minneapolis, MN, 2010).

26. On the consumer movement as a transnational force, see Matthew Hilton, *Prosperity for All: Consumer Activism in an Era of Globalization* (Ithaca, NY, 2009). For the pioneering movement in the United States, see Lawrence Glickman, *Buying Power: A History of Consumer Activism in America* (Chicago, IL, 2009).
27. See, for example, Elihu Katz and Paul F. Lazarsfeld, *Personal Influence: The Part Played by People in the Flow of Mass Communications* (Glencoe, IL, 1955).
28. The argument for Americanization through mass consumption and mass marketing is presented most prominently by de Grazia, *Irresistible Empire*. For a comparative perspective, see also Susan Strasser, Charles McGovern, and Matthias Judt, eds., *Getting and Spending: European and American Consumer Societies in the Twentieth Century* (Cambridge, MA, 1998).
29. On the transatlantic dimension of marketing exchanges in market research and commercial design, see also Jan Logemann, "European Imports? European Immigrants and the Transformation of American Consumer Culture from the 1920s to the 1960s," *Bulletin of the German Historical Institute* 52 (2013): 113–33; and Jan Logemann, *Engineered to Sell: European Emigres and the Making of Consumer Capitalism, 1920s to 1960s* (Chicago, IL, 2019).
30. On the rise of flexible production regimes, see Steven Tolliday, ed., *The Rise and Fall of Mass Production* (Cheltenham and Northampton, MA, 1998); and Michaele Priore and Charles Sabel, *The Second Industrial Divide: Possibilities for Prosperity* (New York, 1984).
31. On the 1970s decline of "manipulative" consumer engineering and the shift to identifying narrow consumer groups, see Norman Kangun et al., "Consumerism and Marketing Management," *Journal of Marketing* 39 (1975): 3–10; Daniel J. Sweeney, "Marketing: Management Technology or Social Process?" *Journal of Marketing* 36 (1972): 3–10; Philip Kotler, *Marketing Management: Analysis, Planning, and Control*, 2nd ed. (Englewood Cliffs, NJ, 1972); and Köhler, *Overcoming Stagnation*, 59–61. On new segmentation strategies based on the AIO or VALS-Approach, see William Wells and Doug Tigert, "Activities, Interests and Opinions," *Journal of Advertising Research* 11 (1971): 27–35; J. T. Plummer, "The Concept and Application of Life Style Segmentation," *Journal of Marketing* 38 (1974): 33–37; and Thomas Drieseberg, *Lebensstil-Forschung: Theoretische Grundlagen und praktische Anwendungen* (Heidelberg, 1995).

PART I

Twentieth Century Marketing—Aspirations and Limits, Costs and Benefits

CHAPTER 2

Professional Marketing as "Consumer Engineering"? A Concept in Transatlantic Perspective

Jan Logemann

In 1971, the German-American market researcher Alfred Politz, an early pioneer of random sampling in consumer surveys, drafted a book-length manuscript on his experiences in the field of marketing titled "How to Produce Consumers—Methods and Illusions."[1] Over the course of his career, from the 1930s to the 1970s, Politz had seen the marketing profession in the United States become a good deal more methodical. Yet this Berlin-trained physicist turned marketing consultant scoffed at the pseudo-scientific veneer that many marketing experts attached to their work by 1970. "The word 'research,'" he wrote, "implies a sort of glamorous intellectual sophistication, and marketing research is a symbol of the modernity of the marketer. Marketing research has become a status symbol, and as such it need not perform; it need only exist."[2] But despite such misgivings, Politz, too, firmly believed in the possibilities of "scientific marketing," which could increase "advertising efficiency," identify the "most important product properties for consumer appeal," discover the "most efficient product design," and craft an "image" for products that created loyalty to brands in "daily consumption behavior."[3]

To Politz, the key to marketing success was statistically sound consumer research. He did not believe, however, that this research existed to actually find out "what the consumer wants." Part of the problem, he thought, was that "consumers do not know what they want and why they act. If the uninfluenced opinions of consumers in the year 1800 had determined

J. Logemann (✉)
Institute for Economic and Social History, University of Göttingen,
Göttingen, Germany

J. Logemann et al. (eds.), *Consumer Engineering, 1920s–1970s*,
Worlds of Consumption, https://doi.org/10.1007/978-3-030-14564-4_2

the development of lighting systems, we would have today merely vastly improved kerosene lamps.... Consumers do not solve problems by answering questions. Research has to solve these questions....”[4] Experts in marketing rather than consumers themselves, Politz believed, advanced modern consumer society. Such attitudes make him a textbook case of a “consumer engineer” (Fig. 2.1).

Politz’ sentiments mirrored the thinking of many marketing experts during the middle decades of the twentieth century. The field had become more professional and methodical since the interwar years, and “consumer engineering” and “scientific marketing” had emerged as concepts entailing the systematic study of markets and consumers. Advertising agencies expanded their use of consumer research, corporations established marketing departments, and the number of specialized consumer research institutions proliferated between the 1930s and the 1960s. Consumer engineering also entailed merchandising in the sense of consumer-oriented product planning and styling as well as sophisticated salesmanship utilizing persuasive advertising. Thus, consumer engineering foreshadowed modern marketing management, yet it frequently retained an overtly manipulative bent. Consumers, to be sure, were no longer simply an irrational mass to consumer engineers:

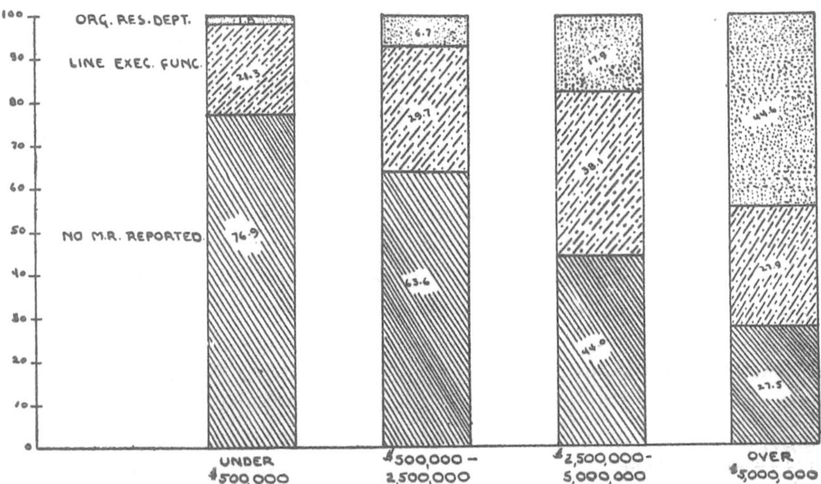

Chart 2. Companies Doing Marketing Research by Size of Company (Net Sales).

Fig. 2.1 U.S. companies doing market research in 1947. By 1947, the majority of large U.S. corporations had an organized research department or conducted market research through line executives. At the same time, only a very limited number of smaller companies engaged in market research activities [“M.R” in this graph]. Besides depicting these facts, this graph and the flow chart in Fig. 2.2 represent artifacts from the professionalization process that fed consumer engineering. Source: Heusner et al., “Marketing Research in American Industry I,” *Journal of Marketing* 11 (1947): 341.

Their actions and motivations could be understood and even predicted with proper psychological or statistical methodology. Still, consumers were seen as susceptible to the influences of artful advertising, creative design, and business innovation. From the perspective of consumer engineers, consumers were still passive recipients rather than active co-creators of a transforming consumer culture. As such, their ideas challenge the very concept of consumer agency, a concept most marketing scholars and historians of consumption are very careful to emphasize today.[5]

To explore the concept of consumer engineering in historical perspective means first and foremost to investigate the history of marketing research and its role in consumer culture. When and why did marketing research become an influential force in business management in the United States and Europe? How did the profession and its self-understanding change to produce such self-assured "consumer engineers" as Alfred Politz? By the 1930s, many marketing experts came to think of themselves increasingly as akin to scientists and engineers in their ability to predict, plan, and shape products, markets, and ultimately consumer behavior. Who were these self-proclaimed "producers of consumers" and what was their background?

In this essay, I trace the rapid development of the marketing profession since the 1930s, focusing especially on the field of market research, which became central to attempts to establish "scientific marketing." The claim to scientific or engineering expertise became pervasive in marketing discourse from the 1930s to the 1950s. Clearly intended to increase the legitimacy and status of the profession, the scientization of marketing intensified its ties to several academic fields. This trend in turn opened up career opportunities for academic refugees and other emigres from interwar Europe, including Politz.[6] I explore the resulting transatlantic and transnational dimension of consumer engineering's development in the final section of this chapter.

At first glance, the notion of consumer engineering appears linked to a specific time and place: the United States, during the middle decades of the twentieth century. Lizabeth Cohen has characterized the era as America's emerging "Consumer's Republic," and questions of consumption loomed large from the New Deal era into the postwar political economy.[7] Increased consumption seemingly pointed the way toward stable economic growth and a more democratic and egalitarian future. Historians have uncovered government policies and cultural changes favorable to the rise of consumerism in American society.[8] Corporate marketing played an important part in this story as well and not simply in the form of ubiquitous advertising.[9] The mid-century expansion of marketing has had a tremendous impact on management strategy and business organization, which business historians have only begun to explore.[10] Consumer engineering entailed a much broader social and economic vision, however, reaching well beyond the corporate world. The movement's protagonists saw themselves not merely as stewards of corporate profits but as engineers of new forms of democratic affluence and societal abundance.[11] In this, they resembled their fellow technocrats in urban planning and other fields in which social engineering was employed in pursuit of high modernity.[12]

Critics of mid-century marketing techniques such as Vance Packard have located the origins of consumer engineering primarily in corporate profit-seeking, which preyed on the social anxieties and vulnerability of consumers.[13] However, professional consumer engineers also shared the broader visions of mid-century social engineering, and they can be seen as part of an effort to methodically create well-functioning and prosperous societies. Such a perspective allows us to recognize the rise of marketing as more than an American business phenomenon. It was an aspect of transatlantic modernity. Since the Progressive Era, social engineering could draw on a vibrant transatlantic discourse about the ills of modern society and the solutions offered by planners, social scientists, and various other experts.[14] Consumer engineers of the interwar years did not just pursue solutions to simple problems of sales management or product design. Many had a much broader agenda, which in some cases even drew on the social reform and design education movements in both Europe and the United States.

The Concept of "Consumer Engineering" and the Rise of "Scientific Marketing"

If consumer engineering was a phenomenon of transatlantic modernity, the term itself was coined in Depression-era America. Earnest Elmo Calkins, a prominent advertising man, characterized "consumption engineering" in 1930 as a new "business science" in which consumer research coupled with consumer-oriented design innovations would create new demand through "artificial obsolescence."[15] Two years later, employees of his agency's design department, Roy Sheldon and Egmont Arens, developed his ideas in *Consumer Engineering: A New Technique for Prosperity.*[16] This book encapsulated many budding trends in the marketing field that would come to the fore in subsequent decades.

"Consumer engineering," Calkins explained in the introduction to the volume, "is shaping a product to fit more exactly consumers' needs or tastes, but in the widest sense it includes any plan which stimulates the consumption of goods."[17] The emphasis on stimulation was a direct reaction to the end of the seller's market of the 1920s and to what Calkins identified as the problem of "under-consumption" during the depression. More consumption, not reduced production, would be the way out of the slump, and Calkins and his collaborators called on business to "engineer a supply of consumers" by creating high-wage employment, making sales-financing available, and by employing the skills of a "new business science" that promised accelerated consumption.[18] A competitive buyer's market with more discriminating consumers would require the systematic efforts of marketing engineers, whose agenda the book detailed.

To Sheldon and Arens, the consumer engineer needed to heed calls for consumer comfort and modernity in design, promoting an ongoing advancement in material living conditions:

> His is a double job, not only to fit the product and the promotion to the existing market ... but to create new needs and stimulate consumption by every possible means.... He plans for the future. Market research and information regarding the consumer are his tools, and these tools he needs and will use in the creation of new consumer acceptance. And the means that he uses them for are the organization and promotion of obsolescence, or, as it has been called, progressive waste...[19]

The authors' program consequently included efforts to introduce modern design and fashion cycles into a wide variety of goods, from textiles to home furnishings. They touted the achievements of new industrial designers in styling goods and in creating products suitable to the machine age.

Sheldon and Arens highlighted the importance of "measuring consumer wants" and surveying markets. They also called for the practical application of academic psychology to marketing problems. Such "humaneering," or the "general adoption in human affairs" of the scientific method, promised to make the world a "much pleasanter place to live in," one without further economic slumps. More than simply advocating a sales agenda, Sheldon and Arens envisioned broader changes as science began to "dominate the business world." Promising reconsideration of social problems which "but a few years ago were only agitated by the Bolsheviks," they exuded faith in "human technology to solve the human problem."[20]

Few marketing experts at the time would have fully embraced this sweeping version of "consumer engineering." In fact, the term itself did not gain wide currency nor was obsolescence openly adopted as a guiding principle of product planning by most corporations. Still, the central elements of the program outlined by Calkins, Sheldon, and Arens flourished in the following decades: Both market research and industrial design saw a tremendous increase in importance. As these two fields professionalized, the study of applied consumer psychology likewise made significant strides in the subsequent two decades. Indeed, the authors of "consumer engineering" were hardly the only marketing professionals to anticipate a prosperous future in the midst of depression. Some dreamed of a "new consumption era" in which "more definitely and scientifically planned campaigns for the consumption of goods" would revolutionize marketing practice and do away with outdated, "spasmodic efforts" of salesmanship and advertising.[21] Others insisted that "prosperity must be made the usual and commonplace" through market analysis and the scientific study of marketing.[22]

Consequently, the practices of merchandising and scientific marketing became more common in American companies. Merchandising, in the terminology of the time, referred to a product planning process that took its cues from customer expectations and desires. It entailed styling and package design as well product portfolio management, all with an eye toward potential sales.[23] Scientific marketing, by contrast, aimed at a thorough professionalization of the marketing field and at the introduction of a well-defined and systematic methodology. American Marketing Association President Frank Coutant observed in 1936 that "on bringing science into marketing, only a start has been made. On marketing research, about two or three millions of dollars a year are being spent.... It is only a drop in the bucket, of course, compared with production research, but it shows that we are on our way to greater efficiency and better profits in marketing."[24] At its core, the drive for scientific marketing lay in the expansion of market and consumer research and the routine application of such systematic knowledge to management decision-making.

The origins of scientific marketing can be traced to at least the turn of the twentieth century. Early calls for a marketing equivalent to the "scientific management" movement optimizing production processes came from Walter Dill Scott in his *Theory of Advertising* (1903) and the works of Arch W. Shaw at Harvard Business School, who in 1911 established a Bureau for Business Research.[25] Marketing professionals and teachers began to organize in associations around 1915, forerunners of the American Marketing Association, which emerged in 1936.[26] The practical application of a more systematic approach to marketing was often pioneered by large national advertising agencies. Already during the 1890s, N. W. Ayer & Son had begun to implement a program of campaign planning which by the 1920s included business advice regarding the market position of products, sales organization, and package design.[27] The most prominent "full-service" agency of the interwar years was J. Walter Thompson (JWT), which under the leadership of Stanley Resor publicly embraced a "scientific" approach: "Advertising must be scientifically prepared. Nothing must be taken for granted."[28] In 1921, the agency hired the renowned behaviorist psychologist John Watson to study consumer behavior for their campaigns.

As advertising agencies expanded their service portfolios, they increasingly branched out into the fields of consumer design and market research. The Calkins & Holden advertising agency built up a proactive design department, and the firm collaborated with the famed industrial designer Walter Teague, while their rivals at JWT worked with Norman Bel Geddes. Already during the 1920s, a few industrial designers had begun to establish their own offices, with Teague taking the lead in 1926 followed by other leading commercial designers such as Geddes (1927), Henry Dreyfuss (1929), and French-born Raymond Loewy (1929). Their design studios became widely influential during the 1930s as independent consultants to American industry and as pioneers of the modernist streamlined style that characterized the decade.[29] They became the most prominent among the taste-makers of the mid-twentieth century whose work helped to promote the patterns of the conscious product styling and continuous design changes that the advocates of consumer engineering had demanded. Visions of consumerist progress and abundance, once confined to the design of retail interiors and department store windows, were now "engineered" into the products themselves.

This design trend dovetailed with developments in consumer and marketing research. The beginnings of modern market research can be traced to advertising research by ad agencies and media companies.[30] Charles Parlin's Division of Commercial Research at the Curtis Publishing Company (publisher of the *Saturday Evening Post* and *Ladies Home Journal*) was a pioneer in systematic market research for advertising customers at the beginning of the twentieth century. By the 1920s, several large advertising agencies, such as JWT, routinely engaged in market analysis and consumer research, while national corporations such as Kraft, DuPont, and Procter & Gamble employed the services of professional home economists to advance their consumer research.[31] Even more systematic market and consumer research was offered by specialized research firms. James Cattell's Psychological Corporation offered psychologically informed consumer studies and a "brand barometer" to corporations beginning in 1921.[32] The A. C. Nielsen Company (founded 1923) conducted household inventory panels and similar studies aimed at tracking changing consumer behavior. Others, including George Gallop's American Institute of Public Opinion (founded 1935) and the firms of Archibald Crossley (1926) and Elmo Roper (1937), combined public opinion polling with market studies.[33]

As a concept, market research was well established by the early 1930s. In practice, however, it took another two decades for scientific marketing and systematic consumer research to become widespread phenomena in American industry. Initially, the crisis of the depression hit the marketing field too, with companies closing market research departments. The significant increase in demand for information on markets, competition, and consumers, however, led to an increase in external market research through agencies and independent consultants.[34] By the end of the decade, industry insiders claimed that market research and the ability to forecast, plan, and organize on the basis of data and figures had become virtually indispensable for companies of all kinds.[35] Still, market research and scientific management remained limited primarily to larger firms in the consumer goods sector.

One classic example of early consumer engineering was in the automobile industry, where the sleek streamlined body became dominant during the 1930s and 1940s, and where recurring model changes were part of a systematic effort to entice consumers.[36] General Motors, already a pioneer of segmented marketing in the 1920s, reacted to the depression by institutionalizing its customer research efforts in the 1930s. A new department, led by Henry Weaver, compiled customer feedback through rudimentary questionnaires on consumer preferences and buying habits. Not only were the results utilized in the sales department and for direct mail advertising campaigns but they also impacted product planning and body styling. Market research activities were publicized to paint GM as especially responsive to consumer concerns and desires.[37] Another industry that pioneered systematic marketing research was the film business. Motion picture studios, like other producers of "fashion goods," had for a long time informally tracked changes in audience taste and attempted to forecast the next big trend. By the 1930s and 1940s, however, as production costs soared and planning became more long-term, studios increasingly relied on empirical surveys and "scientific" audience research provided by companies such as Gallup to tailor their products more closely to shifting consumer demand (Fig. 2.2).[38]

Over the course of the 1930s and 1940s, systematic market research slowly became a widespread practice. We can glean this trend from two empirical studies on the role of market research in American companies. The first, a 1937 survey by the U.S. Department of Commerce, asked 550 companies about their market research activities. Over a third of the firms surveyed stated that they were engaged in market surveys, but only 73 companies maintained their own market research departments. Over 40 percent of companies in the consumer goods sector employed market research.[39] This picture was confirmed by a study of nearly 5000 businesses conducted by the AMA's Committee on Marketing Research Activities during the mid-1940s. Here, about 38 percent of surveyed firms stated they were engaged in market research (46 percent among consumer goods producers). Size mattered, as not even a quarter of small companies (with annual sales under $500,000) conducted

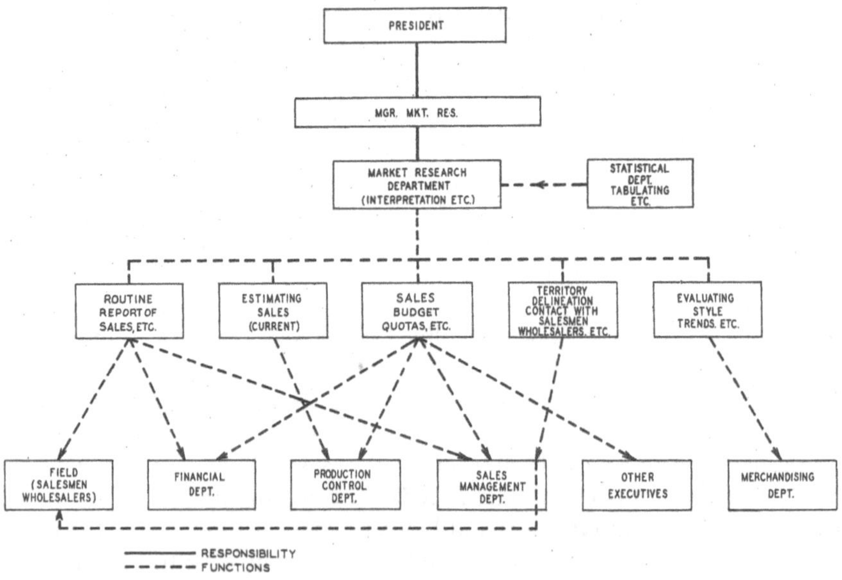

Fig. 2.2 Organizational chart for a consumer goods manufacturer, ca. 1939. New market research departments increasingly occupied a central position in the organization of companies, as this chart illustrates. Source: Elma S. Moulton, *Marketing Research Activities of Manufacturers* (Washington, DC: U.S. Bureau of Foreign and Domestic Commerce, 1939), 19.

research, while that share reached 72.5 percent with the largest firms in the sample (those with annual sales of over $5 million). Especially large consumer goods firms heeded the call for more systematic consumer surveys by market research departments, which produced data not only to predict sales figures and market potential but also to measure advertising effectiveness, develop pricing, and merchandising strategies, not to mention contribute to packaging and product development.[40]

Market research increasingly gained influence on company decision-making processes. Many companies, to be sure, had their research done by "line executives" in departments such as sales. In cases where new research departments were created, however, the majority reported to upper management. In the AMA study, more than half of the firms with such departments noted that their "head of marketing research" participated in regular executive meetings or was actively involved in the company's strategic decision-making.[41] Market research informed departments from sales and merchandising to finance and production. A majority of surveyed firms accordingly expected to grow their own research activities or to employ more outside services. At General Mills, for example, the outside advertising agency was responsible primarily for advertising-related research from copy testing to media analyses, but it was also involved in package design. For research on the products, their market position, and their sales prospects, the company relied on its own sizable research department of twenty-four full-time employees.[42] Large advertising firms also expanded their research capabilities. McCann-Erickson, for example, had created a Central Research and Merchandising Department at its New York headquarters in 1946, for which it hired several renowned marketing experts (including Viennese émigrés Herta Herzog and Hans Zeisel). The department maintained a large library; a research division (for market research, copy tests, and media studies); as well as a merchandising division for the implementation of marketing strategies, which offered advice on everything from sales and packaging to pricing. Yet, the agency still "farmed out" specific tasks to specialized market research companies, which would conduct large sophisticated surveys with the requisite staff of trained interviewers and the tabulating capability of expensive IBM machines.[43]

By 1950, market research and scientific marketing had turned into a complex field and lucrative business, especially for more prominent consumer engineers with consulting businesses. To be sure, according to one (albeit conservative) 1951 estimate, only some 8000 full-time market research professionals were employed in all of U.S. industry. Market research was concentrated in the consumer goods sector, while service sector companies (public utilities and financial companies especially) hardly engaged in market research at all.[44] Nevertheless, in marketing departments, ad agencies, and independent firms, a new type of professional—trained in the methods of psychology or statistics—had become a fixture in the world of American business.

A New Kind of Professional: Marketers as Scientists and Social Engineers

Alfred Politz Research, Inc. (APR) was one of the most prominent of these independent market research firms. The company prided itself in its ability to understand the specific marketing problems of a particular business and to employ statistically sound data gathering.[45] Through such methods, Politz claimed, he could forecast markets and "produce consumers."[46] He credited himself, for example, with providing predictive information leading to Coca-Cola's decision to introduce larger bottle sizes in 1952 and cans in 1954 (with subsequent sales increases). Product and product image were as central as uncovering consumer motivations when it came to understanding consumer behavior and promoting goods that consumers did not yet know they desired.[47] The success of corporate consumer marketing, the postwar consumer engineers argued, depended on scientifically rigorous research conducted by expert consumer researchers.

Alfred Politz exemplified a new generation of marketing experts, professionals who viewed their field as an applied science rather than as a practical art. Born in Berlin in 1903, Politz first came to the United States in 1937. He initially found a job as research director with the polling firm Elmo Roper by relying on his ties to the Parker Pen Company, which he had already advised in Berlin. Afterward, he briefly worked for the advertising firm Compton.[48] In 1943, he launched his own advertising research business, Alfred Politz Research, Inc. This firm included a media division (with clients like *Life* magazine), which studied media and advertising performance (exposure rates, audience sizes) and a products and advertising division, which advised in product development and marketing based on large surveys of consumer behavior and motivations. Politz gained a reputation with his sophisticated random sampling methodology, and his firm attracted numerous corporate clients, including Mobile Oil (formerly Socony Vacuum), U.S. Steel, Bristol Myers, DuPont, and Brown and Williamson.[49] By the 1960s, the independent research consulting firm on Madison Avenue had grown to 220 employees in the central office (85 of whom were highly trained professionals) and an additional 600 full-time field researchers.[50]

Politz was well regarded for his "scientific" rigor and his persona as a scientist turned marketing researcher. A 1977 article in the *Journal of Advertising Research* counted him among the "Founding Fathers" of advertising research in the United States.[51] His reputation as an innovator rested on several improvements to sampling techniques. Politz had introduced "duration sampling" as a means to measure exposure rates of outdoor advertising over a set period of time to gauge, for example, the effectiveness of bus advertising. More importantly, during the 1940s he drew on work at the Census Bureau to develop an alternative to the widely used practice of "quota sampling." This method, which aimed to approximate the overall population in the relative composition of the sample, was flawed, Politz argued.

A more statistically sound approach would be to draw on a large, randomized sample within carefully selected geographic areas. The so-called Politz plan was widely recognized as a new form of "area sampling" in commercial research.[52] Retelling his biography on various occasions during the postwar years, Politz reliably emphasized his doctoral degree in physics from the University of Berlin. Here, he claimed, he had studied with Max Planck and Albert Einstein. He had minored in psychology and in later speeches referred to the experimental Gestalt psychologist Max Wertheimer, another later émigré with whom he had studied in Berlin until the early 1930s. Politz was careful to associate himself with the natural sciences and with the logical rigor of math, a subject he had also briefly taught. In one autobiographical account, Politz joked that, upon arriving in New York, he looked for the profession that made "the most money with the least intelligence. The answer was advertising." And since his language skills were not yet good enough, he went into advertising research, which fit with his scientific background.[53] In reality, however, his career in the United States was hardly a sharp departure from his prior work in 1930s Germany, where he had advised companies on sales and advertising since the late 1920s.[54]

Politz's emphasis on science over experience was indicative of a larger transformation in the marketing profession between the 1930s and the 1950s. Expert status was increasingly linked to a professional identity that saw the market researcher on a par with scientists and engineers. While early marketing men had learned their trade in the business world, in sales, retailing, or advertising, by the early twentieth century, marketing experts came to the field with decidedly academic backgrounds. Hugh Agnew, Paul Converse, George Hotchkiss, Charles Parlin, Stanley Resor, Walter Dill Scott, and Arch Shaw were trained in disciplines like economics and psychology. Later in life, many of them took on university positions or published textbooks on scientific marketing.[55] Their work helped usher in a much broader professionalization process during the 1930s. The number of colleges and universities offering training in marketing nearly doubled between 1930 and 1950, growing from 299 to 588, that is, at a much faster rate than higher education overall and expanding also the breadth of specializations from advertising and sales management to market research.[56]

Increasingly, people employed in marketing thus came with specialized training. The number of publications on specific aspects of marketing and marketing research grew in similar fashion. A comprehensive 1951 bibliography on American marketing research, for example, lists over 100 titles published between 1930 and 1949, more than twice the number published in all years leading up to 1930.[57] The 1936 founding of the *Journal of Marketing* as an academic periodical for the field, finally, gave perhaps the most significant impetus for the further development of the field.[58]

Within its pages, the marketing field saw a vigorous debate over the question of how "scientific" marketing already was and to what degree it should strive to fully emulate the natural sciences. Lyndon Brown's 1937 handbook,

Market Research and Analysis, devoted an entire chapter to the general concept of the "scientific method" and its particular application in fields such as psychology, sociology, or statistics. His aim was to familiarize the businessman with the "rapid growth of scientific method in marketing" and to emphasize the importance of logical and scientific methodology in market research.[59] Marketers proudly surveyed the growing body of knowledge in their field, and by the early 1950s, many confidently characterized "marketing science" as well on its way to becoming an independent area of scientific inquiry.[60]

Indeed, market research was one of several marketing fields to make significant methodological strides in the 1930s and 1940s. Consumer psychology, especially the study of motivations and the dynamic development of attitudes, also benefitted greatly from exchanges with academic psychology. The simplistic behaviorist models of the 1920s were now augmented by new approaches from social psychology, Gestalt psychology, as well as Freudian concepts of subconscious desires.[61] Survey research and especially statistical sampling techniques underwent a similar revolution during these decades. Panel studies emerged as a popular method to measure long-term trends in consumer behavior and attitudes.[62] Large survey institutes like Gallup and Roper vastly improved the "quota sampling" approach, while others championed randomized "area sampling."[63] As the field became more complex, methodological controversies emerged that pitted, for example, quantitative survey researchers against those who preferred the more qualitative methods drawn from psychology. At the same time, especially enthusiastic champions of "scientific marketing" anticipated a more unified "theory of marketing." In 1948, marketing experts Wroe Alderson and Reavis Cox argued that a shared body of knowledge had accrued that made it possible to "establish truly scientific criteria for setting up hypotheses and selecting the facts by means of which to test them." As a science in its own right, the authors felt, marketing offered a critique of classical economics by pursuing an institutional analysis of the role of transactions and economic entities. Human behavior, too, could be studied in market situations in collaboration with psychology, sociology, and statistics to provide a better understanding of how and why economic actors act.[64]

Others were more restrained in their assessment of marketing as a science. Although both practitioners and academics interested in marketing "find the time-worn theories of neoclassical economics to be unsatisfying or downright inapplicable," a Boston University professor, Kenneth Hutchinson, surmised, marketing was not a science: "it is rather an art or a practice, and as such much more closely resembles engineering, medicine, and architecture…." To Hutchinson and others like him, marketing was a practical science or a profession that heavily drew on scientific methodology. "Engineers and physicians are trained to approach their problems in this spirit of scientific inquiry; marketing men are learning rapidly to follow their examples."[65] The analogy to doctors and especially to engineers was a recurring theme in this debate. "Most of us are so close to the area of engineering, that there is surely little need to labor the point," noted Lyndon Brown, pointing to the successful incorporation of an analytical approach with scientific experimentation into the engineering profession as a model.[66] Drawing on psychology, statistics, the social sciences, or economics, "marketing engineering[,] which is in reality human engineering, has the task of getting the right article into the possession of the right individual at the right time and at the right price."[67] Such a vision of marketing as a technical science fused the ideas of scientific marketing and consumer engineering.

Claims of scientific expertise frequently opened doors in the business world, as Politz's case suggests. One consequence of the discourse regarding "scientific marketing" was a close proximity between commercial marketing and academic research around mid-century, with many marketing experts pursuing careers that crossed the lines between business and academia.[68] University research centers in survey and audience research, such as those established by the émigré sociologist Paul Lazarsfeld in collaboration with Princeton and Columbia Universities, could count on market studies to support their budgets. Just like John Watson with JWT during the 1920s, many university-trained psychologists found employment with corporations, market research institutes, or ad agencies as staff members in newly created marketing departments or as external consultants. Their scientific credentials created high expectations among many businessmen, as the marketing professor Edmund McGarry observed: "[businessmen] are prone to look upon a scientific expert as one who has remarkable and mysterious powers of foresight. He must be a prophet who can foretell, where profits are to come from. He is expected to know the unknown, to foresee the unforeseeable."[69] There were some limits to the outsider status enjoyed by the "scientific" marketing expert, especially when academic culture collided with business culture. The innovations of scientific marketing were occasionally met with disdain by middle management in the sales department, where they could appear as an unwelcome departure from business as usual. Market researchers, furthermore, who spent too little time getting to know existing business practice, who came across as overly scientific and technical, or who needlessly "belabored the techniques" and presented "riddles instead of results" could have a difficult time getting heard by management.[70] Perfection in sampling methods, Henry Bund of the Research Institute of America observed, dramatically increased costs. Moreover, "scientific and pseudo-scientific mumbo-jumbo" was likely to scare new clients and corporate executives away rather than attract them.[71] Politz therefore insisted that marketing consultants needed to thoroughly research the economic challenges faced by each individual company and to provide concrete answers to relevant questions in a language that management could understand: "Research is finished when the interpretative predictions are finished, ready for the use of management."[72] Consumer engineers, so the promise, would use scientific methods to offer practical solutions to marketing problems.

Overall, the persona of the marketing expert as scientist proved advantageous for marketing professionals at mid-century. As their success continued in the postwar years, consumer engineering and scientific marketing were no longer simply tied to overcoming the depression of the 1930s. Instead, these movements culminated in the postwar years of abundance with efforts to continuously expand material consumption to previously unknown levels. The Populuxe design style of the 1950s now almost openly embraced the concept of obsolescence with an ever-changing array of color changes and annually updated styling features for automobiles, refrigerators, and a plethora of other consumer goods.[73] Consumer research and psychology, too, witnessed a boom in the postwar years with new approaches such as psychoanalytical motivation research.[74] This enthusiasm for consumer engineering drew on a broader anticipation of boundless prosperity during this era of high modernity and on a widespread belief in the near unlimited potential of science and engineering to improve the condition of humankind in general and consumers in particular. Consumer engineers saw themselves as experts at the forefront of engineering a modern consumer society of democratic abundance and individual happiness.[75]

No American Exceptionalism: Transatlantic Careers of Consumer Engineers

To many outside the United States, the promises of consumer engineering and of modern, professional marketing based on scientific methodologies embodied the American Dream of material abundance. The widespread notion of postwar European societies' so-called Americanization, described by contemporaries and historians alike, has frequently been tied to changes in the production, distribution, and consumption of goods after World War II.[76] Not surprisingly, American consumer engineers were eager to get involved with the European economic recovery in the 1950s. Ernest Dichter, like Politz, another European émigré who had established himself as an independent market researcher, urged American companies to tend to the "unsatisfied needs of Europe today."[77] Dichter observed trends and lingering differences in consumer habits: Europeans "would <u>like</u> to have as substantial [a] breakfast as Americans," he noted by way of example in an essay for the trade journal *Business Abroad*, but they had not yet been "stimulated enough" to spend on cereals or pancakes and waffle mixes. The market researcher made similar observations regarding furniture and other goods, but stressed that Europeans still tended to hold on to goods for too long. They were only now on the "verge of accepting the concept of obsolescence." To overcome traditional notions concerning the immorality of waste, Dichter felt that U.S. firms could succeed by promoting "the idea of rejuvenation and replacement—to sell the American concepts of modernization, disposable products, and 'trade-ins.'"[78] If only properly analyzed by consumer studies and effectively guided by advertising, Europeans, too, could experience the joys of the modern consumer cornucopia.

It would be far too simple, however, to understand postwar Europe's embrace of mass consumption as solely the consequence of American influences on marketing techniques.[79] Instead, interwar Europe had seen its own developments in marketing, design, and consumer psychology. These trends, moreover, had influenced the emergence of modern marketing in the United States in ways that make it difficult to view the consumer engineering practiced by Politz or Dichter as entirely "foreign" to postwar European marketing. Advertising in German-speaking Central Europe, for example, became increasingly organized and professionalized during the 1920s and early 1930s.[80] American agencies such as JWT and McCann had entered the German market and offered advertising pretests and market analyses.[81] While many German admen rejected such systematic approaches to their profession, emphasizing instead intuition and artistic genius, an emerging trend toward more scientific marketing can be discerned in interwar Europe as well. Marketing guru Hans Domizlaff pioneered branding efforts in the tobacco industry, working with elaborate segmentations of price and quality; Domizlaff understood brand marketing as a "social technology" central to modern economies.[82] Advertising research and ad reception studies became established at German universities, while at Vienna's university the *Wirtschaftspsychologische Forschungsstelle* was set up in 1930 as a center for market studies and consumer motivation research.[83] Founded by Paul Lazarsfeld, this last institution was soon conducting sophisticated market surveys for companies from various German-speaking countries. In Germany, the Nuremberg *Institut für Wirtschaftsbeobachtung* became an institutional center for marketing studies, which by the 1930s was succeeded by the *Gesellschaft für Konsumforschung* (GfK).[84] The GfK would play a central role in the German consumer economy under National Socialism and, after the war, emerged as one of Europe's premier market research operations.[85] The Scandinavian countries, France, the Netherlands, and especially Great Britain also had histories of market research dating back to the 1920s and 1930s, histories which informed their postwar marketing development.[86]

While several actors involved with the GfK embraced economic liberalism, other early European market researchers came from a more radical background. Lazarsfeld's survey research center in Vienna, for example, was influenced by Viennese social reform movements, and several of Britain's leading market researchers of the interwar years were heavily involved in social progressivism and social planning movements.[87] The foremost designers in interwar Europe evinced similar links to social reform traditions. Product designers in the German *Werkbund* movement, for example, sought to standardize household goods and create furniture and appliances for model working-class housing projects. At the same time, the famous Bauhaus school created a radical design curriculum that stressed a strictly functionalist modernism but also strove to introduce notions of "good form" into mass production. While many Bauhaus designs initially targeted upscale market segments, the school was not averse to commercial applications and ultimately aimed to provide designs for affordable mass-market products.[88] The postwar international style and the design modernism of many consumer-engineered American goods were thus not at all foreign to European consumers. Alongside postwar transfers from the United States were indigenous European marketing traditions, which postwar Europeans could connect with.

These interwar trends in Europe, moreover, left their mark on the very emergence of consumer engineering in North America. In fact, in their 1932 treatise on consumer engineering, Sheldon and Arens repeatedly looked to Europe for examples of innovation and inspiration. If America was the land of resource abundance and a burgeoning consumer industry, Europe was still the continent to which Americans turned for trends in fashion and style. Interwar European centers such as Paris, Vienna, and Berlin still represented the vanguard of modernity to these proponents of consumer engineering, especially with regard to artistic design and academic research. Sheldon and Arens's treatment of the style experiments of "Professor [Franz] Kruckenberg's" streamlined "äero-express" and the color and design variations for luxury trains proposed by "Professor Joseph Hoffmann" of the *Wiener Werkstätten* was almost deferential.[89] They introduced Kem Weber, a German immigrant designer who had studied under *Werkbund* co-founder Bruno Paul, as exemplary for a new generation of designers who had emancipated themselves from traditional craftsmanship in order to devise forms appropriate to the machine age and mass production.[90] With regard to psychology, the authors of *Consumer Engineering* listed Carl Jung, Sigmund Freud, and Alfred Adler as examples of a "new psychology" from Europe, which they thought might inspire future advertising research and related efforts in "Humaneering."[91]

This American infatuation with European design and thought led to a vibrant transatlantic exchange in design and consumer research during the 1930s.[92] A significant number of European artists and scholars established careers in American marketing after they had to flee Nazi rule in Europe because of their Jewish background or political leanings. One prominent example was the group around Paul Lazarsfeld's Vienna *Wirtschaftspsychologische Forschungsstelle*. Lazarsfeld's work on consumer motivations was received with much interest in the United States, and he pursued a stellar career in social, media, and market research in the decades following his emigration.[93] His background in Viennese psychology opened doors for him on the American scene because, as American market researcher Alexis Sommaripa observed in 1934, "Vienna [is] the present center of the science of psychology [and] has developed very important methods of analysis as applied to consumer needs."[94] Lazarsfeld's "Vienna school" of market research gained influence in the American profession over the coming decades and included such prominent figures as Herta Herzog (McCann-Erickson) and the already mentioned Ernest Dichter.[95] European modernist designers were met with similar enthusiasm by some leaders of American industry. The Chicago Association for Arts and Industries, for example, whose members included Marshall Fields, Harold McCormick, and Harold Swift, set out during the late 1930s to find a Bauhaus artist to open a new and decidedly modernist design school. While their eventual hire, the photo-artist Lazlo Moholy-Nagy, would have a conflicted history with the Chicago business community, the American Bauhaus he established influenced the growing design profession in the United States at a time when consumer engineering and modernist design were at their peak.[96]

Postwar Europe was therefore hardly virgin territory for many elements of the consumer engineering concept. To be sure, American advertising agencies now exerted a modernizing force across the continent more strongly than ever before. In Germany and elsewhere in Europe, subsidiaries of the U.S. agencies offered a "full service" model of marketing consulting and set the standard for professional and scientific conduct in advertising.[97] But returning émigrés such as Dichter were also intent on modernizing European marketing. Dichter influenced European developments through the consulting work that his New York-based firm did for companies and institutions, playing on his expertise as an American expert of modern marketing methods, albeit one with European roots. With regard to American clients, Dichter positioned himself even more directly as a transatlantic translator and cultural broker. In numerous commissioned studies and articles published in trade journals such as *Business Abroad*, he gave advice to American businesses seeking to enter European markets. He alerted them to the necessity of understanding local conditions, which market research could help them account for.

Former émigrés like Dichter frequently invoked their transatlantic expertise and emphasized their background as migrants between the continents. In advertising his motivation research studies to American companies, Dichter carefully pointed out that he was an expert in marketing because of his profession and degree and an expert in Europe because of his migration experience. "[Europeans] accept me and probably many others; in my particular case because I can combine European answers with American know-how.... I do speak their languages and they will sort of hug me and say, 'Well, you're really one of us.'"[98] His background became a prominent asset in his marketing career, leading him to reflect on the irony of his immigrant status: "isn't it funny that most of the marketing people that really made good in the States, quite a number of them happen to be people from Vienna or Germany [and] went to college there ... Alfred Politz, Professor Lazarsfeld, Ernest Dichter ... [They] have come back to you as American experts but whom are you kidding?" Without European experts, America would not have had modern marketing in the same form; however, Dichter noted, he could only have succeeded in the United States.[99] From there, he and others were able to "re-import" modern marketing after the war in the guise of consumer engineering, developed in part from marketing traditions that had been shaped between Europe and the United States during the 1930s and 1940s.[100]

Conclusion: Limits of Consumer Engineering

These transnational exchanges in consumer research and design show that consumer engineering and scientific marketing were hardly foreign elements of a perceived Americanization process in postwar Europe. The eventual critique of consumer engineering had a similarly transnational character by the late 1950s and early 1960s. Vance Packard's attacks on overt consumer manipulation (*The Hidden Persuaders*, 1957) and "planned obsolescence" (*The Waste Makers*, 1960), for example, were widely disseminated and discussed on both sides of the Atlantic.[101] They contributed to an increasingly skeptical public perception of consumer marketing efforts. Critics of mass consumption on the political left increasingly focused on the same aspects of consumer psychology that the consumer engineers had championed. What to marketing experts like Dichter and Politz had been the satisfaction of legitimate and quasi-natural desires was to critics such as Erich Fromm and Herbert Marcuse now merely the satisfaction of artificially stimulated fantasies in one-dimensional personalities bent on materialistic consumption. Many of the critics drew on notions of cultural manipulation in mass media and society developed by Theodor Adorno and other members of the Frankfurt School, whose transatlantic careers were closely interwoven with those of consumer engineers such as Paul Lazarsfeld.[102]

The very premise of what Sheldon and Arens had called "humaneering" thus came under public scrutiny.[103] Concerns about consumer manipulation were picked up by the consumer movement of the 1960s and became coupled with a growing environmentalist awareness of the "limits of growth" by the early 1970s. Occasionally, consumers on a grassroots level even began to rebel against the world of goods proposed by self-proclaimed marketing experts.[104] The idea of engineered prosperity, which had propelled marketing developments from the 1930s to the 1950s, stood on increasingly shaky ground.

Despite such critiques, marketing did not become less important to the consumer goods industry. On the contrary, the marketing field became even more specialized and professionalized during the 1960s and 1970s, increasingly relying on quantitative, more data-driven approaches. Market segmentation gained in importance, as marketers broke down the consuming mass to target specific groups. Consumer psychology, too, attained a new level of sophistication, when the field turned to more cognitive approaches.[105] As the scientific marketing profession matured, however, its practitioners became somewhat less grandiose in their promises and instead provided the necessary knowledge to selectively target specific consumer segments. As Ingo Köhler suggests in his contribution to this volume, companies increasingly made marketing central to their management practice by actively integrating marketing research and consumer feedback into their overall corporate strategies. In part as a reaction to the critiques leveled by the consumer and environmental movements, the self-understanding of marketing professionals shifted from one of consumption experts engaged in the unapologetic "engineering" of consumers and markets to that of more modest interpreters of consumer wishes for corporations aiming to serve them.

Did scientific marketers as consumer engineers in the end simply serve idealized consumers as the ultimate arbiters of mass consumption? Such an interpretation, of course, was in part merely a reincarnation of the ideology of service-oriented consumer capitalism, which regained popularity during the latter part of the twentieth century. In part, however, it was also rooted in a changing understanding of mass communication and of the role of expertise in society. At mid-century, public relations gurus such as Edward Bernays were fully convinced that consumers and the public at large depended on technocrats of various guises and could be influenced and manipulated almost at will by advertisers and marketing experts employing an array of modern media. Such "engineering of consent" by expert "technicians," according to Bernays, was "the application of scientific principles and tried practices to the task of getting people to support ideas and programs."[106] In the post-war decades, however, communications experts—including such pioneers of consumer psychology as Paul Lazarsfeld—came to view persuasive communication as a more complex process taking place in a dynamic social field and requiring the active participation of "opinion leaders" and audience members. The type of mass communication on which modern marketing relied appeared less and less as a one-way street and more like a complex process over which consumer engineers could only exert limited control. And while it surely never fully disappeared, the notion that the expert designer, expert engineer, or expert marketer actually knew better than the consumer what the consumer desired fell out of favor, whereas the notion of consumer agency gained traction. While consumer engineering accelerated the trend toward scientific marketing and modern marketing management, its overtly manipulative bent could ultimately not be squared with the ideal of informed and sovereign consumers.

Notes

1. Alfred Politz, "A. P. Book (Draft #1)," December 22, 1971, Politz Papers, St. Johns University, box 1, folder 3.
2. Ibid., 5–6.
3. Ibid., 6.
4. Alfred Politz, "Creative Market and Opinion Research," Address before Boston Conference on Distribution, October 21, 1952, Politz Papers, St. Johns University, box 3, folder 9.
5. For a discussion of agency in consumer history, see David Steigerwald, "All Hail to the Republic of Choice: Consumer History as Contemporary Thought," *Journal of American History* 93 (2006): 385–403.
6. See Jan Logemann, "European Imports? European Immigrants and the Transformation of American Consumer Culture from the 1920s to the 1960s," *Bulletin of the German Historical Institute* 52 (2013): 113–33.

7. Lizabeth Cohen, *A Consumers' Republic: The Politics of Mass Consumption in Postwar America* (New York, 2003).
8. See, for example, Meg Jacobs, *Pocketbook Politics: Economic Citizenship in Twentieth-Century America* (Princeton, NJ, 2005); and Gary Cross, *An All-Consuming Century: Why Commercialism Won in Modern America* (New York, NY, 2000).
9. A still classic treatment: Roland Marchand, *Advertising the American Dream: Making Way for Modernity, 1920–1940* (Berkeley, CA, 1985).
10. Richard Tedlow, *New and Improved: The Story of Mass Marketing in America* (New York, 1990); Roy Church and Andrew Godley, eds., *The Emergence of Modern Marketing* (London, 2003); and Hartmut Berghoff, Philip Scranton, and Uwe Spiekermann, eds., *The Rise of Marketing and Market Research* (New York, NY, 2012).
11. See Daniel Horowitz, "The Émigré as Celebrant of American Consumer Culture," in *Getting and Spending*, ed. Susan Strasser (Cambridge, UK, 1999), 149–66.
12. On the notion of high modernity, see James C. Scott, *Seeing Like a State: How Certain Schemes to Improve the Human Condition Have Failed* (New Haven, CT, 1998). On social engineering, see Kerstin Brückweh et al., eds., *Engineering Society: The Role of the Human and Social Sciences in Modern Societies, 1880–1980* (Basingstoke, 2012).
13. Vance Packard, *The Hidden Persuaders* (New York, NY, 1957); and Vance Packard, *The Waste Makers* (New York, NY, 1960).
14. See Daniel Rodgers, *Atlantic Crossings Social Politics in a Progressive Age* (Cambridge, MA, 1998).
15. Elmo Calkins, "The New Consumption Engineer and the Artist," 1930, cited in Jeffrey Meikle, *Twentieth Century Limited: Industrial Design in America, 1925–1939* (Philadelphia, PA, 1979), 70.
16. Roy Sheldon and Egmont Arens, *Consumer Engineering: A New Technique of Prosperity* (New York, NY, 1932).
17. Ibid., 1.
18. Ibid., 11–13.
19. Ibid., 55–56.
20. Ibid., 95–96.
21. Herbert Hess, "The New Consumption Era," *American Marketing Journal* 1 (1935): 16–25.
22. Myron Heidingsfield and Albert Blankenship, *Market and Marketing Analysis* (New York, NY, 1947), 3.
23. See Kazuo Usui, *The Development of Marketing Management: The Case of the USA, c. 1910–1940* (Farnham, UK, 2008), Chapter 4.
24. Frank Coutant, "Scientific Marketing Makes Progress," *Journal of Marketing* 1 (1937): 226–30, here 230.
25. See Peggy Kreshel, "Advertising Research in the Pre-Depression Years: A Cultural History," *Journal of Current Issues and Research in Advertising* 15 (1993): 59–75; and Douglas Ward, "Capitalism, Early Market Research, and the Creation of the American Consumer," *Journal of Historical Research in Marketing* 1 (2009): 200–23. On "scientific marketing," see esp. Usui, *Development of Marketing Management*, Chap. 3.

26. On the early development of the profession, see Wilford White, "The Teaching of Marketing...," *National Marketing Review* 1 (1935): 1–8. See also D. G. Brian Jones, "A History of Historical Research in Marketing," in *Marketing Theory*, ed. Michael J. Baker and Michael Saren (London, 2011), 51–80.
27. Ralph Hower, *The History of an Advertising Agency: N. W. Ayer & Son at Work 1869–1939* (Cambridge, MA, 1939), 254–78. On the development of the advertising industry as an institution fostering demand during this era, see also Charles McGovern, *Sold American: Consumption and Citizenship, 1890–1945* (Chapel Hill, NC, 2006).
28. Sam Meek, "New Client Presentation," 1928, JWT Archives, cited in Kreshel, "Advertising Research," 66.
29. On the role of design offices during the 1920s and 1930s, see Meikle, *Twentieth Century Limited.*
30. See, for example, Lawrence Lockley, "Notes on the History of Marketing Research," *Journal of Marketing* 14 (1950): 733–36.
31. See Carolyn Goldstein, *Creating Consumers: Home Economists in Twentieth-Century America* (Chapel Hill, NC, 2012), Chap. 5.
32. Henry Link and Irving Lorge, "The Psychological Sales Barometer," *Harvard Business Review* 14 (1935): 193–204.
33. With regard to consumer research before and during the Great Depression, see Sarah Igo, *The Averaged American: Surveys, Citizens, and the Making of a Mass Public* (Cambridge, MA, 2007); as well as Daniel Robinson, *The Measure of Democracy: Polling, Market Research and Public Life, 1930–1945* (Toronto, 1999), 15–18, 39–63.
34. On the impact of the depression, see Howard Hovde, "Recent Trends in the Development of Market Research," *American Marketing Journal* 3 (1936): 3–19.
35. Willard E. Freeland, "Scientific Management in Marketing," *Journal of Marketing* 4 (1940): 31–38.
36. David Gartman, *Auto Opium: A Social History of American Automobile Design* (London, UK, 1994).
37. Roland Marchand, "Customer Research as Public Relations: General Motors in the 1930s," in *Getting and Spending*, ed. Strasser et al., 85–109.
38. Gerben Bakker, "Building Knowledge About the Consumer: The Emergence of Market Research in the Motion Picture Industry," *Business History* 45 (2003): 101–27. On the increasingly systematic forecasting in various "Fashion goods" industries, see Regina Blaszczyk, *Imagining Consumers: Design and Innovation from Wedgewood to Corning* (Baltimore, MD, 2000); and Veronique Pouillard, "The Rise of Fashion Forecasting and Fashion Public Relations, 1920–1940: The History of Tobe and Bernays," in *Globalizing Beauty: Consumerism and Body Aesthetics in the Twentieth Century*, ed. Hartmut Berghoff and Thomas Kühne (New York, 2012), 151–69.
39. Elma S. Moulton, *Marketing Research Activities of Manufacturers* (Washington, DC: U.S. Bureau of Foreign and Domestic Commerce, 1939). The study was conducted in cooperation with the American Marketing Association, with Frank Coutant, Alexis Sommaripa, Ferdinand Wheeler, and Paul Converse, among others, on the advisory committee.

40. Heusner et al., "Marketing Research in American Industry I," *Journal of Marketing*, no. 11 (1947): 338–54; and Heusner et al., "Marketing Research in American Industry II," *Journal of Marketing*, no. 12 (1947): 25–37. The study was conducted in cooperation with the National Association of Manufacturers. Its members were sent surveys, of which 4786 usable forms (36% of those sent out) were returned.
41. Heusner et al., "Marketing Research in American Industry I," 348–52.
42. Gordon Hughes, "The Relationship of Advertiser and Agency in Research," *Journal of Marketing* 14 (1950): 579–80.
43. Steuart Henderson Britt, "Research and Merchandising in a Modern Advertising Agency," *Journal of Marketing* 13 (1949): 506–10.
44. Donald Longman, "The Status of Marketing Research," *Journal of Marketing* 16 (1951): 197–201. The role of market research in product planning or sales was not yet universally accepted, Longman complained, and business managers frequently did not champion a "scientific attitude" toward marketing.
45. Alfred Politz and Edward Deming, "On the Necessity to Present Consumer Preferences as Predictions," *Journal of Marketing* 18 (1953): 1–5.
46. The draft of his unfinished autobiography bore the title "How to Produce Consumers—Methods and Illusions." See "A. P. Book (Draft #1)," December 22, 1971, Politz Papers, St. Johns University, box 1, folder 3.
47. Ibid., chapter entitled "Product, the Majesty." Politz, however, warned against emphasizing only "image" in advertising while losing sight of the product. For all his focus on understanding consumers, he still remained partially wedded to a product-centered approach to marketing.
48. Alfred Politz, "Highlights of My Biography," April 23, 1982, Politz Papers, St. Johns University, box 1, folder 1.
49. In 1945, the advertising trade publication *TIDE* ran an in-depth article on the "revolutionary," yet expensive Politz method of random sampling. See "Politz Plan," *TIDE*, June 15, 1945, reprinted in Hardy, ed., *Politz Papers*. On his client list, see "Some Highlights of Achievements," December 1, 1960, Politz Papers, St. Johns University, box 2, folder 2.
50. See "Alfred Politz Research Inc." [c. 1964], and Jane Elligett, "Alfred Politz Research Inc.," August 16, 1982, Politz Papers, St. Johns University, box 2, folder 1.
51. Advertising Research Foundation, "The Founding Fathers of Advertising Research," reprinted from *Journal of Advertising Research* (June 1977), in Paul F. Lazarsfeld Archive, University of Vienna, folder "About PFL 2" (blue series).
52. See, for example, Robert J. Williams, "Recollections of Alfred Politz, Aug.–Sept. 1982," PP St. Johns, box 1, folder 2.
53. A. P., "Highlights of My Biography," April 23, 1982, Politz Papers, St. Johns University, box 1, folder 1.
54. "Resume," March 7, 1940, Politz Papers, St. Johns University, box 1, folder 1.
55. See John Wright and Parks Dimsdale, *Pioneers in Marketing* (Atlanta, GA, 1974).
56. Harold Hardy, "Collegiate Marketing Education Since 1930," *Journal of Marketing* 19 (1955): 325–30.

57. David Revzan, *A Comprehensive Classified Marketing Bibliography* (Berkeley, CA, 1951), 76–83.
58. The *American Marketing Journal* (est. 1934) and the *National Marketing Review* (est. 1935) merged in 1936 to become the *Journal of Marketing*.
59. Lyndon Brown, *Market Research and Analysis* (New York, NY, 1935), v and 4.
60. Paul Converse, "The Development of the Science of Marketing: An Exploratory Survey," *Journal of Marketing* 10 (1945): 14–23; or Robert Bartels, "Can Marketing be a Science?" *Journal of Marketing* 15 (1952): 319–28.
61. See, for example, Albert Blankenship, "Psychological Difficulties in Measuring Consumer Preference," *Journal of Marketing* 6 (1942): 66–75, which emphasizes the influence of Paul Lazarsfeld on consumer motivation research. See also Ferdinand Wheeler, "New Methods and Results in Market Research," *American Marketing Journal* 2 (1935): 35–39.
62. Thomas Stonborough, "Fixed Panels in Consumer Research," *Journal of Marketing* 7 (1942): 129–38; and Alfred Root and Alfred Welch, "The Continuing Consumer Study: A Basic Method for the Engineering of Advertising," *Journal of Marketing* 7 (1942): 3–21.
63. Ralph Cassady, "Statistical Sampling Techniques and Marketing Research," *Journal of Marketing* 9 (1945): 317–41.
64. Wroe Alderson and Reavis Cox, "Towards a Theory of Marketing," *Journal of Marketing* 13 (1948): 137–52, here 139.
65. Kenneth Hutchinson, "Marketing as a Science: An Appraisal," *Journal of Marketing* 16 (1952): 286–93.
66. Lyndon Brown, "Towards a Profession of Marketing," *Journal of Marketing* 13 (1948): 27–31.
67. Hess, "New Consumption Era," 18.
68. One contributor even proposed a revolving doors model: H. R. Nissey, "Exchange Professorship Idea Applied to Commercial Research," *Journal of Marketing* 5 (1940): 43–44.
69. Edmund McGarry, "The Importance of Scientific Method in Advertising," *Journal of Marketing* 1 (1936): 82–86.
70. William Marsteller, "Putting the Marketing Research Department on the Executive Level," *Journal of Marketing* 16 (1951): 56–60.
71. Henry Bund, "Does Marketing Research Know Its Own Market?" *Journal of Marketing* 15 (1950): 198–205.
72. Politz and Denning, "On the Necessity," 5.
73. Thomas Hine, *Populuxe* (New York, NY), 1986.
74. Lawrence Samuel, *Freud on Madison Avenue: Motivation Research and Subliminal Advertising in America* (Philadelphia, PA, 2010).
75. This exuberant link between consumer abundance and democratic politics was construed most directly in the publications of consumer researchers Ernest Dichter and George Katona. See Daniel Horowitz, "The Émigré as Celebrant of American Consumer Culture," in *Getting and Spending*, ed. Strasser, 149–66.
76. The most influential recent discussion of Americanization through mass consumption is Victoria de Grazia, *Irresistible Empire: America's Advance Through Twentieth-Century Europe* (Cambridge, MA, 2005).

77. On Dichter and his transatlantic career in motivation research, see, for example, Stefan Schwarzkopf and Rainer Gries, eds., *Ernest Dichter and Motivation Research: New Perspectives on the Making of Post-War Consumer Culture* (New York, NY, 2010).
78. Ernest Dichter, "What Are the Unsatisfied Needs of Europe Today?" article for *Business Abroad*, typescript, n.d., Hagley Museum and Library, Ernest Dichter Papers, box 167.
79. The argument regarding the indigenous European tradition is also made by Stefan Schwarzkopf, "Managing the Unmanageable: The Professionalization of Market and Consumer Research in Post-War Europe," in *Transformations of Retailing in Postwar Europe After 1945*, ed. Ralph Jessen and Lydia Langer (Farnham, UK, 2012), 163–78.
80. See Gerulf Hirt, *Verkannte Propheten? Zur 'Expertenkultur' (west-)deutscher Werbekommunikatoren bis zur Rezession 1966/67* (Leipzig, 2013).
81. Alexander Schug, "Wegbereiter der modernen Absatzwerbung in Deutschland: Advertising Agencies und die Amerikanisierung der deutschen Werbebranche in der Zwischenkriegszeit," *WerkstattGeschichte* 34 (2003): 29–51.
82. On Domizlaff's work at Reemtsma, see Tino Jacobs, "Zwischen Intuition und Experiment: Hans Domizlaff und der Aufstieg Reemtsmas," in *Marketinggeschichte: Die Genese einer modernen Sozialtechnik*, ed. Hartmut Berghoff (Frankfurt a.M, 2007), 148–76.
83. See Claudia Regnery, *Die Deutsche Werbeforschung 1900–1945* (Münster, 2003); and Ronald Fullerton, "Tea and the Viennese: A Pioneering Episode in the Analysis of Consumer Behavior," in *Advances in Consumer Research*, ed. Chris Allen and Deborah John (Provo, UT, 1994), 418–21.
84. Georg Bergeler, *Die Entwicklung der Verbrauchsforschung in Deutschland und die GfK bis zum Jahre 1945* (Laßleben, 1959).
85. Jonathan Wiesen, *Creating the Nazi Marketplace: Commerce and Consumption in the Third Reich* (Cambridge, UK, 2011); and Wilfired Feldenkirchen and Daniela Fuchs, *Die Stimme des Verbrauchers zum Klingen bringen: 75 Jahre Geschichte der GFK Gruppe* (Munich, 2009).
86. See Schwartzkopf, "Managing the Unmanageable"; and Clodwig Kapferer, *Marktforschung in Europa: Methoden Einzelner Länder* (Hamburg, 1963).
87. Stefan Schwartzkopf, "A Radical Past? The Politics of Market Research in Britain, 1900–1950," in *The Voice of the Citizen Consumer: A History of Market Research, Consumer Movements, and the Political Public Sphere*, ed. Kerstin Brückweh (Oxford, UK, 2011), 29–50.
88. Frederic Schwartz, "Utopia for Sale: The Bauhaus and Weimar Germany's Consumer Culture," in *Bauhaus Culture: From Weimar to the Cold War*, ed. Kathleen James (Minneapolis, MN, 2006), 115–38.
89. Sheldon and Arens, *Consumer Engineering*, 44–47.
90. Ibid., 173–74.
91. Ibid., 99.
92. For a more detailed discussion of these transfers, see Logemann, "European Imports."
93. On Paul Lazarsfeld and his role in transatlantic exchanges in the social sciences, see Christian Fleck, *A Transatlantic History of the Social Sciences: Robber Barons, the Third Reich and the Invention of Empirical Social Research* (London, UK, 2011).

94. Letter Alexis Sommaripa (Business Advisory and Planning Council, Dept. of Commerce) to Dexter Keezer (Dir. Consumer Advisory Board, NIRA), January 16, 1934, in Paul F. Lazarsfeld Archive, University of Vienna, folder "Biographie 1933–46."
95. On the Vienna school, see Hans Zeisel, "Die Wiener Schule der Motivforschung," keynote address for the Congress of the World Association for Public Opinion Research (WAPOR) and the European Society for Opinion and Market Research (ESOMAR), August 21, 1967, in P.F.L.-Archive, University of Vienna, folder "Lazarsfeld Vienna Marktforschungsstelle."
96. On American Bauhaus, see James Sloan Allen, *The Romance of Commerce and Culture: Capitalism, Modernism, and the Chicago-Aspen Crusade for Cultural Reform* (Chicago, IL, 1983); and Paul Betts, "New Bauhaus and School of Design, Chicago," in *Bauhaus*, ed. Jeannine Fiedler and Peter Feierabend (Cologne, 2000), 66–73.
97. Harm Schröter, "Die Amerikanisierung der Werbung in der Bundesrepublik Deutschland," *Jahrbuch für Wirtschaftsgeschichte* 38, no. 1 (1997): 93–115.
98. Ernest Dichter, "Business Abroad Article—(Rough Copy)," March 28, 1967, Ernest Dichter Papers, Hagley Museum and Library, box 169.
99. Ibid.
100. On Dichter's role as a transatlantic translator of marketing knowledge, see also Jan Logemann, "Consumer Modernity as Cultural Translation: European Émigrés and Knowledge Transfers in Mid-Century Design and Marketing," *Geschichte und Gesellschaft* 43 (2017): 413–37.
101. Daniel Horowitz, *Consuming Pleasures: Intellectuals and Popular Culture in the Cold War* (Philadelphia, PA, 2012).
102. Adorno had developed aspects of his critique of the "culture industry" while working alongside Lazarsfeld on the well-known "Radio Research Project," which was partially supported by CBS. See Theodor Adorno, "Scientific Experiences of a European Scholar in America," and Lazarsfeld, "An Episode in the History of Social Research: A Memoir," in *The Intellectual Migration: Europe and America, 1930–1960*, ed. Donald Fleming and Bernard Bailyn (Cambridge, MA, 1969), 270–337 and 338–70, respectively.
103. A scare concerning so-called subliminal advertising marked an early high point of this critique of psychological marketing during the late 1950s. See Kenneth Lipartito, "Subliminal Seductions: The Politics of Consumer Research in Post-World War II America," in *Rise of Marketing*, ed. Berghoff, 215–36.
104. On critiques of postwar mass consumption in general, see Daniel Horowitz, *The Anxieties of Affluence: Critiques of American Consumer Culture, 1939–1979* (Amherst, MA, 2004). On organized consumer activism, see Lawrence Glickman, *Buying Power: A History of Consumer Activism in America* (Chicago, IL, 2009).
105. Harold Kassarijian, "Scholarly Traditions and European Roots of American Consumer Research," in *Research Traditions in Marketing*, ed. Giles Laurent, Gary Lilien, and Bernard Pras (Boston, MA, 1993), 265–79.
106. Edward Bernays, "The Engineering of Consent," *The Annals of the American Academy of Political and Social Sciences* 250 (1947): 113–20, here 114.

CHAPTER 3

What Does "Fast Capitalism" Mean for Consumers? Examples of Consumer Engineering in the United States

Gary Cross

One marker of modernity is rapidity of change: popular music, movies, and TV programs come and go, of course, but so-called durable goods are almost as ephemeral. We live in an era of fast capitalism, which also means fast consumption, a particularly intensive form of commodity culture resulting from marketing and technological innovations that led to an increasingly rapid pace of production and purchase, creating profit through fast turnaround of investment. Although the consumer's quest for change (especially in fashion goods) predates this process, this sped-up production and consumption cycle increased consumer expectations regarding convenience and change, which in turn encouraged further technological and marketing innovations. Although consumer culture, marketing, and technology all played interactive roles in this process, historians have tended to stress marketing innovations, including those in advertising.

Predating the 1930s consumer engineering described by Jan Logemann in Chapter 2, fast capitalism comprised most of the same stimulative elements. As Philip Scranton notes, a major theme of modern merchandizing is the transformation of once traditional and even traditionalized goods marketed as heritage and for durability (like furniture) into products that quickly come in and out of fashion. Fast capitalism also meant planned obsolescence, made famous by Vance Packard more than a half century ago. The term "fast capitalism" was only introduced in the late 1980s, however, when Ben Agger argued that

G. Cross (✉)
Department of History, Pennsylvania State University, University Park, PA, USA

J. Logemann et al. (eds.), *Consumer Engineering, 1920s–1970s*,
Worlds of Consumption, https://doi.org/10.1007/978-3-030-14564-4_3

a new order had emerged during the economic crises of the 1970s (inflation and the decline of American hegemony) that led to "just-in-time" batch production designed for ever narrower and changing markets. The erosion of labor's power and of the welfare state as well as the rise of globalization contributed to the decline of classic mass production and consumption, but its "fast" successor was also fostered by new technologies and business processes that reduced the time required for product development and delivery to market. Others associate the era of speed with an even more recent phenomenon, the shift from the production and consumption of durable goods to the selling and buying of sensations in the so-called experiential economy, in particular with the rise of digital technology and new forms of leisure in the 1980s.[1]

As valuable as all this is, these common "postmodernist" interpretations, associated with David Harvey, for example,[2] tend to ignore capitalism's longer history of rapidity. I argue that fast capitalism has origins in the generation around 1900 and is rooted in a cluster of technological innovations, corporate innovations in product design and distribution, and consumers' rising expectations of and desire for novelty. Given the theme of this book, I'll also consider how these transformations have accelerated since the 1930s, and, for a bit more specificity, I'll concentrate on media consumer goods, especially recorded music.

While a cardinal feature of production for profit is the rapid turnaround of investment, technological and marketing constraints severely limited this turnaround until the end of the nineteenth century. That was when a dramatic compression of the product life cycle occurred. It came from many directions. Faster shipping and communication moved goods more quickly from factory to shopping bag, but new packaging and labeling methods also reduced set-up and manufacturing times. Technologically innovative products like phonographs as well as movie cameras and projectors (along with their software of records and film) accelerated the pace of novelty emerging in the 1890s (and developing further in the next decade) still more.[3]

Soon after 1900, manufacturers of a wide range of goods from automobiles to household appliances introduced frequent, even annual model changes, but there was also an explosion of novelty and fashion goods from toys to knickknacks. Moreover, new methods of persuasion induced consumers to adapt more rapidly to change. For example, weekly or daily exposure to magazines, newspapers, and their continuously changing advertising promoted the latest models of new domestic appliances and cars as well as innovations in toiletries, foods, and novelties. This first era of fast capitalism extended until the Great Depression.

As noted years ago by Jeffrey Meikle and Andre Forty, the common-sense assumption that product and marketing innovation slowed during the economic downturn of the 1930s is wrong. If anything, innovation accelerated, not only in product design and marketing but also in technology. The very fact that sales decreased dramatically after 1929 motivated a wide-ranging effort in consumer engineering to bring back anxious shoppers. Thus came streamlined cars (and refrigerators) as well as double features at the movies, tabletop radios, and a faster pace of change on the pop music hit parade. Accelerating waves of ultramodern furnishings, appliances, packaged foods, cars, and much else along with popular enthusiasm for exuberant materialism (what Tom Hine called the "Populuxe") followed the depression and war.[4] By the 1960s, planned obsolescence was supplanted by personal purchases of cars, TVs, and other formerly "family" goods, leading to an ever denser, more individualized consumer experience. The 1970s brought not only post-Fordist segmented consumption but a technological and marketing transformation that quickened the pace of consumption still further. Affluent people from the USA and other advanced nations experienced a new wave of innovation, especially in analog entertainment technologies. From the 1980s, the trend toward innovation continued in digital devices, especially for the rapidly changing personal computer and related accessories. Consumer expectation of the new became an annual ritual. Fast capitalism (and consumer engineering), then, can be understood not only as a form of consumer manipulation but as an expectation that shaped personal behavior and social interaction.

Fast capitalism made for fast people. But this meant much more than a rapidly moving culture of ephemeral and superficial identities. People increasingly accustomed to and expecting novelty experienced dramatically new attitudes about life: Shorter attention spans, but also less resistance to change and a proclivity to mark time less by seasonal and other natural durations than by the introduction of new products and media. Commercial fads, ephemeral fashions, and a rapidly passing, if short list of media hits defined shared experience. Fast capitalism produced other responses endemic today: not just individual identification with time-specific consumer goods but commodities that defined entire generations. The novel produced narrow cohorts of consumption (beginning with the young) that manifested as nostalgia for past fashion later in the life course and divided even subsets of generations. Yet fast capitalism also led to a reaction to all this: individual pursuit of the unchanging, engagement with seasonal and ritual recurrence, and even identification with bygone eras, all in an attempt to mollify and retard the bewildering pace of change.

A Generation of Accelerated Commodity Change, 1890–1930

This process began or at least was accelerated in the two generations after 1890. New products like phonographs, snapshot cameras, motion pictures, canned foods, bottled soft drinks, packaged cigarettes, and cars transformed the way Americans and Western Europeans listened, watched, imbibed, and moved. The coming of new household appliances in everything from toasters and electric irons to vacuum cleaners and electric stoves, refrigerators, and radios produced a regular expectation of material progress, especially with the "new and improved" in routinely updated products. Radical and continuous changes in fashion, cosmetics, grooming devices (like safety razors), novelties, and even toys and furnishings made it hard to keep up. This blizzard of innovation led to a welter of confusing options and new emphases along with the excitement of adopting ever new and wider assortments of things. Setting and even advancing the pace of change was the rapid rise and fall of entertainment celebrity and styles along with novelty and fad marketing as, for example, in board games, fashions, and children's fantasy toys and other playthings. These "soft" industries at the vanguard of fast capitalism were especially directed toward the young.

Let me briefly illustrate this with the phonograph and recording, which came together around 1900. An oligopoly of three producers—Victor, Edison, and Columbia—transformed Edison's original novelty for capturing the voice for playback (first as a business machine) in a hardware–software complex of continuously "improving" players and a constant output of recordings for a home entertainment market. The phonograph also represented a dramatic change in entertainment based on a new business model: the mass commercial distribution of notable voices and musical ensembles from central locations to home sites. The phenomenon of a mass-produced durable commodity for comfort (or pleasure) in the home was itself relatively new: Predecessors might include the cast iron stove, the piano, the sewing machine, or even entertainment or toy items like the stereoscope, but not a lot more than these.[5] The appliancing of the home meant more than easing domestic tasks and raising standards of living. It also had the interesting effect of *privatizing* certain types of pleasure, especially those that could be commercialized, shifting these pleasures from public places and social gatherings into private domestic spaces. The phonograph also created access to a larger geographic (and eventually global) culture of reproduced voice and music. But what it did most was speed up the circulation of commodities. There was the ever "improving" hardware of the "talking machine" and then even more the continuous production and retailing of recordings—breaking sharply from the "durable" model of the stove, piano, dining table, and other common household goods.

Aggressive advertising and retail promotion familiarized consumers with the phonograph and built the Big Three into its main purveyors, each introducing continuous technological advances: Edison's 4-minute Amberol record of 1901 and Victor's Victrola of 1907, for example.[6] All of this encouraged rising expectations and a presumption of inevitable obsolescence—that the "old" would soon pale in comparison with the new. The phonograph largely introduced a cardinal principle of modern merchandising, often linked to consumer engineering, a progressivist consumption, based on the association of personal advance over time through product improvement. But you didn't even have to wait for new models to climb the ladder of enhancement. In the 1890s, the big phonograph companies developed a technique copied a generation later with great success by General Motors and other car companies, rolling out a "full line" of products graduated by features and price. In 1896, for example, Edison offered a range of phonographs based on motor and horn size. By 1899, he had added an entry-level device (the "Gem") marketed to children, with the expectation that as adults users would graduate to the pricier models.[7]

This expectation of turnover was radically accelerated with the mass-duplicated recordings sold to individual consumers for personal use. This was an early example of the "razor and razor blade" marketing that induced repeated purchases, again a major merchandising tool built into consumer-engineered products. Commercial sound recording also created a new kind of fusion of the public and private, recreating fast-changing celebrity entertainment in the parlor—a site that had in Victorian times commonly been associated with cultural stability (and thus had represented a bulwark against the turmoil of the market that the recording now exemplified).

The object of commercial recording, as historian David Suisman has shown, was to create musical hits—popular but usually ephemeral ditties. The result was a new type of sensory experience: two- or three-minute punctuations of musical pleasure consumed in about the time it took to smoke a cigarette or eat a candy bar (these too being manifestations of the emerging fast capitalism of mass consumption). And for the first time anywhere, the voices and music of distant celebrities were immediately accessible and part of daily life, even for those who had never attended a scheduled speech or live performance.[8]

The phonograph record was essential in this process. As important was a nearly simultaneous development: the emergence in the 1890s of Tin Pan Alley—the commercialized song industry, which created the modern hit tune. Dominating commercial music from about 1890 to 1955, it was part of the revolution in mass commodification. For sheet music publishers, success required tunes whose fashionability attracted mass sales. Integral to the hit business was the continual replacement of such tunes with new ones, an excellent example of the modern consumer economy of disposable goods. Because the success of songs was impossible to predict and they were "turned over" quickly, there had to be a continuous flood of songs.[9] Because they were few, simple, and ubiquitous in the soundscape, satiation inevitably followed enthusiasm.[10] Edison ads from 1905, for instance, directed their appeals at up-to-date listeners who had heard a new tune at the theater and wanted to play it at home until they had "mastered both music and words." Edison aimed to use his records to feed an ever-moving conveyor belt of novelty.[11]

Victor, however, was especially adept at recognizing that they were selling phonographs to get people to buy records. This was made plain when the company introduced its Victor IV model in 1911. Priced at $15, it was hardly a profitable item for dealers. But the company insisted that this entry-level machine could serve as a wedge or commercial conduit, opening "homes to Victor Music." It was a machine that sped up consumption.[12]

All of this produced more than the sale of phonographs, records, and other novelties. Even more than the upsurge of new appliances, the acceleration of sound sensations (as well as those of sight, taste, and motion) transformed how audiences and consumers experienced time (anticipating the future and recalling the past while shaping daily experience).[13] The fast capitalism of the phonograph and record accustomed listeners to expect a continuous onslaught of novelty, eliminating the wait for the next hit of sensual intensity (traditionally the festival) and radically reducing the time of exposure to the same sound experience. Instead of a lifetime (perhaps reoccurring in the ritual seasonal singing of a folk song), a given sound experience might only last a few weeks.

More subtly perhaps, this form of fast capitalism seems to have impacted the young with lifelong implications in memory and age-segmented taste. From the beginning of recorded music, manufacturers understood the attraction of their products to youth and the value of associating their songs with memories of youth. Generational identities were built around formative encounters with new gadgets and product styles that left elders behind. New things let people break with their pasts and create a succession of selves (for example, in fashionable clothes, cosmetics, and novelties). What made the turn of the twentieth century especially significant is that many goods were not merely substitutes for homemade or craft goods but instead were true novelties. Home phonographs, roll film cameras, candy bars, cars, and much else did not exist before the 1890s and early twentieth century. The array of novelty is certainly unprecedented in human history. These new consumer goods did not necessarily have an immediate appeal, nor did customers always understand their function or potential. They had to be worked into the habitual world of people. This was the case, for example, for canned soups and Jell-0, which were widely marketed to homemakers early in the twentieth century. An obvious route to new customers was to appeal to the young whose habits were not yet fully formed, to appeal to their youth and presumed openness to change. As a result, the young became early adapters of new goods and technologies.

The linkage between youth and fast capitalism went further than appeals to generational identity and age difference. New goods were also associated with the new patterns of parenting and childhood experience that emerged shortly after 1900. Middle-class parents began buying their children increasingly varied clothes, books, and above all toys. This culmination of a romantic, but also materialistic, trend to indulge children reflected a more permissive culture of childrearing (a complex product of reduced childhood mortality, a progressive societal rejection of child labor, and new ideas about psychological development). Moreover, children's toys became repositories of contradictory adult attitudes toward rapid economic and cultural change. While Noah's arks and circus playsets reminded parents in 1900 of their own childhoods and suggested a timelessness to the young, fads like the Teddy Bear of 1906 offered parents a way to share a romantic embrace of the new with their offspring. Gifting children also let adults recover their memories of wonder, often lost in the satiation of daily consumption, in the (hopefully) delighted child. Because of parental gifts, young middle-class children increasingly experienced constant novelty as a basic part of their childhoods. This often meant that memories of childhood (and nostalgia for it) were defined and marked by identification with these first memories of novel consumer goods.[14]

All this was particularly evident in the fast markets of the phonograph record. With the coming of this good, not only were the "classics" preserved as never before but ephemeral hits survived years after they were first recorded, living now in the form of "standards" or "oldies," the music of each generation's youth played years later in life. Because popular recordings came and went so quickly, individual tunes were closely linked to a brief period of time in a listener's life. Thanks to the record, nostalgic memories of first loves and carefree youth were evoked by a brief tune, heard unchanged again and again throughout life. These ideal markers of memory were often shared with others, frequently from other places but of the same age at the time of the recordings' intense, but ephemeral exposure to a broad national, even international market. In this way, these popular tunes served as hooks on which to hang recollections of the past, like the parade of toys, dolls, and cars that emerged with modern consumer culture. The ephemeral consumer good created the possibility of modern nostalgia.[15]

At the same time, the novelty of the home phonograph clashed with the traditional longing for timelessness and privacy, materialized in the parlor as the site of a quiet retreat from the ever-changing and boisterous street.[16] But the phonograph industry proposed to resolve this contradiction with the promise that a talking machine in the home offered an escape from disorderly public space. The parlor, associated with the piano and fine furniture in Victorian times, was no obvious place for a machine like the phonograph, so Victor had to convince tastemakers otherwise. One solution was the introduction in 1906 of the Victrola, its mechanical works hidden in a four-foot-high cabinet of piano-finished mahogany. The company's 1909 trade catalog suggested that the Victrola was suitable for the "drawing room" in that it "conveys no hint of its purpose" except for the crank for the spring motor.[17] Thus, the fast merchandizing of the phonograph and record produced both fast culture and (somewhat ironically) a longing to recover a time lost to it. Elements of this pattern would be repeated in other fast consumer sectors—most obviously in toys, fantasy entertainment, and fad products, and somewhat less obviously in cars, furnishings, and clothing.

Consumer Engineering and Commodity Speed-Up in the 1930s

As is well known, the Great Depression saw efforts to increase consumer demand in "saturated" markets as consumer engineers designed goods for rapid sale and repeated purchase. One obvious way to increase sales was to go downmarket. Luxury car sales dropped from 150,000 in 1929 to 10,000 in 1937. Surviving manufacturers like Lincoln, Packard, and Cadillac decreased their prices and offered economy models. Companies that did not follow this strategy (including Pierce-Arrow and Stutz) disappeared. Low-priced cars increased from 52 percent of sales in 1926 to 73 percent in 1933. This did not mean that new cars were of lower quality. Rather, to attract scarce customers, manufacturers raised the standard of the "middle and low range" in their product lines. Henry Ford abandoned his Model A in 1932 for a far more powerful and stylish car with a V-8 engine. Other nonessentials also grew cheaper. Cigarette prices dropped back to ten cents a pack. Decca reduced the price of a phonograph record to thirty-five cents (compared to the competition's seventy-five-cent disk). When weekly movie attendance dropped from 90 million in 1929 to 60 million in 1932, exhibitors began offering double features.[18]

In hopes of ferreting out customers, retailers offered bargains and convenient shopping. By 1930, downtown Chicago stores stayed open Saturday nights to lure commuters back into the city on the weekend. Other department stores stayed open Thursday evenings. Most important were developments in discount retailing. In 1930, Michael Cullen introduced a no-frills, self-service supermarket to bargain-hunting, suburban New Yorkers. He expanded to eight stores within two years, drawing in shoppers with massive displays of groceries and cutting costs with self-service. There were many imitators of this business model, including cheap clothing, furniture, and plumbing supply retailers, which sprang up in old hotel garages and bankrupt factories. All this set the stage for suburban discount retailers like K-Mart, Target, and Wal-Mart in the mid-1960s and later big-box specialty stores for electronics, hardware, and even pets. Price, not service, quality, or status was becoming the key in American retailing, undermining the influence of the lavish central city department stores of the late nineteenth century. This feature of Depression-era consumer engineering distinguishes it from earlier efforts to move goods.[19]

Yet consumer engineering seems to have been primarily directed toward the middle-class consumer rather than the downmarket shopper. It was this relatively affluent group that consumer engineers hoped could be induced to spend more. As noted by Ernest Calkins in 1930, the product designer had to "dig in deeper and anticipate wants and desires not yet realized, but foreshadowed by trends and implicit in the habits and folkways" of the nation. As important was the need to manufacture goods that might be replaced before they wore out or were fully consumed.[20]

This effort could sometimes mean technological improvements, like Ford's radical shift from the 4-cylinder Model A to the V-8 of 1932 or the introduction of automatic transmissions, radios, and improved heaters in the mid-1930s. Still, new styles and designs by themselves could bring buyers back and convince Americans that the future was an endless horizon of spending.[21] Examples of this approach were efforts to turn traditional goods into fashionable commodities in furniture, appliances, and even home power tools. Especially important was streamlining, with a sleek, forward-looking design replacing the boxy or mechanical appearance of so many products.[22] This futuristic message was reaffirmed in the design of buildings at the world's fairs of Chicago, San Francisco, and especially New York in the 1930s as well as in the design of a new generation of locomotives.[23] While streamlining suggested speed, even the 1935 Super-Six Coldspot refrigerator, created by Raymond Loewy for Sears, had a streamline appearance with its rounded corners and hidden motors. This trend also appeared in radios, which were increasingly housed in colorful "space-aged" plastic instead of the traditional wooden cabinetry. Streamlining suggested forward motion and a positive future in spite of the depression. Along with all this came the hard sell and heavy radio advertising. The core of consumer engineering was to sell to a cautious consumer with money in their bank accounts.[24]

All this is rather familiar, but what is sometimes less recognized is the aggressive efforts of merchandisers to expand sales to young people and to the parents of young children during the depression. These efforts too represented a step beyond the first stage of fast capitalism at the beginning of the twentieth century. The 1930s saw the full flowering of the popular licensed image or name stamped on a consumer good, evident especially with Disney-branded products but also many other media or storybook characters. Licensing gave manufacturers leverage over store owners, but it also helped increase retail sales by reducing the need for trained sales staff and in-house promotions.[25] Walt Disney was the master of character licensing in the 1930s, first turning his crude Mickey Mouse cartoon of 1928 into a licensing bonanza,[26] beginning with a Mickey doll in 1930 and followed with Mickey's increasingly iconic image on everything from watches and lamp shades to toys and coloring books. These products, in effect, advertised for each other while promoting Disney cartoons. Disney took this marketing magic a step further in 1937 when he licensed the images of the animated feature film *Snow White and the Seven Dwarfs* before the public had even seen them in the movie, giving merchandisers time to roll out figurines and much else to coincide with the enthusiasm garnered by the later appearance of the movie. Disney had developed a marketing strategy that would become common after World War II, coordinating the appearance of licensed goods and movie spectaculars to create special moments of fantasy consumption.[27]

Although product licensing covered a wide assortment of goods, this and other marketing gimmicks were especially directed toward children. While discretionary spending for toys and other kids' stuff was down in the 1930s, merchandisers found a solution: selling cheap, often single toy figures.

The collecting habit, long central to children's play, had begun to shift from gathering stones from nature and leftover goods from adult consumption (trade cards or even cigar boxes) to buying and collecting the inexpensive military figures and bubblegum cards sold directly to kids.[28] In the thirties, a commercialized fantasy world for children emerged, one based on kids' radio shows set apart from adults. This development set the stage for the extraordinary fast pace of children's commodity culture that emerged by the end of the 1970s—most evident in the extraordinary synergy between George Lucas's Star Wars movie trilogy and a flood of licensed toys and other products.[29]

This drive to segment markets by age once again particularly impacted phonographs and records. Despite the depression, enterprising entertainers found that high school students with odd jobs and indulgent parents eagerly bought bobby socks and swing records in the 1930s. The depression kept teens in high school longer and thus extended their contact with the consumer peer culture that emerged in school halls and cafeterias. Benny Goodman's clarinet attracted thousands of teenagers to his New York concert appearance in the winter of 1937. Teens found ways of purchasing used, often junked cars, and restoring, customizing, and enhancing their speed through an aftermarket parts and service industry as well as their own crafts. The extraordinarily large inventory of used cars from the 1920s (especially the Model T) made this possible.[30] Still, the child and teen consumer market was limited by the Depression and parental resistance. This would change during and especially after World War II.

The Fast Capitalism and Consumer Engineering of the Postwar

After 1945, the quest of many Americans for long-deferred luxuries coincided with a dramatic rise in disposable income for symbolic and pleasure goods ranging from fashion furnishings, gadgetry, appliances, and vehicles to age-segmented music and media. In 1946, personal consumption was 21 percent higher in real money terms than in 1941. The generation born after World War II was the largest in American history, twice the size of the previous generation. There were 70 percent more children under fifteen in 1960 than there had been in 1940.[31] All this compounded the prewar trend toward marketing to youth and to child-focused couples. Another trend from the 1930s continued: the marketing of durables to the classes rather than the masses, so to speak, selling cutting edge goods to upwardly mobile middle-class households. Americans bought new cars for the latest step-up feature, like automatic transmissions and electric windows. Research confirmed what advertisers had come to realize in the 1930s—that the young, upwardly mobile were better customers than the less affluent.[32] By the mid-1950s, 85 percent of new cars were purchased by only 47 percent of American families. As a result, carmakers saw a limited market for any cheap basic vehicle (seen in the failure of low-priced cars in the early 1950s, until the VW Beetle found buyers reacting to the excesses of planned obsolescence), while the less affluent bought used cars.[33]

Postwar fast capitalism fulfilled the dreams of at least some of the consumer engineers of the 1930s. Goods increasingly were sold for style and fashion rather than utility. Everything was temporary—house, car, and even the family in some cases. These styles were popularizations of often experimental and elite designs from the 1920s and 1930s that ordinary American consumers had once shunned in preference for traditional wooden and cloth-covered furniture, often in ornate Victorian-like styles. But in the "conservative 1950s," some consumers switched to formerly elite modernist styles, including Art Deco with its sleek and geometric lines or the austere and functional designs of the International Style (dubbed Machine Age Modern in the USA).[34] Furniture as well as cases for clocks and radios came in plastic, replacing craft with a machine-based aesthetic.[35] Other postwar advances included molded plywood, fiberglass, and cast aluminum—making possible the novel designs of chairs, tables, sofas, and lamps by Charles Eames and Russel Wright.[36]

Nevertheless, no phase of fast capitalism after 1945 moved with the tempo of the popular music industry, and its vanguard consumers were youth. A powerful combination of technological and demographic changes made this development possible. While the phonograph and recording industry saw decline with the advent of radio and later the depression, phonograph records regained some of their past glory with the development of the Long Playing (LP) record by Columbia in 1948. LPs made it practical to record whole symphonies and musicals, for example, on a single disk. This no doubt deepened the music culture of mostly older Americans, especially with the coming of high fidelity and stereophonic records after 1957 and phonograph equipment to match. But in the short run, the introduction of the 45 RPM record in 1949 had a greater impact. The 45 record included a single song on either side like the old 78s but was smaller, more convenient, and rugged. More importantly, their production was fast and was directed toward teens. Cheap 45s were conveniently available at drug and even food stores as well as record retailers, often for less than half a dollar, and were purchased weekly by millions of American youth in the 1950s.[37]

Added to this age-segmented entertainment market was the shift of adult consumers from network radio (formerly featuring live cross-generational music) to TV after 1950, and with this the ceding of much of radio to youth. When adults abandoned radio, stations scrambled to find listeners to attract advertising dollars. One prominent solution, adopted by Todd Storz of Omaha, Nebraska, in 1953, was to abandon the live music broadcasts that had often reached a wide age range and instead to air a small list of recordings that appealed to fad- and fashion-conscious youth. In effect, the radio became a personal jukebox (similar to the coin-operated record player common in diners and soda fountains in the 1930s, but free). This new role for the radio was especially attractive to youth, to whom the jukebox had appealed. Storz built an empire in the Midwest of all-hit radio stations that played a continuously changing but small range of records at a time. This approach was really an intensified form of the pattern established by Edison and Victor a half century before: Repetition and fast turnover marked the way that youth consumed music.[38]

But a different sort of music was also on offer. By 1948, announcers playing records on air promoted country and rhythm and blues tunes outside the Tin Pan Alley mainstream. Though starting in Los Angeles and Memphis, the most famous of these disc jockeys (DJs) were Alan Freed (from 1951 in Cleveland and New York) and Robert Smith (aka Wolfman Jack from 1964 who developed a national audience from high-power radio stations in Mexico). These young DJs appealed to youth across class, race, and region.[39] Added to the shift toward 45s and youth-oriented DJ radio was the emergence of the transistor radio in 1957 and, more subtly, making the car radio a standard feature even in the cheap used cars purchased by teens in the 1950s. All this sped up the turnover of music commodities. Already in 1949, retailers reported that the average hit record stayed on the charts for only three months.[40]

Music appealing to the young was not new to the 1950s, but with the shift of radio and recording to youth, popular commercial tunes were sung by the young for the still younger by the mid-1950s. That music was, of course, rock and roll. What made this music distinct was that it was primarily vocal rather than instrumental; it abandoned the wind instruments of the previous big band era for guitars and sometimes pianos; and it featured a heavy beat. The musical style and content of lyrics were often wild, raw, and sometimes sensuousness, deriving, as they did, from rock's predecessors, hillbilly and rhythm and blues. Rock tunesmiths abandoned the sentimental ballads of Tin Pan Alley and embraced the tastes and topics of the working class and minorities, appealing to the rebellious offspring of the respectable white middle class.[41]

Pushing the logic of fast capitalism to extremes, this powerful combination of youth-oriented 45s turned out weekly by the record companies and Top-40 radio playing the two-minute tunes of rockers led to the demise of Tin Pan Alley. By 1956, almost all the Top 40 was rock for the kids.[42] This transformation reinforced age segmentation in music consumption and generational division, the latter marked by repeated "moral panics" over new music styles.

Conclusion: Some Ironies of Fast Capitalism

It may be surprising that the culmination of the logic of a youth-based fast capitalism was a new kind of nostalgia. It was based not on a longing for a past place, culture, or regime but on past consumer goods and experiences.

The increasingly rapid coming and going of manufactured commodities may have helped mark newly emerging identities of the young, but subsequently that fast-paced consumption was often disquieting. Such uncertainty resulted from a rather distinctly modern phenomenon. People found identity and meaning in specific goods, but consequently felt that their selfhoods were threatened when those things disappeared. The nostalgic impulse came from a desire to get them back. But what people wanted to recover was often the consumer goods of their formative years—especially from the earliest years of recalled childhood and the coming-of-age years of youth.[43]

Given how fast rock songs came and went, it shouldn't be surprising that the term "oldies" dates from as early as 1957, when the New York DJ Alan Fredericks played the not-so-old rock hits from 1954 to 1956. But the longing to hear again the popular tunes associated with youth became an obsession for many who had grown up with the rock of the 1950s at the end of the 1960s. Following on the heels of the turbulent 60s, perhaps inevitably, the 50s icon Elvis Presley attracted large crowds of middle-aged, middle-class fans for a performance in Las Vegas in 1969; and this was followed by a revival of 1950s rock in the early 1970s. This pattern has continued with each subsequent age cohort.

This phenomenon may impact only a minority, but it suggests more than an anxious longing to recover the past in an era of ever invented futures. It reinforces a key factor in consumer cultures—the formation of "memory communities" around goods (even musical ones). This has often been the case in the past. Such is, for example, the function of heirlooms (as devices to interweave generations). But, fast capitalism has produced a different sort of consuming community, goods that link narrow age groups, cohorts consisting of often widely dispersed and otherwise unrelated individuals who share a common exposure to an ephemeral and often quite superficial consumer good or experience (like a song) at the same time and often at the same age. Instead of places or events shaping these brief "generations," goods link otherwise separated individuals. They cope with the ever accelerating pace of change that continually robs them of their identities by rooting themselves psychologically in what seems to be "timeless," but, in fact, is ephemeral—that is, their childhoods.[44]

Fast capitalism, with its origins in clusters of technological and marketing innovations and spurred on by economic trends like the Great Depression and the postwar upsurge in income, including that of youth, both fostered and responded to increasing consumer expectations of a rapid turnover of goods. Although fast capitalism increased people's rates of consumption, it also produced more contradictory consumer experiences: the longing for the novelty fix side by side with nostalgia for the simple life, perhaps manifested in past ephemeral consumer goods; the blending of the recurrent with the new (as in modern Christmas); or the return of the old as the new (as in fashion). Among other issues, the dilemmas of diminishing returns on innovation and the persistence of consumer longing for repetition, recurrence, and stability have limited the ability of consumer engineering to promote never-ending novelty. Thus, along with transforming business and the economy, fast capitalism has changed people, how they cope with time, and how they relate to each other.

Notes

1. Ben Agger, *Fast Capitalism* (Urbana, IL, 1988).
2. David Harvey, *The Condition of Postmodernity: An Inquiry into the Origins of Cultural Change* (New York, 1991).
3. Gary Cross and Robert Proctor, *Packaged Pleasures: How Technology and Marketing Transformed Desire* (Chicago, 2014).
4. Tom Hine, *Populuxe* (New York, 1987).
5. Note, esp., *John Crowley, Invention of Comfort: Sensibilities and Design in Early Modern Britain and Early America* (Baltimore, MD, 2001).
6. Examples of such advertising in *Edison Phonograph Monthly*, October 1912, 3–5; May 1914, 3; September 1914, 153; and July 1916, 3; as well as in *Collier's*, November 28, 1908, 61, and March 19, 1910, 6. See also Allen Koenigsberg, *Edison's Cylinder Records, 1889–1912* (New York, 1969), xxii–lvi; C. Fabrizio and George Paul, *Antique Phonograph Advertising* (Atglen, PA, 2002), 50–51; A. J. Millard, *America on Record* (New York, 1995), 66–68, 78–81; Oliver Read and Walter Welch, *From Tin Foil to Stereo: Evolution of the Phonograph* (New York, 1976), 165; and James Weber, *Talking Machine Advertising: A History of the Berliner Gramophone and Victory Talking Machine* (Midland, ON, 1997), 94–95.
7. Roland Gelatt, *The Fabulous Phonograph 1877–1977* (New York, 1977), 71; National Phonograph Company, "The Phonograph and How to Use It," 1900, Hagley Museum Archives; "Edison Diamond Disc Phonographs," 1914, Hagley Museum Archives.
8. David Suisman, *Selling Sound: The Commercial Revolution in American Music* (Cambridge, MA, 2012). For the integration of music clips in advertising, see Timothy Taylor, *The Sounds of Capitalism: Advertising, Music, and the Conquest of Culture* (Chicago, 2012).
9. David Jansen, *Tin Pan Alley: The Composers, the Songs, the Performers and Their Times* (New York, 1988), xv–xvi.
10. Ibid., xx, 3.
11. *Edison Phonograph Monthly*, December 1903, 12 and 14; April 1904, 7; April 1905, 13; August 1911, 11.
12. *Voice of the Victor*, October 1911, 6; and Victor ad in *McClure's*, September 1905, 2.
13. Cross and Proctor, *Packaged Pleasures*, Chapters 5–6.
14. Gary Cross, "Wondrous Innocence: Print Advertising and the Origins of Permissive Child Rearing in the U.S.," *Journal of Consumer Culture* 4, no. 2 (2004): 183–201.
15. Michael Chanan, *Repeated Takes: A Short History of Recording and Its Effects on Music* (London, UK, 1995), 12–13 and 19–20; and Mark Katz, *Captured Sound: How Technology Has Changed Music* (Berkeley, CA, 2010), 29 and 66–70.

16. Katherine Grier, *Culture and Comfort: Parlor Making and Middle-Class Identity, 1850–1930* (Washington, DC, 1998); and Mihaly Csikszentmihalyi and Eugene Rochberg-Halton, *The Meaning of Things: Domestic Symbols of the Self* (New York, 1981).
17. Victrola XVI ad, 1907, in Arnold Schwartzman, *Phonographics: The Visual Paraphernalia of the Talking Machine* (San Francisco, 1993), 48; Victor Victrola leaflet, 1910; Victor/Victrola Catalogue, 1909; "Will There Be a Victrola in Your Home This Christmas?" 1915, Hagley Museum Archives.
18. "Ford's V-8 to Be Seen," *Business Week*, February 13, 1932, 5; and David Gartman, *Auto Opium: A Social History of American Automobile Design* (London, UK, 1994), 105.
19. "Department Store Branches," *Business Week*, October 1, 1930, 10; and "Night Shopping," *Business Week*, November 10, 1934, 14.
20. Ernest Calkins, "The New Consumption Engineer, and the Artist," in *A Philosophy of Production: A Symposium*, ed. George Frederick (New York, 1930), 107–29; and Ernest Calkins, "What Consumer Engineering Really Is," in *Consumer Engineering*, ed. Roy Sheldon and Egmont Arens (New York, 1932), 169–71.
21. Jeffrey L. Meikle, *Twentieth-Century Limited: Industrial Design in America, 1925–1939* (Philadelphia), 4, 52–54, 59, and 101–110; and Adrian Forty, Objects of Desire (New York: Pantheon, 1986), 156–60. See also William Lough and Martin Gainsborough, *High-Level Consumption: Its Behavior; Its Consequences* (New York, 1935); and Henry Link, *The New Psychology of Selling and Advertising* (New York, 1934).
22. "Brave New Model World," *Business Week*, January 11, 1933, 3–4; "Detroit Gets Ready in Big Style," *Business Week*, October 10, 1936, 17–18; "Automatic Transmission—It's Here," *Business Week*, May 22, 1937, 18–19; and Gartman, *Auto Opium*, Chapter 5.
23. Robert Rydell, *World of Fairs: The Century-of-Progress Expositions* (Chicago, 1993), 123–24; and Roland Marchand, *Creating the Corporate Soul: The Rise of Public Relations and Corporate Imagery in American Big Business* (Berkeley, CA, 1998), 301–11.
24. "An Appraisal of Radio Advertising Today," *Fortune*, September 1932, 3; Erik Barnouw, *A Tower in Babel* (New York, 1966), 109–10 and 238; Susan Smulyan, *Selling Radio: The Commercialization of American Broadcasting, 1920–1934* (Washington, DC, 1994), 126–32; and William Paley, *Radio as a Cultural Force* (New York, 1934), 104–5.
25. Gary Cross, *Kids' Stuff: Toys and the Changing World of American Childhood* (Cambridge, MA, 1997), Chapter 4.
26. Norman Kline, *Seven Minutes: The Life and Death of the American Animated Cartoon* (London, UK, 1993), 17, 53, and 91–95.
27. "An Excellent Season," *Playthings Magazine*, January 1934, 34; and "Mickey Mouse Looks Forward to 1936," *Playthings Magazine*, February 1936, 56–57.
28. Richard O'Brien, *Collecting Toys* (Florence, AL, 1990), 175–76, 188, 197–210, and 229–31; and Peter Johnson, *Toy Armies* (Garden City, NY, 1981), 105.
29. Cross, *Kids' Stuff*, Chapter 7.

30. Gary Cross, *Machines of Youth: America's Car Obsession* (Chicago, 2018), Chapter 2; Kathleen Franz, *Tinkering: Consumers Reinvent the Early Automobile* (Philadelphia, PA, 2005), 5–23, 41, 45, 55, 108, and 147; and H. F. Moorehouse, *Driving Ambitions: An Analysis of the American Hot Rod Enthusiasm* (Manchester, UK, 1991), 27–32 and 42–44.
31. "Our Backlog for Spending," *U.S. News and World Report*, August 30, 1946, 55; and U.S. Bureau of the Census, *Historical Statistics of the United States* (Washington, DC, 1965), i: 15.
32. "People Are Changing Their Buying Habits," *U.S. News and World Report*, January 27, 1956, 100–2; "Marketing," *Business Week*, November 22, 1952, 110–18; "The More People Buy, the More They Want," *U.S. News and World Report*, April 15, 1955, 77–80; "How Consumers Take to Newness," *Business Week*, September 24, 1955, 41–43; and George Katona, *The Mass Consumption Society* (New York, 1964), 269.
33. "New Cars: Who Buys Them?" *U.S. News and World Report*, March 14, 1958, 84–86; and "Cars," *Collier's*, August 21, 1953, 18.
34. Leslie A. Piña, *Fifties Furniture* (Atglen, PA, 2005), 7, 13, and 31.
35. Stephen Fenichell, *Plastic: The Making of a Synthetic Century* (New York, 1996), Chapter 5.
36. Sylvia Katz, *Plastics: Common Objects, Classic Designs* (New York, 1984), 11–15, 70–71, and 77–78.
37. Mark Coleman, *Playback: From the Victrola to MP3, 100 Years of Music, Machines, and Money* (New York, 2003), 39, 59–68, and 76–85; and Greg Milner, *Perfecting Sound Forever: An Aural History of Recorded Music* (London, UK, 2009), 109–12.
38. Marc Fisher, *Something in the Air: Radio, Rock, and the Revolution That Shaped a Generation* (New York, 2007), 5–15.
39. Arnold Passman, *The Deejays* (New York, 1971); and John Jackson, *Big Beat Heat: Alan Freed and the Early Years of Rock & Roll* (New York, 2000).
40. Edward Ward, G. Stokes, and K. Tucker, *Rock of Ages: The Rolling Stone History of Rock & Roll* (New York, 1986), 231; and Katona, *Mass Consumption Society*, 269.
41. Glen Jeansonne, David Lurhrssen, and Dan Sokolovic, *Elvis Presley, Reluctant Rebel* (Santa Barbara: Praeger, 2011), 122–26; and Kerry Segrave, *Anti-Rock: The Opposition to Rock 'n' Roll* (Hamden, CT, 1988).
42. Jansen, *Tin Pan Alley*, 280–88.
43. I develop this argument in *Consumed Nostalgia: Memory in the Age of Fast Capitalism* (New York, 2015).
44. Mihaly Csikszentmailhalyi, "Why We Need Things," in *History from Things: Essays on Material Culture*, ed. Steven Lubar and W. David Kingery (Washington, DC, 1993), 20–29.

CHAPTER 4

A Theoretical Exploration of Consumer Engineering: Implicit Contracts and Market Making

Andrew Godley and Keith Heron

The growing literature exploring the emergence of modern marketing has concentrated on the periodization of different marketing techniques coming into usage, the retailing of different product categories, the internationalization of retail formats, and advertising practices.[1] But recent research has begun to focus on deliberate attempts to elicit consumer spending on novel products by firms and marketing specialists. This more recent literature explores how specialists, in particular designers and market researchers, in the middle decades of the twentieth century began to move away from a product-focused approach to one that placed the consumer at the center of marketing initiatives. This development was also associated with the move away from marketing as simply a promotional activity toward strategic marketing instead. Now marketing management informed the entire organization of activities within the firm.[2]

The near paradox of this mid-century movement was that while its adherents were intent on the primacy of consumer interests, consumer agency was viewed with suspicion. In 1952, the German–American market researcher Alfred Politz emphasized that "consumers do not know what they want and why they act."[3] With consumers so resistant to the active search for answers to their problems, specialists had to step into diagnose and solve their problems for them.[4] These specialist market researchers and product designers developed tools and techniques to elicit the explication of previously

A. Godley (✉) · K. Heron
Henley Business School, University of Reading, Reading, UK

J. Logemann et al. (eds.), *Consumer Engineering, 1920s–1970s*,
Worlds of Consumption, https://doi.org/10.1007/978-3-030-14564-4_4

unarticulated consumer preferences. This was consumer engineering. The historical debates on consumer engineering, on whether or not it was beneficial to or exploitative of consumers, are summarized elsewhere in this volume. This chapter aims to use economic reasoning to explain why consumer engineering was so successful.

From a theoretical perspective, this description of the relationship between producers and consumers is one that is characterized by information asymmetries. The sellers have information about the product that the buyers do not possess. Producers believe they have a product that will solve a consumer problem, but consumers typically do not know whether the product will solve their problem or not. Using information economics theory and exploring the implications of information asymmetries, this article will explore a theoretical explanation for the rise and significance of consumer engineers in the mid-twentieth century, suggesting why consumer engineering became significant at a certain time and in certain sectors rather than others.

The result of this theoretical exercise is the suggestion that producers of novel and complex consumer goods, especially of durable goods, have to engage in market-making innovation as well as product innovation. Market-making innovation describes a set of contractual (or more often quasi-contractual) agreements designed to overcome consumers' reluctance to purchase a product. This reluctance to purchase is driven not by the product, but instead by the nature of the transaction. Transactions between consumers and producers can be very simple. But they can also become very complicated. One of the principal drivers of transactional complexity is the presence of information asymmetries.

Setting Out the Problem of Information Asymmetries: Moral Hazard and Adverse Selection in Effects in Consumer Markets

The transactional relationship under consideration is between firms and consumers.[5] Firms sell novel products to consumers. Consumers buy these novel products, about which they have little information, from firms. Under such conditions of uncertainty, consumer purchases are decisions made on the basis of crude estimates of expected future utility.[6] There is a risk such estimates may turn out to be wildly inaccurate. Consumers in fact only acquire sufficient information to make an informed judgment about the utility of a purchased novel product at some point after the formal completion of the contract, meaning these transactions share characteristics of incomplete, open-ended contracts and their associated risks. Producers may seek to disseminate information to overcome such risks, but consumers are unlikely to take such information at face value, as producers may be less than fully transparent in order to complete and profit from the transaction.

This is not the case for all novel consumer goods. For many new products, consumers are well placed to be able to test the firm's claims because for many products, "search goods" in Nelson's terminology, consumers can sample or test goods before purchase.[7] Nelson differentiated search goods from others, which are sufficiently complex in nature that consumers are unable to gain sufficient information prior to purchase, which he called "experience goods." Transactions involving the latter possess similar characteristics to open-ended, incomplete contracts because novel experience goods are acquired in faith by consumers. Only through actually experiencing them after purchase is the consumer genuinely able to judge whether the product has met ex ante expectations. Substantial experimental evidence from behavioral economists conclusively shows that poorly informed consumers facing complex products typically prefer *not* to purchase the product, rather than run the risk of making an incorrect decision.[8] Economists call this risk to transactions from the relative ignorance of one party the adverse selection effect.

Nelson went on to identify a class of goods where consumers would not even be able to judge the utility after experiencing them: credence goods.[9] For some quasi-open-ended transactions, there is also the additional risk of moral hazard where one party has the power to exploit the other without being detected, so where sellers can exploit buyers' gullibility. This leads to what Akerlof described as the "lemons" problem.[10] In markets for credence goods characterized by information asymmetry, where the seller possesses more information than the buyer and where the buyer suspects that the seller may act opportunistically, the buyer will insist on a discount in the price to reflect the cost of insuring against their possible exploitation by the seller (or of the purchase turning into a "lemon," the American slang expression for dud cars). Without such price cuts, consumers will withdraw from the market as the risk of them losing out to opportunistic sellers appears too great. In some markets, the reduction in price demanded by consumers to insure them against the risks of moral hazard may be easily absorbed or passed on to suppliers. But in markets characterized by very high sunk costs, producers may not be able to pay the consumers' implicit insurance premium. To overcome such a strong propensity to consumer withdrawal, producers must invest in developing communication channels not only to disseminate relevant information about the product itself but also to convince consumers of their trustworthiness.[11] The penalty of continued consumer suspicion of opportunistic producer behavior is lower prices, lower profits, and even market breakdown.

The probability that an experience good will become a credence good depends on the extent of the threat of moral hazard. For example, there are several kinds of experience goods that spur repeat demand; the products are consumed typically shortly after purchase, leading to further repeat purchases, subject to some satisfaction threshold being met. Consumers here are neither able to consume at the point of purchase (like most services) nor to sample before purchase (like search goods), but they are able to benefit from the information about the product generated by their previous purchases. The risks of novelty and the dependence on the producer's promise are not eradicated, but are modified to one where producers commit to ensure future purchases are consistent with previous ones.

For novel durable goods, however, consumers are more dependent on an entrepreneur's promise because the transactions are not repeated purchases (and so consumers possess no information from previous purchases), but also because once a durable good has been purchased, consumers have less incentive to continue sampling and testing alternatives thereafter. Consumer durables like computers or automobiles might be typical of these products. Furthermore, consumer durables are typically more expensive and are treated as quasi-investment goods. The possibility of a bad purchase therefore represents a higher long-term risk to consumer utility because of the time required before the expense can be fully amortized and the product replaced.

Figure 4.1 summarizes this first step of setting out the problem posed by information asymmetries. It illustrates that many transactions for novel goods and services are unaffected by either moral hazard or adverse selection effects and so face minimal risk of consumer withdrawal. For example, when both adverse selection and moral hazard effects are low, in Box 1 (with novel search goods like clothing perhaps), consumers are sufficiently informed to pursue their own self-interest and fully commit to transactions. In Box 2, low product complexity means minimal risk of adverse selection effects, but the open-ended nature of the contract exposes consumers to the risk of moral hazard. Entrepreneurial entry into these types of markets (domestic construction services perhaps) would have to devise contractual strategies to avoid lemon-style insurance-related discounts (through stage payments perhaps).

In some markets for complex experience goods, Box 3, consumers face the risk of adverse selection (it is too complex for them to know ex ante whether the product will meet expectations), but consumption is sufficiently coincident with the moment of purchase to make the risk of moral hazard minimal. These markets might be composed of nondurable goods and services. In order to overcome the risk of complexity, entrepreneurs may seek to build incrementally on existing products and services, thus enabling consumers to draw comparisons either from their own or others' previous transactions.

Fig. 4.1 Moral hazard, adverse selection, and the risk of consumer withdrawal

Moral hazard	- Adverse selection	Adverse selection +
+	2. Open-ended incomplete transactions	4. Novel complex consumer durables
-	1. Search goods	3. Complex nondurables (repeat goods)

For entrepreneurs engaged in markets like Box 4, where entrepreneurs are introducing novel, complex, non-incremental durable goods, consumers in the target market possess little relevant information and have little prospect of independently accessing such information so as to make an informed decision. There is therefore a high risk of adverse selection effects influencing consumer reception. Moreover, because consumers have to pay up front, but will have open-ended requirements, there is a strong risk of moral hazard. Such markets, often for novel, high-tech durable products with high intellectual property content, for instance, are a common feature of the entrepreneurship literature.[12] Yet focusing on the characteristics of such markets from the consumer's perspective should lead to the conclusion that without appropriate market-making innovations, these are markets with a high risk of consumer withdrawal and so high rates of entrepreneurial failure regardless of the merits of the novel product itself.

Producer Response: Market-Making Innovation and Implicit Contracts

Nelson's focus on the different properties of consumer goods is helpful because it indicates how producers might respond with different advertising strategies when engaging with risk-averse consumers in transactions characterized by varying degrees of information asymmetries. While this was an advance on Akerlof (who, as Stiglitz reminds us, ignored the desire of producers to supply more information[13]), for the purposes of this article, Nelson's typology does not go far enough in explaining the difficulties facing entrepreneurs in responding to such information asymmetries. Indeed, there is nothing in Nelson's analysis that necessarily leads to an entrepreneur having to invest in a market-making response. Alternative institutional solutions could easily be envisaged (standards, regulations, independent arbiters, etc.) to overcome the problems with such transactions caused by information asymmetries.[14] To understand why in most consumer goods markets it is producers who take on the role of reducing the risk of consumer withdrawal from the threats of adverse selection and moral hazard rather than any other party to the transaction, it is important to explain why consumers find it so difficult to specify their wishes in advance of purchasing a product.

Overcoming Costly Pre-purchase Specification with Credible Commitments and Implicit Contracts for Novel Products

Another way to conceptualize Nelson's demarcation between credence, experience, and search goods is to understand that when consumers are unable to specify their requirements prior to purchase, they will only be able to make an informed judgment of a product's utility after experiencing it. Consumers are able to assess search goods, the look and feel of the fabric, for example, and so acquire sufficient information about the good's likely utility before they purchase it. For credence and experience goods, by contrast, making such an assessment is impossible.

It is this inability to specify requirements before a purchase that so powerfully demarcates consumer demand from business demand for novel complex products. Businesses typically have a much greater understanding of the specification required for any particular new product, and so business-to-business markets are often characterized by tenders and other sorting techniques to ensure better matches between buyer and seller.[15]

In the absence of clear specification from consumers, producers engage in some guesswork in order to better identify more exactly what it is that consumers desire but are unable to articulate. Producers may invest in market and consumer research to acquire partial support for their decisions. But no market research can provide perfect information, and so, in the end, producers have to opt for a particular product or design with less than perfect information about consumer desires.[16] An entrepreneur making investment decisions in the face of just such an absence of consumer specifications is what Casson describes as exercising entrepreneurial judgment.[17] It is this adoption of specific techniques by producers (often using specialist assistance) to better understand unarticulated consumer desires that historians have discussed as consumer engineering.

Having made their decision, producers have to communicate with their target audience about their particular novel product. But given that the real underlying consumer demand factors remain unarticulated, producers engage in communicating with consumers through tacit information like branding, logos, and other forms of product and corporate imagery, using vehicles such as advertising, sponsorship, public relations, and so on. Producers invest in such intangible information with the aim of leading consumers to recognize congruence between their unarticulated desires and what the firms are offering.

Producers of complex consumer goods therefore have to communicate with prospective consumers in order to convince them that the particular complex product is the solution to consumers' problem. But they have to do so in such a way that overcomes any reluctance to deal with complexity (adverse selection) and mistrust (moral hazard). This is market making. What makes it particularly difficult is that consumers are so unwilling to prespecify their requirements that producers have to communicate solutions to consumers without articulating what are, in effect, quasi-contractual commitments.

The need for innovation in market making is therefore the outcome not of information asymmetries per se, but rather of the evidently very high costs to consumers of articulating more clearly their required specification pre-purchase. If producers found market making more costly, then consumers would have a stronger incentive to specify their own requirements and then invest in a search for the most suitable providers. Such a market, like most business-to-business markets, would involve much reduced marketing costs, but much greater specification and search costs. Given the expense of market-making innovations like brands and reputations, it is reasonable to infer that consumers find it very costly to engage in any rigorous specification process. It is not so much that consumers "do not know what they want" (Politz) but that they discover that it is too expensive for them to find out.

Producers therefore have to provide sufficient relevant information to consumers more cheaply than consumers can discover it themselves.[18] Moreover, it is firms that typically have the stronger incentive to resolve the risk of consumer withdrawal rather than consumers because firms' investments in sunk costs associated with production are significantly greater than any individual consumer's search costs. It is producers, therefore, that will invest in consumer engineering and other market-making strategies in order to make the markets for complex consumer goods work to all parties' satisfaction. When consumers typically do invest in pre-purchase specification (for example, in self-designed house construction), there is much less incentive for producers to invest in brand creation (house builders, to continue the example, merely tender bids on price and quality).

In some consumer goods sectors, then, typically complex durable goods, where repeat purchases are rare, amortization costs are high, and consumers find pre-purchase specification very costly, producers face the strongest incentive to provide intangible product-specific information to consumers. Firms see a real economic benefit to investing in consumer engineering and other market-making innovations. If consumers believe the intangible information offered by producers, the risks and hence the costs to contracting are reduced, and so consumers will transact and they too will enjoy the economic benefits of the transaction.

Such market-making solutions involve by definition the ability to meet a consumer's unarticulated, open-ended requirements and so require a firm to go beyond the explicit contract of exchange—transferring the rights to a good for a given price—to an implicit contract, where the producer communicates to the consumer that it will meet all their product-associated demands, whether understood at the moment of transaction or not, whether codified or not, and until some point in the future when consumer uncertainty falls away approximately to zero. Such a commitment to unspecified consumer requirements therefore represents unfunded guarantees to future expectations. Implicit contracts are costly but necessary market-making innovations.

Okun defined implicit contracts as "invisible handshakes" or "arrangements that are not legally binding but that give both sides incentives to maintain the relationship."[19] Substantial anecdotal or partial evidence of the pervasiveness of implicit contracts can be drawn from a variety of contexts in which relationship is preferred to contract. Examples occur in the business history literature on complex infrastructure projects,[20] in the international management literature on German and Japanese corporate governance systems,[21] and in the cross-cultural management literature on Chinese managers' decision-making,[22] to list but a few.

The economic literature on implicit contracts makes clear, however, that markets so characterized are only able to function in the presence of supportive social norms. The most significant norm to be observed in experimental data is reciprocity.[23] Reciprocity's importance in the behavioral economics literature derives from its ability to enable markets characterized by implicit contracts to function. It overcomes what Avner Greif has called "the fundamental problem of exchange."[24] But this observation implies that a transactional relationship between entrepreneurs and consumers based on implicit contracts exhibits more similarities with a "prisoner's dilemma" view of the world than does the conventional understanding of price-taking free markets. Credible and long-term commitments to repeated exchange introduce significant constraints on both parties' freedom of action, with consumer engineering characterized by producer promises to consumers. When this marketing strategy succeeds, it is because consumers are able to judge from the evidence of the transaction that the producer has kept the promise. The principle of reciprocity then leads consumers to keep on purchasing, and producer reputation is enhanced. On the other hand, should consumers detect from the evidence of consuming that producers are reneging, trust will break and the transactional relationship will fail.

Implicit contracts have been particularly influential in the economics of the labor market, where the empirical observation of lower-than-expected levels of volatility in employment and wages over the course of a business cycle has been explained by "the hypothesis that contract wages embody implicit payments of insurance premiums by workers in favourable states of nature and receipts of indemnities in unfavourable states."[25] The equivalent of this wage rigidity in labor markets is price rigidity in consumer markets. The literature here emphasizes that risk-averse consumers interpret any change in price or quality that appears to favor producer interests as producer opportunism, and so producers face a strong incentive to maintain price and quality to avoid consumer boycotts.[26] Once "the firm draws a clientele with attractive implicit contracts, any deviation unfavourable to consumers is seen as a violation of these contracts."[27] The strongest empirical support for this is provided by Young and Levy's excellent analysis of Coca Cola's seventy years' persistence with price rigidity, where the real price of Coca Cola was held almost constant for over seventy years. There is also Godley's interpretation of Singer's enormous investment in its international sales organization. Neither the cheapest nor technologically the best sewing machine, Singer was nevertheless able to enjoy a dominant global market position for several decades.[28]

To sum up, the first difficulty facing producers of novel complex durables is communicating to inarticulate consumers that such goods might meet their needs. Because most complex durables possess strong elements of basic multifunctionality, it is difficult for producers to signal likely post-purchase usage to potential consumers through conventional promotion strategies. Product complexity and consumer inability to prespecify requirements suggest that an appropriate market-making solution to overcome the risk of adverse selection would be for an entrepreneur to invest in signaling mechanisms to disseminate information that allows consumers to judge how they might use the product. Historians' research on consumer engineering could here focus on the nature of signaling mechanisms adopted by such producers.

The second difficulty relates to the open-ended nature of transactions. The explicit contract is a spot transaction (or a near-spot transaction in cases of installment purchases). But consumers will be aware of the risk of moral hazard, as producers simply may not keep promises. For novel durable goods, producers may initially offer attractive servicing and repair terms but subsequently change terms, for example. Entrepreneurs seeking to overcome consumer propensity to withdraw because of the risk of moral hazard would therefore need to make credible commitments not to change service conditions in ways that might adversely affect consumers. But because consumers' future requirements remain unspecified at the point of transaction, such a commitment must be made through an implicit contract.

It follows that if implicit contracts are the preferred solution to overcoming the threat of consumer withdrawal in markets for complex consumer goods, entrepreneurs will need to invest in market-making innovations that reduce the risks to consumers of adverse selection and moral hazard. Historians of marketing might here want to explore the relationship between product design and contractual design to better explain the significance of the nature of the contractual transaction as a market-making innovation.

The most complete market-making response would be a comprehensive presales demonstration and after-sales service that met all information requirements for consumers of novel durables, much as has been described for Singer.[29] Such an investment would be hugely costly for entrepreneurs, but it would signal a credible, market-making commitment to elicit consumer trust at the market's point of entry. This scenario would represent the ultimate and most expensive example of consumer engineering.

Given the expense associated with such a market-making innovation, entrepreneurs might simply pass on the costs of after-sales services to consumers in the form of an explicit list of prices for a variety of services.[30] But charging the market rate for after-sales services opens up the possibility of third parties establishing themselves as competing sources of such services. In the long run, competition in the provision of after-sales service is unlikely to impact firm strategy, but at the point of market entry where the need to elicit trust with consumers is the key to successful market making, competition in after-sales service may undermine the credible commitments needed for the relationship between entrepreneur and consumer to begin. Thus, producers will prefer to subsidize their after-sales services and so deter competitor entry. Because the cost of such a subsidy has to come from product revenues, premium pricing strategies have to be employed by producers. Otherwise, the subsidy for market-support services is not viable. The provision below cost of after-sales support and advice to consumers of complex durables should therefore overcome much of the risk of potential consumer withdrawal.[31] The implication is that historians of consumer engineering need also to take full account of producers' pricing strategies as another element of the relationship with consumers unable or unwilling to articulate their desires.

Conclusion

This discussion of the theory of implicit contracts and market making takes as its point of departure theoretical insights drawn from information economics about the consequences for information asymmetries in market relationships and the high probability for these to lead to market failure of some sort. The chapter then suggests that adapting game theory insights from "prisoners' dilemma"-type scenarios suggests that the solution to such complex transactions lies in producers cultivating consumers' trust in their ability to solve consumers' problems. This insight can readily be applied to the rapid growth of consumer engineering during the middle decades of the twentieth century. This was the period of the consumer revolution and the introduction of many novel, but complex consumer goods. But because consumers did not articulate their desires or prespecify their requirements, it fell to producers to communicate the benefits of these novel products and why they would solve consumer problems. The criticism from consumer engineers of the time was that consumers "do not know what they want" (Politz). But the conclusion of this theoretical introduction would be that a better interpretation of consumer behavior was that consumers discovered that it was too costly for them to decide what they wanted.

Marketing materials shifted during the early decades of the twentieth century from being dominated by explicit product information to growing use of imagery and other forms of tacit information. As the twentieth century progressed, producers increasingly moved to place consumers at the center of their marketing initiatives. Indeed, as the concept of strategic marketing emerged, so consumer requirements, rather than engineering constraints, became increasingly central to product design. Consumer engineers like Politz therefore had to develop tools and techniques to both identify consumer desires and then persuade firms to adapt their offerings in order to make these markets function optimally.

Notes

1. Andrew Godley and Haiming Hang, "Collective Financing Among Chinese Entrepreneurs and Department Store Retailing in China," *Business History* 58, no. 3 (2016): 364–77; Andrew Godley and Alessandra Tessari, "Made in Italy. Made in Britain. Quality, Brands and Innovation in the European Poultry Market, 1950–1980," *Business History* 56, no. 7 (2014): 1057–83; Andrew Godley and Haiming Hang, "Globalization and the Evolution of International Retailing: A Comment on Alexander's 'British Overseas Retailing, 1900–1960'," *Business History* 54, no. 4 (2012): 529–41; and Andrew Godley and Bridget Williams, "Democratizing Luxury and the Contentious 'Invention of the Technological Chicken' in Britain," *Business History Review* 83, no. 2 (2009): 267–90.
2. D. G. Brian Jones and Mark Tadajewski, eds., *The Routledge Companion to Marketing History* (Abingdon, 2016); Ingo Köhler and Jan Logemann, "Towards Marketing Management: German Marketing in the 19th and 20th Centuries," in ed. Jones and Tadajewski, 371–88.
3. Quoted by Jan Logemann in Chapter 2 of the present volume.
4. Andrew Godley and Mark Casson, "'Doctor, Doctor...' Entrepreneurial Diagnosis and Market Making," *Journal of Institutional Economics* 11, no. 3 (2015): 601–21.
5. This section is adapted from Andrew Godley, "Entrepreneurial Opportunities, Implicit Contracts and Market Making for Complex Consumer Goods," *Strategic Entrepreneurship Journal* 7, no. 4 (2013): 273–87.
6. For the purposes of theory building, we are ignoring state intervention, warranty provision, comparison Web sites, or other institutional innovations to overcome the threat of opportunistic behavior in open-ended contracts in this section. Equally, the focus is on goods rather than services, where consumption is mostly simultaneous with production and so where transactions are mostly spoted rather than sharing the open-ended characteristics emphasized here.
7. See Philip Nelson, "Advertising as Information." *Journal of Political Economy* 82, no. 4 (1974): 729–45.
8. Godley, "Entrepreneurial Opportunities" discusses this. This seemingly counter-intuitive level of risk aversion shown by consumers in laboratory experiments conforms exactly with McCloskey's interpretation of why some English regions failed to adopt enclosure methods during the Agricultural Revolution. See Dierdre McCloskey, "The Enclosure of Open Fields: Preface to a Study of Its Impact on the Efficiency of English Agriculture in the Eighteenth Century," *Journal of Economic History* 32 (March 1972): 15–35.
9. See Uwe Dulleck, Rudolf Kerschbamer, and Matthias Sutter, "The Economics of Credence Goods: An Experiment on Role of Liability, Verifiability, Reputation, and Competition," *American Economic Review* 101 (April 2011): 530–59, for an excellent recent review.
10. George A. Akerlof, "The Market for 'Lemons': Quality Uncertainty and the Market Mechanism," *Quarterly Journal of Economics* 84, no. 3 (1970): 488–500.
11. See Koehler in this volume.

12. See Gary Dushnitsky and Dovev Lavie, "How Alliance Formation Shapes Corporate Venture Capital Investment in the Software Industry: A Resource-Based Perspective," *Strategic Entrepreneurship Journal* 4, no. 1 (2010): 22–48; and Albrecht Enders et al., "The Long Tail of Social Networking: Revenue Models of Social Networking Sites," *European Journal of Management* 26, no. 3 (2008): 199–211.
13. Joseph E. Stiglitz, "The Contributions of the Economics of Information to Twentieth Century Economics," *Quarterly Journal of Economics* 115, no. 4 (2000): 1452.
14. Richard N. Langlois, "The Vanishing Hand: The Changing Dynamics of Industrial Capitalism," *Industrial and Corporate Change* 12, no. 2 (2003): 351–85; and Christian Kleinschmidt, "Comparative Consumer Product Testing in Germany," *Business History Review* 84, no. 1 (2010): 105–24.
15. Obviously, these are points on a spectrum rather than separate categories of behavior. IBM's position of dominance in the business machine market for decades was based on the tagline, "No one was ever fired for buying IBM," indicating that where information asymmetries arise in B2B markets, a similar pattern of behavior to that described here for consumer markets emerges.
16. Brian K. Orme, *Getting Started with Conjoint Analysis: Strategies for Product Design and Pricing Research* (Madison, WI, 2006), Chapter 2.
17. See Mark Casson *The Entrepreneur: An Economic Theory* (Cheltenham, 1982); and Mark Christopher Casson, "Entrepreneurship and the Theory of the Firm," *Journal of Economic Behaviour and Organisation* 58, no. 2 (2005): 327–48. For historical applications, see Mark Casson and Andrew Godley, "Entrepreneurship and Historical Explanation," in *Entrepreneurship in Theory and History*, ed. Youssef Cassis and Ioanna Pepelasis Minoglou (Basingstoke, 2005); and Mark Casson and Andrew Godley, "Revisiting the Emergence of the Modern Business Enterprise: Entrepreneurship and the Singer Global Distribution System," *Journal of Management Studies* 44, no. 7 (2007): 1064–77.
18. Firms obviously gain from economies in pooling common characteristics of consumer demand specifications.
19. Arthur M. Okun, *Prices and Quantities: A Macroeconomic Analysis* (Washington, DC, 1981), 49–50.
20. Maria Eugénia Mata, "The Role of Implicit Contracts: Building Public Works in the 1840s in Portugal," *Business History* 50, no. 2 (2008): 147–62.
21. Tim Jenkinson and Colin Mayer, "The Assessment: Corporate Governance and Corporate Control," *Oxford Review of Economic Policy* 8, no. 3 (1992): 1–10.
22. John L. Graham and N. Mark Lam, "The Chinese Negotiation," *Harvard Business Review* 81, no. 10 (2003): 82–91.
23. See, for example, Robert Axelrod, *The Evolution of Cooperation* (New York, 1984); Ernst Fehr and Simon Gachter, "Fairness and Retaliation: The Economics of Reciprocity," *The Journal of Economic Perspectives* 14, no. 3 (2000): 159–81; and Simon Gächter and Benedikt Herrmann, "Reciprocity, Culture and Human Cooperation: Previous Insights and a New Cross-Cultural Experiment," *Philosophical Transactions of the Royal Society B* 364, no. 1518 (2009): 791–806.

24. Avner Greif, "Cultural Beliefs and the Organization of Society: A Historical and Theoretical Reflection on Collectivist and Individualist Societies," *Journal of Political Economy* 102, no. 5 (1994): 912–50; and Avner Greif, "The Fundamental Problem of Exchange: A Research Agenda in Historical Institutional Analysis," *European Review of Economic History* 4 (2000) 251–84.
25. Sherwin Rosen, "Implicit Contracts: A Survey," *Journal of Economic Perspectives* 23, no. 3 (1985): 1144–75, here p. 1145; Costas Azariadis and Joseph E. Stiglitz, "Implicit Contracts and Fixed Price Equilibria," *Quarterly Journal of Economics* 98, Supplement (1983): 1–22.
26. Elke Renner and Jean-Robert Tyran, "Price Rigidity in Customer Markets," *Journal of Economic Behaviour and Organization* 55, no. 4 (2004): 575–93.
27. Okun, *Prices and Quantities*, 154.
28. See Andrew T. Young and Daniel Levy, "Explicit Evidence on an Implicit Contract," June 21, 2010, Emory Law and Economics Research Paper No. 4–05 and Bar Ilan Univ. Pub Law Working Paper No. 8–05, http://dx.doi.org/10.2139/ssrn.739984; Andrew Godley, "Pioneering Foreign Direct Investment in British Manufacturing," *Business History Review* 73, no. 3 (1999): 394–29; Andrew Godley, "The Global Diffusion of the Sewing Machine, 1850–1914," *Research in Economic History* 20 (2001): 1–45; and Andrew Godley, "Selling the Sewing Machine Around the World: Singer's International Marketing Strategies, 1850–1920," *Enterprise and Society* 7, no. 2 (2006): 266–314.
29. Godley, "Entrepreneurial Opportunities."
30. In principle, the costs of presales demonstration could also be passed on to consumers in the same manner. But the obvious desire of producers to induce the transaction here obscures the same logic.
31. And following on from the previous note, the same logic applies in principle to presales demonstration services, but is likely to be obscured in practice.

PART II

Consumer Engineers and Transatlantic Exchanges at Mid-Century

CHAPTER 5

Shopping Malls and Social Democracy: Victor Gruen's Postwar Campaign for Conscientious Consumption in American Suburbia

Joseph Malherek

The Viennese architect and urban planner Victor Gruen (1903–1980), who emigrated to the United States after Hitler's annexation of Austria in 1938, is best remembered as the inventor of the suburban shopping center and of the downtown pedestrian mall. This is the legacy for which he has been both celebrated and maligned in scholarly and popular accounts alike.[1] Gruen himself was ambivalent about his American career, and after repatriating to Austria in 1968, he made it his mission to protect Europe from the kind of garish commercial developments that had perverted his original vision for the shopping center. The depth of Gruen's disappointment was the inverse of the height of idealism that motivated his original vision for the shopping center, which he had seen as an organized, pedestrian-only community space that would serve as a city center for the rapidly growing postwar suburbs. It was a triumph of rational planning in the era of the Cold War, when such efforts at social engineering were often suspected of being communistic and in opposition to the ideals of "free enterprise." Along with Elsie Krummeck, his wife and business partner, Gruen first articulated his idea of the shopping center in a 1943 article for a special issue of *Architectural Forum* titled "194X," in which visionary architects imagined new building types for a hoped-for period of postwar prosperity.[2] His vision finally came to fruition in the spring of 1954 with the opening of Northland, a mammoth shopping center in suburban Detroit that set the mold for dozens of other shopping centers designed

J. Malherek (✉)
George Washington University, Washington, DC, USA

J. Logemann et al. (eds.), *Consumer Engineering, 1920s–1970s*,
Worlds of Consumption, https://doi.org/10.1007/978-3-030-14564-4_5

by Gruen, and for thousands of others designed by his imitators, over the next quarter-century.

This chapter looks at Gruen's postwar advocacy for the shopping center concept and the ways in which its implementation was a conscious effort on the part of developers, retailers, and their architectural consultants to engineer built environments that would facilitate a pleasant, leisurely, and free-spending consumer experience.[3] The liberty of American-style consumption required the rational planning of a Viennese socialist. For Gruen, who was as much urban planner as he was architect, the building of shopping centers was an opportunity to create wholly new towns from scratch according to his ideal of pedestrian spaces. He was grateful to be supported by "merchant princes," department store magnates motivated by more than profits; a sense of pride in their communities inspired them to invest in building something big and bold that would have lasting value. The influence of great city planners like Le Corbusier and the Viennese planners Camillo Sitte and Otto Wagner was clear in Gruen's shopping centers, which merged modernism with a traditional reverence for the pedestrian ideal of the city square, which Gruen reimagined as the pedestrian mall.[4] Also evident, and perhaps more significant, was the progressive impulse of the Austrian Social Democratic Party and its massive public housing projects in Vienna, the *Gemeindebauten*, initiated in 1919. These "people's palaces," with shared interior courtyards, were part of an effort to create an environment of proletarian socialization, designed with the explicit purpose of instilling in inhabitants communitarian values and a socialist consciousness.[5] Along with Rudi Baumfeld, a childhood friend who would remain his lifelong confidant and business partner, Gruen had won a prize in a design competition for a public housing project near the beginning of his architectural training.[6] Remarkably, many of the features of these complexes—which included kindergartens, playgrounds, swimming pools, meeting rooms, medical and dental clinics, libraries, lecture halls, and shops—would reappear in Gruen's original conception of the shopping center, which was closer to an ideal town than the purely commercial venture it eventually became.

Gruen was an ardent Social Democrat, and his commitment to democratic values and the possibility of encouraging them in the built environment did not wane when he was in the USA, despite his role in creating an emblem of consumer capitalism. In applying his professional training and political sensibility to the burgeoning consumer economy, Gruen was part of a wave of émigré professionals that included the sociologist Paul Lazarsfeld, a fellow Viennese Social Democrat and occasional participant in Gruen's agitprop political cabaret, who would become an innovative market researcher and media analyst on the American scene. These émigrés brought with them the political values and aesthetic sensibilities that characterized Jewish intellectual life in Central Europe between the world wars. Whereas scholars like Victoria de Grazia have emphasized the export of American values, business practices, and marketing methods to Europe,[7] this chapter considers Gruen as an importer of European political ideals and design ideas, which would produce a distinctly American building type in the shopping center. For Gruen, Vienna served as the urban paradigm, a city where he learned that architecture encompassed not just physical structures but the public spaces between them. Architects were not merely servants of developers and their private interests. They also fulfilled the critical social function of engineering spaces in which individuals could express themselves as members of a community through consumption, that vital element of the post-World War II economy. Finally, I consider Gruen's later years, when he repatriated to Vienna and, ironically, became an evangelist against the kind of urban redevelopment that he had witnessed in the USA. The collapse of commercial life in city centers was partly due to the explosion of suburban shopping centers, which Gruen feared would spread to Europe.

Selling the Idea of the Shopping Center

Gruen began his American career in the late 1930s designing storefronts, shop interiors, and department stores, first in New York with fellow architect Morris Ketchum and then in Los Angeles with the designer Elsie Krummeck. When he and Krummeck split in the late 1940s—personally and professionally—Gruen founded his own firm, Victor Gruen Associates (VGA), and he focused on making his vision for the shopping mall a reality. He had already cultivated a reputation as a thoughtful analyst of retail architecture and its psychological effects on paying and prospective customers. When addressing audiences of retailers and designers, Gruen was philosophical about the theatrical elements of the store, but he also expressed an intimate knowledge of the technical requirements to produce an almost magical effect on the shopper. He said that stores led a "double life," as "factories with machinery" that were concealed by their "gayer" side as showplaces for merchandise, designed inside and out to arouse consumers' desires. Gruen maintained that the work of designing a commercial structure was not so different from the business of the theater in that it required keen attention to "showmanship." Indeed, Gruen had a background in theater as an actor, manager, and producer for Vienna's Political Cabaret, an agitprop theater troupe, which had been forced underground in the 1930s. After Hitler's Anschluss of Austria in 1938 drove its members into exile, Gruen reconstituted the Viennese performers in New York as the Refugee Artists Group, keeping its antifascist, social-democratic ethos in two successful revues. Gruen's experience staging such productions informed his professional career through his belief that an intelligent design could create the right "atmosphere," a feeling of restfulness, luxury, and good taste that would encourage shoppers, usually women, to linger longer and spend more money.[8]

Gruen was unimpressed by what passed for a "shopping center" in the late 1940s, and in 1949, he claimed that no center "in the real sense of the word" had yet been constructed. The so-called shopping centers that had been developed merely used the "old formula" of "more or less correlated" stores on two sides of a busy highway. Postwar suburban shopping areas were typically located in "Miracle Miles" along main thoroughfares. These strips taxed shoppers' nerves with noise, gasoline odors, the danger of crossing busy streets, and even the steady reflection of moving objects—cars—in the show windows of stores. They were, Gruen said, nothing more than newly created Main Streets with all of the disadvantages and none of the advantages of the Main Street setup. While the downtown stores were designed to serve the pedestrian, suburban stores served only the driver. Developers had failed to change the design of shopping centers for the suburban context. They made no attempt to incorporate themselves into the character of the residential neighborhood, and they employed garish designs in a "never-ending race" to attract the attention of shoppers.[9]

The main design feature of the shopping center Gruen envisioned was to segregate pedestrian traffic from automobile traffic, parking, and store deliveries in order to create "psychological comfort" for shoppers. The stores of a shopping center did not face the street. Instead, they lined colonnades that surrounded a central courtyard or landscaped area—the *mall* that would later become a synecdoche for the total idea of the shopping center. The mall would be "enlivened" by such things as kiosks and juice stands, and it would be landscaped with trees, shrubbery, flower beds, and fountains, which gave it the character of a large park. "It is difficult to prove that a tree ever sold one penny's worth of merchandise," said Gruen, but "the eye needs respite from observing thousands of cars and large groups of buildings." The communal atmosphere would be encouraged through benches, walkways, and public announcement boards, which would invite "leisurely shopping." This "inward-looking" orientation was intended to create a restful atmosphere in which patrons would spend long periods of time strolling, socializing, having meals, and, of course, purchasing goods. Rather than seeing a strip of individualized stores, patrons would tend to think of the complex as a whole, and the mall plan with shops on both sides had the advantage of doubling the frontage along any particular strip.[10]

Designed with the perspective of the shopper in mind, nothing was to interfere with the pleasantness of the shopping experience. All of the service areas, utilities, and functional elements of the shopping center were to be hidden from the shopping areas. Service roads would run on a lower level to underground receiving areas, and in no place would the service roads cross any roads or walkways that were used by customers (Fig. 5.1). Foot traffic would be directed from the parking lots to the center, and direct access to individual stores would not be permitted from the parking areas. This was an important element of the plan: Shoppers would be exposed to other shops even if they only intended to visit one, and the single entrance and exit to shops facilitated the proper display of "impulse" items. As he had done in his earlier designs of shopfronts, which made creative use of exterior arcades to funnel potential customers into the showroom, Gruen reimagined the retail space

Fig. 5.1 Victor Gruen on Margaret Arlen's television show, January 25, 1953. Gruen explains a key principle of his shopping center design to TV host Arlen, the use of underground tunnels to segregate delivery truck traffic from customer car traffic and pedestrian areas. Source: Victor Gruen Papers, Manuscript Division, Library of Congress, Washington, DC.

in ways that were meant to engineer consumers. His shopping center would be more than the sum of its parts: Individual stores would benefit from being part of a collective, and they would also be served by the co-location of a large department store, which would serve as an "anchor." The entire development would have a cohesive architectural treatment, and tenants would be subject to certain restrictions on the size of signs, the use of neon, and the choice of colors and materials in storefronts. Yet they would be given the freedom to express their individuality so long as they did it in a "harmonious and esthetically pleasant manner." Gruen proposed other amenities such as theaters, exhibit halls, public meeting rooms, and even nurseries where mothers could deposit their small children as they shopped. Overall, the center was designed to be more than just a place for suburbanites to shop. Consumers would associate the shopping center with "all activities of cultural enrichment and relaxation," argued Gruen.[11]

With the help of Larry Smith, a real estate analyst and economic advisor who would become a key partner, Gruen's concept of the shopping center evolved to become a social theory and a financial arrangement as well as an architectural plan. Writing in 1952 in the journal *Progressive Architecture*, Gruen and Smith defined the shopping center as a "conscious and conscientious cooperative effort by many private commercial enterprises to achieve a specific purpose: more and better business." But while the center was a cooperative commercial enterprise, it would also serve a social function by filling the "vacuum" created by the absence of civic "crystallization points" in the suburbs. Gruen and Smith acknowledged that city centers were shrinking, in terms of both population and social importance, while the suburbs were expanding. The regional shopping center would serve as a "satellite" downtown area to provide the social function of a city center for suburbanites. But it was also an opportunity to build a better downtown, designed "scientifically" to disguise the "ugly rash" on the body of cities, namely the utilitarian elements, those smokestacks, electrical lines, roadways, and signs that had accumulated ad hoc. In contrast, the shopping center would be a planned, coordinated design that would produce a pleasing atmosphere with "magnetic powers" to attract people and keep them there. (Some later observers described this as the "Gruen effect.") It would be a pedestrian oasis in an automobile age, with conformity, but not uniformity, as its aim. Gruen drew inspiration from his native Vienna as well as Turkish and Arabian bazaars and the commercial arcades of nineteenth-century Paris, which were the product of a cooperative effort by merchants to create a safe, weather-protected space for shoppers. While he accepted the dominance of the "auto-borne" consumer in postwar suburban life, he ultimately aimed to extract that consumer from her car for a pleasant stroll along a shopping mall.[12]

Northland

By the late 1940s, Gruen was commuting frequently between Los Angeles and New York on business (and to visit his mistress, Lazette van Houten, who would later become his third wife). One day in 1948, he found himself stranded in Detroit, where his plane had made an emergency landing due to bad weather. He decided to make use of his time there by visiting the famous J. L. Hudson department store. The mammoth Hudson's was a landmark in downtown Detroit. Occupying an entire city block, it was a bulwark of consumption in an increasingly desolate city center. Yet even an institution like Hudson's was threatened by the new wave of postwar suburbanization and the trend to decentralization, driven by the democratization of automobile transportation. Though he was warned that it would be impossible for an outsider, and particularly a Jew, to get a meeting with Oscar Webber, the president of the company, Gruen persisted in engaging Webber's subordinates, and eventually on a later visit got a meeting with Webber himself. Despite Webber's reluctance to diminish the mightiness of the downtown store with smaller satellites, Gruen managed to convince him of the wisdom of planning suburban branch stores around his own "shopping towns," and that Gruen was the man for the job. This gave Webber the opportunity to take on the role of more than a merchant: He could become a civic leader.[13]

Gruen introduced his plan for Northland, which would be the first built of several planned centers, to the Detroit Chapter of the American Institute of Architects in January 1952.[14] The plan called for sixty different types of merchandising and service facilities, ranging from dress shops to cigar kiosks, with parking space for 5500 customers' cars and 900 employee cars. The entire center would cover eighty acres, but an additional 100 acres surrounding the plot would be held "in reserve" as a buffer against the residential area, and for the future expansion of the center's shops and parking lots. Northland was designed specifically for the customer behind the wheel, but the design strictly segregated customer car traffic from delivery truck traffic, which was directed to underground tunnels. Each store would have access to these basement loading docks. The shops would also be integrated by a central heating and air conditioning system. Gruen designed a space for pedestrians at the core of the center that would be completely free of automobiles—the signature feature of his centers. Covered colonnades would provide shoppers protection from the weather. The spaces between buildings would follow the pattern of European cities—landscaped as parks, courts, plazas, and malls that would provide a commercial-free respite from shopping. The Hudson's branch store (at 470,000 square feet, the largest ever built to that point) would be at the heart of the store group, surrounded on three sides by tenant buildings. The idea was to direct customers through the inner malls with the hope of creating an intensity of pedestrian traffic "comparable to downtown streets." While each shop along the mall would be free to express its own character, all would be subject to certain controls designed to create a pleasant harmony rather than a "dissonant" relationship between adjacent shops. A standard lettering type for all signs, set in Mondrian-like frames, was created by a graphics consultant to further integrate the collection of shops. Gruen also believed that the shopping center should be a community "focal point," and so his plans included club rooms, meeting halls, a public auditorium, a common kitchen, public toilets, and a nursery "where children can be checked while Mother shops."[15]

When it opened in March 1954, the $22.5 million, 80-store Northland Center was an immediate sensation for the shopping public, exceeding all sales expectations with daily visits of forty to fifty thousand customers. It was also a revelation for architects and developers. *Architectural Forum* called it a "planning classic" on the level of Rockefeller Center in New York. It was the "first modern pedestrian commercial center" based on the "market town" plan that was both physically and psychologically suited to shopping. In this sense, it was a "rediscovery" rather than an invention. It had all of the "visual vigor" of downtown but with an architectural unity imposed by Gruen. Even the center's public sculptures were, according to Gruen, an "integral portion" of the architectural treatment of the outdoor space. Northland was immediately recognized as a potential model for city planners looking to revitalize "blight-spotted decaying shopping districts" downtown. "The things we learn in building shopping centers are the things that can save the cities," said Gruen. He believed that the success of Northland was proof that, even in the heightened Cold War context of American "free enterprise," planning could be socially acceptable, not communistic.[16]

Reviews of Northland in the popular press were just as enthusiastic as the celebratory accounts in the trade papers. The journalist Dorothy Thompson, writing for the *Ladies Home Journal*, called Northland a "tiny city" and a "model of enlightened planning." It was the perfect example of "social co-operation" between merchants, architects, sculptors, artists, and civic-minded citizens, and yet it was "entirely the creation of private enterprise." While shopping had been typically regarded as an exhausting activity, a job, Thompson managed to shop at Northland for six hours, she claimed, without feeling any fatigue. The labor of shopping was transformed into the pleasure of consumption.[17] *Life* magazine called it the "most elegant" of the new shopping centers in the USA, having the air of a bazaar with its fanciful sculptures, fine architecture, music, and "pure gaiety." *Family Circle* observed that this "spirit of gaiety" created an atmosphere friendly to children and adults alike. *McCall's* profiled a resident of suburban Detroit who exclaimed that Northland was "like a park with stores!" that made shopping so "fun" that even her husband was eager to join her on Saturday shopping trips. About a year into Northland's operation, the *New York Times* called it a "fabulous success" that was projected to have sales of $80 million for the first year, $30 million more than initial projections. By 1960, the 50,000 shoppers who daily visited Northland, accommodated by 10,000 parking spaces, would be driving more than $100 million in annual sales.[18]

Shopping Center Evangelism

Gruen was not the only shopping mall designer. The first shopping center implemented in a "completely planned fashion" was Seattle's Northgate, designed by John Graham, which opened in 1950. Gruen's former colleague Morris Ketchum was also busily designing centers, and his Shoppers' World opened near Boston in 1951. But Gruen was perhaps the most articulate and visionary, and his firm had completed fifteen shopping center designs by the fall of 1954.[19] By the fall of 1955, in addition to the large regional centers like Northland, there were an estimated 1000 smaller shopping centers in operation with another 2000 under construction or in the planning stage. The new centers served a surging suburban population, which was growing at four times the rate of the country as a whole.[20]

Gruen was more than an architect or contractor. He was the spokesman of a movement for a "truly new building type." Because the shopping center was a new concept, he had to convince town planners, developers, financiers, and the general public that the idea had both commercial and social value, and that there was a right way to do it that required "conscientious, scientific planning." Gruen believed that the chaos of the free market was insufficient to engineer efficient spaces of consumption. He spoke out against the "archaic hodgepodge" of unplanned, "anarchistically-growing" shopping districts in favor of his planned, integrated shopping *centers*, which avoided the "honky-tonk" appearance of the "helter-skelter" alternative. Rather than one long mall, Gruen's many malls and courts made more efficient use of space, and they concentrated customer traffic. Gruen sometimes also "stacked" his shopping streets with two levels of storefronts facing his malls, effectively doubling the selling space. The centralization of services and utilities, furthermore, made operations cheaper for tenants and allowed them to devote their space completely to merchandising.[21]

Gruen understood the shopping center as an organization of separate architectural elements into an integrated whole that was coordinated with the surrounding area and its sociological composition. He made the case for what he called "premerchandising," that is, the deliberate selection of tenants to produce a balanced retail market in the center that maintained competition while avoiding redundancies. Premerchandising was one of many ways in which the planned shopping center relied on the studies of economic analysts, traffic consultants, and other specialists who lent their knowledge to the planning of the center. Gruen did not withhold his disdain for the unplanned, haphazard suburban development of the postwar years, and he laid much of the blame for the "vast desert" of unhappy shopping on the "tyranny" of the automobile, which was in his opinion the cause of much poor urban planning. After Northland was built and its success was proven, Gruen had a ready example of his ideal of the planned shopping center, which was predicated on the separation of automobile and shopper, producing the pleasant atmosphere of "untroubled joy" on the pedestrian malls. Despite the prevalence of the automobile, Gruen insisted that people still were not only willing but happy to walk, so long as they were in a pleasing environment. Centers like Northland were, according to Gruen, natural heirs to the Greek agora and the European and New England towns where commerce, culture, and society were woven together in town centers. Moreover, the shopping center idea was not just for the suburbs. Gruen immediately recognized it as a model for the redevelopment of American downtowns, a mission that would come to define his later career.[22]

Southdale

Gruen's work for Oscar Webber on the Northland shopping center led directly to a major contract with the Dayton Company of Minnesota, which operated the Dayton's department store. Like Webber, the Dayton brothers were what Gruen called "merchant princes." The members of this kind of family business were motivated not only by commercial interests but also by a desire to improve the reputation of their family "empires." They felt a responsibility to future generations, and they tended over their stores in a "paternalistic" manner, as though they were little fiefdoms. Gruen believed that these were the ideal clients for a designer of shopping centers, and it did not hurt that Webber, a close friend of the Dayton family, virtually insisted that the brothers hire Gruen for the job.[23]

In June 1952, Donald C. Dayton, president of the company, announced plans for a $10 million "shopping and residential project" in the Minneapolis suburb of Edina. Envisioned as a "satellite downtown" serving a population of 250,000 within a fifteen-minute drive, it would resemble Northland and other Gruen-designed projects with its emphasis on social and cultural integration in the community. It was to be the first of several suburban centers ringing the city. In addition to the shopping center, the ambitious development plan called for a school, a park, a playground, an amusement center, restaurants, nurseries, office buildings, a medical center, an auto service station, and a fire station. The center would only occupy eighty-six acres of a 500-acre plot purchased by the Dayton Company. The "buffer" zone surrounding the center was meant to control future development and prevent parasitic "commercial slum areas." Indeed, the Dayton Company planned to profit from this "blight-proof" area by leasing the property, whose value would have increased due to the very presence of the center.[24]

But Southdale also included an important innovation that distinguished it from Northland. The harsh Minnesota climate permitted only 126 "ideal weather shopping days" a year, so the center would be connected by malls and a central plaza that were completely closed off from the outdoors. While working on another department store project for Dayton's, Gruen had experienced the extreme climate of Minnesota with its very cold winters and very hot summers, and he became convinced that a covered and "climatized" public area was required for Southdale. Gruen called this an "introvert" design, and he made comparisons to the Galleria Vittorio Emanuele in Milan and the nineteenth-century arcades and classic department stores in European cities. Open shopfronts would face malls and courts that would be centrally heated in the winter and cooled in the summer to maximize efficiency. The glass enclosure would be "scientifically lighted" to give visitors the illusion of being out-of-doors in a paradise of "perpetual spring." Gruen's central market square would be surrounded by "stacked" streets—two levels of store frontage.[25]

The architectural and retail professions were generally very kind to Gruen's Southdale design. The trade journal *Architectural Forum* marveled at the success of the artificial environment, which "uncannily" conveyed the feeling of a metropolitan downtown within the confines of a single building. Yet Southdale was not exactly downtown. It was an "imaginative distillation" of downtown's magnetic elements—the variety, the lights and color, the business and bustle. According to the *Forum*, it actually improved on downtown by eliminating dirtiness and chaos, and by adding sidewalk cafes, art, plants, attractive walkways, a charming central court, and the many quaint lanes leading to it. While other shopping centers had fallen short in their efforts to mimic downtown, Southdale made the real Minneapolis downtown appear "pokey and provincial" relative to its manufactured metropolitan atmosphere. The new center was, the journal gushed, more than the sum of its parts.[26] But not everyone was impressed. After a visit to Southdale shortly after its opening, the renowned architect Frank Lloyd Wright called it a "barracks" wholly lacking in imagination and with "as much life as a cardboard box." "You have tried to bring downtown out here," said Wright dismissively, referring to the center's suburban setting. "You should have left downtown downtown."[27]

Planning in the Postwar Era

Gruen's experience working on downtown redevelopment elevated him as a public figure, but it also exposed him to the political and ideological frustrations of working in the American system. Gruen was particularly bothered by antipathy to the concept of *planning* that he so frequently encountered, often from business interests like the parking garage owners who rallied to defeat his visionary plan to create a pedestrian-only zone in downtown Fort Worth, Texas. Described in one account as "one of the most articulate men in his profession," Gruen became increasingly outspoken. "Planning" was practically a dirty word in the USA, almost as bad "as if Lenin had invented it," he said. Gruen, an old Viennese Social Democrat, lamented that his adopted country suffered from the notion that planning was "a terrible thing, like socialism or worse, and that we have to leave everything to rugged individualism." Gruen argued that the success of shopping centers like Northland was proof that planning meant good business, and that some merchants seemed to know this better than politicians. He scoffed at absurd outcomes from the obstinate idea that any kind of planning presented a threat to liberty: "How much liberty does a man have sitting in a 90-mile-an-hour car in a frozen traffic jam?" Indeed, Gruen annoyed many businessmen in the automobile industry with his persistent critiques of American car culture and its ruinous effect on cities. He also faced the wrath of those who saw the automobile as a precious commodity and status symbol.[28]

What Gruen called "democratic planning" sought to enrich human life by producing a "physical and sociological framework" that did not force individuals to conform, but rather created the "shapes and patterns" in which harmonious coexistence and individual expression were possible. He sought to calm the nerves of those who saw the "threat of socialism" in urban redevelopment and renewal by reminding them that the projects were constituted by a partnership of private businesses, community leaders, and government officials. Moreover, he noted that private enterprise and private consultants designed, constructed, and profited from those projects. The goal of planning was not to autocratically determine people's actions, but to establish the basis for the "greatest achievable individualistic expressions" that could coexist harmoniously. By the mid-1960s, as the role of government in building public infrastructure and preserving the social welfare became more firmly established during the Kennedy and Johnson administrations and through "urban renewal" efforts, Gruen witnessed wider public acceptance of the idea of planning, to the point where it became fashionable. Gruen was even invited to work on the planning plank for Kennedy's 1960 presidential campaign platform.[29]

Gruen cemented his status as the guru of the shopping center with the 1960 publication of his *Shopping Towns USA: The Planning of Shopping Centers*, which became a veritable bible among shopping mall planners.[30] Gruen wrote the book with Larry Smith, the economic analyst with whom he had collaborated on many projects, including Northland. The book examined nearly every technical aspect of mall planning from the perspectives of an architect and an economist, but it also advocated the idealist vision of the shopping center that Gruen had been refining for more than a decade. The term "shopping towns" was justified, the authors felt, because shopping centers, in their ideal form, ought to take on the characteristics of "urban organisms" that served myriad human needs and activities. Gruen and Smith presented planned shopping centers as the solution to the "amorphous conglomeration" of suburbia in which merchants struggled to organize their activities. They assuaged the fears of businessmen worried about the authoritarian effects of planning, assuring them that it would create a vibrant, stimulating environment that would encourage the "pursuit of happiness."

Gruen believed that Americans had concentrated their efforts on improving private living standards while neglecting the public environment. In many ways, Gruen was not a great architect of buildings. Individually, his structures were inconspicuous and unremarkable. Instead, he excelled as a planner of public spaces that also had a commercial component. He believed that the spaces between buildings were at least as important as the buildings themselves. Indeed, Gruen came to regard himself as an "environmental" architect who concerned himself with the total man-made and "man-influenced" environment. The architecture of an individual structure became "pathetically inconsequential," Gruen argued, when it was surrounded by the "anarchy" of industrial and commercial slums. Even when he was designing store interiors, he was interested in creating the proper atmosphere through "psychological lighting," which could affect the mood of the shopper. Gruen had always been sensitive to the "noisiness and disorderliness" of the kind of street signs and billboards that cluttered shopping strips, each seeking to attract more attention than the next, creating a total visual cacophony. His shopping centers—with their nondescript exteriors, introverted character, and pleasant courtyards accented with modern art—were an attempt to ameliorate the environmental chaos of the commercial strip. He knew that schemes to maximize the profit potential of every bit of space—such as a plan to convert the space over the main waiting room in New York's Grand Central Terminal into three stories of shops and bowling alleys—failed to comprehend the "psychological lift" that came from a pleasant environment.[31]

A Reorientation Toward Europe

By the mid-1960s, Gruen's firm had designed more than forty shopping centers, and it had established satellite offices in New York and Chicago in addition to its base in Beverly Hills. VGA also operated temporary project offices in cities where it had major clients, such as Detroit, Minneapolis, and San Francisco, and it maintained an international clientele in Australia, South America, and Europe. Its projects included not only shopping centers, but also public buildings, churches, schools, office buildings, banks, exhibitions, and New Towns. By 1966, Gruen's six partners and staff of nearly 300—which included not only architects and engineers, but also transportation planners, merchandising analysts, graphic artists, interior designers, economists, and other specialists—began to operate more independently of him.[32]

In response to the increasing demand for his consulting services abroad, Gruen founded Victor Gruen International (VGI), which began in Gruen's Bel Air home but was eventually based in Vienna. Though VGI was originally conceived as a branch of VGA, Gruen eventually dissolved his relationship with his old firm and reestablished himself in Europe. At the opening of the new VGI office in May 1967, Gruen promised to combine his American experience with the European tradition; however, he generally disclaimed the moniker of "American expert" when speaking to European audiences. He claimed to be a cosmopolitan, citing his intimate knowledge of the fundamental differences between the social and cultural conditions on both sides of the Atlantic and referring to his work experience on several continents. He emphasized that the first thirty-five years of his life were spent in Vienna, where he had been educated and had opened his first architectural office. While he acknowledged his role as a pioneer of regional shopping center design, he insisted that he was a generalist in the "much wider battle area of the manmade urban environment." Indeed, he had stated his urbanist passions clearly in his 1964 book, *The Heart of Our Cities*, advocating for the critical role of planning in reviving American downtowns, which by then had become decayed and chaotic largely through the dominance of the automobile.[33] Gruen warned that America's "urban crisis" and the disfiguration of the cityscape, most strikingly in Los Angeles, threatened Europe, too. "During the 29 years I have spent in the United States up to now, I have seen the tragedy with my own eyes," said Gruen, gloomily. "You as Europeans have been spectators in the audience of the great American urban tragedy."[34]

Gruen's frustration with the American system had mounted over the years, and he grew increasingly disenchanted and pessimistic about the possibilities for reform. The postwar years in the United States had been a time of great technological and sociological change, but the rapid pace of change had led Americans to make "mistake after mistake" as they failed to recognize the "essential supremacy of human values." Gruen felt that his city planning designs, more important to him now than his shopping centers, were repeatedly stymied by the question of racial integration. He came to see the failure of U.S. society to live up to the ideals of the Declaration of Independence, namely, that all men were created "equal." He also detested the "one-sided pursuit for ever more money and ever more materialistic growth" that seemed to define American ideology. He began to resent the artificiality and unhealthiness of the "air-conditioned life" in which he found himself living in Los Angeles, and he even sympathized with his children and other "hippies" as they protested against a life defined by material things. The last straw, perhaps, was the "urban crisis" in the USA, characterized by slums, white flight, and riots, all of which Gruen believed to stem from the "weak" sense of urbanity that plagued American cities. The impossible situation led Gruen to view the entire country as almost a lost cause, and he began to see it as his mission to save Europe from a similar fate.[35]

In the spring of 1968, Gruen founded the Victor Gruen Foundation for Environmental Planning, with an office in Los Angeles, electing himself as president. Upon reaching his sixty-fifth birthday on July 18, he formally resigned from the presidency of VGA and moved his base of operations to Vienna, where he directed VGI. For a time, he also had a separate company based in Switzerland called Victor Gruen Planning and Architecture. He confessed to leading a "gipsy life," going back and forth between Vienna, Los Angeles, and New York, and also working in France, Belgium, Italy, and Germany. By the early 1970s, however, he had settled more permanently into the city of his birth, where he lived and worked for most of the remainder of his life.[36]

Gruen had gone from being the inventor of the shopping center to being its most enthusiastic and articulate evangelist to being, toward the end of his life, its fiercest critic because of what it had become, a thing devoid of the idealism that had motivated his original designs. As he reestablished himself in Vienna in the 1970s, he took on the cause of warning European city planners not to make the same mistakes that had occurred in the United States over the past thirty years. He lamented the fact that the "environmental and humane" concepts which were the basis for his original vision of the shopping center had been completely forgotten in favor of arrangements whose only merit was commercial profitability. Shopping centers were no longer the projects of the "merchant princes" like Oscar Webber and the Daytons of Minnesota, the ambitious clients who had the wherewithal to realize Gruen's vision. Now they were planned by "anonymous" real estate enterprises with no interest in building a legacy or strengthening a community. Instead, these faceless corporations were only interested in making money. At the same time, Gruen reluctantly admitted that suburban shopping centers had delivered the final "death blow" to the suffering central cities by driving out nearly all commercial activity there.

As tragic as this history was in the USA, Gruen felt that it would be even more tragic in Europe because American cities were relatively young and their downtowns had never had as much "to offer" as the traditional European central city. Gruen feared that the urban character of cities like his beloved

Vienna was threatened by the development of "uni-functional" shopping centers, which produced a "monoculture" that compromised the essential variety of urban life. He developed this theme in his 1973 book *Centers for the Urban Environment*, in which he expressed a new environmentalism and sought to atone for his sins as father and evangelist of the shopping center, while remaining proud of Northland and Southdale as ideal types.[37]

Toward the end of his life, however, Gruen's mood shifted somewhat. "The shopping centre is an extreme but by no means the only expression of the effort of substituting naturally and originally grown mixtures of various urban expressions by an artificial and therefore sterile order," said Gruen in London in 1978, speaking before an audience of shopping center owners who were probably expecting a different tone from the inventor of the shopping mall. The result was the creation of "functional ghettos" on the model of Le Corbusier. These developments served only a single use. They introduced the forced obligation of transportation between them as opposed to livability within them. Gruen said that the conventional shopping center was a thing of the past and that the members of his audience should focus on creating "multi-functional" centers "for tomorrow." While he regretted the way that shopping centers had developed, he stuck to the values that he had articulated in his original concept.[38]

Gruen did not soften his criticism after his declaration in London, and in the last few years of his life, he became as well known for his antipathy toward shopping centers as for being the man who had invented them. "I refuse to pay alimony for those bastard developments," he famously said of the ubiquitous malls built by "fast-buck promoters and speculators." He felt that these developments were a perversion of his original concept. As he preached the values of urbanity, namely, direct human communications, the easy and free exchange of ideas and goods, and the easy access to a multiplicity of choices, he urged audiences to forget about the "conventional" shopping center. Shopping centers had been reduced to standardized malls, which appeared the same whether in Detroit or in Houston. They were, with few exceptions, fully enclosed no matter what the climate. Rather than being islands of urbanity in the suburban desert, these shopping centers completely lacked identification with their surrounding communities and had no purpose other than merchandising. Gruen even supported a successful campaign to stop the construction of a mall near Burlington, Vermont, which would have constituted "premeditated murder of a city by robbing it of practically all its retailing."[39]

Gruen's success as an architect of consumer environments with shops, department stores, shopping centers, and downtown pedestrian malls was the product of his upbringing in the urban density of Vienna during its transition to modernity, his politicization as a Social Democrat in the new Republic of Austria after World War I, the traumatic experience of his emigration to the United States as victim of Nazi persecution, and, finally, his eagerness to establish himself as a forward-thinking professional in his adopted homeland. His personal trajectory made his vision for the shopping center unique, but it was precisely the idealism behind is original design that led him to sour on the shopping center as it ultimately developed. He had masterfully engineered the ideal consumer environment, but the demands of capitalism had evacuated the communal, democratic experience that was to have been at its core.

Notes

1. There are two book-length biographies on Gruen: M. Jeffrey Hardwick, *Mall Maker: Victor Gruen, Architect of an American Dream* (Philadelphia, PA, 2004); and Alex Wall, *Victor Gruen: From Urban Shop to New City* (Barcelona, 2005). Other secondary accounts include Richard Longstreth, *City Center to Regional Mall: Architecture, the Automobile, and Retailing in Los Angeles, 1920–1950* (Cambridge, MA, 1997); and Lizabeth Cohen, *A Consumers' Republic: The Politics of Mass Consumption in Postwar America* (New York, 2003), Chapter 6. More recently, Gruen's achievements as a specifically modern architect have been examined by David Smiley in *Pedestrian Modern: Shopping and American Architecture, 1925–1956* (Minneapolis, MN, 2013). Gruen's autobiography was only recently published in the original German and in English translation: Victor Gruen, *Shopping Town: Memoiren eines Stadtplaners (1903–1980)*, ed. Anette Baldauf (Vienna, 2014); Victor Gruen, *Shopping Town: Designing the City in Suburban America*, ed. and trans. Anette Baldauf (Minneapolis, MN, 2017). An early version of the original manuscript for his autobiography is Victor Gruen, "Biographische Notizen," April 2, 1975, in box 76, folders 7–8, Victor Gruen Papers, Manuscript Division, Library of Congress, Washington, DC (hereafter: Gruen LOC).
2. "Shopping Center: Gruenbaum & Krummeck, Designers, Hollywood, Calif.," *The Architectural Forum*, May 1943.
3. For a discussion of Gruen's formative years in Vienna and his early career in the USA, see Joseph Malherek, "Victor Gruen's Retail Therapy: Exiled Jewish Communities and the Invention of the American Shopping Mall as a Postwar Ideal," *Leo Baeck Institute Year Book* 61 (2016): 1–14.
4. On the work of Sitte and Wagner, which bridged the nineteenth and twentieth centuries, see Carl E. Schorske, *Fin-de-Siècle Vienna: Politics and Culture* (New York, 1981), 25–100.
5. On the Gemeindebauten, see Helmut Gruber, *Red Vienna: Experiment in Working Class Culture, 1919–1934* (New York, 1991), 45–80; and Eve Blau, *The Architecture of Red Vienna, 1919–1934* (Cambridge: MIT Press, 1999).
6. Victor Gruen, "Biographische Notizen," 30 and 51. See also Gruen, *Shopping Town* (2017), 38.
7. Victoria de Grazia, *Irresistible Empire: America's Advance Through Twentieth-Century Europe* (Cambridge, MA, 2005).
8. "Commercial Buildings: Prototype Supermarket," *Progressive Architecture*, July 1956; Victor Gruen, "Modernized Store Layout," speech at Store Modernization Show, July 8, 1947, in box 1, binder 1, Victor Gruen Papers, American Heritage Center, University of Wyoming, Laramie, Wyoming (hereafter: Gruen AHC); Victor Gruen, "Modernization for More Efficient Operation," speech at N.R.D.G.A., San Francisco, June 14, 1948, in box 1, binder 1, Gruen AHC; and Victor Gruen, "Notes for Talk to Be Delivered to the

Southern California Display Club," May 26, 1949, in box 1, binder 1, Gruen AHC; Gruen, "Biographische Notizen," 30–44.

9. Victor Gruen, "What's Wrong with Store Design?" *Women's Wear Daily*, October 18, 1949, 62; Victor Gruen, "What to Look for in Shopping Centers," *Chain Store Age*, July 1948; and Victor Gruen, "Yardstick for Shopping Centers," *Chain Store Age*, February 1950.
10. Victor Gruen, "What to Look for in Shopping Centers," *Chain Store Age*, July 1948; and Victor Gruen, "Yardstick for Shopping Centers," *Chain Store Age*, February 1950. See also Longstreth, *City Center to Regional Mall*, Chapter 11.
11. Victor Gruen, "What to Look for in Shopping Centers," *Chain Store Age*, July 1948.
12. Victor Gruen and Lawrence P. Smith, "Shopping Centers, the New Building Type," *Progressive Architecture*, June 1952; Victor Gruen, "The Planning of Shopping Centers," *Michigan Society of Architects Monthly Bulletin*, February 1952, 15–25, in box OV19, Gruen LOC; Victor Gruen, "The Chains' Stake in Planning the Center," *Chain Store Age*, May 1954; and Victor Gruen, *Centers for the Urban Environment: Survival of the Cities* (New York, 1973), 14.
13. Gruen, "Biographische Notizen," 121–28 and 181; Gruen, *Shopping Town* (2017), 109–17.
14. Victor Gruen, "Shopping Centers," address delivered before the Detroit Chapter of the American Institute of Architects, January 16, 1952, in box 1, binder 1, Gruen AHC.
15. "Northland Center," planning book, n.d., in box 22, folder "Shopping Centers—Northland Center (Detroit, MI), 1954," Gruen AHC; Gruen, *Centers for the Urban Environment*, 28.
16. "Northland Center, Detroit," *Michigan Tradesman*, March 24, 1954; "Northland: a new yardstick for shopping center planning," *Architectural Forum*, June 1954; Sterling Soderlind, "Architect Says Southdale Planned as 'Cultural Center' for Its Patrons," *Minneapolis Sunday Tribune*, March 14, 1954; and Gruen, *Shopping Town* (2017), 142.
17. Dorothy Thompson, "Commercialism Takes—and Wears—A New Look," *Ladies Home Journal*, June 1954.
18. "20th Century Bazaar," *Life*, August 30, 1954; "Adventure in Shopping," *Family Circle*, September 1954, 49; Eleanor Pollock, "The $290 Pair of Shoes," *McCall's*, March 1955; "Sales of Center Surprise Owners," *The New York Times*, February 22, 1955; and "Victor Gruen: Biographical Data," [ca. 1963], in box 5, folder "Speech File 1963," Gruen AHC.
19. "Living by Design," transcript of television broadcast on WOR-TV, January 19, 1954, in box 1, binder 1, Gruen AHC; Victor Gruen, "The Shape of Things to Come," speech at Chain Store Age 14th Annual Seminar, Philadelphia, February 26, 1968, in box 3, vol. XVI, Gruen AHC.
20. Genevieve Smith, "Shopping Centers: More, Bigger, Better," *Printers' Ink*, November 25, 1955, 21.
21. Victor Gruen, "Financing Shopping Centers," address delivered at the Annual Savings and Mortgage Conference of the American Bankers Association, New York City, March 4, 1953, in box 1, binder 1, Gruen AHC; "$25 Million Shopping Center Is Announced," *Independent* [Pasadena, CA], May 3, 1953; Victor Gruen, "Twelve Check Points for Regional Planned Center," *Women's Wear Daily*, December 28, 1953.

22. "Northland: A Regional Shopping Center for Detroit, Michigan," *Michigan Society of Architects Monthly Bulletin*, March 1954, 33–48, in box 27, folder "Shopping Malls—Northland (Detroit, MI), 1954–1955," Gruen AHC; "Shopping Centers," *Art Digest*, November 15, 1954; Victor Gruen, "Dynamic Planning for Retail Areas," *Harvard Business Review* 32 (November–December 1954): 53–62; and Gruen, *Shopping Town* (2017), 129.
23. "Biographical Material, Annotated Chronology," in box 20, folder 19, Gruen LOC; Gruen, *Centers for the Urban Environment*, 33; Victor Gruen, "Shopping Centres, Why, Where, How?" speech for Third Annual European Conference of the International Council of Shopping Centres, London, February 28, 1978, in box 5, folder "Speeches, 1970–1978," Gruen AHC; and Gruen, *Shopping Town* (2017), 131.
24. "Dayton Company Announces $10,000,000 Shopping Center Project in Edina-Richfield," *The Minneapolis Star*, June 17, 1952; Sterling Soderlind, "Architect Says Southdale Planned as 'Cultural Center' for Its Patrons," *Minneapolis Sunday Tribune*, March 14, 1954; and "Dayton's Again Takes the Lead with Southdale," *The Dayton News*, July 1952, in box OV-4, Gruen LOC.
25. "The New Southdale Center," promotional brochure, [ca. 1952], in box OV-4, Gruen LOC; Gruen, "Biographische Notizen," 220–23; "New Thinking on Shopping Centers," *Architectural Forum*, March 1953; untitled document, [ca. 1956], in box 1, vol. II, Gruen AHC; and Gruen, *Centers for the Urban Environment*, 33.
26. "Southdale Shopping Center," *Architectural Forum*, April 1957.
27. Joe F. Kane, "Minneapolis Crucified by Architect," *Rapid City Journal* [from Associated Press], November 19, 1956. Wright berated Gruen in person over his disgust at the Southdale design, which he considered to be a desecration of nature. Gruen believed that Wright was anti-urbanist: Whereas Gruen saw himself as creating public spaces for the masses, he felt that Wright mainly made buildings for rich people. Gruen, *Shopping Town* (2014), 303–4.
28. "New City," Talk of the Town, *The New Yorker*, March 17, 1956, 33–34; "How to Judge a Town by Its Planning: An Interview on Plant Site Selection with Victor Gruen, Architect and Urban Planner," *Management Methods*, 1960, box 13, Gruen AHC; Jim Doyle, "Urban Life in America: Nice Houses…Shabby Cities; Fine Bathtubs…Poor Parks," *Toledo Blade*, February 21, 1960; Frank Mulcahy, "Scarcity of Land for Urban Use Stresses Need of Proper Planning," *Los Angeles Times*, February 7, 1960; and Gruen, *Shopping Town* (2014), 288.
29. Victor Gruen, "Urban Planning for the Sixties," Annual Proceedings of the United States Conference of Mayors, Chicago, May 11–14, 1960, box 34, folder "Manuscripts, 1962–1978," Gruen AHC; Victor Gruen, "The Architect's Role in Urban Renewal," speech at seminar of the Michigan Society of Architects, Detroit, April 7, 1961, box 2, volume X, 1961, Gruen AHC; "The Economic and Social Significance of Urban Renewal," *Architectural Metals*, August 1962, 10–26; Victor Gruen, "The Meaning and Value of Master Planning," remarks at Goodyear meeting, Phoenix, January 13, 1964, box 2, volume XIII, Gruen AHC; and Gruen, "Biographische Notizen," p. 190.
30. Victor Gruen and Larry Smith, *Shopping Towns USA: The Planning of Shopping Centers* (New York, 1960).
31. Victor Gruen, "Store Designing for the 'Feminine Touch': Famed Store Designer Tells Interior Secrets," *West Coast Feminine Wear*, April 29, 1947,

12; Victor Gruen, "Design with Light," speech, January 31, 1950, in box 4, folder "Speeches—1943–1952," Gruen AHC; Victor Gruen, speech at State A.I.A. Convention, Avalon, Catalina Island, October 3, 1947, in box 5, folder "Speeches, 10-3-47," Gruen AHC; Emily Genauer, "Art and Architecture Happily Wed, New Shopping Center Exhibit Proves," *New York Herald Tribune*, April 3, 1955; Victor Gruen "The Need for an Urban Planning Philosophy," speech before the Washington, DC Section, Institute of Traffic Engineers, May 14, 1957, in box 1, volume V, Gruen AHC; Victor Gruen, "Grand Central Terminal: Notes Concerning Proposed Changes," 1960, in box 2, volume VIII, Gruen AHC; Victor Gruen, "The Changing City: Environmental Architecture," *Matrix* 1, no. 2 (Summer 1962), in box 31, folder, "Articles, 1962," Gruen AHC; Victor Gruen, "Environmental Architecture," in *The People's Architects*, ed. Harry S. Ransom (Rice University, November 1964), 55–61, in box OV65, Gruen LOC; and Victor Gruen, letter to the editor, *Arts & Architecture*, November 1965.

32. "Organization for Efficient Practice: Victor Gruen Associates," *Architectural Record*, October 1961; and "Victor Gruen Associates," brochure, [ca. 1967], in box 74, folder 7, Gruen LOC.
33. Victor Gruen, *The Heart of Our Cities: The Urban Crisis, Diagnosis and Cure* (New York, 1964).
34. Victor Gruen, "The Regional (Shopping) Center," *Technical Bulletin* 104 (June 1963), 25–29; "Shopping Malls—General, 1960–1963," in box 27, Gruen AHC; "Rough Translation of Victor Gruen's Address at the Occasion of the Opening of the European Office," May 18, 1967, in box 5, folder "Speeches 1967–1973," Gruen AHC; Victor Gruen, talk for Congresso Internazionale, Milano, October 14–16, 1967, in box 3, Volume XV, Gruen AHC; Victor Gruen, letter to Herman Guttman and Victor Gruen Associates, [ca. 1972], in box 8, Gruen AHC; "Victor Gruen: Biographical Data," [ca. 1963], in box 5, folder "Speech File 1963," Gruen AHC; and Gruen, *Shopping Town* (2014), 325.
35. Victor Gruen, "Schizophrenia in Urban Planning," speech at the Victor Gruen Foundation for Environmental Planning, Los Angeles, April 30, 1970, in box 5, folder "Speeches, 1970–1976," Gruen AHC; Victor Gruen, "The Future of the City and the Central Business District," lecture at the University of California, Riverside, May 24, 1972, in box 3, vol. XVIII, Gruen AHC; Victor Gruen, "Two Americans in Austria: Bicentennial Reflections," *Vienna News*, October 7, 1976, 4–5; and Joyce Haber, "Victor Gruen: Architect, Dreamer and Doer," *Los Angeles Times*, September 18, 1966.
36. "Biographical Data," *Outline to Public Relations Material for Book*, n.d., in box 10, folder "Biographical Information, Victor Gruen 1903–1980," Gruen AHC; "Background Information," The Victor Gruen Foundation for Environmental Planning, n.d., in box 13, folder "Professional Files, Victor Gruen Foundation, 1968," Gruen AHC; Gaby Janoschek, letter to Arthur Lawrence, November 6, 1968, in box 5, folder "Speech Requests," Gruen AHC; Victor Gruen, letter to Jerome Biblit, January 14, 1969, in box 5, folder "Speech Requests," Gruen AHC; Kemija Gruen, letter to John Crosby, January 17, 1969, in box 5, folder "Speech Requests," Gruen AHC; Gaby Janoschek, letter to John Nolen, January 27, 1969, in box 5, folder "Speech Requests," Gruen AHC; Victor Gruen, letter to Stewart L. Udall, February 12, 1969, in box 11, folder 4, Gruen LOC; Gruen, "Biographische Notizen,"

212; Maggie Savoy, "Architect Plans Cities for Humans," *Los Angeles Times*, June 5, 1969; and Gruen, *Shopping Town* (2014), 327–28.

37. Victor Gruen, *Centers for the Urban Environment: Survival of the Cities* (New York, 1973). Gruen simultaneously published a German version of the book, *Das Überleben der Städte: Wege aus der Umweltkrise* (Vienna, 1973).
38. Victor Gruen, "Shopping Centres, Why, Where, How?" speech for Third Annual European Conference of the International Council of Shopping Centres, Hilton Hotel, London, February 28, 1978, in box 5, folder "Speeches, 1970–1978," Gruen AHC.
39. Ian Menzies, "His Love for Shopping Malls Is Turning Sour," *Boston Sunday Globe*, April 23, 1978; William Severini Kowinski, "The Malling of America," *New Times*, May 1, 1978, 30–55; Neal R. Peirce, "The Shopping Center and One Man's Shame," *Los Angeles Times*, October 22, 1978; and "A Pall over the Suburban Mall," *Time*, November 13, 1978, 72.

CHAPTER 6

Consumer-Based Research: Walter Landor and the Value of Packaging Design in Marketing

Bernard Gallagher

Three distinct elements that advanced consumer convenience came together to make the United States a more competitive marketplace in the first half of the twentieth century: individual packaging for products, the expansion of self-service stores in urban and suburban areas, and the rise of industrial design. These key developments were well-established when Walter Landor (1913–1995) toured the United States in 1939. Using consumer-based research from the beginning of his industrial design business in 1941, he took advantage of the new competitive marketplace, creating designs for packaging, labels, and branding that made him successful and promised increased sales of his clients' products.

This chapter presents Landor as a "consumer engineer" who contributed to the practice of consumer-oriented marketing by pre-testing his designs for his clients. To ensure that his designs touched the consumer emotionally, Landor's firm conducted consumer-based research, and when projects grew in scope and complexity, he adopted additional research methods. Creating designs that made the ordinary more enjoyable, he embraced this facet of consumer engineering from early in his career. This chapter identifies key moments in Landor's career and examines contemporary case studies that highlight the interplay of package design and perceived product or brand attributes that research-based design aimed to evoke.

B. Gallagher (✉)
Independent Historian, Laurel, MD, USA

J. Logemann et al. (eds.), *Consumer Engineering, 1920s–1970s*,
Worlds of Consumption, https://doi.org/10.1007/978-3-030-14564-4_6

Walter Landor—A Transatlantic Biography

During the second half of the twentieth century, Walter Landor, a pioneer in graphics design for packaging and corporate branding, produced some of the most recognized packages, labels, and brands.[1] He saw the importance of a visual symbol for the success of a company and understood that the connection between the customer and the brand was as significant for his clients as the products they produced. In his fifty years of work, his list of clients grew constantly, beginning with local companies in the San Francisco Bay area and eventually expanding to international corporations around the globe.

Soft-spoken and with a slight hint of an accent, Walter Landor was born in Munich, Germany. He grew up surrounded by artists, many from his own family, along with their social and professional connections. His professional development began at home with his father, Fritz Landauer, a noted Jewish architect of synagogues in early twentieth-century Germany who had been influenced by the Bauhaus school.[2] The apprentice-like training he received from his father expanded young Walter's aptitude and his interest in continuing his training and education as an architect. When it came time for him to advance to the next level to learn architectural drafting, however, he realized his own capabilities were limited. Thus, he later recalled, "I decided that I would concentrate on designing everyday products that would make life more pleasant and more beautiful and appeal to the mass audience."[3]

So Landor turned to the study of design, also drawing on "the privilege [of having been] brought up in an environment where the ideas of the Werkbund and the Bauhaus" concerning industrial design had been very influential.[4] It became apparent to him that he wanted to pursue industrial design in order "to create a more aesthetically beautiful environment, to increase the everyday enjoyment of life through design."[5] On the basis of his initial training from his father and in view of trends in the new schools of design in Germany, he recognized the potential and power of design, how it could affect the emotions of people, and decided to focus his career on designing for the mass market.

In 1931, he was sent to Great Britain as an exchange student to study art and to improve his proficiency in English. The head of the household where he lived noticed his interest in design and introduced him to a friend at a local advertising agency, where Landor then interned in copywriting and marketing. He went back home to Munich but returned to London and enrolled at Goldsmith College of Art in London, where he studied under Milner Gray, an established industrial designer. Shortly after graduation, he was offered a job at Gray's advertising and marketing company, where he was assigned to design packages constructed of plastics (a newly developed material).[6] In 1935, Misha Black joined the company, and together Gray, Black, and Landor formed International Design Partnership (IDP). A year later, Landor also became a Fellow of the Royal Society of Industrial Artists in Great Britain.[7]

While Walter continued his career in England, his family (father, mother, and sister) remained in Germany. During the rise of the Nazi Socialists, the League of German Architects banned his father from producing any additional work as an architect. In 1937, Walter's parents and sister emigrated to England, and later his father set up shop as a designer of cemetery monuments in London.[8]

In 1939, the IDP team, including Landor, traveled to the United States to install their portion of the British Pavilion at the New York World's Fair. During his time there, Landor met the American industrial design giants Raymond Loewy, Walter Teague, and Henry Dreyfus. With war approaching in Europe and wanting to stay longer in the United States, he took some time away from the World's Fair and decided to travel across the country. His plan was to meet with other industrial designers and to learn about potential business opportunities from his professional contemporaries in America. He also wanted to see for himself "how American industrial designers had succeeded so miraculously, so dramatically, more than we had in London."[9] In contrast to his professional academic background, he found that American industrial designers had a variety of experiences. As self-styled celebrities who embodied all things modern in styling and design, American designers showcased their products and promised to bring contemporary design home to the consumer.[10]

Eventually, Landor made his way to Los Angeles in hopes of finding a job. Hearing that there was a need for professional industrial designers in San Francisco, he decided to travel up the coast to explore his prospects there. Although San Francisco was not an industrial city, he found some food processing companies in the area and realized that that might mean an opportunity in terms of labeling and packaging. Before starting his own design business, however, he taught industrial design at the California College of Arts and Crafts in Oakland, California, in January 1940. In the front row was Josephine Martinelli, an artist and designer, who he would marry. After spending just a brief period in San Francisco, he decided to settle in the Bay area. In 1941, Walter and Jo, his wife and business partner, established Walter Landor and Associates. In a 1993 interview, he recalled that San Francisco served as his gateway to the rest of the world.[11]

During his career, Walter Landor would demonstrate a versatility in industrial design for everything from the graphics on packages for retail foods and beverages to the carrier markings for commercial aviation and the corporate symbols for giants in banking and finance. His design work underscored the growing importance of product packaging and brand image in mid-century mass marketing.

Packaging, Consumer Design, and the Use of Research

Retail packaging in all its forms is found on the shelves of supermarkets, hardware stores, pharmacies, and a variety of specialty stores. It touches nearly everything we purchase. The average modern supermarket stocks "tens of thousands of different products that line the shelves"; however, shoppers are in contact with packaging without really noticing it. During an average trip to the store, packaging competes for the buyers' attention. While pacing through the aisles, customers have only a limited time to select the product they want from the shelf.[12]

In the postwar shopping environment, the trend in retail selling was toward self-service supermarkets, so packaging played an increasing role in selling the product inside the package. The package by itself, rather than staff, had to promote the product and carry the manufacturers' message about it. Through its visual themes and appearance (colors, shapes, physical structures, graphics, and fonts), the package had to convince the customer that the product was worth purchasing.[13] To that end, the designer of the package needed to communicate the product to the consumer, not just "describe the contents and how to . . . use [it]." The point was that "symbolic designs convey direct or indirect messages about the product and its quality and value."[14] The role of the package helped consumers to make their decisions. It also became convenient for the shopper to select a product off the shelf, make an impulse purchase, or simply ignore the item, and then continue down the aisle. The good design of a package could help boost the sales and profits of the right product, while the wrong package could cause even a good product to fail. In a 1956 interview, Walter Landor summarized the purpose of well-designed packaging: to sell, "the package itself must do the talking."[15]

By the postwar years, business leaders were thus aware that the package had grown into an important selling and advertising tool. While industrial design was supposed to make things look better, packaging design needed to do more. The designer also needed to know if the new package would make the sale. To achieve the goal of designing successful packaging for his clients, Landor adopted several methods. In particular, outcomes needed to be pre-tested with consumers. Thus, his approach throughout the design process for each client required close teamwork between designers and researchers.[16]

Landor drew upon empirical consumer research integrated with creativity to develop successful packaging and label designs for his clients. The design process for a new account usually began with a review of the current and previous graphics and packaging used by the client and its competitors. The visual aspects of imagery, colors, designs, graphics, and fonts along with the general appearance of the packaging were discussed. Design elements were proposed for the project and added to the array of tools at the designers' disposal. The initial review process was necessary for Landor's team to get a feel for the value of the existing brand designs and product images and the extent to which they sustained product recognition or brand equity with the consumer.[17] From the outset of the process, the preliminary review sessions established a road map for testing the effectiveness of the designs, which would be corroborated by Landor's research group.

In the early 1950s, Landor began to take prototypes of his packaging and label designs into supermarkets to solicit responses from shoppers. Typically, he would present two or three comparable packages to individual shoppers and ask which one they liked best. He would then ask which one they would more likely purchase, all while an assistant recorded the answers. It did not take long for some supermarket managers to see Landor, often in a lab coat, stopping and asking shoppers questions, and soon the store manager would ask him to leave.[18]

To avoid these confrontations while gathering answers to questions about the designs, the Institute for Design Analysis, a Landor affiliate, was installed alongside his studios. The Landor researchers at the Institute also built a supermarket laboratory "to help designers and clients visualize the new packages in the real-life context of grocery shelves" in a more controlled environment.[19] Shoppers would be randomly invited from the street to participate in a supermarket buying study. They were given a budget and tasked with buying certain types of products, including those of Landor's client and the client's competitors. The researchers would watch the invited shoppers from an inconspicuous location as they passed through the aisles with their shopping carts. Afterward, the designers and researchers would meet with the shoppers, individually or in groups, in an interview room to gather additional data about the packaging. Often the shoppers would be stopped and interviewed in the mock supermarket in order to get an immediate response to their decision about one packaged product versus a similar product fora different brand that they had put in their carts.[20] The inventory in the mock supermarket would be rotated over time with ten to twenty-five different designs for the client's products in order to determine how well each version connected with the shoppers (Fig. 6.1).

Fig. 6.1 Setting up the supermarket lab. Source: The Walter Landor Design Collection, Archives Center, National Museum of American History.

By comparing results, the top three or four designs would rotate in again until a final two or three could be presented to the client, along with the interview feedback and supermarket data, for the client's consideration and approval.[21] The research team eventually utilized five techniques to gather data for the designs under consideration: individual interviews, panel sessions, observations in the supermarket laboratory, interviews with real grocery shoppers, and at-home interviews.[22] Landor used these methods of consumer research and interview feedback extensively for testing the designs of his packages (Fig. 6.2).

He also employed a number of techniques beyond consumer research to develop the final package design or brand image. One such technique he established was regularly scheduled meetings with his designers in a sort of free-for-all roundtable of the project team along with the senior designers and Walter. These meetings were designated sessions for internal presentations of the designs that provided objective critical reviews known throughout the company as "crit sessions." The ideas and suggestions of these meetings were then shared among the project team members in a cross-team, in-house review to gather ideas and creative suggestions from additional perspectives

Fig. 6.2 Interviewing a shopper. Source: The Walter Landor Design Collection, Archives Center, National Museum of American History.

and viewpoints. Based on the findings from their research and rounds of feedback, including on the background of the client's existing and historical imagery, colors, designs, graphics, and fonts were presented and discussed.

From the results of the research, Landor and his team would determine the two or three most "receptive" examples of designs that would be presented to his clients. The choices (and often the comments) made by the interview subjects would enable Landor's teams to develop creative designs, always with the client's best interests in mind (per their directions) as the team developed their final drafts for each project. At the same time, his studies were never meant to be "full-scale" or comprehensive. He usually recommended that his client contract with an independent research group to reach their own conclusions.[23]

The increased sales and product recognition he achieved in the supermarket for his clients enabled Landor to summarize the importance of the consumer-centered process this way: "Consumer research aids in the selection of the chosen design, and often is used to continue the study of the effectiveness of the selected package once it is launched. Consumer research makes its special contribution from initial market studies to post-design evaluation."[24]

The Attributes of Successful Packaging According to Landor

Through the initial contact and interview with the client's leadership, who presented the particular intentions for their products along with the basic attributes and aims of their packaging, Landor and his team of researchers and designers explored multiple designs based on the rounds of research and matched them into design features for their clients. These attributes or features of the designs varied from attempts to attract and motivate the consumer to informative labels or whimsical graphics to purposeful seasonal holiday packaging, all in order to highlight the latest product or strengthen an existing family of products.[25]

Shortly after the end of World War II, Landor began to build his design portfolio, starting with Safeway at both the corporate level and in their supermarkets. In 1947, he designed their corporate annual report and then worked on several packaging and labeling projects for in-house brands of Safeway products.[26] For Safeway's in-house frozen food brand, Bel-air, he described two graphical attributes for the packaging of frozen vegetables and concentrated fruit juices as "informative" and "appealing to taste buds"; that was the message that the package label communicated to consumers. The designs uniquely included the leaf-like symbol that identified the brand name, the name of the product, and an illustration of the prepared product that would help the early 1950s homemaker visualize what to expect as she prepared daily meals for the family.

The name and the leaf-like symbol for Bel-air provided the appeal of freshness of the packaged food in the supermarket freezer section, and the curvature of the symbol worked well, whether on packaged boxes of frozen green beans or strawberries or on cans of frozen orange juice or lemonade. The visualization of a prepared serving of corn, peas, or mixed vegetables presented a more "convincing" reason to purchase the Bel-air brand of frozen foods rather than a competing brand.[27]

Over time, Landor identified more than 30 key attributes of creative components for successful, brand-sustaining packaging. Their functions ranged from attracting shoppers' attention to identifying the brand and the product inside the package to informing shoppers or presenting an appealing appearance, while targeting buyers with designs that matched the appropriate pricing categories. As individually packaged goods were developed into important components in advertising and marketing, including in connection with what Jerry Janowski calls "total marketing," advertisers discovered that packaging could serve as another medium for promoting products.

The story of packaging beer illustrated the changes. It "[had] been bottled and sold in glass and ceramic containers since the mid-nineteenth century. Prior to that time, if you wanted a beer 'to go,' you had to have a bucket or jug on hand to take the frothy brew home from your local tavern." By the mid-twentieth century, however, there were a variety of ways to buy beer along with the multiple "layers" of containers and packaging from which to choose. Beer was sold in bottles or cans, held conveniently together in six-pack cartons, and shipped and stored in cases of twenty-four. At each layer, the packaging helped to make the sale of the beer to the customer. From a case on a pallet and a six-pack on a shelf or in a cooler to the bottle or can in the hand of the consumer, beer packaging served as an advertisement in the marketplace.[28] From this model with layers of advertising and marketing at each level of the distribution chain, American businesses began to see packaging "in terms of its overall advantage to the entire distribution system, particularly to the end of the line—the consumer."[29] To reach this design goal of "total marketing," Walter Landor set about identifying the key elements or components of "total design" in packaging and labels.

One early notable example of Landor's use of such a design approach was for Sick's beer, in which the redesign for Sicks' Select went beyond the placement of labels and brand names on bottles and cans to include a "total design" for the product. The Seattle Brewing and Malting Company was established in 1893 by Andrew Hemrich, the son of a German brewmaster, and following the end of Prohibition in 1933, Fritz Sick, a brewer from Baden, Germany who emigrated to Canada in 1883, purchased the brewery.[30] His son, Emil Sick, took over the family business and decided that it was time to update and modernize the look of their popular beer Sicks' Select. The existing label appeared old and this was an opportunity for Walter Landor to rejuvenate the visual appeal of the label. It would also demonstrate that the new design would increase the product's ability to sell itself in self-service stores with more distinctive and attractive packaging.

While working on the project, Landor was aware that individually packaged goods had developed as an important component in advertising and marketing; and he set out to expand on this insight with a "total marketing" approach to the redesign. Landor started with identifying the key elements or components in packaging and labels, and he was able to use some of the existing elements in the design for sustaining the brand. Both the brand name "Sicks' Select" and the number "6" needed to remain the key visual elements in the final design and both needed to be "clearly readable from a distance."[31]

Landor extended the project by placing the two primary design elements of the Sicks' Select brand onto larger packaging components, such as four six-pack cartons in a case of cardboard shipping containers. Printing on the shipping cartons also provided an opportunity to advertise the brand name. The "shipping cases were re-designed to become forceful advertising mediums at no extra printing cost. When stacked, they maintain that high-quality look of the foil label, in spite of the printing limitations applying to shipping cases."[32] He also displayed the script "Sicks' Select" and the distinctive "6" on smaller components, such as the tops of the cans and bottle caps (Fig. 6.3).

The frequent display of the name on various parts of the label in a Germanic script, reflecting its heritage and also projecting its role for advertising and marketing, had the role of reinforcing the brand on the shelf at the store and in the hand of the consumer.[33] An editor of *American Brewer* in 1949 summarized the intended impact of the packaging design for Sicks' Select: "Landor's contention that 'every inch counts in modern merchandising' is borne out by the manner . . . in making the consumer feel that real care and perfection has gone into this particular bottle of beer."[34]

Landor's design of Sicks' Select labels drew the attention and recognition from other breweries. In the beer label competition at the annual conference of the Small Brewers Association (SBA), he won first prize. His success in the beer label competitions continued. He won several design awards over the next three years from the Brewers Association of America. In 1952, Landor was invited to deliver the keynote address at their annual meeting, and in his presentation, "Gentlemen, Your Label is Showing. Is It Selling Beer for You?" He emphasized that the proper label is necessary for product loyalty and sales and then outlined the attributes for the final design of a successful beer label to his audience in terms of drawing "attention from a distance, brand emphasis, distinctive character, [and conveying] quality" to the customer. For Landor, the beer label needed to "look like beer, project a sales story, reproduce powerfully [in advertising, and] adapt effectively" to various packaging and displays. He mentioned his work with three clients—Gettelman and Stag, in which the brand names stood out and the labels worked on all packages—cartons, cans, and at any angle in hand of the consumer. He singled out his third client, Karl Gretz, a small brewer, in which the design hit the attribute of quality "to give his can an authentic premium look." With members of top management from many breweries at the association meeting, his speech opened doors to new clients, especially brewers in

Fig. 6.3 Sick's Select labels, before and after. Source: The Walter Landor Design Collection, Archives Center, National Museum of American History.

the Midwest markets of Milwaukee and St. Louis, as well as those in Texas.[35] His success escalated as brewers there were attracted to the work of a West Coast designer who understood their brand loyalty, sales, and expansion goals.

Landor's work for the Lone Star Brewery provides another example of his efforts in developing effective and comprehensive brand designs. As in many areas of America during the nineteenth century, German immigrants in Texas started breweries and introduced lager-style beers to ale-drinking Americans. In 1883, Adolphus Busch, with a group of San Antonio businessmen, started the first mechanized brewery in Texas, the Lone Star Brewery in San Antonio.[36]

The business grew during the first quarter of the twentieth century; however, after the repeal of Prohibition in 1933, the brewery did not resume production. Then in 1940, Peter Kreil, a brewer from Munich, Germany picked up the Lone Star brand and put his own recipe into production. Sixteen years later, the Lone Star brewery, under new company leadership headed by Harry

D. Jersig, was one of the thriving breweries in Texas. He was not content with a "leave-well-enough-alone" attitude; he wanted to expand his brewery to an even larger customer base. By this time, Landor's track record with re-branding breweries convinced Jersig to redesign the packaging and labels at a time when the brewery was still growing. So he reached out to Walter Landor to do the work. Landor was elated that Lone Star was doing well in a not so "highly competitive" market nor were its sales declining. It was often customary to expect a designer to rescue a product to "halt further sales decreases," but the management at Lone Star had the "foresight and courage to redesign" the entire line of packaging and labels to create a new "family identity" for the different beers.

The redesign by Landor targeted self-service retail stores and every step from bottling to delivery to customer. In addition, the expanded placement of the new graphics by Landor's design team became Lone Star's company identity, visible at "every step which the public comes in contact with Lone Star." The scope of the "total design" program went beyond cases, bottles, and cans to include letterheads, signage on delivery trucks, and driver uniforms. Commenting on the importance for "total marketing" of the new graphics on the delivery trucks, Landor remarked, "Each time a delivery truck makes a delivery, the truck passes the eyes of people. The design of the brewer's message on that truck either communicates something of importance to people or it fails utterly to leave an imprint and a future sale has been lost." The Landor designs for Lone Star won four awards at the Brewers Association of America as the new labels offered both "eye appeal" and "family identity" attributes. The Package Designers' Council presented Landor with an award in the category of "Best Coordinated Packaging" for the designs of "labels, cans, bottles, crowns, 6-packs, shipping cases, trucks, drivers' uniforms, etc."[37]

Breweries continued to play a prominent role for Landor into the 1970s. His clients included local or regional breweries such as Lucky Lager and Regal Pale Ale as well as national brands like Falstaff, Miller Lite, and Sapporo of Japan.

Beyond Beer: Landor's Impact on the Design Profession

In 1952, Walter Landor became a founding member of the newly formed Packaging Designers' Council (PDC), a professional association for industrial designers who specialized in the design of packages. With most major industrial design companies headquartered in New York or Chicago, Landor's election to the PDC enabled him to advertise his services nationally in articles or press releases in which he claimed that he was the only industrial designer on the West Coast.[38] With each new project, he chipped away at the monolithic domination of design firms in the East. Two years later, he declared in a press release, "New York's title as the top design city in the nation is being challenged by San Francisco. Landor has been bringing a fresh western

Fig. 6.4 Mock-up of how Spreckels Sugar label would appear on TV. Early television advertisers struggled with selling effective commercials. Many ads were uninspiring and often used existing packages to promote their products. Source: The Walter Landor Design Collection, Archives Center, National Museum of American History.

approach and new imagination to the field of design."[39] Whether or not it was true, he had thrown down the gauntlet. He wanted everyone to know that San Francisco was full of new ideas and that his designs offered new opportunities for success.

The concept of "total marketing" went beyond the packaging designs for beer and beverages in general to encompass many other products, including such everyday household staples as, for example, sugar. Landor's client Spreckels Sugar, founded by immigrant-entrepreneur Claus Spreckels in 1863, had become the largest beet sugar refinery west of the Mississippi River. Spreckels, born in Germany, was an entrepreneur and industrialist who had major sugar interests in Hawaii and encouraged the growth of sugar beets in California.[40]

In 1956, the vice president of Spreckels, William H. Ottey, spoke about the need to redesign existing packaging and the importance of an updated visual design to help "win the competitive battle of the self-service shelf." Walter Landor was retained to develop the packaging for all five products with the attributes of an "attention getting" pattern that would allow the customer to identify the Spreckels brand "without actually having to read the name" and would work well "in all forms of advertising and promotional media." Following the feedback from focus panels, the designers at Landor understood that the packaging for Spreckels sugar also needed to be bold, clean, and identifiable with a standout brand mark. As part of the "total marketing" requirements, the designs included layers from the individual packaging for both one-pound and five-pound packages as well as the shipping cases. After in-store consumer testing of several graphics and visuals for the packages, the final designs with the prominent-sized "double-S" on an hourglass-shaped white background highlighted the packaging for Spreckels Sugar (Fig. 6.4).[41]

The back and side panels of the package displayed informative details with serving suggestions, and the photographic images of pies and cakes made the package itself a marketing campaign when the product was in a home. Another desirable design attribute the packaging needed was "to insure TV'isibilty"—this at a time when the commercials for Spreckels sugar was telecast on snowy black-and-white television sets.[42]

New Horizons Aboard the Klamath: Corporate Identity Designs and Global Clients

Instead of settling for larger office space to accommodate his growing staff of designers and researchers, in 1962 Landor bought the retired ferryboat *Klamath* as an attraction to showcase his work. His architects had the three levels gutted and then re-fabricated the interior to be his company's headquarters with design studios, again including a mock-up of a supermarket and study rooms for conducting consumer research. Away from the noise of downtown city and traffic, the *Klamath* provided an idyllic setting for creativity and imagination, where "only the sea gulls can interrupt the meeting." It was the perfect setting for his staff of creative associates.[43]

Soon, the *Klamath's* unique character made the boat a San Francisco landmark, and Landor took advantage of its celebrity, opening it for symposia, parties, and social fundraisers. One particular activity on board the *Klamath* was the annual visits to San Francisco by the Harvard Business School as part of an executive marketing program. Landor opened his doors (gangplank) to these executives to take a glimpse at his products and services. Of course, it was beneficial to Landor as well since it was "a major marketing opportunity for contacts, and the *Klamath* was a glamorous location."[44]

During its twenty years aboard the *Klamath*, Landor's company expanded as the list of clients rapidly grew. Corporate leaders came to San Francisco to see what was different about the office on a ferryboat. They wanted to experience the unconventional atmosphere of a design company that produced such creative and financially rewarding results. They came from different industries and with larger projects for Landor's steam to create new types of graphic designs. As the size and scope of projects grew beyond packaging and labels for retail products on supermarket shelves, Landor began to design larger graphic systems that evolved into corporate identity and the field of branding.

While retail packaging remained vital to Landor's business, two new industries sought out his services while aboard the *Klamath*. The first was commercial airlines, that is, international carriers that wanted to adopt new modern graphics on their aircraft and other points of contact with air travelers. The second industry was banks and financial institutions, which required modern corporate branding and signage that connected personally with the public for their businesses. These two industries transported Landor and his company's services from packaging and labels and propelled him into large-scale corporate branding from the 1960s through the 1980s.

Seeking exposure in a country noted for its high-fashion designers, Landor set up his first international office in Rome, Italy in 1967, and landed the design project for new graphics and markings on Alitalia, the national airlines of Italy. The interviews conducted by Landor's team with international air travelers revealed there was a disconnect between Alitalia's self-image and its actual reputation. Although the carrier was a global international airline, it appeared to be a small domestic airline and was in desperate need of a modern international image. The technical challenge for Landor was that the graphics needed to be applied to a variety of aircraft, such as 747s and DC-10s, as well as to flight uniforms, interiors, tickets, and printed materials.[45]

Backed with the results of the surveys, Landor's team of designers developed the graphics that reinforced two important visual elements: the graphics competed "for top visibility—but also to symbolize the vibrant spirit of the Italian people."[46] The new designs replaced the Italian national flag on the tail section and removed the old bow-and-arrow symbol of ancient Rome from the fuselage while it embraced Italy's national colors.[47] Summarizing the Alitalia project, Rodney McKnew, a program director for Landor, recapped the dramatic changes, "Here was an airline that practically had no reputation at all to really show for themselves." He continued to describe the rationale for the shape of the slanted first letter, "[the aircraft] had a vertical stabilizer that was the 'A' in Alitalia."[48] Just as Landor's processes in packaging and labels had been successful for his earlier clients, his first venture with the graphic design of an airline also enhanced the status of Alitalia as an international airline and attracted more aviation clients. The list of international and U.S. airlines that subsequently came to the ferryboat in San Francisco in search of new, modern graphic designs that distilled their essence included British Airways, Thai Air, Hawaiian Airlines, Japan Air, SAS, and Allegheny Air.

The second type of business that came to Landor to recast their corporate identity was the financial institution in need of a new brand. Based in California, Bank of America provided a variety of financial services ranging from personal checking and savings accounts to large corporate business transactions. However, while the strength of Bank of America was the size of the company, consumer surveys by Landor's researchers found that, in the eyes of individuals and small business clients, the institution appeared too big. Bank of America was not attracting "new, smaller, perhaps younger depositors," who perceived the institution as impersonal and oriented toward large corporate accounts.[49]

Fig. 6.5 Bank of America logo, before and after. Source: The Walter Landor Design Collection, Archives Center, National Museum of American History.

Reinforcing this image was the bank's prominent signage for large business services although each branch of the bank was a full-service office that handled accounts for individuals and young families alike. While looking to consolidate the different types of outdoor and advertising symbols and the signage under one umbrella, Landor's designers developed the "BA" monogram.

Initially, the management of Bank of America was certain that there was value in its current trademark, the "old sailing ship," but feedback from Landor's consumer research proved, "most people thought it was the trademark for the Encyclopedia Britannica." The existing equity in the image did not resonate with typical consumers. In addition, they found that many people were intimidated by banks; therefore, Landor wanted to take the design attributes into a different direction (Fig. 6.5).[50]

To Landor, the new symbol for Bank of America communicated "something quite wonderful and strange happening between [the letters B and A.]. The majority of the people see a bird. It was conceived as a bird from the start. It suggests softness and gentleness, a non-threatening symbol more like an old-time monogram. It's a very personal statement."[51] The new graphics eliminated the bulkiness and impersonality of the old signage. In its place, the new identity for the Bank of America had a friendlier, "personal quality" attributes that spoke to average depositors and their everyday banking needs.

Conclusion

Walter Landor and his firm produced some of the most recognized packaging, labels, and brands in the mid-twentieth century. As a consumer engineer integrating consumer feedback into his designs, Landor sought to determine if existing packaging and design features either needed subtle tweaks or to embrace new graphic symbols to replace the existing package design. Backed by his research findings, Landor would meet the leadership of the companies during project review sessions and convince them of the direction of the project. If necessary, he would refine the prototype design and solicit feedback and only then identify the best two or three based on this process. Landor followed this approach with every new project, while admitting at times that to arrive at a final design, more research was needed "with the customers of the industries to see how they perceive the company and its products and its services."[52] With this process, Landor claimed he was able to determine the best designs for his corporate clients at a time when differences among brands were "getting smaller," thereby putting "a tremendous burden on the designer of the package" to make them distinctive, recognizable, and appealing to consumers.[53]

Landor also presented himself as an advocate for the consumer who paid close attention to the feedback he received from consumer testing. Each design was tested for a positive reaction via consumer research in which the design solved "a problem in communication—rapid communication." It was not enough to create an artistically pleasing design; the design needed to capture the attributes of the product, brand, or company in order, as he put it, "to arrive at a design solution which satisfies us aesthetically and emotionally ... yet truly communicates to a mass audience.... [T]hat is our responsibility."[54] Throughout the mid-twentieth century, business leaders in industries ranging from retail foods and beverages to commercial aviation, banking, and finance relied on Landor and his design firm. His case demonstrates that not all Mad Men were located on Madison Avenue: at least one was on the West Coast, on a ferryboat on the Bay.

Notes

1. For additional biographical reading, see Bernard Gallagher, "Walter Landor," in *Immigrant Entrepreneurship: German-American Business Biographies, 1720 to the Present*, vol. 5, ed. R. Daniel Wadhwani (German Historical Institute, Washington, DC, June 8, 2011), https://www.immigrantentrepreneurship.org/entry.php?rec=69.
2. Sabine Klotz, *Fritz Landauer (1883–1968): Leben und Werk der Jüdischen Architekten* (Berlin, 2001).
3. Ken Kelley and Rick Clogher, "The Ultimate Image Maker," *San Francisco Focus*, August 1992, 67.
4. "Obituary: Walter Landor. Herald of the Corporate Image," *The Guardian*, June 16, 1995, 13.
5. Sylvia Rubin, "How Logic Led to Logos," *San Francisco Chronicle*, August 28, 1992, E5.
6. Veronique Vinne, "The Brand Named Walter Landor," *Graphis* 321, May/June 1999, 103; and Kelley and Clogher, "Ultimate," 67 and 114.
7. "Bassett Gray Becomes a Partnership," *Advertiser's Weekly*, May 23, 1935, 256; and "Walter Landor, Designer Pioneer, Dies at 81," PR Newswire Association, Inc., Financial Section, June 11, 1995.
8. "Fritz Landauer: Architect and Designer of Grave Monuments," Alumni Biographies, Technical University of Munich, http://www.150.alumni.tum.de/biografie/fritz-landauer/.

9. Carla Marinucci, "Designing Man," *San Francisco Examiner*, October 1, 1989, E5.
10. Thomas Hines, *The Total Package: The Secret History and Hidden Meanings of Boxes, Bottles, Cans and Other Persuasive Containers* (New York, 1995), 113.
11. Kelley and Clogher, "Ultimate," 114; Vinne, "Brand," 103; and "Walter Landor, Designer Pioneer, Dies at 81," June 11, 1995.
12. Hines, *Total Package*, x; and Marianne Rosner Klimchuk and Sandra A. Krasovec, *Packaging Design: Successful Product Branding from Concept to Shelf* (Hoboken, NJ, 2006), 35.
13. Arthur D. Little, Inc., *The Role of Packaging in the U.S. Economy: Report to the American Foundation for Management Research* (Washington, DC, 1966), 71.
14. Stanley Sacharow, *The Package as a Marketing Tool* (Radnor, PA, 1982), 46.
15. "Packages Must Speak for Themselves," *San Francisco Call-Bulletin*, November 23, 1956, 13.
16. Donald Short and Robert J. Stovell, "Packaging for People," *Human Factors* 8, no. 4 (August 1966): 307–8.
17. "The Landor Way: How One Designer Uses Consumer Research to Stimulate Package Design Creativity," *Good Packaging Yearbook*, offprint (n.d.), 1–7, Landor Design Collection, Archives Center, National Museum of American History; Klimchuk and Krasovec, 37; and Walter Landor, "Design Moves Merchandise if It Moves People," *Good Packaging Yearbook*, July 1957, 83.
18. Lewis Lowe (designer and fine artist), transcript of interview by Jessica Myerson, April 20, 1993, Landor Design Collection.
19. Short and Stovell, "Packaging," 309; and Vinne, "Brand," 104.
20. "The Super Market Lab: Pre-testing Package Design," *Sales Management* 84, no. 9 (May 6, 1960), 38–39.
21. "Landor Way"; and "Super Market Lab."
22. "Landor Way."
23. "Landor Way."
24. Short and Stovell, "Packaging," 309; and "Landor Way."
25. "Landor Way"; and Landor, "Design Moves Merchandise," 83–94.
26. "Walter Landor's Package Designs Honored by Art Museum," *Ad Age—San Francisco Advertising Club*, April 7, 1948, unpaginated offprint, Landor Design Collection.
27. Landor, "Design Moves," 83–94.
28. Jerry Jankowski, *Shelf Space: Modern Packaging Design* (San Francisco, CA, 1998), 36.
29. Stanley Sacharow, *The Package as a Marketing Tool* (Radnor, PA, 1982), 41.
30. Gary Flynn, "The History of Rainier Beer," Brewery Gems, http://www.brewerygems.com/rainier.htm; Peter Blecha, "Rainier Beer—Seattle's Iconic Brewery," HistoryLink, Online Encyclopedia of Washington State History, http://www.historylink.org/File/9130; and "This Is the Label ... That Boosted Sales of This Beer ... and It's Printed on Kaiser Aluminum Foil," *Good Packaging*, advertisement, November 1949, 13.
31. "Six Keys to Profit Labeling," *American Brewer*, December 1949, unpaginated offprint, Landor Design Collection.
32. "Design for Selling More Beer," *Western Brewing and Distributing*, unpaginated offprint, Landor Design Collection.
33. "Six Keys."

34. "Design for Selling More Beer."
35. Walter Landor, "Gentlemen, Your Label Is Showing. Is It Selling Beer for You?" *Brewers' Association of America: Bulletin No. 1139*, February 12, 1953, 1–8.
36. Michael C. Hennech and Tracé Etienne-Gray, "Brewing Industry," Texas State Historical Association, June 12, 2010, https://tshaonline.org/handbook/online/articles/dib01.
37. "Lone Star's Redesign Program," *American Brewer* (July 1955).
38. "Package Design Elects Landor," *Western Advertising*, December 29, 1952, 1.
39. Walter Landor and Associates, "Western Designer Wins Top Awards," Press Release, October, 1954, Landor Design Collection.
40. UweSpiekermann, "Claus Spreckels: Robber Baron and Sugar King," in *Immigrant Entrepreneurship: German-American Business Biographies, 1720 to the Present*, vol. 2, ed. William J. Hausman (German Historical Institute, Washington, DC, June 7, 2011), https://www.immigrantentrepreneurship.org/entry.php?rec=5; and "Spreckels Sugar History," Spreckels Sugar, http://www.spreckels-sugar.com/history.aspx.
41. "How Spreckels Planned and Developed a Stronger Family of Packages," *Sales Management*, April 15, 1956, unpaginated offprint, Landor Design Collection.
42. Walter Landor, "Design Moves Merchandise," 90.
43. "Reconversion of Old Ferry Boat into Practical Office Building," *American Journal of Building Design* (January 1966): 18; and K. R. MacDonald, "How a Ferry Boat Became a Floating Office Building," *The Office* (October 1965): 76.
44. Jean Emery Gomez, transcript of interview by Jessica Myerson, September 16, 1993, Landor Design Collection.
45. "Package and Design Magazine Features Landor: An Inside Look," June 4, 2016, https://landor.com/thinking/landor-creating-the-worlds-most-agile-brands; and Peter McDonald, "How the New Visual Image Was Created," *Winged Arrow*, October 1969, 1–4.
46. Stan MacLean, "Designers Specialize in Airline Corporate Identity Projects," *Airfare*, January 1975, 64.
47. Barbour, "Times of the Signs," *The Washington Post*, July 4, 1976, 2; and "Alitalia Begins Image Change Campaign," *Aviation Week and Space Technology*, November 17, 1969, unpaginated reprint, Landor Design Collection.
48. Rodney McKnew et al., transcript of interview by Jessica Myerson, July 5, 1993, Landor Design Collection.
49. Marty Olmstead, "Man of a Thousand Designs," *PSA Magazine*, March 1980, 83.
50. Olmstead, "Man of a Thousand Designs," 83; and Kelley and Clogher, "Ultimate," 66.
51. Kelley and Clogher, "Ultimate," 66; and McKnew et al., interview, June 2, 1993.
52. "Walter Landor on Design, Branding, and Landor" (interview), 1977, https://www.youtube.com/watch?v=S5jxx_0on5k.
53. Martin Rossman, "Art of Package Design: The Subtle Salesman," *Los Angeles Times*, October 10, 1965, M1.
54. "Pioneers: Walter Landor," *Communication Arts*, January/February 2000, 118.

CHAPTER 7

German-Style Consumer Engineering: Victor Vogt's *Verkaufspraxis*, 1925–1950

Uwe Spiekermann

Mid-twentieth-century "consumer engineering" in the United States was a vision of marketing experts on how to establish and manage a capitalist consumer society with steady economic growth and a rising level of wealth for the broad majority of the population.[1] Targeting the "citizen consumer," it promoted the promise that everyone could earn a good living and that the "American dream" could be realized by a large portion of society. At the same time, consumer engineering was a professionalization strategy, "an enticing expression to one who wishes to dignify his calling with a professional label."[2] The consumerist gospel of these experts was informed by the American system of manufacturing, consumer goods that were standardized, as well as an efficient and rationalized organization of distribution and sales.[3] The growing U.S. wealth and consumer goods output garnered intense interest among European businesspeople, politicians, and experts before World War I, during the 1920s, and after the Allied victory in World War II. This article will focus on a particular group of these intermediaries led by the German publisher and entrepreneur Victor Vogt. A representative of the German standardization movement and driven by his assessment of Germany's defeat in World War I, he and a larger group of business practitioners and consultants tried to inform German businesspeople about American principles of business, marketing, and consumer goods sales—and to formulate a suitable "German" response.

U. Spiekermann (✉)
University of Göttingen, Göttingen, Germany

J. Logemann et al. (eds.), *Consumer Engineering, 1920s–1970s*,
Worlds of Consumption, https://doi.org/10.1007/978-3-030-14564-4_7

As a platform of information and interaction for practitioners in production, the wholesale trade, and retailing, Vogt established the monthly journal *Verkaufspraxis* (roughly: Sales Practices) in 1925. The trade journal was, at least until the Great Depression, a clear advocate of American business and sales methods. At the same time, however, it tried to merge these with a pronounced German understanding of entrepreneurship and business culture.[4] Published from 1925 until 1943 and again from 1949 until 1964, it held a leading position in the German market for business advice literature during two periods of intense "Americanization."[5]

Victor Vogt and the Journal *Verkaufspraxis*

Neither Vogt nor *Verkaufspraxis* have found recognition in historical research.[6] Not even a Wikipedia article offers any biographical or institutional basics. This lacuna, however, says nothing about the significance of Vogt, his group of experts, or his journal. Instead, it reflects the one-sidedness of marketing and consumption historiography, which focuses predominantly on advertising journals and the gurus of consumer engineering, while neglecting the practical work of entrepreneurs in the consumer goods industries.[7] In addition, the tradition of German business studies has been neglected, as have American-German knowledge transfers, and interwar business practices (Fig. 7.1).

Victor Vogt was born on April 16, 1887, in the Silesian middle town of Frankenstein as the son of the banker Richard Vogt.[8] After studying economics, he completed a commercial apprenticeship at his father's bank, before starting work for the Deutsche Bank in Paris and London.[9] His interest in organizational studies and journalism developed in the United Kingdom, not in the United States.[10] He returned to Germany in 1912, where he worked two years for the Berlin Bankhaus S. Bleichröder, before taking over the editorial office of the journal *Organisation: Zeitschrift für praktische Geschäftsführung, Reklame und Plakatkunst* (Organization: Journal for Practical Business Management, Advertising, and Poster Art) in April 1914 and becoming proxy director (*Prokura*) of its Charlottenburg-based publishing house in June 1914.[11] From 1915 to 1919, he served as an officer of the German Army and was severely wounded in late 1916.[12] Discharged from active service, he additionally took over the editorial office of the *Deutsche Büro-Zeitung* (German Office Newspaper) and worked as a consultant to banks and merchant houses. Vogt was surely one of the representatives of the early rationalization movement, which started already before the war and was deeply influenced by American ideas of scientific management and corresponding German traditions.[13] In 1920, the publisher and consultant also started his first business, co-founding an injection molding firm in the town of Birkenwerder.[14] The combination of theoretical knowledge and practical experience that had marked his career to this point would become his hallmark in the following decades.

In the early 1920s, Vogt published his first advice books, which were intended to help rationalize the daily routines of managing manufacturing

Fig. 7.1 Victor Vogt, 1925. Source: *Verkaufspraxis*, no. 3 (1925/26): 2.

and marketing. He taught the use of filing cards and registries, and he co-authored an impressive 644-page overview of office machines available in Germany and the United States.[15] This last book was discussed (and used) on both sides of the Atlantic.[16] Indeed, despite the common notion of Europe being "Americanized," there was never just a one-way flow of traffic in ideas and practices in business organization and rationalization.

Vogt wrote his books at the same time he was consulting for many firms. In the early 1920s, he developed office organization systems and new types of "rational" office furniture intended to embody his ideas about efficient business management. Vogt produced and promoted his innovations through the Büro-Einrichtungsfabrik Fortschritt (Progress Office Furnishings Factory) in Freiburg i. B., which was founded in 1901 by Otto Skrebba and employed up to several hundred people.[17] From 1925 until his death in 1960, Vogt acted as a director of this important producer of office equipment.[18]

Vogt's business activities can help to broaden our perspective to include Germany's prosperous and industrious Southwest. After the hyperinflation of 1923, Victor Vogt started another long-lasting collaboration, this time with Julius Hans Forkel. Beginning in 1914, Forkel had published regularly updated maps of the war situation and founded (with the financial support of the publisher and bookseller Franckh'sche Verlagsbuchhandlung) an eponymous publishing house for business in Stuttgart in 1919.[19] Since 1991 part of Hüthig Publishers, this small firm would not only publish Vogt's books and *Verkaufspraxis* but also become one of the most successful purveyors of business advice literature during the Weimar and especially the Nazi periods. Although most of Forkel's books on marketing, sales, advertising, and business practices were written by German business experts, translations of core books from the American debate were an important element of its portfolio.[20]

Vogt was Forkel's most successful author. In 1926, he published *Taschenbuch der Geschäftstechnik*, a compendium of business techniques, which combined his own business experience with a detailed analysis of U.S. and British literature.[21] Already in 1926, Vogt added a new book on sales psychology for salesmen and shop assistants, co-authored with the American specialist Frederick A. Russell.[22] Vogt's largest and most important book *Absatzprobleme* (Marketing Problems) appeared in 1929.[23] Based on the detailed expertise of the U.S. literature, this detailed guide was intended for executives and salesmen in the consumer goods industries. Revised several times, it was used in (West) Germany until the 1980s. Vogt also published several smaller pamphlets on branding and distribution techniques during the early Nazi period.[24] By then, however, he was first and foremost active as editor, columnist, and author of the journal *Verkaufspraxis*.

The journal's mission was clear-cut and ambitious:

> This new monthly reveals how the successful American and Englishman achieve their great sales revenues. It treats the many interesting American and English books and journals on selling in which practitioners reveal their business secrets

without hesitation. The material suited for increasing sales in the German context is offered in a beautifully produced journal.[25]

Verkaufspraxis was established in 1925 as an interface between business theories and business practices, between the Anglo-Saxon world and Germany. Consequently, the target audience was not academics or even advertisers but instead entrepreneurs, executives, managers, and salespeople in the consumer goods industries. Whereas advertising agencies played an increasingly dominant role in the United States and the United Kingdom, in Germany their functions were partially discharged by expert intermediaries working for trade journals like *Verkaufspraxis*.

Circulation figures are always a tricky business, but *Verkaufspraxis* was certainly the most widely read journal in the field of business administration, business practices, and advertising. In 1929, the journal had some 12,000 subscribers and a total print run of 14,000.[26] Even in 1930, after the start of the world economic crisis, the print run was still 11,480.[27] In April 1929, Vogt and the Verlag für Wirtschaft und Verkehr also established a supplement to *Verkaufspraxis* called ***Bausteine: Blätter zur Förderung des geschäftlichen und persönlichen Erfolgs*** (Building Blocks: Newspaper for the Promotion of Managerial and Personal Success). Its perforated pages could be torn in two and collected in a business card file. The supplement was included until 1932. All in all, *Verkaufspraxis* was a commercial success. Its economic foundations were sounder than those of most of its more specialized competitors.[28]

Working for Recovery, Fighting for National Strength: Partial Adoption of U.S. Consumer Engineering Techniques in the 1920s

Although the term "consumer engineering" was not coined until 1932, the idea behind it was already common in the 1920s, in both the United States and Germany. The American advertising executive Ernest Elmo Calkins (1868–1964), whose work was deeply influenced by his European experiences, promoted similar ideas a few years before he wrote the preface to "Consumer Engineering."[29] He defined the term as "a latent dynamic force, inherent in things [that] occasionally manifested strange phenomena."[30] To some degree, it had already shaped the 1920s, even without the catchphrase, which functions as a simple marker for historians, who often ignore the manifold related publications and activities before the Great Depression and their lure of hope and change in the marketplace. The phrase "consumer engineering" was a commercial narrative from the early 1930s. It was used by successful marketing moneymakers during the 1940s and 1950s to promote their own work. Nonetheless, a simple retrospective of the term's usage hides more than it uncovers.

Consumer engineering was based on the idea that experts, courageous leaders in their specific fields of expertise, should and could rationalize and improve the commercial sphere for the public good. Similar to the older idea of "social engineering," which aimed to pacify class struggles already before World War I, consumer engineering sought to harmonize conflicting interests in an authoritative way, that is, through the use of expert knowledge.[31] In the United States, such ideas were deeply shaped by the transformative experience of economic planning during World War I and by the moral crusade of the fair trade movement during the interwar years, which pushed for retail protection from chain stores through price maintenance. Both stood in deep contrast to a free market society and demanded modesty, integrity, and respect for all actors in the spheres of production, trade, and consumption.[32] It was more than coincidence that Aldous Huxley's novel *Brave New World* was written in this period (Fig. 7.2).[33]

A project of business and knowledge elites, consumer engineering stood in strict opposition to cooperative ideals of modern consumer societies and to the "consumerism" advocated, for instance, by U.S. economist Sidney A. Reeve or, in the German case, Franz Staudinger.[34] These two men had already offered dreamworlds of a steady and affordable supply of standardized consumer goods in which everyone got a square deal. Matters were further complicated by a plethora of "bright modernity," including new colors, new printing technologies, new media, and new materials.[35]

As the director of the Fortschritt office furnishings factory, Victor Vogt encountered such visions of modern consumption and produced modern and aesthetic durables—furniture, filling cabinets, office stationeries, and organizational forms. Vogt's growing interest in marketing and rationalization was also deeply rooted in his war experiences, however. "Organization" was not just a key slogan of the 1910s but was also crucial to the war effort. Soldiers, material, and foodstuffs had to be "organized." For many patriotic Germans, like Vogt, Germany's defeat resulted from a lack of organization in the civil sector. The adoption of U.S. and British business models and consumer

Fig. 7.2 "You are your customer's advocate." This image of the same man as both a lawyer and a businessman was supposed to promote *völkisch* self-restraint among business's consumer experts. Source: *Verkaufspraxis* 15 (1940): 192.

engineering techniques by Victor Vogt and his *Verkaufspraxis* represented a tribute to victorious enemies in war and superior competitors in peace. Advanced efficiency in business and the consumer sphere were supposed to help Germany rebuild by recapturing important domestic and foreign markets. New knowledge and improved methods also had an important social impact for bourgeois experts like Vogt and his staff. Such expertise would help sustain and improve the position of honest and diligent businessmen facing the rigid measures mandated by the Treaty of Versailles, which severely undermined the competitiveness both of German exports and of goods made in Germany for the domestic market.[36]

Vogt, Forkel, and many of the hand-picked authors of *Verkaufspraxis* were deeply shaped by the experiences of World War I, not to mention Germany's relatively weak position in business after the Revolution of 1918–1919 and the emergence of the Weimar welfare state. For these authors, business rationalization represented a continuation of the war in an honourable, fair, and individual way. Vogt saw himself as a kind of general training officers for a larger battle. He and his collaborators understood rationalization and the adoption of consumer engineering as crucial elements in the reconfiguration of Germany's intellectual and material life.[37] They wanted to form a new army of business experts and consumer engineers that could compete with those in the United States and Great Britain.[38] Vogt captured the guiding principle behind their understanding of business practices in the final sentence of his business handbook: "Bees do not obey; the spirit of discipline guides them."[39]

Consequently, the U.S.–German knowledge transfer was only partial. Vogt was particularly interested in the fair trade movement and American crusades to purify business and improve morality. Less interesting were the management techniques of leading corporations.[40] Although the German experts were impressed by U.S. growth rates and wealth, they perceived the United States predominantly as a young, enthusiastic nation, eager to innovate and to learn quickly. These were the attributes that could help Germany to rebuild its earlier leading position in international business, innovation, and service.

In other words, we face the apparently paradoxical situation that Vogt and *Verkaufspraxis* were not interested in "Americanizing" German business at all, not if we understand "Americanization" as a monolithic, unidirectional knowledge transfer.[41] On the contrary, Vogt and his associates saw American (and British) business methods not as worthy of outright adoption but rather as tools that could help repair and improve German business.[42] In contrast to the dominant ideas of American rationalization and in accordance with the U.S. fair trade movement, Vogt and his colleagues advocated cooperative "German" business ethics of "live and let live" and a particular understanding of functional differentiation in business.[43] Specifically, they believed that producers, wholesalers, retailers, and consumers performed specific functions for both their own benefit and for the common good. Competition was accepted but limited by mutual respect for other actors in the market sphere. They were convinced of the higher quality and uniqueness of German goods and services, even if scarce economic resources and a smaller domestic market got in the way. Consequently, Victor Vogt and *Verkaufspraxis* offered only a partial adoption of U.S. consumer engineering techniques based on the staff's business expertise, social position, national pride, and market-liberal convictions.[44]

This partial adoption of American (and British) ideas about rationalization and consumer engineering techniques still offered a broad range of new ideas and information for German business executives in production, the wholesale trade, and retailing. Vogt believed that an inventive nation like Germany had no substantial problems in production, although more efficiency was necessary. Instead, he saw increasing sales as the core challenge. Moreover, accomplishing this "feat" would require "a broad range of qualities, skills, and knowledge."[45] Selling, however, was not a material interaction between two parties but the establishment of long-lasting business relations.[46] In accordance with ideas developed by the Canadian-British author and editor Herbert N. Casson, *Verkaufspraxis* authors understood selling as a "service" delivered for the satisfaction of the customer, who was often another business, namely, a retailer or a wholesaler.[47] Vogt advocated scientific and psychological sales methods, based on general rules and as expressions of personality and individuality.[48]

It is possible to identify efforts of knowledge transfers in at least eight areas:

First, the journal informed readers about ongoing efforts in rationalization and the broad field of applied Taylorism. Punch cards, developed and propagated by the German-American immigrant entrepreneur Herman Hollerith, were presented and discussed as well as U.S. cost accounting equipment.[49] The authors introduced workflow studies that evinced a specific interest in standardization methods and in eliminating inefficient routines in business administration and the promotion and sale of consumer goods.[50]

Second, *Verkaufspraxis* had a strong focus on market and consumer analysis.[51] Contributing authors presented American and British examples that emphasized clearly defined categorizations and predominantly quantitative methods. At the same time, however, the journal covered quite different qualitative approaches.[52] Consumer typologies, for instance, were discussed, mostly based on a combination of psychological research and practical knowledge.[53]

Third, the staff wanted to take King or Queen Consumer seriously.[54] Victor Vogt, who wrote an introduction to every issue, constantly emphasized the crucial role of service for economic success. The authors presented many illustrated proposals to improve sales organization and to treat consumers with respect and courtesy.[55]

Forth, consumers were understood as the vanishing point of any economic (and social) reform. Although Vogt and his practitioners were entrepreneurs and managers, they turned their perspective toward the economic interests of all—which meant the ubiquity of consumers and consumer interests. At the same time, however, consumers had to learn to fulfill their role in society. This included education and guidance by experts, by business leaders, who would accomplish their noble mission, if need be, by fighting "consumer torpor."[56]

Fifth, the staff of *Verkaufspraxis* was particularly interested in rationalizing points of sale.[57] They offered a lot of advice about the statistical acquisition of empirical data on sales volumes and rhythms, and they evaluated the growing number of formulas and methods for forming such knowledge.[58] At the same time, the journal's experts were attracted to the "modern" psychology of shopping, discussing its consequences for organizing salesrooms and arranging consumer goods in them.[59]

Sixth, the authors understood selling as a profession whose requisite knowledge, ethos, and skill set could be learned and improved on. The rationalization of selling was linked to the systematic training and education of shops assistants and salesmen.[60] The German journal was fascinated by quite simple American teaching tools, questionnaires for shop assistants and shop owners, and their hidden idea of programing people with the superior knowledge of sales experts.[61]

Seventh, *Verkaufspraxis* had a specific interest in analyzing American and British advertising, as it was practiced by advertising agencies both abroad and in Germany. New trends were presented, and examples of appealing aesthetics were offered.[62] Of particular interest were the advertising campaigns by Anglo-Saxon multinationals, which became both competitors of and models for midsize German firms.[63]

Eighth, many articles dealt with purchasing motives and how to create consumer desire with new goods, better service, and more effective communication.[64] Although mostly resulting from business practice and everyday psychology, the journal offered early forms of motivational research long before this method was developed in more detail by Austrian-German immigrants in the United States.[65]

Vogt and *Verkaufspraxis* were convinced that this partial adoption of American (and British) consumer engineering techniques would help German business gain ground in domestic and foreign markets and likewise enable German consumers to afford cheaper goods and an increased material standard of living. At the same time, the journal's large readership not only indicated relevant resonance among readers but also underlined a core difference between the Anglo-Saxon and the German markets. Although the number of marketing and advertising consultants and agencies was growing in Germany, the consumer market there was still deeply shaped by individual entrepreneurs and managers.[66] Vogt's permanent appeal to readers' individualism, personality, moral and honesty was grounded in the different social structure of Germany's business community.

The Great Depression, however, undermined this agenda of partial adoption. On the one hand, the economic slump hit the United States hard: "The American 'Economic Miracle' has come to an end" was one telling reaction in *Verkaufspraxis*.[67] On the other hand, the establishment of a presidential dictatorship in Germany led to intensified market interventions by the state. As with the national-liberal economists of the so-called Freiburg School, who developed the guiding principles of the West German social market economy and neoliberalism in the early 1930s,[68] this development eventually led to a reinterpretation of the role of the state—and then of the racial state—by Vogt and *Verkaufspraxis*' authors.

The Crisis of National-Liberalism and the Emergence of the Interventionist (Racial) State

Vogt and *Verkaufspraxis* exemplify the intellectual and conceptual consequences of German liberalism's decline. Organized in the left-liberal German Democratic Party (DDP) and the national-liberal German People's Party (DVP), liberalism manifested itself in the former as a guardian of German republican and constitutional traditions, whereas its representatives in the latter were generally perceived as aligned with heavy industry. The DDP represented the self-employed bourgeoisie and most German Jews, while the DVP represented national and nationalist entrepreneurs, managers, and the propertied. Both liberal parties had a stronghold in the German Southwest.[69] We do not know Vogt's party preferences, but his lead articles combined ideas of a free market economy with a basically peaceful policy of revising the postwar order.

Typical for Vogt was a puzzling national-liberal mix of economic self-help, an elitist code of ethics, and resolute nationalism.[70] Vogt envisioned a corporatist state, where everybody would work efficiently in his position and act voluntarily for the common good of the German *Volk* or people.[71] From May 1929, Vogt became more political in his columns. As an entrepreneur, he strenuously opposed the Weimar Republic's welfare state, which he believed was undermining morality and self-reliance.[72] He complained about the heavy tax burden, which he perceived as a hefty penalty for private initiative. Still some months away from the Wall Street Crash of 1929, he was remained convinced that the emerging economic crisis could be handled by rekindling the entrepreneurial spirit. He welcomed the new authoritarian direction of German politics after the collapse of the great coalition in March 1930. State and individuals had to restrain themselves in order to overcome the economic and psychological crisis.[73] But he still believed in self-help and the entrepreneurial spirit, which would serve the common good.[74] Therefore he strenuously rejected the Federal emergency Act of June 27, 1930, paving the road to a planned economy and to serfdom.[75]

Vogt was convinced that business did not exist for politics, but reasonable politics were a precondition for prosperous business.[76] At the same time, he argued that political opinions should not interfere with the conduct of business.[77] In contrast to most representatives of the *Mittelstand*, the large group of midsize and smaller entrepreneurs, craftsmen, and retailers, he defended corporations and large-scale firms, department and chain stores, as long as they were founded on sound economic principles.[78] But he also believed in an economy with a large number of small and middle-sized firms and shops run by independent entrepreneurs.[79] This was similar to the ideas of the United States fair trade movement. Vogt, however, warned that their trust in state-help was a dangerous illusion.[80] He attributed the economic crisis to excessive state activity. He instead wanted to see a "new democracy" in business life, based on the cooperation of entrepreneurs, experts, and firms.[81] Voluntary chains, which were on the rise in the United States, could be one answer, purchasing cooperation and local and regional communities of interest another.[82] Cooperation could combine the spirit of free entrepreneurs and independent managers with the efficiency and lower costs of large business organizations. Vogt's ideas were typical for the early 1930s, when the search was on for a third way between capitalism and communism. Another author expressed the mood soon after the economic crisis began:

> From the New World comes intoxication over the reign of machines and numbers. The dollar as ultimate authority. Business is everything. Every man only worth what he earns. From the East reverberates the gospel of the masses. Equal rights for all. Everybody worth the same as the next person. No independent individualized existence, only the collective (*Allgemeinheit*). Caught in the middle: the German.[83]

A different economic order seemed necessary to achieve an overarching sense of accomplishing prosperity and defending independent business. Vogt himself anticipated an end of marketing as consumer engineering before it had even been put into practice: "It is not possible to develop a larger demand for the people and afterwards expect partial relinquishments."[84] He argued for an extension of public relief works to create additional income and facilitate higher rates of consumption—before the National Labor Service was founded in June 1931. But the focus of *Verkaufspraxis* articles shifted from the consumer to the internal workings of the consumer goods and retailing industries.[85] Consumer engineering efforts did not match the realities of high levels of debt, declining rates of production and consumption, or mass impoverishment.

During the crisis, Victor Vogt and *Verkaufspraxis* maintained their course. Editor and staff complained about the ongoing economic slump, the fatalism of most German people, and the growing levels of state intervention. Vogt criticized the leading political parties, especially the Social Democrats and the Nazi party for economic ideas involving more state planning and regulation: "Economic-interventionist experiments won't pave the way for recovery. Only a return to character [*Persönlichkeit*] and individual achievement will."[86] He recommended fundamental optimism and a noble attitude, praising Henry Ford as a role model.[87] In contrast to many representatives of heavy industry, he argued courageously against autarky.[88]

Vogt expected the Great Depression to be a moral watershed. The enticement of foreign capital and the promise of more efficient production methods had led to neglect limitations in German business after the heavy losses caused by World War I and then hyperinflation.[89] Steady reconstruction work was necessary. Believing the economic crisis to have been the result of widespread corruption in business and state affairs, moreover, he saw need for fresh entrepreneurial integrity.[90] Vogt used harsh arguments against white-collar crime and its only modest punishment, a stance he shared with National Socialists.[91] Vogt advocated a public pillory and other rigid changes in the treatment of corrupt business leaders. "Weaklings, washouts, profiteers, and notorious fraudsters" should be expelled from the community of honest businessmen.[92] This should still be an internal affair of the professionals, but the state could support such efforts. But Vogt did not stop there. He also directed his furor against those consumers who had been corrupted by bargains and consumer credit. If they had supported honest businesses, the crisis would be less deep. Consumer engineering was based on the short-term perspective of economic men and women.[93] A true consumer would reflect on the long-term consequences of his purchases for local communities, the social order, and the well-being of all Germans. Vogt argued for a culture of mutual respect, which paradoxically he found from 1933 in National Socialist governmental measures and in the actions of other business representatives.[94]

Cooperation and Community: Consumption Engineering and the "Rational" Nazi State

Germany's turn from a presidential to a National Socialist dictatorship in 1933 did not change the format of *Verkaufspraxis*. In clear ignorance of the significance of the historical changes, Vogt welcomed "the great purge" and applauded the recovery of "free entrepreneurship."[95] And he welcomed other state interventions, for instance, advertising regulations, as markers of a new, fair order.[96] Although the Hitler cabinet intensified its regulatory and intervention efforts, most entrepreneurs understood this turn as part of a renewal and as unavoidable exceptional measures for recovery.[97]

Vogt and *Verkaufspraxis* continued their work under National Socialism, although they were critical of the "social" agenda of the Nazi party and government. The journal maintained its core agenda, supplying information and advice for businesses. Self-help and improvement remained the core topics, although advertising and internal business organization became more important from the mid-1930s. In his lead articles, Vogt supported the new National Socialist government and Germany's successful revision of the Versailles treaty. The national perspective was strong, but *Verkaufspraxis* was neither explicitly racist nor anti-Semitic.[98] Meanwhile, the journal's strong market position played an integral role in the Forkel publishing house's becoming a major player in the fields of business and law during the Third Reich.

Important gradual changes occurred in the journal's content during the 1930s, however. U.S. consumer expertise was still relevant, but the number of articles on the subject declined from the beginning of the Great Depression.

The United States was no longer the unchallenged model of modern business, whereas Germany's economic star was on the rise again after 1933–1934. *Verkaufspraxis* still presented and discussed U.S. innovations and improvements, but these became additions to the stories of growing performance by German firms and experts.[99] This changing flow of ideas reflected Vogt's conviction that Germany was no longer dependent on U.S. consumer engineering techniques because it had established a more advanced form of self-reflective *consumption* engineering. This point is crucial for understanding varieties of consumerism. Here, the consumer was understood in a more noble position of self-constraint. Consumption engineering was a German alternative to the U.S. (or Western or capitalist) way of consumer engineering. In contrast to Calkin's use of this term in 1930, which was very similar to "consumer engineering" in 1932, this consumption engineering was a manifestation of the anticipated needs of the (German) people's community. At least six main characteristics of consumption engineering were perceived by the authors of pieces in *Verkaufspraxis* and many other specialist publications as crucial during the Nazi period.[100]

First, as with neoliberal ideas emerging in the early 1930s, they thought a strong state should establish a legal and economic framework for the consumption sphere and guarantee security and order there.[101] This caused limitations and hardships because the state was now seen as an expression of the racial, material, and cultural foundation of the German people.[102] Such state activity, however, was necessary in a world of competing states, empires, and races.

Second, the authors understood the economy as an organic entity with functional differentiation. Production, wholesaling, retailing, and consumption each represented distinct rationales and followed different logics. Their internal relations were based on honor, service, and mutual respect. This facilitated further "rationalization," guided by experts but accepted and specified by the different segments of the supply chain.[103]

Third, the articles portrayed competition as the law of life. The experiences of other national communities could be included and transfers of knowledge from outside Germany remained important, but economic performance could no longer be restricted to individual profit or well-being. The dominant goal of business was to strengthen the German community.[104] Advertising was still necessary, but simply to maintain continuity in the consumption of relevant and proven products, not to create need or stimulate desire, not to spawn new markets.[105] Vogt's credo in 1933 was simply: "Be critical toward new desires!"[106]

Fourth, consumption was understood both as a necessity and as an expression of the individuality and creativity of the German people. While consumer engineering was understood as a general toolbox for Western capitalist societies, consumption engineering should express the spirit and the economic needs of individual nations. Mass and bulk production would not fit for Germans as a nation of high and tasteful culture. Consumption engineering would foster batch and customer production and support a world of goods and services in accordance with Germany's traditions (Fig. 7.3).

Fifth, the individual consumer should and could trust in the services of production and trade.[107] His or her personal desires had to be directed to the priorities and needs of the German community[108]: "Previously, business beheld its great mission in fulfilling the public's wishes, in following its ideas. Business was the public's true servant. Its purpose in life was the will and the command of the customers.... Today another will directs business—the will of the state."[109] Thus, experts had to reinterpret consumers' desires. Appeals to their "subconscious" became exhortations to a racially inflected national or *völkisch* mission instead of invocations of the promise goods held for increasing individual pleasure.[110]

Finally, consumption should serve the German community first.[111] Domestic aliens to the German community and foreign members of other communities had to take a back seat to the racially defined German people's needs, even if this meant the demise of such groups.

It cannot be the task of this article to analyze Vogt's and his journal's transition under National Socialism in detail. Eventually, Vogt made his arguments as a party member and so wrote about "our National Socialist Weltanschauung" or worldview.[112] Further, he declared his support not only for Germany as a (racial) state but also for Adolf Hitler's "Weltanschauung."[113] His transformation into an eager supporter of the National Socialist government was typical for the large majority of formerly national-liberal entrepreneurs.[114] They still had adequate breathing room and were able to make independent business decisions.[115] Even during the war, they were still talking about the synthesis of an economy obliged to the needs of the Volk and the "creative" (*schöpferisch*) private initiative and self-reliance of businessmen.[116] By now, Vogt was obviously arguing in large measure against his convictions of the early 1930s. His reversals included going against his earlier preference for small and midsize firms, and against his strong emphasis on state intervention as an efficient, necessary, and sometimes superior mode of business practice.[117] Now, only the state and responsible consumption engineers could guide the majority of consumers toward fulfilling their true role in the economy.

For Vogt and *Verkaufspraxis*, World War II became a proving ground for this model of consumption engineering, which entailed a voluntary commitment to offering leadership in identifying improved sales methods and to communicating to consumers improved ways of consumption. The task was challenging, but the journal's experts now had to prove their mettle as "home front soldiers."[118] They saw their attitude, conduct, forbearance, and ability to think in terms of the common German good as legitimations for their leadership role in the German community.[119] Consumers had to do their part too. Their role in national community was different, but their values needed to be the same as those of the business and consumption experts.

Although he constantly expressed his desire for peace and the undisturbed conduct of business, Vogt was a willing supporter of Nazi Germany's war effort.[120] He accused "England" as the driving force behind the war and praised his own government for its wise preventive efforts.[121] After

Fig. 7.3 Expanding evidence and adding value: Man in the focus of experts, 1929. Source: *Uhu* 5, no. 10 (1928/29): 86.

Germany's defeat of France, he welcomed the opportunities that a new Europe and a new colonial empire governed by Germany promised.[122] He favored large-scale planning in Europe's East and West.[123] The United States no longer represented a model for Germany, whereas the closer connections with Germany's European neighbors he supported were eventually conducive to European cooperation after Germany's defeat in 1945.

The limits and, of course, the failure of consumption engineering during the Nazi period were obvious.[124] In the context of this book, however, it is more important to realize that German experts—and probably those of other nations and empires too—developed models for economic improvement that were meant to function as alternatives to Anglo-Saxon approaches to consumer engineering.[125] The development of such alternatives also conditioned German experts' attitudes toward ostensibly Western models in the early postwar period.

Reluctant Acceptance: New Ways of Selling and Advertising in 1949–1950

By the time *Verkaufspraxis* had been relaunched in December 1949, Victor Vogt had been replaced as editor by Gottlieb Friedrich "Fritz" Seitz (1890–1966), who had worked as advertising director at Robert Bosch GmbH since 1940. Previously an officer in the German Army, he had managed a furniture factory in occupied France from 1916 and was responsible for several popular journals—published by the Franckh'sche Verlagsbuchhandlung in Stuttgart, including *Kosmos* (Cosmos), *Amerika und Wir* (America and Us), and *Basteln und Bauen* (Making and Building). During the 1920s, he acted in multiple capacities as publisher, advertising consultant, lobbyist for executive employees, and promoter of German culture in the Southwest. Like Vogt, he had been both nationalist and liberal, playing an active role for the DDP in the early 1920s.[126] He later joined the SA and was a committed National Socialist.[127]

Seitz, Vogt, and Forkel signed the first postwar editorial of *Verkaufspraxis* but offered no explanation for Vogt's replacement.[128] During the war, Vogt's Fortschritt office furniture company had converted its production over to military needs, for instance, by developing organization tables for commando posts, and it used forced labor.[129] From 1944, the Freiburg firm built tail units and aircraft fuselages for Messerschmitt.[130] Although Freiburg endured several heavy bombings (the British Operation Tigerfish destroyed large parts of the historic center as well as some midsize industrial firms, killing some 2800 people in November 1944) Fortschritt remained relatively unscathed.[131] By late 1949, Vogt's dedicated support of the National Socialist government no longer presented an obstacle to continuing his business career in the French occupation zone.[132] Still, Vogt did not contribute additional articles to the first postwar volume. Nonetheless, Seitz' reprinting of two volumes of valuable articles from earlier issues of *Verkaufspraxis* emphasized continuity with Vogt's direction.[133]

In principle, the relaunched *Verkaufspraxis* faced quite similar circumstances as the journal had at its beginning in 1925. Rationalization and transfers of business expertise were seen as necessary for recovery from the war. "It is proper to again seek success in free competition and in foreign markets."[134] Former models of market research and consumer analysis had to be reinstituted after the end of rationing and with the reestablishment of a market society. The hardships of war and especially of the postwar period made efficient basic provisioning of goods a necessity of the time, although the eventual seller's market of the postwar years slowed down this process. Self-service concepts had been already discussed in the 1920s and were implemented from the late 1930s, but now the U.S. example seemed to offer new methods namely for the cheap and efficient distribution of goods.[135] The United States became a model once again. Its advanced advertising methods and techniques were of particular interest.[136]

In 1949–1950, however, it was not yet necessary to discuss and implement the newest U.S. methods in consumer engineering. Instead, *Verkaufspraxis* offered adaptations and refinements of German and U.S. models from the late 1920s.[137] The adoption of U.S. expertise was again only partial, but Germany's total defeat and West Germany's role in the Cold War led to an intensified orientation toward the Western superpower. In addition, it was necessary to earn foreign currency, U.S. dollars, on the world market. Partial adoption of U.S. methods also enabled closer cooperation with Western and Southern European neighbors, who had to solve similar economic problems after the war. Nevertheless, it is striking how *Verkaufspraxis* continued to follow wartime thinking. As already mentioned, Europe, dominated by Germany, had been the focus of many editorials after 1941. In fact, it was common to talk about "us Europeans."[138] During the war, the journal had also analyzed the situation in European states conquered by Germany.[139] *Verkaufspraxis* has supported the creation of a new European order, especially a greater economic zone under German supremacy.[140] In the immediate postwar period, the journal, run predominantly by former National Socialist supporters and party members, developed close ties to France, Italy, Switzerland, and Britain, even if U.S. examples became dominant.[141]

There was no immediate transfer of U.S. consumer engineering in the early postwar period—although consumers received renewed attention.[142] The rationale for such distance to U.S. influences was threefold. First, *Verkaufspraxis* was still promoting the idea of severe cultural and economic differences between both countries. Second, its authors took for granted that German graphic design still offered superior aesthetic quality in advertising and even product design. Third, postwar experts also remained skeptical of the overcommercialized advertising methods prominent in the United States.[143] In addition, the severe differences in purchasing power and in the basic needs of most consumers shaped the transfer of commercial models from the United States. Consumer engineering was not perceived as a model for overcoming the economic obstacles of the postwar era, but as a bundle of measures typical for a buyer's market. It would take years, they thought, before Germany's economic situation brought about such circumstances.

Adoption and Alienness: Some Conclusions

The example of Victor Vogt and *Verkaufspraxis* adds important perspectives to our understanding of the interrupted career of consumer engineering techniques in Germany from the 1920s to the 1950s. First, while common narratives about German marketing are based on branded consumer goods and fancy print advertisements, the consultants and practitioners of the *Verkaufspraxis* group represented not only a different business sector, closer to business practice, but also different consumer goods, most notably durables. Their outreach to producers, wholesalers, retailers, and consumers alike allows a more nuanced understanding of German business and sales culture in the mid-twentieth century.

Second, although U.S. consumer engineering techniques were discussed and adopted even before the term was coined in 1932, their transfer to Germany was never an affair of the heart. It was triggered by the promise of economic reconstruction and a rising standard of living, but it was embedded in a culture of global competition, not in a culture of universal acceptance of the American model of manufacturing, selling, advertising, and consumption.

Third, the adoption of U.S. consumer engineering techniques and ideas in Germany was restrained by external shocks, like the Great Depression and World War II. National traditions, nationalistic desires, and the rise of National Socialism led to the alternative German concept of *consumption* (not consumer) engineering during the 1930s and early 1940s. This idea comprised an amalgam of an organic understanding of society, faith in the merits of free and creative entrepreneurship, the values of the so-called Mittelstand, and ideas about social hierarchies and the appropriateness of modern consumerism. Although such consumption engineering—especially in its racialized version—was no longer propagated after World War II, adherence to it severely slowed the adoption of U.S. consumer engineering models in the 1950s and 1960s. The historical experiences of the Great Depression and National Socialist rule helped the national-liberal establishment in Germany to make peace with the idea of a social market economy (with a strong welfare state and wide-ranging regulation) and to accept the need to cooperate with European neighbors to the West and the South.

Finally, the partial adoption of U.S.—or Western—ideas of consumer engineering by Victor Vogt and the *Verkaufspraxis* group calls into question the common scholarly use of "Americanization" as a unidirectional flow of expertise and the expression of a superior, more promising model for the future. Vogt's study of U.S. business practices captured a broad variety of ideas, often contradictory to the perspective of consumer engineering. America offered a broad variety of business models; the fair trade movement, oligopolistic cooperation, and the widespread reception of economic planning should not be marginalized in analyses of America's influence on Germany. German experts like Vogt treated U.S. ideas as implements in a well-appointed toolbox, deciding on their own which to use or not use in response to the challenges Germany faced as a modern consumer society.

Notes

1. The concept is usually traced back to the Great Depression, when experts like Roy Sheldon and Egmont Arens pushed for "a totalized approach," in *Consumer Engineering: A New Technique for Prosperity* (New York, 1932), one "that advocated psychological and behavioural study to learn consumer preferences and the retooling of business to meet them." See Charles F. McGovern, *Sold American: Consumption and Citizenship, 1890–1945* (Chapel Hill, NC, 2006), 228. For a broader perspective, see Lutz Raphael, ed., *Theorien and Experimente der Moderne: Europas Gesellschaften im 20. Jahrhunderts* (Cologne, 2012); and Thomas Etzemüller, ed., *Die Ordnung der Moderne: Social Engineering im 20. Jahrhundert*, ed. Thomas Etzemüller (Bielefeld, 2009).
2. George D. Olds, Jr., "Review of Sheldon and Arens, Consumer Engineering," *Management Review* 21, no. 5 (1932): 157–58, here 157.
3. David A. Hounshell, *From the American System to Mass Production, 1800–1932: The Development of Manufacturing Technology in the United States* (Baltimore, MD, 1985); Roland Marchand, *Advertising the American Dream: Making Way for Modernity, 1920–1940* (Berkeley, CA, 1985); and Gary Cross, *An All-Consuming Century: Why Commercialism Won in Modern America* (New York, 2000).
4. *Verkaufspraxis* was advertised as "the journal of psychological sales methods, of seeing into the buyer's soul, of 'customer service.' Wherever businessmen reveal their secrets of success in trade journals, *Verkaufspraxis* evaluates [those methods]. Imitating the foreign—that awful German custom—is not promoted, but whoever does it better is [this journal's] teacher." W. H. Wolff, *Jugend: Wege zu einer neuen Käuferschaft* (Stuttgart, 1928), 238.
5. See Mary Nolan, *The Transatlantic Century: Europe and America, 1890–2010* (Cambridge, UK, 2012), esp. Chaps. 3–4; Egbert Klautke, *Unbegrenzte Möglichkeiten: 'Amerikanisierung' in Deutschland und Frankreich (1900–1933)* (Stuttgart, 2003); Volker R. Berghahn, "The Debate on 'Americanisation' Among Economic and Cultural Historians," *Cold War History* 10 (2010): 107–30; and Victoria de Grazia, *Irresistible Empire: America's Advance Through Twentieth Century Europe* (Cambridge, MA, 2005), predominantly offers one-dimensional and one-sided stories instead of a history of transatlantic entanglements.
6. Stefan Bauernschmidt, *Fahrzeuge auf Zelluloid: Fernsehwerbung für Automobile in der Bundesrepublik des Wirtschaftswunders: Ein kultursoziologischer Versuch* (Bielefeld, 2011), 135, mentions Vogt's definition of market research but does not provide additional information. Alexander Schug, "Werbung und die Kultur des Kapitalismus," in *Die Konsumgesellschaft in Deutschland 1890–1990: Ein Handbuch*, ed. Heinz-Gerhard Haupt and Claudius Torp (Frankfurt a.M., 2009), 355–69, here 359, n23, only uses Vogt's book *Absatzprobleme* to back his conclusions about general developments in advertising. Marius Lange, *Zwischen Demoskopie und Diktatur: Unternehmerische Öffentlichkeitsarbeit in Deutschland, 1929–1936* (Frankfurt a.M., 2010), examines the articles of eight *Verkaufspraxis* volumes on public relations.
7. A good example of this tendency: Gerulf Hirt, *Verkannte Propheten? Zur 'Expertenkultur' (west-)deutscher Werbekommunikatoren bis zur Rezession*

1966/67 (Leipzig, 2013). Although it offers a good number of biographical sketches, it does not question standard narratives about German market research.

8. The private banking house Richard Vogt & Co. was established in 1887 in Frankenstein, Silesia; *Berliner Börsenzeitung*, September 20, 1887, 16. In 1891, Vogt and the Schlesische Bankverein formed a limited partnership; "A Forgotten Predecessor Established 150 Years Ago: Schlesischer Bankverein," *Bank and History*, no. 11 (2006): 1–3, here 2; *Berliner Börsenzeitung* May 1, 1891, 13; and *Berliner Börsenzeitung*, March 11, 1904, 2.
9. Richard Vogt & Co. cooperated closely with Deutsche Bank; see *Volkszeitung* [Berlin], August 29, 1897, 2.
10. Johann Joseph Kaindl, *Werbefachleute* (Wien, 1921), n.p.
11. *Berliner Börsenzeitung*, June 16, 1914, 29. In 1922, the journal was renamed *Zeitschrift für Betriebswirtschaft, Verwaltungspraxis und Wirtschaftspolitik* (Journal of Business Management, Administrative Practice and Economic Policies). In a parallel development, the *Organisatoren-Verband* (Federation of Organizers) was founded in Berlin, and it still exists today, having been renamed *Gesellschaft für Organisation* (Society for Organization) in 1926.
12. During the first half of 1917, he was replaced by the retiree Karl Wolit as managing director of the *Organisation Verlagsgesellschaft mbH*; *Berliner Börsenzeitung*, December 29, 1916, 14.
13. See Robert Kanigel, *The One Best Way: Frederick Winslow Taylor and the Enigma of Efficiency* (New York, 1999); and Wolfgang König, *Geschichte der Konsumgesellschaft* (Stuttgart, 2000), 47–72.
14. *Berliner Börsenzeitung*, November 12, 1920, 29.
15. Victor Vogt, *Die Karthothek, ihre Anlage und Führung* (Berlin, 1920); Victor Vogt, *Die Kartei, ihre Anlage und Führung*, 2nd ed. (Berlin, 1922); and Victor Vogt and Ludwig Brauner, *Illustriertes Orga-Handbuch erprobter Büro-Maschinen* (Berlin, 1921). Historical research predominantly focuses on the rationalization of blue-collar work, whereas the intense debates on white-collar work are often ignored. See Timo Luks, *Der Betrieb als Ort der Moderne: Zur Geschichte von Industriearbeit, Ordnungsdenken und Social Engineering im 20. Jahrhundert* (Bielefeld, 2010).
16. "Hand-Book of Approved Office Machines," *Business Equipment Magazine* 52 (1922): 382.
17. Carola Schark, "Wo früher in Haslach Büromöbel hergestellt wurden, steht heute das Gutleutviertel," *Badische Zeitung*, April 7, 2015. The firm's product range can be gleaned from Victor Vogt, *Taschenbuch der Geschäftstechnik*, 3rd ed. (Stuttgart, 1927), 2, 872–73; and *Verkaufspraxis* 4, no. 2 (1928/29): cover and iii.
18. See Landesarchiv Baden-Württemberg, Abt. Freiburg, W 134, Nr. 047363g Bild 1 at http://www.landesarchiv-bw.de/plink/?f=5-1966505-1, for a series of images from Vogt's 70th birthday, including of his wife Odette Vogt, neé Crespy; "Direktor Victor Vogt 70 Jahre alt," *Baden-Württemberg* (1957): 46; and "Direktor Victor Vogt †," *Baden-Württemberg* (1960): 72.
19. "50 Jahre Forkel-Verlag," *Börsenblatt für den Deutschen Buchhandel* 24 (1968): 3335.
20. See, for instance, Werrett Wallace Charters and Max Eichler, *Verkaufspsychologie für den Einzelhandel: Erfahrungen über die Kunst erfolgreicher*

Kundenbehandlung (Stuttgart, 1926); Natalie Kneeland, *Psychologisch falsche und richtige Ladenverkaufsgespräche: 135 Fälle aus dem Einzelhandel* (Stuttgart, 1927); and Claude C. Hopkins, *Propaganda: Meine Lebensarbeit* (Stuttgart, 1928).

21. Victor Vogt, *Taschenbuch der Geschäftstechnik*, 2 vols. (Stuttgart, 1926).
22. Frederick A. Russell and Victor Vogt, *Verkaufspsychologie für reisende Kaufleute: Erfahrungen über die Kunst erfolgreicher Kundenbehandlung* (Stuttgart, 1926), which was based on Russell's 1924 *Textbook of Salesmanship*. The sixth edition of this book was revised and republished as Victor Vogt and Ernst Dülken, *Technik des Reise-Verkaufs: Tausend Erfahrungen über bessere Abschlüsse für den reisenden Geschäftsmann und seine Firma, in ein System gebracht und kritisch beleuchtet* (Stuttgart, [ca. 1930]).
23. Victor Vogt, *Absatzprobleme: Das Handbuch der Verkaufsleitung für Erzeuger, Groß- und Einzelhändler*, 2 vols. (Stuttgart, 1929).
24. Victor Vogt, *Der neue Artikel: Praktische Überlegungen vor, während und nach seiner Einführung* (Stuttgart, 1933); and Victor Vogt, *Vertriebstechnik: Wie der Fabrikant und der Groß-Händler durch richtigen Kräfte-Einsatz zum Erfolg kommen* (Stuttgart, 1934).
25. Victor Vogt, *Taschenbuch der Geschäftstechnik*, 3rd ed. (Stuttgart, 1927), 2, 878.
26. Vogt, *Absatzprobleme* (1929), 2, 896.
27. Vogt and Dülken, *Technik des Reise-Verkaufs* (1930), 561.
28. In the field of business administration, there was the *Zeitschrift für handelswissenschaftliche Forschung*, *Betriebswirtschaft*, *Annalen der Betriebswirtschaft*, and the *Zeitschrift für Betriebswirtschaft*. Business practices were discussed in the *Zeitschrift für Organisation*, *Betriebsführung*, and *Wirtschaftlichkeit*. Best known to historians are the leading advertising journals of the period such as *Die Anzeige*, *Gebrauchsgraphik*, *Die Reklame*, *Seidels Reklame*, and *Wirtschaftswerbung*. See Kurt Schmalz, "The Business Periodicals of Germany," *Accounting Review* 5 (1930): 231–34.
29. Ernest Elmo Calkins, *The Business of Advertising* (New York, 1915); Ernest Elmo Calkins, "The New Consumption Engineer and the Artist," in *A Philosophy of Production: A Symposium*, ed. J. George Frederick (New York, 1930), 126–28; Ernest Elmo Calkins, "The Job of the Consumption Engineer," *Merchandising and Selling* 15, no. 28 (1930): 60–62; and "Urges Advertising to Push Prohibition," *New York Times*, May 20, 1930, 23. See also Fred Beard, "Forgotten Classics: The Business of Advertising, by Earnest Elmo Calkins (1915)," *Journal of Historical Research in Marketing* 7 (2015): 573–83; and Regina Lee Blaszczyk, *Imagining Consumers: Design and Innovation from Wedgwood to Corning* (Baltimore, MD, 2000), 137–38.
30. Earnest Elmo Calkins, *'Louder Please!' The Autobiography of a Deaf Man* (Boston, 1924), 4–5, who used this sentence to describe the beginnings of modern advertising in the late nineteenth century.
31. "New Profession Appears: Promoters of 'Social Engineering' Find a Fruitful Field," *New York Times*, October 15, 1899, 8; and William H. Tolman, *Social Engineering*, with intro. by Andrew Carnegie (New York, 1909).
32. This did not mean backwardness; see Susan V. Spellman, *Cornering the Market: Independent Grocers and Innovation in American Small Business* (New York, 2016).

33. Aldous Huxley, *Brave New Work* (New York, 1932).
34. Sidney A. Reeve, *Modern Economic Tendencies: An Economic History of the United States* (New York, 1921). See also Lawrence B. Glickman, "Rethinking Politics: Consumers and the Public Good during the 'Jazz Age,'" *OAH Magazine of History* 21, no. 3 (2007): 16–20; and Lawrence B. Glickman, *Buying Power: A History of Consumer Activism in America* (Chicago, IL, 2009), 202. On Staudinger, see Uwe Spiekermann, "Medium der Solidarität: Die Werbung der Konsumgenossenschaften 1903–1933," in *Bilderwelt des Alltags: Werbung in der Konsumgesellschaft des 19. und 20. Jahrhunderts*, ed. Peter Borscheid and Clemens Wischermann (Stuttgart, 1995), 150–89.
35. See Regina Lee Blaszczyk and Uwe Spiekermann, "Bright Modernity: Color, Commerce, and Consumer Culture," in *Bright Modernity: Color, Commerce, and Consumer Culture*, ed. Blaszczyk and Spiekermann (New York, 2017), 1–34; and Regina Lee Blaszczyk, *The Color Revolution* (Cambridge, 2012).
36. *Verkaufspraxis* was launched in October 1925, when the German economy was hit by a recession. Vogt emphasized the "floods of our need" and talked about Germany's "miserable situation." In this context, rationalization appeared as a kind of necessary economic purification requiring ruthless implementation; Victor Vogt, "Aussichten und Einsichten," *Verkaufspraxis* 1, no. 3 (1925/26): 3–4. A similar assessment: Paul Gunkel, "Nachdenkliches zum Jahresbeginn," *Verkaufspraxis* 1, no. 4 (1925/26): 3–4.
37. Such ideas were also discussed and implemented by the German *Mittelstand* movement, which was dominated by mid-sized retailers. On their moral and partial adoption of "modern" sales methods, see Uwe Spiekermann, "'Der Mittelstand stirbt!' Der Kampf zwischen mittelständischem Einzelhandel und Warenhäusern in Deutschland 1896–1938," in *Das Berliner Warenhaus: Geschichte und Diskurse*, ed. Godela Weiss-Sussex and Ulrike Zitzlsperger (Frankfurt a.M., 2013), 33–52, esp. 44–51.
38. The USA was explicitly perceived as a "superior opponent"; "Deutschland und die Wirtschaftserfolge Amerikas," *Verkaufspraxis* 1, no. 6 (1925/26): 19–21, hier 19.
39. Vogt, *Taschenbuch der Geschäftstechnik*, 2: 853.
40. "Edward A. Filene, amerikanischer Warenhausbesitzer," *Verkaufspraxis* 1, no. 4 (1925/26): 32–34.
41. This is the dominant perspective in Harm Schröter, *Americanization of the European Economy: A Compact Survey of American Influence in Europe Since the 1880s* (Dordrecht, 2005).
42. "Was wir von den Amerikanern lernen können," *Verkaufspraxis* 1, no. 2 (1925/26): 36–37.
43. Victor Vogt, "Kaufmännischer Ehrenkodex," *Verkaufspraxis* 1, no. 6 (1925/26): 3–6.
44. On the history of marketing in the Weimar Republic, see Uwe Spiekermann, "'Der Verbraucher muß erobert werden!' Marketing in Landwirtschaft und Einzelhandel in Deutschland in den 1920er und 1930er Jahren," in *Marketinggeschichte: Die Genese einer modernen Sozialtechnik*, ed. Hartmut Berghoff (Frankfurt a.M., 2007), 123–47.
45. Victor Vogt, "Verkaufspraxis," *Verkaufspraxis* 1, no. 1 (1925/26): 3–5, here 3. Vogt's analysis accorded with that of American experts, who criticized that in Germany "the art of sales practice is still in its infancy"; Günther Stein,

"Mängel der deutschen Exportmethoden: Amerikanische Kritik deutscher Reklame," *Berliner Tageblatt*, May 11, 1928, 8.

46. "Kunden sind Kapital," *Verkaufspraxis* 1, no. 1 (1925/26): 6.
47. Casson, one of the most productive authors on business and technology in the first half of the twentieth century, and from 1915 editor of *The Efficiency Magazine*, had probably impressed Vogt, who referred to him several times. See, for instance, Victor Vogt, "Der Einzelwille in der Geschäftsleitung," *Verkaufspraxis* 1, no. 2 (1925/26): 33; and "Ich verstehe den Verkauf von A bis Z!," *Verkaufspraxis* 1, no. 7 (1926/27): 2.
48. Vogt's emphasis on the virtue of personality was also based on private experiences. In his hometown of Frankenstein, a local grocer was able to compete with a Berlin-based chain store because of his compassion for his customers; Victor Vogt, "Persönlichkeit," *Die Uhrmacherkunst* 7 (1927): 15–16, here 15.
49. Georg Lang, "Die Lochkarte als Hilfsmittel bei der Kundenwerbung," *Verkaufspraxis* 3 (1927/28): 99–106; and F. Grüner, "Eine mechanisierte Kundenkartei," *Verkaufspraxis* 2 (1926/27): 626–32. At the same time, the magazine propagated more common ways of data mining. See "Die Verkaufskartothek," *Verkaufspraxis* 1 (1925/26): 21–23. For the USA, see Josh Lauer, "Making the Ledgers Talk: Customer Control and the Origins of Retail Data Mining, 1920–1940," in *The Rise of Marketing and Market Research*, ed. Hartmut Berghoff, Phillip Scranton, and Uwe Spiekermann (New York, 2012), 153–69.
50. Fritz Heinrichs, "Ingenieur und Vertrieb," *Verkaufspraxis* 5 (1929/30): 736–38.
51. I[rene] M. Witte, "Marktanalyse," *Verkaufspraxis* 1, no. 8 (1925/26): 27–30; Max Eichler, "Terra incognita," *Verkaufspraxis* 3 (1927/28): 403–8; P. H. Crodel, "Lernt eure Kunden kennen!," *Verkaufspraxis* 4 (1928/29): 293–95; and J. Kurt Herzfeld, "Marktanalyse auf statistischer Grundlage," *Verkaufspraxis* 4 (1928/29): 750–52.
52. W. H. Wolff, "Wandlungen in der Kundschaft," *Verkaufspraxis* 5 (1929/30): 74–76; and "Ein Verkaufslaboratorium," *Verkaufspraxis* 5 (1929/30): 490–92.
53. "Sechs Kundentypen," *Verkaufspraxis* 3 (1927/28): 83–85.
54. "Der König im Reiche des Handels," *Verkaufspraxis* 1, no. 1 (1925/26): 20; and "Der Verbraucher ist König," *Verkaufspraxis* 2 (1926/27): 220.
55. Theodor Lach, "Werbet um die Frauen!," *Verkaufspraxis* 5 (1929/30): 245–47; and Paul Wandslebe, "'Service' ... wie ihn der Kunde sieht," *Verkaufspraxis* 5 (1929/30): 291–93.
56. Victor Vogt, "Der Jungbrunnen der Wirtschaft," *Verkaufspraxis* 1, no. 7 (1925/26): 3–7, hier 5.
57. See "Neue amerikanische Verkaufsmethoden, die den Umsatz steigern," *Verkaufspraxis* 1, no. 5 (1925/26): 32–33, which also evinced a positive understanding of self-service, a sales method that had not yet been introduced in Germany; I[rene] M. Witte, "Chain Stores," *Verkaufspraxis* 1, no. 7 (1925/26): 36–39; "Ladenbau," *Verkaufspraxis* 1, no. 10 (1925/26): 9–12; and Karl Berg, "Selbstbedienungssystem," *Verkaufspraxis* 4 (1928/29): 248–50.
58. Victor Vogt "Verkaufs-'Wissenschaft'?," *Verkaufspraxis* 2 (1926/27): 323–29; and Richard Brauns, "Der Lagerumschlag im Einzelhandel," *Verkaufspraxis* 4 (1928/29): 46–48.

59. "Wie sollen unsere Verkaufsräume eingerichtet sein?," *Verkaufspraxis* 4 (1928/29): 540–42.
60. "Verhandlungstechnik," *Verkaufspraxis* 1, no. 1 (1925/26): 26–30; P. M[ax] Grempe, "Verkaufsschulen," *Verkaufspraxis* 1, no. 8 (1925/26): 36–40; "Was sollen wir unsere Verkäufer lehren?," *Verkaufspraxis* 1, no. 10 (1925/26): 36–39; Bruno Birnbaum, "Eine Hochschule der Verkaufskunst," *Verkaufspraxis* 1, no. 12 (1925/26): 20–23, which deals with Lucinda Prince; "100 Regeln für das Verkaufspersonal," *Verkaufspraxis* 2 (1926/27): 603–8, 698–703; F. M. Manasse, "Die Verkäuferschule von General Motors in Berlin," *Verkaufspraxis* 5 (1929/30): 30–36; and A. Schirmer, "Mehr sprachliche Schulung!," *Bausteine* 1 (1929/30): 255–56.
61. Victor Vogt, "Reisender gesucht," *Verkaufspraxis* 2 (1925/26): 282–89.
62. "Was sagen uns die beiden amerikanischen Bildanzeigen," *Verkaufspraxis* 1, no. 2 (1925/26): 16–18; Fritz Körner, "Neue Wege der Anzeigen-Reklame?," *Verkaufspraxis* 1, no. 12 (1925/26): 20–24; Helmut Biegel, "Neue Wege für das Inserat im Fachblatt," *Verkaufspraxis* 4 (1928/29): 83–88; "Booklets," *Verkaufspraxis* 4 (1928/29): 136–39; "Die technische Anzeige!," *Verkaufspraxis* 4 (1928/29): 610–14; "Ein Königreich für eine Idee … ," *Verkaufspraxis* 5 (1929/30): 11–18; and [Hans] Wündrich-Meissen, "Deutsche Reklame im Lichte der 'Berliner Illustrirten,'" *Verkaufspraxis* 5 (1929/30): 162–69.
63. Pet Hayne, "Das Lichtbild als Werbehelfer," *Verkaufspraxis* 3 (1927/28): 225–39.
64. Victor Vogt, "Kauf-Motive: Befruchtung der Praxis durch die Theorie," *Verkaufspraxis* 1, no. 9 (1925/26): 3–7; and Hans Wündrich, "Bedarfsweckung durch positive und negative Momente?," *Verkaufspraxis* 4 (1928/29): 234–38.
65. See Mark Tadajewski, "Remembering Motivation Research: Toward an Alternative Genealogy of Interpretive Consumer Research," *Marketing Theory* 6 (2006): 429–65; Dirk Schindelbeck, "Vom 'Mehrwert' erfolgreicher Produktkommunikation: 'Einfühlung' und 'Leidenschaft' als ethische Leitlinien bei Ernest Dichter und Hans Domizlaff," *Medien & Zeit* 4 (2005): 18–23; and Hartmut Berghoff, Phillip Scranton, and Uwe Spiekermann, "The Origins of Marketing and Market Research: Information, Institutions, and Markets," in *The Rise of Marketing and Market Research*, ed. Berghoff, Scranton, and Spiekermann, 1–27, here 6–8.
66. There was, of course, some advice for hiring such experts; see "Was kostet ein Werbeberater?," *Verkaufspraxis* 4 (1928/29): 495–96.
67. "Amerika … der Konkurrent," *Verkaufspraxis* 5 (1929/30): 749–53.
68. See Ralf Ptak, *Vom Ordoliberalismus zur Sozialen Marktwirtschaft: Stationen des Neoliberalismus in Deutschland* (Opladen, 2004).
69. See Bruce B. Frye, *Liberal Democrats in the Weimar Republic: The History of the German Democratic Party and the German State Party, 1918–1933* (Carbondale, IL, 1985); and Ludwig Richter, *Die Deutsche Volkspartei 1918–1933* (Düsseldorf, 2002).
70. Victor Vogt, "Geschäftsmoral als Erfolgsfaktor!," *Verkaufspraxis* 1, no. 2 (1925/26): 3–4, here 4.
71. Victor Vogt, "Der Jungbrunnen der Wirtschaft," *Verkaufspraxis* 1, no. 7 (1925/26): 3–7, here 7. The German term "Volk," sometimes rendered inadequately as "people" or the similarly pronounced "folk" in English, refers to the nation or the constitutive people, but it also denotes more, namely, a

collective entity based not only on legal factors but also a shared history, language, and culture. "Volk" is an oscillating term that can be used in a racist or a progressive manner. See Jörn Retterath, *'Was ist das Volk?' Volks- und Gemeinschaftskonzepte der politischen Mitte in Deutschland 1917–1924* (Berlin, 2016).

72. Victor Vogt, "Vater werden ist nicht schwer ... ," *Verkaufspraxis* 4 (1928/29): 453–57.
73. Victor Vogt, "Der Fluch der bösen Tat," Verkaufspraxis 6 (1930/31): 581–84.
74. Victor Vogt, "Heraus aus der Sackgasse!," *Verkaufspraxis* 5 (1929/30): 581–85.
75. Heinrich Gillmann, "Die Preissenkungsaktion der Regierung," *Verkaufspraxis* 5 (1929/30): 699–701; and Heinrich Gillmann, "Die Preissenkung marschiert!," *Verkaufspraxis* 5 (1929/30): 726–28.
76. Victor Vogt, "Und sie bewegt sich doch!!," *Verkaufspraxis* 5 (1929/30): 709–13.
77. "Politik gehört nicht ins Geschäft!," *Verkaufspraxis* 5 (1929/30): 25.
78. "Die guten Warenhausanzeigen," *Verkaufspraxis* 8 (1932/33): 143–45.
79. "Wo liegt die Stärke des kleinen Betriebes?," *Verkaufspraxis* 6 (1930/31): 613–17.
80. Victor Vogt, "Hilf Dir selbst, Einzelhandel!," *Verkaufspraxis* 5 (1929/30): 5–10, here 5.
81. Victor Vogt, "Vom Absolutismus zur Demokratie," *Verkaufspraxis* 5 (1929/30): 197–201, here 198.
82. Walter Friedrich, "'Freiwillige' Kettenläden-Organisation," *Verkaufspraxis* 6 (1930/31): 374–75; Victor Vogt, "Diese Erkenntnis fehlt dem Zwischenhandel!," *Verkaufspraxis* 7 (1931/32): 323–26; Fritz Kiesler, "Konkurrenten können zusammenarbeiten!," *Verkaufspraxis* 7 (1931/32): 583–86; and "Bilden sich Interessengemeinschaften?," *Verkaufspraxis* 8 (1932/33): 175–77. The U.S. situation was analyzed by Spellman, *Cornering the Market*, 117–36.
83. Fr. v. Hüllesheim, "Vom Persönlichen," *Bausteine* 2 (1930/31): 447–48, here 447.
84. Victor Vogt, "Das blecherne Zeitalter," *Verkaufspraxis* 6 (1930/31), 325–29, here 328.
85. An exception was Pauschek, "Die Kehrseite der Medaille," *Verkaufspraxis* 7 (1931/32): 347–49, which argued in favour of a general consumer perspective to overcome the crisis.
86. Victor Vogt, "Der unbekannte Wirtschafts-Soldat," *Verkaufspraxis* 7 (1931/32): 579–82, here 580. Similar Victor Vogt, "Wann wird das Geschäft wieder besser?," *Verkaufspraxis* 7 (1931/32): 515–18.
87. Victor Vogt, "Gesundung," *Verkaufspraxis* 6 (1930/31): 389–93.
88. Victor Vogt, "Kaufleute, wahrt Eure heiligsten Güter!," *Verkaufspraxis* 7 (1931/32): 643–47, esp. 646; and Werner Arendt, "Propaganda-Autarkie?," *Verkaufspraxis* 7 (1931/32): 693–94.
89. Victor Vogt, "'Produktionsmittel'?—'Konsumgüter'??," *Verkaufspraxis* 7 (1931/32): 5–8, esp. 5.

90. Victor Vogt, "Gestern noch auf stolzen Rossen … ," *Verkaufspraxis* 5 (1929/30): 69–73. See Annika Klein, *Korruption und Korruptionsskandale in der Weimarer Republik* (Göttingen, 2014), esp. sec. 3.
91. Victor Vogt, "Unser Wunschzettel für Weihnachten," *Verkaufspraxis* 7 (1931/32): 131–34, here 131.
92. Victor Vogt, "Vom kommenden Kaufmanns-Denken," *Der Materialist* 53, no. 11/12 (1932): 6–7, here 6.
93. "Der Kunde von heute," *Verkaufspraxis* 6 (1930/32): 94–95.
94. Although with some distance, practitioners and academics in the fields of business studies supported National Socialism with only few exceptions. See Peter Mantel, *Betriebswirtschaftslehre und Nationalsozialismus: Eine institutionen- und personengeschichtliche Studie* (Wiesbaden, 2009); Peter Mantel, "'Eine vollkommen unpolitische Disziplin': Zur Entwicklung der modernen Betriebswirtschaftslehre im ersten Halbjahr ihres Bestehens," *Die Hochschule* 19 (2010): 148–64.
95. Victor Vogt, "Die Wiedergeburt des 'ollen, ehrlichen' Kaufmanns," *Verkaufspraxis* 8 (1932/33): 387–90, here 387.
96. "Staat—Gesetz—Geschäft," *Verkaufspraxis* 9 (1933/34): 369–71.
97. The debate on the position of entrepreneurs in Nazi Germany is still going on. See Peter Hayes, "Corporate Freedom of Action in Nazi Germany," and Christoph Buchheim and Jonas Scherner, "Corporate Freedom of Action in Nazi Germany: A Response to Peter Hayes," *Bulletin of the German Historical Institute* 45 (2009): 29–41 and 43–50, respectively.
98. Despite the economic exclusion of Jewish Germans, a piece entitled "Fight Prejudices" appeared as late as 1939; see "Vorurteile bekämpfen!," *Verkaufspraxis* 14 (1939): 458.
99. "Gute amerikanische Weihnachtswerbung," *Verkaufspraxis* 14 (1939): 96–97; and "Verbesserungen gut gezeigt," *Verkaufspraxis* 14 (1939): 416.
100. The following points are based on Uwe Spiekermann, "From Neighbour to Consumer: The Transformation of Retailer-Consumer Relationships in Twentieth-Century Germany," in *The Making of the Consumer: Knowledge, Power and Identity in the Modern World*, ed. Frank Trentmann (Oxford, UK, 2006), 147–74. For a broader perspective, see Martina Steber and Bernhard Gotto, eds., *Visions of Community in Nazi Germany: Social Engineering and Private Lives* (Oxford, UK, 2015).
101. Victor Vogt, "Leben und leben lassen!," *Verkaufspraxis* 14 (1939): 283–87.
102. This included limits to the growth of individual firms and to the switching of employment; see Victor Vogt, "Die Geschichte vom Hund und seinem Knochen," *Verkaufspraxis* 14 (1939): 353–57.
103. Victor Vogt, "Concerto grosso," *Verkaufspraxis* 14 (1939): 139–43, here 142–43.
104. Victor Vogt, "Sieg des Gemeinschaftsgedankens," *Verkaufspraxis* 15 (1940): 107–10.
105. "Werbung! Der Regulator des Betriebes, nicht der Umsatzmotor," *Verkaufspraxis* 14 (1939): 75–77.
106. Vogt, *Der neue Artikel*, 16.
107. "Was muß der Kunde lernen, damit er den vollen Nutzen der gekauften Ware hat?," *Verkaufspraxis* 15 (1940): 345–46.

108. "Kundenerziehung tut not!," *Verkaufspraxis* 16 (1941): 53–55; and "Selbstzucht!," *Verkaufspraxis* 16 (1941): 73–76.
109. Victor Vogt, "Die Entthronung des Käufers," *Verkaufspraxis* 14 (1939): 495–99, here 496.
110. "Alle sind Wettbewerber!," *Verkaufspraxis* 14 (1939): 251–53, here 252. The German "völkisch" is the adjectival form of "Volk," but its meaning does not oscillate in the same way. See note 71 above.
111. This included "peace" between worker and employer as the foundation of further rationalization; see Victor Vogt, "Concerto grosso," *Verkaufspraxis* 14 (1939): 139–43.
112. Victor Vogt, "Leben und leben lassen!," *Verkaufspraxis* 14 (1939): 283–87, here 285.
113. Victor Vogt, "Freiheit, die ich meine," *Verkaufspraxis* 15 (1940): 5–8, here 8.
114. For the general debate on Nazi morality, see Claudia Koonz, *The Nazi Conscience* (Cambridge, UK, 2003); Wolfgang Bialas, *Moralische Ordnungen des Nationalsozialismus* (Göttingen, 2014); and Wolfgang Bialas and Lothar Fritze, eds., *Nazi Ideology and Ethics* (Newcastle, 2014), esp. Chap. by Bialas, "Nazi Ethics and Morality ...".
115. "Wo stehen wir? Was gibt uns die Zukunft zu tun auf?," *Verkaufspraxis* 14 (1939): 23–27.
116. Victor Vogt, "Bauskizzen der Friedenswirtschaft," *Verkaufspraxis* 17 (1942): 3–6, here 6. The mixed system of state intervention and private initiative was praised as a key element of Germany's economic success; see Victor Vogt, "Das Geheimnis der Mischung," *Verkaufspraxis* 17 (1942): 37–40.
117. Victor Vogt, "Um das Los des 'kleinen Mannes'," *Verkaufspraxis* 14 (1939): 69–73, here 69–70; and Victor Vogt, "Die Entthronung des Käufers," *Verkaufspraxis* 14 (1939): 495–99, here 498–99.
118. Victor Vogt, "Die Sendung," *Verkaufspraxis* 16 (1941): 369–72.
119. Victor Vogt, "Haltung," *Verkaufspraxis* 16 (1941): 403–6; and "Es kommt auch 'mal wieder anders," *Verkaufspraxis* 15 (1940): 72–75.
120. Victor Vogt, "Müßiggang ist aller Laster Anfang!," *Verkaufspraxis* 14 (1939): 605–8; and Victor Vogt, "Freiheit, die ich meine," *Verkaufspraxis* 15 (1940): 5–8.
121. "Was würde Knigge dazu gesagt haben," *Verkaufspraxis* 14 (1939): 641–43.
122. Victor Vogt, "Die Neue Linie," *Verkaufspraxis* 15 (1941): 145–48.
123. Victor Vogt, "Führungsaufgabe der Zukunft," *Verkaufspraxis* 16 (1941): 297–300. See (not only for the murderous consequences) Isabel Heinemann, *Rasse, Siedlung, deutsches Blut. Das Rasse- und Siedlungshauptamt der SS und die rassenpolitische Neuordnung Europas* (Berlin, 2003); and Thomas Müller, *Imaginierter Westen. Das Konzept des 'deutschen Westraums' zwischen politischer Romantik und Nationalsozialismus* (Bielefeld, 2009).
124. See Tim Schanetzky, *"Kanonen statt Butter": Wirtschaft und Konsum im Dritten Reich* (Munich, 2015), although it ignores relevant Anglo-Saxon historiography and underestimates the ideological dimension of National Socialist consumption.
125. See S. Jonathan Wiesen, *Creating the Nazi Marketplace: Commerce and Consumption in the Third Reich* (Cambridge, UK, 2011), esp. 24–41, although

it underestimates the significant prehistory of these visions of consumption, which were already discussed before World War I.

126. Biographical details: Nachlass Friedrich Seitz, Landesarchiv Baden-Württemberg, Abt. Hauptstaatsarchiv Stuttgart, Q 2/30, https://www.deutsche-digitale-bibliothek.de/item/HS7RAR5P7GP4AGTYXBZNSGWOEJI4WFFA.
127. Joachim Scholtyseck, *Robert Bosch und der liberale Widerstand gegen Hitler 1933–1945* (Munich, 1999), 340 and 353.
128. [Julius Hans] Forkel, Victor Vogt and F[ritz] Seitz, "Was zur 'neuen Verkaufs-Praxis zu sagen ist," *Verkaufs-Praxis* 24 (1949/50): 3–4.
129. Bernd Boll, "Zwangsarbeiter während des Zweiten Weltkriegs in Baden," *Zeitschrift des Breisgau-Geschichtsvereins 'Schau-ins-Land'* 111 (1992): 179–203, here 181. Vogt mentioned the general change: "The present situation already shows that foreigners at a lower cultural level can be used for this purpose. Their achievements are generally good, although their use in large numbers may not seem very desirable for racial reasons" (Victor Vogt, "Probleme des Nachwuchses," *Verkaufspraxis* 17 [1942]: 207–10, here 208).
130. Gerd R. Ueberschär, *Freiburg im Luftkrieg 1939–1945* (Würzburg, 1990), 201.
131. Ulrich P. Ecker, *Freiburg 1944–1994. Zerstörung und Wiederaufbau* (Waldkirch, 1994), 31.
132. Norbert Frei, *Vergangenheitspolitik. Die Anfänge der Bundesrepublik und die NS-Vergangenheit* (Munich, 1996).
133. *VP-Auswahl: Die besten Aufsätze aus früheren Jahrgängen der Stuttgarter Verkaufspraxis, Zeitschrift für die Verkaufs-, Absatz- und Geschäftsförderung in Fabriken, im Groß- und im Einzelhandel*, comp. Fritz Seitz, 2 vols. (Stuttgart, 1949). This edition included only articles from the journal's early years. In October 1949, Forkel also launched *VP-Briefe: Monatsblätter zur Verkaufs-Praxis*, a journal specialized in the professional needs of sales agents.
134. *VP-Auswahl*, 1: 3.
135. Gustav Adolf Bischoff, "Ratio auf dem Marsch. Ein Gespräch über den Beispiel-Laden der Fachgruppe Lebens- und Genußmittel," *Verkaufspraxis* 17 (1942): 125–29.
136. "Gepaarte Anzeigen wieder beliebt," *VP-Auswahl* 1: 25–31; "Durch farbige Anzeigen Textilien verkaufen? Von neuartigen amerikanischen Vertriebsmethoden," *VP-Auswahl* 1: 52–57; Fritz Wiedemann, "Warum nicht Bequemlichkeit und Entspannung verkaufen?," *VP-Auswahl* 2: 107–10; "Der Weihnachtsmann als Verkaufshelfer," *VP-Auswahl* 2: 164–68; and "Gefrorener Sonnenschein in Dosen," *Verkaufspraxis* 24 (1949/50): 16–23.
137. Fritz Wiedemann, "Verkaufs-Psychotechnik," *Verkaufspraxis* 24 (1949/50): 224–26; [Claude C. Hopkins], "Vom Erfolg der Pepsodent-Werbung," *Verkaufspraxis* 24 (1949/50): 139–44 (reprint from Hopkins, *Propaganda* [1928]); Fritz Wiedemann, "Charakter und Erfolg," *VP-Briefe* 1, no. 3 (1949/50): 9–13; and Fritz Wiedemann, "Farben helfen verkaufen," *VP-Briefe* 1, no. 6 (1949/50): 13–16.
138. Victor Vogt, "Bauskizzen der Friedenswirtschaft," *Verkaufspraxis* 17 (1942): 3–6, here 3.
139. W. Haas, "Werbung in Frankreich," *Verkaufspraxis* 17 (1942): 7–16; and "Ein französischer Kalender für deutsche Soldaten," *Verkaufspraxis* 17 (1942): 45–49.

140. Victor Vogt, "Absatzplanung in der Neuordnung," *Verkaufspraxis* 17 (1942): 327–30, 365–68. See Richard Evans, *The Third Reich at War, 1939–1945* (New York, 2008), esp. 321–402; and Mark Mazower, *Hitler's Empire: How the Nazis Ruled Europe* (New York, 2008), esp. 553–75.
141. "Die Stimme seines Herrn," *Verkaufspraxis* 24 (1949/50): 41–45; and "Gegen die hutlose Mode," *Verkaufspraxis* 24 (1949/50): 88–93.
142. Carl Graeser, "Die Bedeutung des Verbrauchers für die Wirtschaft," *VP-Briefe* 1, no. 2 (1949/50): 11–14.
143. "Nach 20 Jahren: Wandlungen von Marken-Anzeigen in amerikanischen Frauen-Zeitschriften," *VP-Auswahl* 1: 73–78.

PART III

Consumer Engineering Practices in Postwar Europe

CHAPTER 8

Consumer Credit as a Marketing Tool: The French Experience in European and Transatlantic Comparison, 1950s–1960s

Sabine Effosse

A 1958 brochure aimed at shop owners in the Cetelem consumer credit network advised, "never make two sales, i.e., the sale of the appliance and the sale of the credit package; make just one sale, i.e., the sale of the appliance on credit."[1] If buying new durable consumer goods on credit (vacuum cleaners, washing machines, fridges, and so on) does not sound unusual in advanced consumer societies of the early twenty-first century, Cetelem's sales advice was by no means self-evident in mid-twenty-first-century France, a country that was in large parts still very rural even by the mid-1960s.

Saving was emphasized, not taking out consumer loans to satisfy mere wants and desires.[2] According to the saying, "a rich man pays his debts," consumer credit was perceived as an emergency loan and was primarily used for food (putting something on one's tab at the local grocer) or essential textiles (clothing and household linen) by the working classes. In this context, convincing a broader section of the French public to buy on credit so as to enjoy modern comforts without delay posed a significant challenge to marketing experts in postwar France. For them, what we are calling "consumer engineering" in this book meant first of all creating "modern" shoppers uninhibited by any conservative resistance to incurring debts for non-emergencies.[3]

S. Effosse (✉)
Department of History, University of Paris Nanterre, Nanterre, France

J. Logemann et al. (eds.), *Consumer Engineering, 1920s–1970s*,
Worlds of Consumption, https://doi.org/10.1007/978-3-030-14564-4_8

Three groups of social actors sought to meet this challenge in postwar France. First, there were manufacturers who understood that they needed to sell more to increase production and profits. Seeking to increase consumer demand with credit, they teamed up with commercial banks to set up new institutions that specialized in consumer finance—our second group of actors. Among these, Cetelem, founded in 1953, stood out as particularly successful. Postwar France presented an unusual case in consumer credit because of its legislation on banking, which had been nationalized in December 1945. Whereas new consumer credit options were made available to consumers in neighboring countries in the postwar era via pre-existing networks, for example, finance houses in the United Kingdom and savings banks in Germany,[4] French financial authorities preferred to see dedicated organizations for financing household spending set up that had no access to public resources. This requirement precluded using the nationalized banks, which left no suitable networks through which to distribute consumer credit.

So Cetelem opted to collaborate with a third group of actors—retailers, usually small family businesses—as part of its commercial strategy to attract customers. Already in contact with consumers, actors in this last group were particularly well placed to identify customers' requirements as well as assess their creditworthiness. In fact, they could offer credit at the point of sale, as was done elsewhere in Europe.[5] As key participants in the sale of credit, retailers received credit institutions' full attention in terms of both recruitment and sales training. At the beginning of the 1960s, however, retailers saw their role restricted.

Legislative changes affected the profitability of consumer credit institutions and led to strategic repositioning and internal organizational changes—with regard to decisions about the locations of branch offices, for example, and in terms of early steps in the computerization of their processes. The approach centered on a credit application completed at the point of sale was succeeded by one focused on customers' consumer credit track records. This development was made possible by the systematic data collection achieved with early computer systems. Accordingly, financial institutions contacted "good payers," namely people who repaid their loans on time directly. They offered these consumers new products intended to boost their loyalty, such as revolving loans, the origins of which date back to the mid-1960s. This trend became more pronounced after 1969, when France adopted monthly salaries for all, ten years after Germany and Sweden.[6]

But how did French consumers react to the implementation of the consumer credit–focused commercial strategies of the postwar era? Were they won over by credit and thus persuaded to buy more things? To a certain extent, yes. Although the average debt level of French residents remained lower than that of their UK and German counterparts at the end of the 1960s, there is no denying that the creation of new consumer credit institutions in France had altered social practices. From an instrument once looked down on, once used by the working classes to buy food or semi-durable goods, credit had become a commonplace means of enjoying the comforts available in an affluent society. Adopted by the salaried middle classes, it undoubtedly drove many households' first purchases of new durable household goods and automobiles. This evolution highlighted how credit helped change understandings of French domesticity, not to mention customary consumer behavior. With favorable credit terms and retailers trained to put customers at ease, credit marketing paved the way toward more "modern" consumer attitudes. The shift from a culture of austerity and thriftiness to affluence and spending redefined the meaning of credit, a process in which the emerging baby boomer generation and changing gender roles played key roles.

In this chapter, I show how major players in the French consumer goods industry brought French buyers to spend and consume in new ways. How did these automobile and appliance manufacturers succeed in convincing consumers to enjoy new items before paying for them?[7] In the first section, I assess how French industrial companies managed to convince investment banks to set up new lending organizations in the first place, even though the regulatory environment favored production over consumption. I also examine the extent to which increases in consumer purchasing power during the 1950s were fostered by the creation of the new consumer credit companies as well as by their efforts to promote a new way of buying.[8] The emerging working society afforded by full-employment conditions during the postwar economic boom years, or *trente glorieuses*, offered new opportunities to expand the consumer credit market by changing habits in family budget management. Incomes became more regular, more predictable, while the fear of falling into debt faded.

In the second section, I turn to the retailer as intermediary between financial institution and consumer. I show their key role in attracting buyers on credit and examine how potential customers reacted to their sales pitches. This section also considers the tools involved in training shop owners and any sales staff. What roles, for example, did marketing advice books and training seminars play? What kinds of arguments did retailers employ to persuade consumers? Finally, in the third section I focus on strategic developments in the lending industry, as lenders learned to extract value from their customer files at the beginning of the 1960s by directly marketing credit to "good payers" in new "customer loyalty" schemes.

Financing Private Individuals' Consumption as an Opportunity for Growth?

The common impression that household spending was transacted in cash until the twentieth century and in credit thereafter is misleading.[9] In fact, consumer credit has been around a long time in its traditional form. Retailers extended it to increase sales, while customers used it to finance the purchase of consumer goods within the literal meaning of the term, that is, goods intended to be used up or depleted. For ordinary European family budgets, credit was primarily used to purchase foodstuffs (by running a tab at the butcher's, for instance) and then textiles (necessary household linen and items for daughters' dowries), furniture, or even bicycles, as a result of industrialization and gradual increases in living standards.[10]

A new kind of credit emerged alongside this familiar sales-driven kind between the two World Wars. Now came the loans introduced by manufacturers of new semi-durable consumer goods—cars, radios, and gas stoves, for instance—as part of the second wave of industrialization. Following Henry Ford's model in the United States, European automotive manufacturers began to set up "modern" consumer credit subsidiaries in the 1920s, integrating these into systems in which parties outside the credit companies acted as intermediaries between buyers and sellers. In France in 1938, in fact, 25 percent of passenger vehicles, a truly big-ticket item, were sold on credit, prefiguring postwar trends in consumer credit.[11]

Widespread destruction in Continental Europe reinvigorated the need for credit in the wake of World War II. Although consumer credit was available to households in the United Kingdom via finance houses, or in Germany via savings banks, the situation in France was more complicated. Bank lending, which had been nationalized since 1945, was expected to support industrial reconstruction and therefore production. Financing for household needs was virtually non-existent. At the same time, pent-up demand for durable household goods was huge.

Faced with this gap, some industrial companies became involved in setting up new financial organizations in order to expand their market by offering credit to private individuals. After reviewing the situation in the United States, industry leaders were convinced of the importance of this project. However, they needed to obtain the cooperation of French financial authorities in order to enable "safe" consumption spending on credit, that is, spending that did not increase domestic inflation.

"You Need to Sell to Produce": Manufacturers' Lending Initiatives

The crash of 1929 had a profound effect on manufacturers. Even though the goal since the beginning of industrialization had been mechanization and rationalization in order to produce more, the crash revealed the need to have a broad and solvent consumer market in order to sell an increasingly large amount of goods. Credit sales provided one solution to this perceived need.

The issue arose again in similar terms during the reconstruction process immediately after World War II, especially for "new" European industries such as household appliances. In fact, even though there were a large number of American imports, including the *Frigidaire* brand before the war (*frigo* even became a synonym for refrigerator in French), the European industrial boom (embodied in the rise of Electrolux and Arthur Martin, for example) raised the issue of how to sell goods that had become more plentiful but that were still expensive.

In fact, the cost of washing machines and fridges amounted to several months' salary for a French factory worker. Accordingly, despite the success of the *Salon des arts ménagers* (Household Arts Show), which reopened its doors in 1948, the new goods often remained out of reach for young married couples or housewives dreaming of "American kitchens."[12] The issue was not just price but the limited availability of credit offered by manufacturers' subsidiaries or retailers.[13] Because of credit shortages and the priority given to professional capital equipment for bakers, butchers, and the like in France, loans to individuals did not really recover. Only the economic unions, the organizations set up by retailers based on the model adopted by Paris department stores, provided loans of between three and six months to buy textiles (clothing and dowry items) or hardware in certain regions.

The lack of credit to allow households to purchase new durables was increasingly recognized as a core problem. Thus, furniture and household appliance manufacturers had the idea of setting up new organizations that sold credit, in order to create the conditions for a mass market. Seeking institutions that possessed the financial strength required to grant loans on a large scale, the manufacturers turned to banking partners, specifically to two merchant banks that had not been nationalized, Banque Générale Industrielle La Hénin and Union Française de Banques. Accordingly, Sofinco was founded in 1951 as a result of the partnership between the French National Furniture Federation and Banque Générale Industrielle La Hénin. The company, which specialized in financing motor scooters and furniture, experienced a difficult start due to an extremely aggressive marketing policy that encouraged the granting of loans without proper checks on the buyers' creditworthiness. Moving too quickly in hopes of rapid sales expansion, Sofinco's initial lending policy was not sustainable. This was why the second such project in the works, backed by the French Electrical Manufacturers' Association was first subjected to an in-depth review by the partner bank, Union Française de Banques. Viewing the United States as the leading pioneer in consumer credit, Jacques de Fouchier, the bank's managing director, dispatched Boris Méra, its chief executive officer, to observe existing practices there.[14]

"The Wind of Fashion Blows from the West": The U.S. Experience and the Founding of Cetelem

Union Française de Banques demonstrated a great deal of interest in this consumer credit project, which was backed by an association that included large manufacturers (Thomson, Brandt, and Conord) and importers (Frigidaire, Bendix, and Frigeco). Henri Davezac, the association's chairman, intended to "bring happiness to housewives" by developing the sale of household appliances on credit. The idea appealed to Jacques de Fouchier. His bank was looking for new business activities, and the financing of households appeared to be a promising opportunity. However, he asked Boris Méra, his closest colleague, to perform a feasibility study before providing a reply.[15]

Mr. Méra initially focused on Sofinco's experience. He also reviewed the project proposals drawn up by the electrical goods manufacturers Arthur Martin and Frigidaire. Lastly, he spent several weeks on a research trip in New York in October 1952. This trip, which could be compared to the productivity missions that took place immediately after the war, confirmed the attraction of developing sales financed by credit in France. As for the emerging mass retail sector and the Dayton seminars (organized by National Cash Register), which drew a lot of leaders from the French retail industry, the consumer credit experience in the United States, including its promotion by marketers, was seen as a model to follow on the way toward constructing the modern French consumer. Thus, for example, Boris Méra collected advertising documentation from the National Foundation for Consumer Credit that insisted the "wise use" of credit "raises standards of living."[16] The aim in the French case, however, was to adjust French habits, which were still rooted in frugality and rural society.[17]

De Fouchier and Méra took three main ideas from the US experience: the desirability of simplifying processes, especially by eliminating bills of exchange, which had been compulsory in France to that point; the need to have retailers share in the risk inherent in consumer credit; and the speed and profitability gains to be had from mechanizing routine tasks. On the other hand, they had to find a different solution to recovering the costs of loan defaults because French law accorded immediate ownership of items to their purchaser, even those bought on credit, meaning repossession was not possible, unlike in the United States, the United Kingdom, or Germany. The workaround they chose was to combine each consumer loan with an insurance policy that guaranteed repayment in the event that the borrower defaulted due to illness, invalidity, or death.

The simplicity of the process for granting credit observed in the United States, and its potential for adaptation in France convinced Jacques de Fouchier to agree to the proposal made by the French Electrical Manufacturers' Association. Thus, both partners decided to set up a new lending organization. They still had to obtain the authorization of the French financial authorities, however, in an environment where lending had been nationalized.

Converting French Financial Authorities: Supporting Growth and Combating Overpriced Loans

French financial authorities viewed consumer credit with suspicion because it was associated with several perceived ills. The biggest concern was inflation, a recurring problem for the French economy, but consumer credit also stood accused of enabling the purchase of consumer goods through expensive hire-purchase schemes as well as propping up high retail prices. Accordingly, except when used to purchase cars, which were seen more as a productive asset used primarily by self-employed professionals (doctors, notaries, etc.), French financial authorities considered consumer credit illegitimate. They saw consumer credit as a marketing device for the automotive sector only and consequently refused to register any new institutions that might conduct such business.[18]

This entrenched position changed with the improvement of the country's economic situation, however. Since adopting the minister of finance Antoine Pinay's policies in 1952, France had succeeded in stabilizing inflation, permitting the idea of reinvigorating economic activity with lending to emerge. Robert Buron, the minister for economic affairs, therefore favored reinvigorating growth not only via lending to support the manufacture of export goods and the development of housing, both already considered acceptable uses of credit, but also via consumer loans, a novel concept at the time.

Before encouraging the development of consumer credit, however, such credit needed to be regulated in order to prevent abuses, especially in terms of interest rates. Rules to promote "economically sound and socially acceptable credit" were adopted in July 1954. In particular, interest rates were to be published and related statistics gathered for the financial authorities; the amounts and terms of loans were limited in accordance with the goods financed; a minimum equity capital requirement was set for the lending institutions, as was the minimum ratio of shareholder equity to outstanding consumer debt.[19]

One important limitation of the measure was the lack of any cap on interest rates, in contrast to the UK Money Lenders Act of 1927. Only the obligation to display rates was mandated, and that was to encourage competition. To combat usury, financial authorities preferred to exert influence on the size of the lenders, encouraging the creation of "large" entities like Sofinco or Cetelem, which were undoubtedly easier for Banque de France to monitor via shareholder equity and minimum equity capital rules. The regulation also determined which kinds of goods would likely be financed by credit. Although there was no comprehensive list, like in the United Kingdom, the aim was to sell "useful and durable goods" on credit. The term and the cash payment varied depending on whether the goods were considered a priority for the French economy, as major household appliances and cars were.

The question of consumer goods' utility and durability raised the issue of consumption and living standards. The production and consumption of important new consumer goods complemented French home-building policy, which emerged very late in France relative to Germany and was meant to help modernize family life. This situation in France during the postwar boom years resembled that in the United States during the 1930s and in Germany in the wake of World War II. The strong link between home-building policy and the emerging consumer credit market emphasized the role of the latter in modernizing consumers' lifestyles. Making consumer credit available to accompany the new housing coming online reflected how regulators now saw consumer credit as an "investment loan" for improving living standards.

Taking terms that had been used for production and transposing them to households, French authorities promoted consumer credit as "a loan for personal" and "household appliances" that was likely to encourage "the rational fitting out of the home." Against the tense political and social backdrop of 1953–54, consumer credit was presented as a means of improving living conditions. It would supposedly lighten housewives' workloads, too. Freed from domestic tasks by the refrigerator, the washing machine, and the vacuum cleaner, French women could become "queens, like American women," and focus on raising their children. The "new" regulated consumer credit was presented as a means to modernization (80 percent of French homes had no bathroom in 1954) and to the establishment of social harmony. Credit, synonymous with poverty to that point, would now facilitate the purchase of goods linked to comfort and well-being: domestic appliances. In this way, consumer loans appeared explicitly as tools to influence household spending behavior and to engineer, so to speak, a modern consumer experience.

This is exactly what Sofinco and Cetelem, the two financial institutions resulting from the partnership between merchant banks and manufacturers, were supposed to be. Cetelem, founded in 1953, was the first institution authorized to conduct its lending business. By displaying loan rates 25 percent lower on average than those on the market, it intended to promote the "happiness of housewives." Although Cetelem was favored by the regulation and benefited from significant industrial and banking support, however, it was not entering an untouched market. Its first goal, therefore, was to set up a network of shops "accredited" by Cetelem, inasmuch as credit was an ancillary to sales. In other words, Cetelem's first marketing campaign was conducted in the business-to-business (B2B) sector, to use current terminology.

"You Sell, and We Will Do the Rest": The Role of Shop Owners in the Consumer Credit Boom[20]

As the loan was actually arranged at the point of sale at that time, the real customers of credit institutions were not private individuals but shop owners. In direct contact with buyers and materially associated with any potential gains or losses incurred through a credit sale, retailers played two key roles: They promoted purchases on credit to potential buyers, and they helped ensure the successful repayment of loans to the lender through the quality of the information they obtained from potential borrowers in the first place, not to mention the accuracy of their own impressions of these customers. The important dual role of retailers, already observed by Méra in the United States, made recruiting and training shop owners a major issue for any new credit institution.[21] Next came the question of how well retailers got through to their customers and with what pitches. To what extent did customers accept or reject offers to purchase on credit?

"A Good Seller Grants Sound Loans": Recruiting and Training Shop Owners

When it launched its business, Cetelem's goal was to finance 30,000 loan applications per year, at which point its operations would become profitable.

Achieving this aim first meant going directly to the retailers to convince them to offer Cetelem loans to their customers. To this end, the institution set up a "group of commercial inspectors," who were assisted by the experience of Cetelem's industrial shareholders (especially Arthur Martin). For the manufacturers involved in the foundation of Cetelem, the idea was actually to refocus on their core business of producing goods and to leave the marketing process to retailers, to the benefit of the new credit institution.

When the inspectors went out to meet the retailers, they found two characteristic features of the market. First was the broad diversity of the commercial sector that helped supply the French with household appliances; it included electrical installation companies, hardware stores, wholesalers, branch outlets, and more. Second, credit sales were already common practice. According to market research on credit for household appliances carried out in late 1955, around 80 percent of the retailers surveyed sold goods on credit, usually for a term equal to or shorter than one year.[22] These loans were financed either through the retailers' own cash flow (around half of the retailers) or with the assistance of specialized organizations. This information led Cetelem to fine-tune the arguments it proffered retailers to promote its credit products.

Reactions to Cetelem's overtures ranged from indifference to rejection or even indignation. Among retailers who did not extend any credit, the most frequent comment was, "if I offer credit in my store, I am going to attract bad customers and devalue my business image." Some store owners were also shocked by the extensive financial information requested by Cetelem to establish a business relationship.[23] Retailers already affiliated with another credit institution, such as CREG, Radiofiduciaire, or Sofinco, expressed concern about switching to another company. Accordingly, Cetelem's commercial inspectors (read: sales team) put forward several arguments to convince retailers of the benefit of selling on credit and of the quality of Cetelem's service. The first argument, obviously, was that "credit significantly boosts sales." Accordingly, in a brochure entitled "You sell, and we do the rest," Cetelem highlighted the potential for retailers to triple their revenues "at no risk."

In fact, even though the institution required that retailers be associated with the anticipated successful outcome of the loan, the latter no longer needed to draw on their own cash or worry about recovering losses caused by bad loans because Cetelem paid retailers immediately. Cetelem's second argument aimed to reassure shop owners about the lending institution's strength and responsible business methods. As the newest entrant among the new consumer credit institutions, Cetelem needed to establish its legitimacy. As part of this process, Cetelem invited the business owners it approached to visit the institution's head office in Paris, where certain modern services, such as mechanical data processing, were likely to create a favorable impression. Advertising materials, including posters, signs, leaflets, and prospectuses, were also used, following the US model of promoting manufacturers' goods like Frigidaire by the shops.

Cetelem's approach actually paid off. By the end of 1954, it had 2300 accredited correspondents. This accreditation covered the quality of the people selling, the quality of the products they sold, and the quality of the shop's service after the sales. Accordingly, Cetelem, which had been convinced by the US experience, made the satisfaction of its loan customers—the guarantee of timely repayment—the focal point of its development strategy: "What are we selling? A service over and above the appliance."

"Pay for the Comfort of Your Home Little by Little": Customer Responses[24]

Once shop owners had been recruited, they needed to be trained. Such training was important to Cetelem for two reasons. A shop owner had to make potential customers agree to the credit terms on offer as well as assess their repayment capabilities. To "make the credit-based pitch easier," Cetelem drew inspiration from the manufacturers' own credit sales techniques, more specifically the techniques applied by Arthur Martin, Bendix, Frigidaire, and Schneider. Like those companies, Cetelem drew up "practical handbooks for sellers" for its accredited correspondents. The brochure *A few tips for a smooth sale, to try immediately, with no restrictions or embarrassment* insisted on four points: understanding the customer's requirements, potentially directing their desire toward a more expensive appliance, finding out their real objections to credit, and reassuring them by remaining on familiar ground.[25] To succeed, Cetelem reminded salespersons of the watchword, "never make two sales, i.e. the sale of the appliance and the sale of the credit package; make just one sale, i.e. the sale of the appliance on credit." Buying on credit was to become "normalized" in the minds of consumers, something that would become a generally accepted part of appliance purchases.

"Understanding the customer's requirements: [How?] - It's really simple.... If you are selling fruit, explain that it will keep better in a refrigerator; when talking about racing or wrestling, talk about the event that you saw on TV; when talking about furniture, mention how comfortable new armchairs are [for watching TV], and watch the response." To the extent that "there is no question of displaying everything in your store," Cetelem also insisted on the key role played by the prospectus, which would enable shops to raise the customer's awareness. In particular, the salesperson was supposed to suggest that customers return during a "quiet period" to discuss the product. The aim was then to question the customer about the intended use of the appliance that they had their eyes on. This process would enable the salesperson to note the number of children in the family, the family's situation, the customer's qualifications on some occasions, and even the name of their employer. The seller could then present the appropriate appliance. Large families purchased a washing machine more easily, whereas young couples were more likely to purchase a refrigerator. Such conversations would also yield useful information for the loan application.

The promotion of new standards of domestic comfort in face-to-face sales was closely linked with changes in the family and in government family policy. With the baby boom, the French state encouraged mothers to look after children not only for health reasons but also to improve their education level. This changing understanding of the family lay behind the success of salespersons in promoting domestic appliances as a means to free mothers from domestic work in order to focus on training skilled workers and well paid consumers for the future.

Where the choice of products was concerned, the salesperson was meant to stress the benefits of using credit to buy a "high-quality" item, which was supposedly reliable and would therefore be useful. In fact, product ranges were very extensive at the time, which reflected the number of manufacturers. In the case of washing machines, for instance, a so-called heavy-duty washing machine retailed at between 160,000 and 200,000 French francs in January 1955, while a "light-use" machine cost between 70,000 and 80,000 French francs. The idea was to show the customer the benefit of not buying a less reliable machine for cash when they could get a better one "for the same cash price + 12 small monthly installments."[26] In part, this strategy was about "selling more" to consumers, but it was also meant to change consumption habits more generally, getting consumers to think of new consumer goods as long-term household investments.

But what if the customer withdrew or became frightened? "[T]he greatest obstacle remained the price," especially the price of the loan. "The loan is too expensive!" was noted as customers' main objection, the one that sellers had to overcome. To achieve this aim, the salespeople needed to position themselves on ground familiar to the customer.

Reassuring customers included making the use of credit a commonplace. "We all live on credit," like for gas and electricity: "we consume it first, and we pay for it later, but we don't have anything left. In contrast, when we pay for a refrigerator or a washing machine every month, we are consuming, we are paying for it partly with the savings that the appliance enables us to make, and it continues to be useful to us long after the end of the loan."[27] Using references familiar to buyers was highly recommended. A clever salesperson did not talk about interest rates. They presented the rate in the form of a monthly payment and compared it with "a housewife's shopping basket," where possible. "Your customer buys 50 French francs worth of food every week; this is the basis for the monthly installment that you need to suggest to them." Accordingly, in the case of credit offers in rural areas, Cetelem recommended presenting the monthly installments in relation to the price of a single rabbit. Besides the cost of the loan, the other major objection was fear of the future, fear of debt. "What if something happens to me?" In such cases, sellers were supposed to remind the customer that life insurance was attached to every Cetelem loan.

Lastly, where the information requested when opening the loan application was concerned, sellers needed to be prepared to overcome the third objection usually put forward by customers: "Your information requirements are intrusive!" In a country where cash payments were still the ideal, credit had to be used discreetly. Customers were still concerned about any enquiries that could be made with their employer. The salesperson was then supposed to use this opportunity to explain that all the information requested would be used for the proper recovery of the loan, a system that made it possible for customers to benefit from lower rates than Cetelem's competitors offered. The seller also had to remind customers that Cetelem was a bank "and therefore bound by professional confidentiality." Only after the sale had been agreed to would the salesperson fill in the customer's credit purchase application.

Assessing a borrower's creditworthiness, and therefore rejecting that borrower if necessary, was the second aspect in the salesperson's training process. In fact, the successful outcome of the loan was largely dependent on the salesperson: "Your direct contact with the buyers, and your customer knowledge will enable you to assess your customers' solvency and responsible approach better than anyone else; the success of the transactions that we will handle together will largely depend on your judgment and on the information that you will forward to us." The information Cetelem requested about the customer included their job, their monthly income, and their housing situation, in addition to their identity. Generally speaking, having employee status, regardless of whether as an executive, a white-collar worker, or a manual worker, was a major advantage in terms of obtaining a loan. The monthly installments were then set at between 10 and 15 percent of monthly income, both by Cetelem and the other credit institutions.

Cetelem's marketing strategy, which was based on the quality of the salespersons and their service, was a success. The target of financing 30,000 applications in the first year was achieved. Some 100,000 applications were financed in 1954 and 230,000 applications in 1958. By then, Cetelem's sales network included around ten thousand retailers. The main appliances it financed were vacuum cleaners, refrigerators, and washing machines, which together accounted for 87 percent of credit applications, whereas televisions made a small breakthrough of 12 percent.[28]

Cetelem's first few years of existence were therefore a success. The goals set in terms of the number of applications financed were achieved, and the institution ranked second only behind CREG, its historical competitor. Changes in the regulatory environment from 1957, however, and the stagnation of the average loan amount put pressure on Cetelem's financial results. The time had therefore come to adapt to a changing market.

Retaining the Loyalty of "Good Payers": The Customer-Based Approach and Direct Credit as Key Factors in Adapting to the Market

The signing of the Treaty of Rome on March 25, 1957, marked a new stage for the consumer credit market. French industry, and especially the household electrical appliance industry, which was younger than the automotive industry, had to become more competitive in order to deal with its European counterparts, especially its competitors in Germany and Italy. While it undertook internal efforts to modernize, the sector also appealed to state financial authorities for greater flexibility in the terms and conditions of its credit offerings. The authorities, however, firmly intended to demand price reductions in exchange for such concessions, both for the appliances and the loans to finance them. Furthermore, large French banks such as Crédit Lyonnais and Société Générale decided to follow their European counterparts and enter the personal loan market. Faced with change in the regulatory and sales environment, Cetelem refocused its strategy, settling on three areas: increasing the average loan amount in the applications financed, focusing on existing and former customers, and automating the operations that enabled the company to gain a better understanding of its customers as consumers.

The Challenges of Personal Bank Loans and Declining Household Appliance Prices for Financial Institutions

In May 1959, two of the largest nationalized French deposit-taking banks, Crédit Lyonnais and Société Générale, launched a new product for private individuals, "personal loans."[29] This initiative was in keeping with the European framework. In fact, Midland Bank began offering personal loans in 1958, followed by Dutch, German, and Swedish banks. Personal loans represented a small revolution for French banks. Till then these banks had focused on financing the state and companies, only granting overdrafts or advances to private individuals with sufficient property or investment assets to guarantee the loans. Moreover, a flawed interpretation of the causes of the 1929 crash in the United States meant that the banks considered consumer credit a "toxic loan."[30] However, the activities of other European banks in this field, together with the need to find investments that generated returns, drove French banks to invest in the retail market.

Accordingly, Crédit Lyonnais and Société Générale began offering personal loans to finance any exceptional nonprofessional expenses in 1959. These loans were granted for a term of between three months and three years and offered favorable rates, for example, a maximum of 10.6 percent per year in 1959, compared with almost 20 percent to purchase a household electrical appliance with a Cetelem loan.

The differences in rate and term in the products offered by the state-owned banks caused concern among the consumer lenders. They considered the initiative unfair competition and complained to the authorities. In fact, the regulations introduced in 1954 did not permit the banks to offer such personal loans for consumption; however, the authorities did not react for three reasons. First, personal loans were still marginal and accounted for between 4.5 and 9 percent of the consumer loans outstanding between 1959 and 1963. Second, two-thirds of personal loans financed expenditures relating to housing, making personal loans appear primarily complementary to consumer loans, not in competition with them. Finally, the banks new loan offer would encourage competition and likely improve overall credit terms for households.

Faced with these new players in the credit market, the financial institutions had to change their commercial strategy. The consequences of the Common Market increased pressure to do so. The opening of borders and competition from German and Italian products resulted in a fall in the price of consumer goods. Accordingly, fridges sold on average for ten French francs per cubic liter between 1953 and 1955, eight francs per cubic liter in 1961, and five to seven francs per cubic liter in 1963.[31]

The fall in prices of the main goods financed on credit by Cetelem resulted in a decrease in the profitability of its loan applications, to where the amount had become too small to be profitable. Cetelem therefore decided to diversify its business activities and move into the most profitable consumer sector. "Everyone said to themselves: the extraordinary segment is cars," recalled a Cetelem executive. The institution was now determined to penetrate this sector, even though the existing finance offers were broad and long-established. This decision, implemented in 1960, proved delicate. The auto credit market was the preserve of long-established subsidiaries of car manufacturers (DIAC, DIN, and CAVIA) and dedicated banks (SOVAC and COFICA), which together accounted for around 80 percent of car loans.

Accordingly, Cetelem bet on a major innovation to penetrate this highly competitive market: ending the "kick-back" or commission paid to the intermediaries (dealers or garage owners) who brought in the loan applications. Ending this practice made it possible to lower interest rates and offer a major sales argument, especially when directed at a customer base of modest or average means. Besides provoking fierce reaction from established lending institutions, however, this break with existing practice posed the problem of how to penetrate the market without intermediaries. Cetelem then decided to make full use of its experience of financing household appliances by using its customer files—containing over 1.5 million names in 1960—to market car loans directly.

If a commonplace practice today, this idea amounted to a small revolution in the way credit was granted. Although the salesperson had been the customer's sole contact person in terms of their requests for credit until that point, Cetelem made the big leap to direct credit with car loans. As part of the same strategic approach, Cetelem also used all the logistics and financial support of the banking group to which it had been attached since 1959, Compagnie Bancaire. Customers who had a mortgage with this financial group could also see themselves offered a loan to fit out their kitchen, buy a car, or finance new furniture. Cetelem entered this last sector in 1960.

What were the results of this diversification? In the six years between 1959 and 1965, the average amount of each loan increased by 67 percent, while one-third of revenues were now generated by the car sector (18 percent) and the furniture sector (17 percent). However, Cetelem's market share of domestic car loans still only amounted to 4 percent of the financing. Yet this small market share should not hide a major innovation relating to Cetelem's entry into the car loan market where the effect ended up being multiplied by a factor of ten: the systematically use and extraction of value from its customer files. Cetelem broke into the car loan market thanks to its customer files. In fact, a customer's track record had an intrinsic value. It not only enabled the quality of the customer to be assessed, depending on the timeliness of their repayments, but also enabled that customer—as a "good payer"—to be offered a loan that renewed itself as they repaid it. This is how Cetelem established the basis for revolving credit and an even more profound transformation in French consumer purchasing behavior in subsequent decades.

Extracting Value from Customer Files: "Credit in Your Pocket" and Building Customer Loyalty

Cetelem's entry into the car finance market therefore marked a major change for the institution. It processed 300,000 credit applications in 1960, when a customer-based approach was added to the application-based approach. Knowledge of those customers was now considered as an essential commercial and strategic issue. Accordingly, to reward customers who repaid their loans in a timely manner, Cetelem invented the "Good Payer" card in 1961. This card, which was issued as a reward for a responsible approach, enabled a customer who had already repaid a Cetelem loan to be granted another loan "as quickly as possible, with the minimum amount of formalities, and at the lowest possible cost." Customers who were honored in this way considered themselves "special" and Cetelem retained their loyalty. Creditworthiness rather than being free of debt became the marker of the economic integrity for French consumers.

It was specifically the concept of simplifying the granting of a new loan to timely customers that led to the introduction of "a permanent overdraft," or credit reserve. The strategy selected was to offer former customers who had paid off an initial conventional loan a credit reserve that would be topped up as and when they made repayments and that they could use "directly" as they wished. As was the case for many other innovations introduced by Cetelem, this idea came from North America, more specifically from Canada, where an executive at the institution had previously worked.[32]

The major advantage of this new "credit in your pocket" package was that only one file needed to be opened for the same customer, thereby limiting the average review timeframe and administrative costs. Launched in 1965, this package was subsequently successfully developed via partnerships formed with Paris department stores like Galeries Lafayette.

"Credit in your pocket" was not only innovative as a product offering but also reflected a change in the company's relationship with the customer. Whereas salespersons had been the unavoidable intermediaries between the consumer and Cetelem—10,000 correspondents had been accredited by 1963—the institution was now increasingly opting for auto credit and direct access to customers who no longer needed to be sold on the idea of credit. This development was made possible by a change in the company's internal organizational structure, namely the strengthening of its regional operations thanks to the foundation of Compagnie Bancaire, which enabled resource pooling. Consequently, Cetelem had twenty offices in the French provinces, which were connected to seven decentralized branches in 1975, in addition to a stand-alone branch in Paris. This decentralization during the 1960s was primarily supported by increasingly cutting-edge computer equipment.

In fact, when the institution was founded in 1953, its managers took care to mechanize its operations. As specialists in the financing of "small loan applications," which were restricted in terms of refinancing, credit institutions did not have access to public deposits and therefore needed to refinance themselves with partner banks or even Banque de France. This had a cost. The only way to improve profitability lay in cutting overhead. Accordingly, the first computers, two IBM 1401 machines, were installed in 1961, replacing the punch-card entries made with the conventional mechanical data processing techniques of the time.[33] New credit applications were therefore being directly entered into computers by late 1962, and the entire application management process was computerized in 1964. This computerization achieved its dual purpose: big productivity gains (the average number of applications processed per employee increased by 65 percent between 1960 and 1965) and superb knowledge of the customer.

Who Were the "Good Payers"? What Did They Buy on Credit?: From Family Fathers to Young Women from the Salaried Middle Classes

Regarding what the novelist Georges Pérec called the "things," the main goods purchased on credit in France were also the most expensive cars, followed by refrigerators and televisions.[34] However, this triad changed in a decade. Washing machines, fridges, and vacuum cleaners were the goods most often purchased on credit in the 1950s. Increased spending power made cars and televisions the most popular goods in the 1960s, 50 percent of which were bought on credit. Furniture also made a remarkable breakthrough. For many French people whose income was increasing, "comfort became comforting." As homes were built on a massive scale and marriages took place between baby boomers, the amount of furniture purchased on credit grew. Such keenness on furniture and outfitting homes was not specific to France. In West Germany, the use of consumer credit to buy furniture and fabrics for the home also accounted for a significant portion of the loans granted (20% in 1964).[35] This evolution comported with an emerging redefinition of French domesticity, which increasingly focused on improving the "nest," that is, on housing conditions and standards of living.

The profile of the buyers displayed a constant feature; people who purchased on credit were primarily urban employees. But there was also a change, the age of the credit applicant. From the mid-1950s to the mid-1960s, the typical applicant changed from father of a family to newly wed couple. Baby boom children reaching marriageable age from the mid-1960s marked a turning point in behavior where buying on credit was concerned. Baby boomers, who had always known social insurance (introduced in 1945), full employment, and regular salary increases, were no longer scared of credit and did not want to wait in order to enjoy modern comforts.[36] "Why wait to reach the peak of your career, and therefore to be old, in order to enjoy the advantages of this world? I'm relying [*escompter*] on credit thanks to my career."[37] Accordingly, 66 percent of young people took out a loan in the mid-1960s compared to an average of 20 percent among the remainder of the population.

The role played by young wives, and women more generally, in these credit purchases was marked. In fact, women played a dual role in the consumption process: They made purchases for themselves and for the household as a whole. Accordingly, credit institutions systematically emphasized young housewives in their advertising documents and insisted on appliances for the kitchen, which was now located at the center of the home.[38] The "perfect homemaker" wanted "an American kitchen," which meant brand new appliances as seen in magazines and on television. Until February 1966, however, when the reform of the French marriage system went into effect, a married woman could not take out a loan without the permission of her husband. Some financial institutions were aware of this important "new market" and anticipated a change in the law. In fact, Radiofiduciaire, a subsidiary of Philips, created "express credit," repayable in six months, and invited all French women to apply for credit for appliance purchases less than 500 French francs (Fig. 8.1).

At the same time, consumer credit, which had been regulated in 1954, was now primarily used by the middle classes. Although white-collar workers accounted for 8 percent of the French population in 1958, they made 33 percent of household appliance purchases on credit that year, compared with 34 percent for manual workers, who accounted for 29.5 percent of the population. All the surveys carried out by the National Institute of Statistics and Economic Studies confirmed that households who bought goods on credit had an income slightly higher than the average in France—6000–15,000 French francs in 1965 instead of 4000–7000 French francs. Socio-occupational backgrounds also influenced credit use. Employees (white-collar workers, manual workers, and

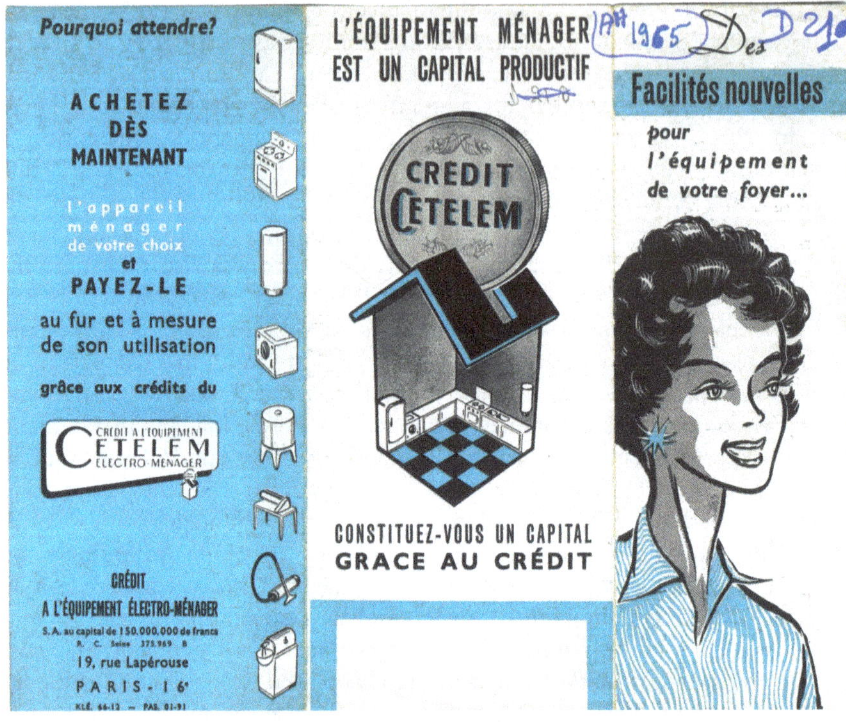

Fig. 8.1 Cetelem advertising leaflet, 1965. The house as piggy bank in the center of this leaflet portrayed consumer credit as an investment dedicated to the modernization of everyday life. The leaflet targeted women in particular, emphasizing how new domestic appliances made housework easier. Source: Archives historiques BNP Paribas Personal Finance—Fonds Cetelem.

middle-ranking executives) comprised the majority of borrowers, whereas the self-employed (farmers, retailers, and tradesmen) were underrepresented.

Regulated consumer credit therefore saw its use expand among the middle classes and the younger generations during the 1950s and 1960s, indicating a broad-based and generational shift in attitudes. Young baby boomer couples, sensitive to material comforts and the "things" described by Georges Pérec, wanted to enjoy the technical advances shown at the *Salon des Arts Ménagers*, for example, without delay. Accordingly, far from having a stigma attached to it, credit became "savings for young people." This change occurred under pressure from industrial companies concerned about expanding their market and accelerating the supply of new consumer goods to French residents via the creation of new financial institutions. If we compare its use in other European countries, however, the development of credit in France remained tightly controlled and restricted. In fact, the average debt per inhabitant was 88 French francs in 1965, compared to 163 francs in West Germany, 212 francs in the United Kingdom, and 1037 francs in the United States.[39]

Lastly, the consumer credit offer in France remained segmented until the liberalization of credit in 1966. Even though most of the financial institutions' customers were manual workers and the middle classes, the beneficiaries of banking loans were mainly executives and self-employed professionals, who were the only ones to have a bank account, a practice still rare in France before the 1969 law regarding the monthly payment of salaries.[40]

Conclusion

To conclude, the French were won over by consumer credit on the basis of three key factors. The first was its "rehabilitation." Once associated with an emergency loan, often with very high interest rates, that was used by the working classes, it became a loan intended for the purchase of semi-durable goods at reasonable rates by the middle classes. This change occurred partly as a result of the private initiatives of manufacturers concerned with broadening their market, merchant banks seeking new opportunities, and government policies seeking to reinvigorate growth through regulated lending. The change in the conditions for distributing credit, due to the arrival of new operators like Cetelem or Sofinco, therefore played an important role.

The second factor involved convincing the French to buy on credit. On that point, the new financial institutions implemented a B2B strategy intended for retailers and salespersons. The sellers got the French "used" to buying on credit in the 1950s. Once they had been trained, their sales pitch relied on their comments (reassuring and making the use of credit commonplace) and on the handbooks provided by financial organizations. The quality of the service, of the item sold, and of the after-sales service was key to this "customer attraction" process. Next, adjusting to changes in the market led these institutions to alter their commercial strategy.

The third factor, the systematic use of the financial institutions' customer files, enabled them to reach consumers directly without having to go through salespersons at the point of sale. This use and extraction of value from borrowers' data, primarily thanks to computing, was essential for broadening the market in the early 1960s from a marketing standpoint. This business-to-customer stage, where credit institutions granted loans directly to consumers, represented a turning point. It was an essential means for increasing the institutions' profitability and boosting their customers' loyalty. For those customers who repaid their loans in the most timely manner, it was also a guarantee of benefiting from the best possible credit conditions and of renewing their loans. This development was all the more remarkable in view of the fact that the need for household appliances was huge when the baby boomers reached marriageable age. For this first generation, which was free of the concerns relating to illness and old age thanks to the introduction of universal social welfare coverage in 1945, the use of regulated credit distributed by credit organizations was no longer perceived as a problem. Credit became the "savings of young people" for those who were keen to enjoy "comfort without delay." Like in Germany in this period, this new generation, whose values had shifted, marked the role of demand in the expanding consumer credit market.[41] It also emphasized how this credit was such an important aspect in the overall consumer engineering scheme: It helped facilitate a whole range of new consumer practices and contributed to fostering "modernizing" consumer lifestyles.

Notes

1. "Quelques trucs pour vendre fluide: A essayer immédiatement, sans contrainte, ni complexe" (brochure for salespeople), 1958, Cetelem archives.
2. Sheldon Garon, *Beyond our Means: Why America Spends While the World Saves?* (Princeton, NJ, 2012).
3. Victoria de Grazia, *Irresistible Empire: America's Advance Through Twentieth-Century Europe* (Cambridge, MA, 2005).
4. Rebecca Belvederesi-Kochs, "Moral or Modern Marketing? Sparkassen and Consumer Credit in West Germany," in *The Development of Consumer Credit in Global Perspective: Business, Regulation, and Culture*, ed. Jan Logemann (New York, 2012), 41–62.
5. Sean O'Connell, *Credit and Community: Working-Class Debt in the UK Since 1880* (Oxford, UK, 2009).
6. Monthly salaries were accompanied by the widespread opening of bank accounts and the option of personal loans based on the "quality" of the customer. See Jeanne Lazarus, *L'épreuve de l'argent: Banques, banquiers, clients* (Paris, 2012).
7. For the archives list, see Sabine Effosse, *Le credit à la consommation en France, 1947–1965: De la stigmatisation à la réglementation* (Paris, 2014), 274–80.
8. See the survey made by the Public Opinion French Institute (IFOP) for the Economic Plan, "Enquête sur les tendances de consommation des salariés urbains. Vousgagnez 20% de plus, qu'enfaites-vous" (Paris, 1955).
9. Jan Logemann and Uwe Spiekermann, "The Myth of a Bygone Cash Economy: Consumer Lending in Germany from the Nineteenth Century to the Mid-Twentieth Century," in *Consommer à crédit en Europe*, ed. Sabine Effosse and Isabelle Gaillard, Special Issue, *Entreprises et Histoire* 59, no. 2 (June 2010): 12–27.
10. For France, see Anaïs Albert, "Working-Class Consumer During the Belle Epoque: Invention, Innovation, or Reconfiguration?" *Annales, Histoire, Sciences Sociales* 67, no. 4 (2012): 731–63.
11. Patrick Fridenson, "French Automobile Marketing, 1890–1979," in *Development of Mass Marketing: The Automobile and Retailing Industries*, ed. Akio Akochi and Koichi Shimokawa (Tokyo, 1981), 127–54.
12. Claire Duchen, "Occupation Housewife: The Domestic Ideal in 1950's France," *French Cultural Studies* 2, no. 4 (1991): 1–11; Claire Leymonerie, "Le Salon des arts ménagers dans les années 1950, théâtre d'une conversion à la consommation de masse," *Consommer en masse*, ed. Sophie Chauveau, Special Issue, *Vingtième Siècle: Revue d'Histoire* 91, no. 3 (2006): 43–56; and Rebecca Pulju, *Women and Mass Consumer Society in Postwar France* (New York, 2011).
13. Gilles Laferté et al., "Le crédit direct des commerçants aux consommateurs: Persistance et dépassement dans le textile à Lens (1920–1970)," *Genèses* 79, no. 2 (2010): 26–47.

14. For the history of consumer credit in the United States, see Louis Hyman, *Debtor Nation: The History of America in Red Ink* (Princeton, NJ, 2011); and Garon, *Beyond our Means.*
15. On the history of Cetelem, see *De la 4 CV à la vidéo. 1953–1983 cestrenteannées qui ontchangénotre vie*, book edited for the 30th anniversary of Cetelem (Paris, 1983); Rosa-Maria Gelpi and François Labruyère (both worked for Cetelem), *The History of Consumer Credit; Doctrines and Practices*, trans. Liam Gavin (New York, 2000; Hélène Ducourant, "Du crédit à la consommation à la consommation de crédits: Autonomisation d'une activité économique," Ph.D. of Sociology, University of Lille 1 (2009); Sabine Effosse, *Le crédit à la consommation en France, 1947–1965: De la stigmatisation à la réglementation* (Paris, 2014); and Gunnar Trumbull, *Consumer Lending in France and America* (New York, 2014).
16. "When you buy your goods, credit wisely used serves you well," advertising poster from the Retailers Credit Bureau in cooperation with the National Foundation for Consumer Credit, 1952, Cetelem Archives.
17. For the German case, see Jan Logemann, "Americanization Through Credit? Consumer Credit in Germany, 1860s–1960s," *Business History Review* 85, no. 3 (2011): 529–50.
18. Sabine Effosse, "French Consumer Credit Policy in the 1950s and 1960s," *Development of Consumer Credit*, ed. Logemann, 183–99.
19. Banque de France Archives, Direction générale du Crédit, box 1331200301/61, box 1331200301/85; and National Credit Council Report, 1955 ("Réglementation du financement des ventes à crédit en date du 28 juillet 1954").
20. Quoted in Effosse, *Le crédit à la consommation*, 129–41.
21. Walter A. Friedman, *Birth of a Salesman: The Transformation of Selling in America* (Cambridge, MA, 2004).
22. Effosse, *Le crédit à la consommation*, 133–35. For Germany: Logemann and Spiekermann, "Myth of a Bygone Cash Economy."
23. Cetelem Archives, inspection report June 9, 1959.
24. Title of a Cetelem poster.
25. Cetelem Archives, Brochure, 1958. For the United Kingdom and the role of doorstep finance agents there, see Liz Mc Fall, *Devising Consumption: Cultural Economies of Insurance, Credit and Spending* (Oxon, 2015), Chap. 3.
26. Cetelem Archives, Brochure, "Quelques trucs pour vendre fluide: A essayer immédiatement sans contrainte ni complexe," 1958.
27. Cetelem Archives, brochure used by Frigidaire, 1959.
28. Cetelem Archives, Annual Report, 1959.
29. Sabine Effosse, *Le crédit à la consommation*, 175–85.
30. Martha Olney, "Avoiding Default: The Role of Credit in the Consumption Collapse of 1930," *The Quarterly Journal of Economics* 114, no. 1 (February 1999): 319–35.
31. Cetelem Archives, Brochure L'Officiel du froid, VIe Journées internationales d'études du Salon des Arts ménagers 35, no. 157 (May 1966).
32. Hélène Ducourant, "Du crédit à la consommation à la consommation de crédits. Autonomisation d'une activité économique" (Ph.D. diss., University of Lille 1, 2009).

33. Bernardo Batiz-Lazo, Juan Carles Maixe-Altes, and Paul Thomes, eds., *Technological Innovation in Retail Finance: International Historical Perspectives* (London, 2011); and Pierre Mounier-Kuhn, *Mémoires vives: 50 ans d'informatique chez BNP Paribas* (Paris, 2013).
34. Georges Pérec, *Les Choses: Une histoire des années 1960* (Paris, 1965).
35. Banque de France Archives, National Credit Council, box 1427200301/312 and 313, "Crédit à la consommation en Allemagne, 1950–1969."
36. Gunnar Trumbull, *Consumer Lending in France and America: Credit and Welfare* (New York, 2014).
37. Henri Durand, *L'abondance à credit* (Paris, 1966), 91.
38. On French women and consumption, see Marie-Emmanuelle Chessel, *Histoire de la consommation* (Paris, 2012). For regarding the Swedish case, see Orsi Husz, "Golden Everyday: Housewifely Consumerism and the Domestication of Banks in 1960s Sweden," *Le Mouvement social* 250 (January–March 2015): 41–63.
39. National Credit Council, Annual Report, 1965.
40. Eighteen percent of French households had a bank account in 1966; see Jeanne Lazarus, *L'épreuve de l'argent: Banques, banquiers, clients* (Paris, 2012), 21–28.
41. Detlef Siegfried, *Time is on My Side: Konsum und Politik in der westdeutschen Jugendkultur der 60er Jahre* (Göttingen, 2006).

CHAPTER 9

Adidas and the Creation of a Transnational Market for German Athletic Shoes, 1948–1978

Thomas Turner

Adolf Dassler, a forty-eight-year-old shoemaker and entrepreneur, established an eponymous specialist athletic shoe factory in Herzogenaurach, a small town in Franconia, in 1948.[1] Situated close to the town's railway, the company had fifty employees. From these relatively modest beginnings, this medium-sized, independently owned business, typical in Germany, experienced phenomenal growth over the next three decades. By the early 1970s, Dassler's business was successful on a global scale. It owned factories in Germany, France, Canada, and Austria. Working with suppliers in Yugoslavia, Australia, Argentina, and Taiwan, it produced 35,000 pairs of shoes a day for sale in 120 countries to the world's sporting elites as well as countless amateur or recreational athletes.[2] By the time of its founder's death in 1978, the firm was selling a vast range of athletic shoes, clothing, and equipment. Indeed, it dominated the international sporting goods markets. If Dassler never became a household name, the brand name of his products, Adidas, certainly did.

Registered in 1949, Adidas is today one of the most recognized brands on the planet, among only a handful of truly global names.[3] Yet overfamiliarity with its branded wares perhaps obscures the remarkable nature of its history. In three decades, a small firm set up by a middle-aged German entrepreneur to supply a niche market grew beyond all expectations into an internationally significant player, the leader by some margin in athletic shoes and a major player in other kinds of sporting goods. Not surprisingly, Adidas's story shows how it used carefully tailored products and marketing efforts to

T. Turner (✉)
Independent Historian, London, UK

J. Logemann et al. (eds.), *Consumer Engineering, 1920s–1970s*,
Worlds of Consumption, https://doi.org/10.1007/978-3-030-14564-4_9

appeal to specific consumer groups, but there was more. Adidas's history also reveals the extent to which shifts in consumption were driven by more general attempts at social engineering in the postwar period. The firm's business was built on its reputation for product innovation, yet the extent to which its accelerating product cycle and broadening range embodied postwar fast capitalism and notions of planned obsolescence (see Chapter 3) is open to question. Moreover, if we accept that consumption is linked to the human desire to engage in social practices, we must consider how shifts in practice stimulated and created markets, and identify the forces and agents that lay behind the social and cultural changes driving consumption. Adidas was, after all, a manufacturer of a niche product that went mainstream. What changed to make that happen, and what caused that change? The firm's rise in the three decades after World War II was by no means inevitable. To understand how and why it occurred means considering how Adidas encouraged the consumption of its products, especially as it moved beyond domestic markets. It also requires examining how Adidas fit within a wider context of postwar change and social engineering.

The Founding of Adidas

By 1948, Dassler was already a veteran of the German shoe industry. He entered the trade after World War I, when he established a small shoemaking business in Herzogenaurach and began crafting athletic shoes in his spare time. These experimental shoes were well received, and in 1924 he formed a partnership with his older brother Rudolf to make and sell footwear to the sports clubs and federations then springing up across Germany. Their firm, Sportschuhfabrik Gebrüder Dassler, grew steadily during the interwar period. After the Nazis came to power in 1933, it supplied sports shoes to the expanding Wehrmacht and benefitted from the regime's emphasis on school and company sport and other forms of physical exercise. By 1936, it was one of Germany's biggest manufacturers of athletic footwear, making shoes for eleven sports. Many athletes at the Berlin Olympics, including Jesse Owens, wore its products; and annual revenues reached 480,000 RM. The firm expanded into a second factory in Herzogenaurach in 1939, but the war disrupted production and brought the company's string of successes to an end.[4] Production resumed in 1945 after Herzogenaurach surrendered to American troops; some of the first postwar products were training shoes made from recycled military tent canvas for GIs stationed nearby.[5] The war, however, exacerbated differences between the brothers. By 1948, long-standing animosity finally resulted in the dissolution of their partnership, with employees asked to choose who to work for. The bulk of the sales and promotional staff stayed with the elder Rudolf, the rambunctious salesman, whereas the technical staff opted for Adolf, the quiet shoemaker.[6] In one factory, on one side of the Aurach river, Rudolf formed the business that became Puma.

In the other, on the opposite side, Adolf set about building Adidas. Thereafter, the brothers' rivalry was channeled into business.

Adolf Dassler brought an athlete's sensibility to shoemaking, constantly pushing for improvement. He enjoyed a variety of athletic pursuits throughout his life. Already as a young man, he was driven by the shortcomings of existing sports footwear to make shoes for himself and his friends. He aimed to cater directly to the needs and desires of athletes and was obsessive in the pursuit of incremental changes that could assist athletic performance. This focus led to constant and systematic experimentation with materials, designs, and production methods. It also meant rudimentary market research in the form of continual discussions with the athletes of various disciplines who wore his shoes. A *Sports Illustrated* reporter described him in 1969 as in love with shoes, "quick-witted but rather shy, more gratified by the entries he makes in the idea book he keeps on his nightstand than by the figures in the company ledger."[7] His constant tinkering, enthusiasm for sport, and technical ingenuity ensured that the firm created products tailored to the needs and tastes of its primary consumers. This approach underpinned the company's success after 1948.

As the firm's patriarch, Adolf Dassler defined Adidas's strategy and shaped its corporate culture. His philosophy and beliefs formed the pillars of the firm's approach to business and its appeal to consumers. Marketing material addressed to retailers of Adidas products stressed that Adidas was dedicated to producing the best footwear for sports, and that it would innovate constantly to achieve this goal. The firm's guiding principle of "The Best for Athletes" was outlined in one of the first Adidas catalogs, printed in summer 1949. In an introductory note, Dassler promised that constant cooperation with the heads of German athletics and the three-time Olympic coach Josef Waitzer (later head of the Bavarian Athletic Federation) would ensure that Adidas shoes always remained up-to-date and that, despite postwar difficulties in obtaining special leathers, they would always be the best athletic shoe available. Photographs of him helping competitors with their shoes at a track and field event indicated his involvement with active sportsmen and sportswomen. "As a sports shoe manufacturer" he wrote, "I consider it particularly important to maintain continuous contact with athletes. The lessons learnt from them indicate the direction of my work." Praise from German athletes and soccer players was included as testimony that he was, indeed, "on the right path." That almost all top German athletes in 1948 wore Adidas footwear was cited as proof of its superiority.[8]

In 1950, Adidas noted that in over thirty years' of "tireless work" the firm's shoes had been "continuously improved and a great many patents and design protections registered." Dassler's determination to craft footwear better to the needs of athletes necessitated a highly specialized product range. The 1950 catalog listed twenty-seven models: seven soccer boots, two track and field spikes, two handball shoes, five ice skates, shoes for field hockey, boxing, wrestling, cycling, fencing, basketball, and tennis, and four shoes intended to be worn during training. All models were positioned in terms of their functionality, designed to enable better sporting performance.[9] Subsequent marketing materials made a virtue of innovation and positioned Adidas in the vanguard of technological progress. As individual models were changed or replaced, the exclamation "New!" peppered catalogs. The celebration of novelty was not confined to the company's products. In 1961, the catalog showed the "functional structure with bright, clean work spaces and modern machinery" at the firm's factory in Scheinfeld, Bavaria, while stylized line drawings in later publications illustrated the unadorned, modern architecture of the firm's German and French factories.[10] Sketches of the company's sites of production signified progress, technology, and resources.[11] As Bernhard Rieger has shown for an earlier period, public relations and marketing that linked science and technology spoke directly to public enthusiasm for innovation and so invested Adidas products with prestige.[12]

The rapidly changing Adidas range encouraged consumption, especially among athletes keen to exploit any small benefit in their pursuit of sporting glory. Adidas's evolving offerings should not, however, be considered simply as an exercise in styling akin to that developed by Harley Earl at General Motors nor as an extension of the fashion-oriented clothing industry. There was more to Dassler's approach than empty marketing or consumer temptation. Experimentation and consultation resulted in real changes and tangible benefits for athletic consumers. In the 1950s, Adidas shoes incorporated fine and lightweight leathers, soft crepe rubber or foam soles, patented heel stiffeners, ventilated uppers, and seams designed to reduce chafing. The firm embraced German technological and industrial expertise, most obviously in its approach to materials and production. German chemical firms had led the world since the nineteenth century and in the 1940s pioneered the production of synthetic rubber and oil-based plastics.[13] As the historian John Lesch has argued, the recovery and renewed prosperity of the chemical industry was a major component of West German postwar economic revival.[14] Adidas applied this expertise to sports footwear, using compounds and materials created by German and Austrian chemical and rubber firms in its shoes. The firm was also an early adopter of manufacturing techniques that transformed the footwear industry, particularly soles attached with adhesives and, later, fully molded sole units. Soccer boots with molded rubber soles were introduced in the late 1950s, and in 1962 the firm launched a range of "6V" training shoes with plastic sole units attached in a new fully automated process. The bespoke machinery, which was pictured in the firm's catalog, was described as "the most modern and progressive machine on the market."[15] *Sports Illustrated* wrote of a "streamlined" operation, with computerized records and specially designed $100,000 machines that soled thirty shoes at a time.[16]

Through relentless product innovation, high-quality manufacturing, and sensitivity to athletes' requirements, Dassler built a successful business.

The firm's connection to the elite, however, was cultivated as much through personal contacts and clever marketing as it was through product excellence. Athletes were welcomed warmly at Herzogenaurach, and many top performers were given free shoes. John Disley, a British bronze medalist at the 1952 Helsinki Olympics, recalled being surprised to receive a pair of Adidas shoes, in his size, compliments of Adolf Dassler, after his victory.[17] This approach, together with the shoes' technical qualities, meant that during the 1950s Adidas became the shoe of choice for many athletes in Germany, and later elsewhere. In desperation, Puma began to pay professional soccer players to switch to wear their boots, and during the 1960s a system of under-the-table payments became established as the Dasslers fought to get the elite into their products.[18] At the 1968 Mexico City Olympics, the two companies gave away some $100,000 in cash and equipment worth about $350,000.[19]

The effort Adidas and Puma put into ensuring that top athletes wore their products indicated the significance of such usage from a promotional perspective. From the outset, Adidas catalogs included images and testimonials of the top stars wearing the firm's state-of-the-art footwear. The 1950 catalog included images of the soccer teams FC Nürnberg, VfB Stuttgart, FSV Frankfurt, and St. Pauli in Dassler's boots. It also noted that the latest Adidas models were worn by Schalke 04 and FC Kaiserslautern. The firm's tennis shoe bore the last name of the leading German player, Hans Nüsslein.[20] A catalog printed after the 1952 Helsinki Olympics noted that twenty-three of the twenty-nine German athletes who finished among the top six in the world did so in Adidas.[21] The firm used its association with the elite to engineer desire among a larger market of aspiring athletes—a tried and tested formula used by sporting goods manufacturers since the late nineteenth century. The implication was that the best wore only the best shoes, and that by buying those shoes more ordinary athletes might perform similar feats of athleticism. Through strategies like these, the firm targeted consumers in the performance-driven sports market.

Although catalogs highlighted the firm's relationships with top athletes, Dassler's decision to brand his shoes with three distinctive stripes was perhaps more significant in wider marketing terms. Before this, sports shoes were largely unadorned and uniform in color, generally black. Dassler's simple visual device of three contrasting stripes transformed press and media coverage into free advertising and made immediately apparent which athletes wore his shoes. As media coverage of sports grew in the postwar era, newspaper, magazine, and television pictures cemented the firm's connection to the elite and carried the brand to a worldwide audience. Sports news was transformed into advertising. One of the most famous images from the 1966 soccer World Cup, for instance, was of Geoff Hurst leaping for joy after scoring in England's quarter-final against Argentina. Hurst is largely out of shot, only his Adidas boots are in the frame.[22] In the tournament's final match, twenty of twenty-two West German and English players wore Adidas boots, their three stripes clearly visible in television pictures broadcast to an estimated worldwide audience of four hundred million.[23] Not surprisingly, during the late 1960s and early 1970s a plethora of branding devices indebted to Adidas's stripes (and Puma's comparable "formstrip") were launched by frightened rivals. These imitations (including the Nike "swoosh") testified to the original's effectiveness in raising popular awareness of Adidas products and generating wider sales.

Global Expansion

In the early postwar period, Adidas focused primarily on West Germany and other German-speaking markets in Europe. Foreign sales were offered mainly as indicators of quality, and in 1950 the firm boasted of exporting to eight countries.[24] That number increased as the decade progressed, with television, Cold War tensions, and easier travel raising the profile and cultural significance of international sports. The firm's connection with the elite athletes who appeared at reinvigorated international contests brought Adidas to the attention of consumers and retailers outside Germany, stimulating demand beyond domestic markets. In this respect, the 1954 soccer World Cup was a pivotal moment.[25] Dassler worked closely with Sepp Herberger, the West German coach, and from 1950 Adidas was the exclusive supplier to the team, providing them with a series of innovative, lightweight boots. The 1954 tournament was the first to be broadcast on television extensively in Europe, and in a final celebrated afterward in Germany as "the miracle of Bern," West Germany overcame a two-goal deficit to beat the favorites, Hungary, three–two. Several West German players wore boots with novel screw-in studs that could be changed to match ground conditions, a feature highlighted by the rain-soaked final.[26] The West German victory was partially ascribed to Dassler's decision use longer studs on the sodden turf, and, more generally, to the technical superiority of their Adidas footwear.[27] Dassler, who joined Herberger and the exhausted players on the pitch after the match, was dubbed "the shoe marshal" by the German press.[28] Adidas milked the publicity, which helped generate interest in the firm's products among a global constituency of players, coaches, and soccer federations as well as among the sporting goods merchants who supplied them. In Germany, the firm soon called its footwear "the athletic shoe of world champions [*Weltbesten*]."[29]

The firm's international reputation was raised further two years later at the Melbourne Olympics. As the only English speaker, Adolf's twenty-year-old son, Horst, was sent to Australia to promote Adidas. Once there, he gave shoes to as many athletes as possible. Those he courted were duly impressed by both the quality of the product and the firm's apparent generosity, and many wore the shoes in competition. The Melbourne, a lightweight kangaroo leather spike developed especially for the games, was a conspicuous presence throughout the event.[30] By the firm's own count, seventy-two

Olympic medals were won and thirty-three world records were set by athletes in Adidas in 1956.[31] Global film, television, magazine, and newspaper coverage helped advertise the three stripes. In the United States, *Life* published a fifteen-page color photo-essay of the games. It contained images of several American medal-winners in Adidas, including a shot of the 400-meter hurdlers on the medal podium. In it, Josh Culbreath, Glenn Davis, and Eddie Southern are wearing blue, white, and red Adidas spikes, respectively. The cover of the same issue showed the American Bobby Morrow winning the 100-meter race in Adidas.[32] From a marketing perspective, Horst Dassler's activity in Melbourne brought the firm's products to the attention of serious athletes around the globe and was, as the firm declared in a catalog printed afterward, an achievement without precedent.[33]

International orders increased throughout the 1950s. The firm's global expansion was, however, haphazard and opportunistic, characterized by personal relationships and serendipity more than systematic strategic intent. As Jeffrey Fear has shown, this was usual for the medium-sized German firms that globalized in the 1970s, with which Adidas's experience in the 1950s and 1960s had much in common.[34] Initially at least, expansion was driven by foreign entrepreneurs who recognized the quality of Adidas products and saw opportunities in their domestic markets. Sales to the United States began in 1953 after Clifford Severn Sporting Goods in California wrote and begged the firm for a shipment of running spikes. The Severn brothers drove around college campuses, building sales by raising awareness of the German shoes among coaches and athletes. Canadian sales developed after Ray Schiele, a German emigre working as a salesman, learned of the firm's boots during the 1954 World Cup. Sensing a market among Canadian soccer players, he begged the Adolf Dassler to send a consignment. Schiele was later placed at the head of Adidas Canada, the firm's first foreign subsidiary. In Britain, the Dasslers initially worked with Stuart Surridge, a sporting goods merchant in London, before in 1961 they established a partnership with Umbro, a family-run sports clothing manufacturer based near Manchester.[35]

Foreign sales were initially to professional or top athletes concerned about performance. Consumers tended to be those who were willing and financially able to invest in a premium product because Adidas products were not cheap. As one British newspaper noted in 1954, Dassler's boots may have been half the weight of those produced in Britain, but they were also twice the price.[36] Nevertheless, the firm's popularity among elite athletes outside West Germany paved the way for a move into foreign mass markets. By 1958, Adidas produced 2000 pairs of shoes a day but had orders for ten times that amount.[37] This was hardly the stuff of "scientific marketing." Adidas pursued a relatively simple strategy. By focusing on technological development, relationship building, and financial payments to sports stars, it sought to get its products onto the feet of as many top athletes as possible, confident that this would stimulate demand further down the sporting hierarchy among a much broader constituency of sports consumers. In this way, the elites were co-opted by the firm as marketing tools. In so doing, Adidas established itself the market leader. Its shoes became those to which many potential consumers aspired.

De-Germanizing the Brand

As its international business grew and it started pursuing mass sales outside West Germany, Adidas began to adapt its products and marketing efforts to appeal to international audiences. Its first two foreign-language catalogs, in English and French–Italian, were printed in 1960. Overtly German model names such as Sieg (victory), Trumpf (trump), Kampf (fight), Schuss (shot), and Leichtgummi (lightweight rubber) were gradually phased out in favor of places, times, and internationalisms. Top-of-the-range models ceased to be called Ass (ace) and Pik-Ass (ace of spades) after these names caused giggles among American athletes.[38] Adolf Dassler morphed into Adi Dassler. Slight shifts in tone and presentation helped transform the firm's image and obscured a nationality still tainted by war and mass murder. Although Adidas benefitted from stereotypical ideas about German quality, tapping into the language of inclusivity and common experience espoused by the rising international sports movement enabled this German firm to recast itself as a partner in the shared endeavor of global sporting achievements. The extent to which this change was a strategic response to increasing international sales or a deliberate attempt to encourage foreign business is difficult to determine. Nevertheless, although the heart of the firm remained rooted in southern Germany, its public face took on an increasingly international aspect as the company sought to appeal to global consumer markets.

These efforts embraced more than corporate image. The firm expanded its product range, targeting sports seldom played in Germany. In 1960, French catalogs included rugby boots—the first time Adidas produced shoes for a game more popular in France and Britain than in Germany.[39] In 1963, a catalog of "American Style Football" shoes was produced for the United States, with one of the new American football models named "Monster-Man."[40] This process of diversification was most visible at the firm's French subsidiary, where the son Horst Dassler was eager to establish his independence. Adidas entered France in 1959, when it purchased an ailing shoe factory in Alsace to make soccer boots for the German market. Horst was sent to manage the facility. Away from his parents and emboldened by his success in Melbourne, he quickly transformed it into an almost entirely separate business.[41] Because his parents closely controlled activity in athletics and soccer, the firm's principal markets, Horst moved into areas in which Adidas had a lower profile and he could have a freer hand.

One of the most notable results of Horst's efforts was the firm's move into the American basketball market in the late 1960s. Basketball models already occupied a minor position in the Adidas range in the 1940s, possibly because there was an American military base outside Herzogenaurach, but the limited popularity of basketball as a spectator and participation sport in the company's principal European markets meant basketball shoes offered neither the mass market sales of soccer and generic training products nor the prestige that came with being linked to the stars of track and field or professional soccer.[42] Throughout the 1950s, the only Adidas shoe suitable for basketball was the Allround, a blue leather boot with welted sponge rubber soles that was sold for a range of activities.[43]

In the United States, basketball was dominated by large American rubber companies, which since the 1930s had benefitted from trade tariffs on imported rubber footwear. The standard shoe among top players was the Converse All Star, a canvas and rubber model that had barely changed since its introduction in 1917 and had been worn by every American Olympic squad between 1936 and 1964.[44] By the mid-1960s, changes to the game were making the "All Star" and similar shoes increasingly ill-suited, yet American manufacturers did little to adapt to the needs of ballplayers. The United States lowered (but did not remove) tariffs on imported footwear in 1966 as part of the Kennedy Round of trade negotiations, presenting Adidas with an opportunity to increase sales in the United States.[45] Chris Severn, an Adidas associate in California, noted the lack of domestic innovation and urged Horst to respond to the latent desire for better footwear among college and professional basketball players. With Severn's help, Adidas France developed new models designed explicitly for basketball, the Supergrip and the high-topped Pro-Model.[46] These shoes incorporated many of the technical advances for which Adidas was known. From a performance perspective, they were in a different league than the dated models produced by American manufacturers. Yet technical innovation was couched in a relatively conservative visual package. Severn had noticed that college athletes more accustomed to the black running spikes produced in America were reluctant to don the blue, red, white, and green shoes made by Adidas.[47] Presumably to avoid upsetting conservative American tastes, the new basketball models aped the lace-to-toe design and black-and-white color schemes of popular shoes like the All Star. Later, a distinctive ribbed rubber toe cap was added to both models.[48] The toe cap was actually developed for tennis to protect against wear when players dragged their feet in a serve, but it performed a similar job in basketball. It may also have been a visual echo of the rubber toe caps on traditional canvas basketball shoes, another attempt to make the shoes appeal to buyers more familiar with Converse and other American products.[49] In 1970, a revised Supergrip was given a new, more aspirational and American-friendly name, the Superstar. A note in the catalog added that it was "For Export," an indication that it had been designed primarily for American buyers.[50]

The new basketball models were unveiled to American retailers in the late 1960s. Although advertised as "the most advanced basketball shoe[s] yet produced," they received a hesitant welcome from coaches and players. Many were not convinced by descriptions of the "long-wearing sole, well-cushioned heel, form insole, arch support, and large heel counter" or the "revolutionary new ankle padding [that] insures [a] comfortable, snug fit and extra ankle protection."[51] Severn pitched the shoes to NBA teams, but only Jack McMahon, coach of the newly formed San Diego Rockets, could be persuaded. The Rockets wore Adidas during the 1967–1968 season. They performed dismally, finishing at the bottom of their division, but their presence in the NBA meant that other teams saw the Adidas shoes and heard Rockets players' recommendations. This exposure allayed many coaches' and players' doubts. Maybe the shoes were, as Adidas claimed, superior to those made by American manufacturers. The following year, the Boston Celtics, the leading professional team of the late 1960s, wore Adidas to victory in the 1969 NBA Championship, and John Wooden, the most influential coach of the era, switched the similarly successful UCLA Bruins from Converse to Adidas. These were watershed changes, and several other professional and college teams followed their lead. Orders multiplied. By 1970, Adidas could legitimately claim that the Superstar was "worn by the best basketball players in the world."[52] Regular television coverage brought the brand's three stripes to the attention of a wide new audience, and although Adidas remained expensive and hard to find in the United States, they became instantly desirable for many high school players and fans.[53] By 1973, around 85 percent of professional players in the United States wore the Superstar, as did many college players. It went on to become one of the firm's most successful models. Around 10 percent of the firm's sales were basketball shoes, nearly all of them produced by Adidas France.[54]

Sport for All

Scholars in the social sciences have demonstrated the connections between consumption and social practice. People buy and use stuff to enable them to perform various actions and activities; goods have no meaning unless they are integrated into networks of understanding connected to practice.[55] In the case of Adidas, the firm was established to cater to a specific niche market: people who engaged in sport. The firm aimed to persuade consumers already in the market for shoes appropriate to their athletic practice to buy Adidas, not other brands, especially not Puma. As Dassler suggested, the firm sought to stimulate desire among an international community of "athletes" and "active people" by catering directly to their needs and providing them with the best. Marketing material presented Adidas footwear as technically innovative, highly functional equipment that aided athletic performance. The material trumpeted the firm's association with the world's sporting elite as a way to generate sales among strivers and novices. As the firm moved into markets outside Germany, it adapted its products and its presentation to suit international audiences, but the fundamental message remained the same.

Adidas did remarkably little, however, to create, or engineer, new consumers for its sports products, and did virtually nothing to stimulate demand where none previously existed. It did not seek to increase popular engagement in the sports practices that drove the consumption of its products. Nor did it attempt to alter these practices. Yet the firm's phenomenal growth over three decades suggests that changes in societal sports practices were happening. Sport was changing, and more people than ever before were doing it. The overall market for sports shoes was increasing at a dramatic pace. It is notable that while Adidas established dominance at international sporting events and in national markets around the world, many of its rivals remained in business. In 1970s Britain, for example, the footwear trade press often noted that sports shoes sales were increasing and that more firms were entering the market.[56] Adidas and other athletic shoe manufacturers were beneficiaries of social changes initiated outside the footwear and sporting goods industries, profiting from the effect these changes had on consumption patterns. Just as the earlier Dassler Brothers firm had benefitted from Nazi programs commanding large sections of German society to engage in regular exercise, Adidas too grew large on the back of state-backed sports and fitness drives in the postwar period. These governmental attempts at social engineering, more than anything the firm did, changed ideas about sport and created a vast market for all types of athletic footwear.

Perhaps it is not surprising that a German firm led the world in the production of this consumer good. The country's history of state involvement in sports dated to the early nineteenth century, giving vociferous Nazi proponents of physical fitness plenty to work with. In the decades after World War II, West Germany led Europe in the implementation of popular programs in sport, creating the conditions necessary for the mass consumption of related products. Formal competition and sports clubs were officially abandoned in the immediate aftermath of World War II because of their Nazification or assimilation by the previous regime, but by the late 1940s the German Athletic Association (Deutscher Sportbund or DSB) emerged as an umbrella organization for the Federal Republic's 87,000 voluntary sports clubs. In explicit contrast to the Nazis emphasis on competition and physical hardening, the DSB adopted an inclusive "sport for all" policy, which, as Ilse Hartmann-Tews has argued, provided a means to rebuild the discredited reputation of organized sport. Clubs affiliated with the DSB were open to all sections of society. The DSB introduced and encouraged different forms of physical recreation were introduced and encouraged, and began efforts to persuade the public about the benefits of regular exercise. In 1959, it launched a "Second Way" campaign outlining the positive social and individual effects of mass involvement in sport, and promoting a range of physical activities across a broad section of German society.[57] Despite these efforts, by the late 1960s West German health insurers were warning that the children of the country's economic miracle were becoming unfit, with 33 percent of men and 40 percent of women overweight.[58] During the 1970s, the DSB responded with a series of wide-ranging "*Trimm Dich, Durch Sport*" (Get Fit, Do Sports) campaigns, which encouraged physical activities of all sorts to improve public health. Television advertising, public information films, brochures, events, and other publicity material all sought to persuade Germans to take up regular exercise.[59]

Promotional activity was matched by investment in sports infrastructure. Starting in 1960, the German Olympic Society embarked on a fifteen-year project to overcome the shortage of facilities that existed after the war. It led to a DM 17 billion construction program that more than doubled the number of athletic fields and sports halls in West Germany.[60] As part of the push for fitness in the 1970s, local governments across Germany created publicly accessible *Trimm* (fitness) tracks and paths in woodlands and parks. These bucolic installations were open to all and provided signposted running trails and equipment for a variety of physical exercises (Fig. 9.1).

These initiatives had a powerful effect on participation rates in West Germany. Between 1960 and 1980, membership in sports clubs affiliated with the DSB increased from around three million to roughly seventeen million, that is, from 6.7 percent of the population to 27.6 percent. Many more people enjoyed sports or physical recreation activities on an informal basis. With rising incomes and the arrival of the leisure society in the 1960s, a broad range of sports and other physical activities were embraced by many Germans.[61]

The influence of this sports policy was felt across Western Europe, with the "Second Way" and other initiatives providing a model for similar programs later adopted by other nations. European governments were not alone in their concerns about physical health. The federal government of the United States was also campaigning to raise activity levels in this period. Concerns about the physical fitness of young Americans were first aired in the mid-1950s when Dr. Hans Kraus suggested that the easiness of postwar life was weakening American children. His research led to the establishment of the President's Council on Youth Fitness in 1956, tasked with educating the American public about fitness. These efforts intensified under John F. Kennedy, who outlined his desire to make physical fitness a defining feature of his administration in "The Soft American," a *Sports Illustrated* article published shortly before his inauguration.[62] Under his direction, the renamed President's Council on Physical Fitness began to publish fitness information and offer technical advice to schools and communities. A series of best-selling booklets suggested possible exercise regimes, while national television and radio campaigns raised awareness. After Kennedy's assassination, these and similar programs were continued by Lyndon Johnson, who increased the emphasis placed on involvement in sports, and his successors.[63] Vast numbers of Americans became engaged, paving the way for the fitness fads and booms of

Fig. 9.1 Running on a West German *Trimm Pfad* in Adidas sports shoes and clothing, 1975. Source: Walter Umminger, *Trimm Trab: Das neue Laufen ohne zu schnaufen* (Frankfurt a.M.: Deutscher Sportbund, 1975, 29. © Deutscher Olympische Sportbund.

the 1970s and 1980s. As in West Germany, these efforts at social engineering prompted shifts in social practices that led to new and altered patterns in the consumption of sports-related products.

Recreational Adidas

Western "sport for all" programs raised the profile of such activity, encouraging mass participation in noncompetitive leisure sports and other forms of physical exercise. Almost as a by-product, these government campaigns created a sizable buying public for comfortable sports footwear and clothing. Not surprisingly, Adidas embraced the possibilities offered by new attitudes toward sport, adapting its marketing and products accordingly. Catalogs for the German market printed in the late 1960s restated the DSB's core messages, and the firm began to offer a variety of brochures, leaflets, and posters that promoted DSB programs.

Perhaps more significantly, "sport for all" offered a way to extract further financial value from the firm's investment in production innovation and technology. Dassler's promise to keep his products up-to-date and the rapid turnover of elite models this effort entailed meant that Adidas amassed machinery and expertise dedicated to products that quickly became redundant from a professional sports perspective. Yet shoes that were seen as out-of-date at the highest level remained entirely functional and more than adequate for the demands of lesser athletes. Mass participation provided an opportunity to extend the life span of shoe models and technologies that otherwise might have been abandoned. This was made apparent in 1970, with the addition in Germany of the Trimm Star to the range, literally Fitness Star. The new model was advertised as an "all round shoe for sport and recreation" and was officially licensed by the DSB, timed to coincide with the first "Get Fit through Sport" campaigns. From a manufacturing point of view, the shoe was not new but rather a reworking of construction processes together with molded sole technology introduced in the early 1960s. The most significant developments were cosmetic. Unlike previous Adidas training shoes, the Trimm Star was made of "brown velour leather" with burgundy stripes. It was not intended to coordinate with colorful sports uniforms but rather with the informal causal wear favored by reluctant athletes and weekend loungers.[64] In 1973, a new color scheme of turquoise and yellow was introduced, celebrated in catalogs as "Colorful—Stylish—Most Comfortable."[65]

The Trimm Star pointed the way forward. As participation in sport increased, Adidas began to court consumers more concerned by fitness and health—and style and fashion—than sheer performance. During the 1970s, the DSB slogan and campaign mascot, Trimmy, began to appear on Adidas shoe boxes, and flat-soled, multipurpose leisure and training shoes became ever more significant within this product range. Alongside highly technical shoes intended for professional athletes, the firm churned out basic, easily manufactured models in a variety of materials and colors, and with different soles, creating choices to suit different activities and budgets. As manufactured objects, these shoes represented recycled innovations from the 1950s and 1960s. Shoes originally designed for Olympians were now sold to novice or more occasional athletes as well as to people unwilling or unable to buy a premium product. By 1972, the Adidas catalog in Germany included nineteen different training shoes, including the Adria, an inexpensive canvas and rubber shoe marketed as suitable for all sports as well as "vacationing, leisure, and camping."[66] Model names reflected new ideas about how Adidas shoes might be worn. Alongside those that conjured images of speed (Gazelle), achievement (Record), and sporting events (Olympiad), a new leisure-oriented range introduced names redolent of vacations and relaxation: Tahiti, Miami, Riviera, and Savanna. One of the firm's best-selling models in the late 1970s was a simple brown and beige training shoe called Tobacco (Fig. 9.2).[67]

During this period, Horst Dassler pushed for the firm to diversify into clothing. Adidas training suits, made of blue, red, green, and white synthetic fabrics with distinctive striped sleeves and pants, were introduced in 1967. Catalogs described the new garments as "ideal for sport und leisure," but showed them modeled by the soccer star Franz Beckenbauer—after whom they were named—in traditional sporting contexts.[68] This approach soon changed. In 1969, catalogs showed the suits being worn by families (including Beckenbauer's) enjoying less strenuous recreational activities, including bicycling, fishing, camping, sailing, and toy slot-car racing.[69] Clothing came to make up a sizeable chunk of the firm's business, especially after Adidas secured a deal to supply officials' outfits for the 1972 Munich Olympics. Designers sought to appeal to consumers interested in style, and Adidas showed a determination to move beyond sports functionality. Training suits began to incorporate elements of popular fashion, and by the end of the decade flared trousers, winged collars, and printed patterns were common in a range of Adidas leisurewear that extended to safari suits.

Adidas's marketing transformed in the 1970s to reflect these developments. The firm still produced highly technical shoes for elite sports, but in marketing materials these "special" models occupied an increasingly diminished position in contrast to the prominence they had enjoyed in the 1950s. Whereas once Adidas's connection to the elite was celebrated, now the firm showed its shoes and clothing being worn in a variety of informal contexts by playful, smiling groups of ordinary—albeit fit and youthful—people. Catalogs included images of families enjoying gentle sports and outdoor activities, and the descriptions suggested the shoes were "ideal for 'fitness enthusiasts' and 'recreational athletes.'"[70] Marketing materials that had once focused almost entirely on elite sports now promoted relaxed informality and physical activity as part of a leisured and consumerist postwar lifestyle.

Fig. 9.2 Trimmy, mascot of the Deutscher Sportbund's 1970s *Timm Dich Durch Sport* campaigns (© Deutscher Olympische Sportbund)

Conclusion

When Adolf Dassler died in 1978, the firm he established had grown into what today might be called a sports-lifestyle brand. Adidas produced and sold a massive range of sophisticated, innovative footwear that catered directly to the needs of accomplished athletes. The firm continued to work to ensure its products were associated with this elite. Adidas shoes and clothing were worn by almost all of the world's top sportspeople and were visible at nearly all of the world's premier sporting events. Ever greater television and media coverage of international and national meets provided the firm with invaluable exposure. It worked in tandem with Adidas's own marketing efforts to ensure the brand remained connected in potential consumers' minds with the very best of sporting achievement. Yet the firm was also one of the world's largest manufacturers of casual shoes and clothing, a key player in the mass market for leisurewear. Supplier factories in Eastern Europe and Taiwan produced simple training shoes based on older Adidas designs and technology in vast numbers. The training suits of the late 1960s became an expanding range of sports and sports-inspired clothing, some of it of only tangential relation to sports. Although the firm's marketing efforts stressed the connection to top athletes, the vast majority of its customers were engaged in far less strenuous activities.

Adolf Dassler's success was grounded in his firm's ability to make shoes that catered to the physical needs of sports consumers, but its aggressive marketing and its ability to adjust to changing market conditions were significant factors in the company's growth after 1948. Wherever it went, the firm built a reputation among elite athletes for high quality, innovative products that was justly deserved. Adidas was just as good at communicating its connection to this elite and exploiting it to encourage consumption within its target market of sports consumers. Yet the firm's move beyond its initial consumer base into a far greater mainstream market owed much to forces over which Adidas itself, initially at least, had little control. The burgeoning athletic shoe and clothing industries after World War II owed their existence to broader efforts at social engineering that had a direct impact on the consumption of these types of product. Recreational and leisure sports were promoted by governmental organizations as a way to increase popular fitness and were made by possible by the same postwar affluence that, ironically, had contributed to worsening health. Without mass involvement in sports, the sports shoe industry would have remained a niche concern. That Adidas came to dominate this new sports market in the 1960s and 1970s was testament to its investment in innovative products, its reputation in the sporting world, and its ability to adjust to new tastes and expectations. If by 1978 it was a very different firm to that of 1948, it was because ideas about sport and the consumers to which it catered had been similarly transformed.

Notes

1. Four principal sources on the firm's history were consulted: Detlef Vetten, *Making a Difference* (Hamburg, 1998); Klaus-Peter Gäbelein, "Adidas—Eine Erfolgsstory aus Herzogenaurach," *Herzogenauracher Heimatblatt* 2 November (2000), accessed 17 July 2017, https://www.herzogenaurach.de/fileadmin/user_upload/Content/Stadtgeschichte/HB_Adidas.PDF; Barbara Smit, *Pitch Invasion: Adidas, Puma and the Making of Modern Sport* (London, 2006); and Keith Cooper, *Adidas: The Story as Told by Those Who Have Lived*

It and Are Living It (Herzogenaurach, 2011). Vetten's and Cooper's are corporate histories produced by the firm; Gäbelein's is a local news story written with assistance from the firm; and Smit's is a popular business history based on interviews with many of the key players.

2. Vetten, *Making a Difference*, 140.
3. Gäbelein, "Adidas," 5.
4. Ibid., 3–4.
5. Dassler training shoe, 1946, Adidas archive.
6. Vetten, *Making a Difference*, 105.
7. John Underwood, "No Goody Two Shoes," *Sports Illustrated*, March 10, 1969, 324.
8. Adidas catalog, 1949, DC-279, 3–5, Adidas archive, Herzogenaurach (author's translation). All Adidas catalogs consulted for this study are in this archive; only the ones in German have been translated by the author.
9. Adidas catalog, 1950, DC-281, 3–4, 7–18 (author's translation).
10. Adidas catalogs, 1961, DC-2, 3, 24, and 1962, DC-268, 40 (author's translation).
11. This point borrows from Dick Hebdige's analysis of how an image of the Innocenti works in Milan was used as a logo on early Lambretta scooter advertisements. See Dick Hebdige, "Object as Image: The Italian Scooter Cycle," in his *Hiding in the Light: On Images and Things* (London, 1988), 102–3.
12. Bernhard Rieger, *Technology and the Culture of Modernity in Britain and Germany 1890–1945* (Cambridge, UK, 2005), 37–39.
13. See Raymond G. Stokes, *Opting for Oil: The Political Economy of Technological Change in the West German Chemical Industry, 1945–1961* (Cambridge, UK, 1994).
14. John E. Lesch, "Introduction," in *The German Chemical Industry in the Twentieth Century*, ed. John E. Lesch (Dordrecht, 2000), 1.
15. Adidas catalog, 1962, DC-268, 31–32, 38 (author's translation). See also Adidas catalogs, 1962, DC-289, 31, and 1964, DC-829, 19.
16. Underwood, "No Goody Two Shoes," 16.
17. John Disley, in conversation with author, April 18, 2011.
18. Smit, *Pitch Invasion*, 82–90.
19. Underwood, "No Goody Two Shoes," 22–31.
20. Adidas catalog, 1950, DC-281, 7–10, 16.
21. Adidas catalog, 1952, DC-5722, 3.
22. The photograph of Hurst is reproduced in Peter Robinson, Doug Cheeseman, and Harry Pearson, *1966 Uncovered: The Unseen Story of the World Cup in England* (London, 2006), 200–1.
23. This success was not cheap. Adidas paid England players £1000 each to wear its boots in the final, the amount each stood to receive if England won the tournament. See Smit, *Pitch Invasion*, 78–90.
24. Adidas catalog, 1950, DC-281, 4.
25. See Vetten, *Making a Difference*, 112–17; and Smit, *Pitch Invasion*, 45–58.
26. On Adidas boot design, see Jean Williams, "Given the Boot: Reading the Ambiguities of British and Continental Football Boot Design," *Sport in History* 35, no. 1 (2015): 94–99.

27. According to Karl-Heinz Lang, one of Dassler's assistants in the 1970s, Dassler's real innovation, and the one that improved the performance of the German team, was his use of nylon studs and soles. Unlike leather, nylon did not absorb water and so did not increase in weight as the match progressed. This meant the German players did not tire as quickly as their opponents. Karl-Heinz Lang, in conversation with author, August 18, 2011.
28. German press clippings reproduced in Vetten, *Making a Difference*, 113 (author's translation).
29. Adidas catalog, 1956, DC-270, 1 (author's translation).
30. See Vetten, *Making a Difference*, 122; and Smit, *Pitch Invasion*, 58–68.
31. Adidas catalog, 1956, DC-270, 1.
32. "A Spectacle of Olympian deeds," *Life*, December 10, 1956, 34–49.
33. Adidas catalog, 1956, DC-270, 4–5.
34. Jeffrey Fear, "Straight Outta Oberberg: Transforming Mid-Sized Family Firms into Global Champions 1970–2010," *Jahrbuch für Wirtschaftsgeschichte / Economic History Yearbook* 53, no. 1 (2012): 125–69.
35. Smit, *Pitch Invasion*, 52–53, 63, 80–81.
36. "What a Dassler!" *Daily Sketch*, November 30, 1954, reproduced in Vetten, *Making a Difference*, 112.
37. Williams, "Given the Boot," 97.
38. Smit, *Pitch Invasion*, 64.
39. Adidas catalog, 1960, DC-258, 18.
40. Adidas catalog, 1963, DC-856.
41. Smit, *Pitch Invasion*, 99–111.
42. Adidas basketball boot, 1949, Adidas archive; Adidas catalog, 1950, DC-281, 15.
43. Adidas "Allround," 1955, Adidas archive; Adidas catalog, 1959, DC-262, 11.
44. Wallace R. Lord, ed., *Converse Basketball Yearbook 1965* (New Malden, MA, 1965), back cover.
45. Mansell G. Blackford and K. Austin Kerr, *B. F. Goodrich: Tradition and Transformation, 1870–1995* (Columbus, OH, 1996), 283; and Alison Gill, "Limousines for the Feet: The Rhetoric of Sneakers," in *Shoes: From Fashion to Fantasy*, ed. Giorgio Riello and Peter McNeill (Oxford, 2006), 377.
46. Smit, *Pitch Invasion*, 104–6.
47. Ibid., 63.
48. Adidas catalog, 1968, DC-312, 22.
49. Karl-Heinz Lang interviewed in Adidas-Salomon AG, *Superstar 35th Anniversary PR Book* (Herzogenaurarch, 2005), 10. Interestingly, Adidas basketball shoes of the 1940s and 1950s included a similarly defunct ankle patch like that on the "All Star," presumably so they conformed to popular ideas of what a basketball shoe should look like.
50. Adidas catalog, 1970, DC-339, 41.
51. Adidas catalog, 1968, DC-319, 15.
52. Adidas catalog, 1970/71, DC-4139, 12.
53. On popular responses to the Adidas "Superstar" and its subsequent repositioning, see Thomas Turner, "German Sports Shoes, Basketball, and Hip Hop: The Consumption and Cultural Significance of the Adidas 'Superstar,' 1966–1988," *Sport in History* 35, no. 1 (2015): 127–55.
54. Smit, *Pitch Invasion*, 105–6.

55. See Donald A. Norman, *The Design of Everyday Things* (London, 1998); Jukka Gronow and Alan Warde, eds., *Ordinary Consumption* (London, 2001); Elizabeth Shove, *Comfort, Cleanliness and Convenience: The Social Organization of Normality* (Oxford, 2003); Elizabeth Shove and Mika Pantzar, "Consumers, Producers and Practices: Understanding the Invention and Reinvention of Nordic Walking," *Journal of Consumer Culture* 5, no. 1 (2005): 43–64; Elizabeth Shove et al., *The Design of Everyday Life* (Oxford, 2007); Elizabeth Shove, Matt Watson, and Mika Pantzar, *The Dynamics of Social Practice: Everyday Life and How It Changes* (London, 2012); and Alan Warde, *Consumption: A Sociological Analysis* (London, 2016).
56. See, for example, "Clarks launch sports range …," *Footwear World*, August 1976, 9.
57. Ilse Hartmann-Tews, "Sport for All: System and Policy," in *Sport and Physical Education in Germany*, ed. Ken Hardman and Roland Naul (London, 2002), 153–64.
58. Rolf-Herbert Peters, *The Puma Story: The Remarkable Turnaround of an Endangered Species into One of the World's Hottest Sportlifestyle Brands* (London, 2007), 45.
59. Hardman and Naul, "Sport and Physical Recreation in the Two Germanies," in *Sport and Physical Education*, ed. Hardman and Naul, 42–43.
60. Frieder Roskam, "Sports Facilities," in *Sport and Physical Education*, ed. Hardman and Naul, 193–95.
61. Hartmann-Tews, "Sport for All," 162.
62. John F. Kennedy, "The Soft American," *Sports Illustrated*, December 26, 1960, 15–17.
63. Julie Sturgeon and Janice Meer, "The First Fifty Years, 1956–2006: The President's Council on Physical Fitness and Sports Revisits Its Roots and Charts Its Future," in *President's Council on Physical Fitness and Sports: The First 50 Years, 1956–2006*, ed. Janice Meer (Tampa, FL, 2006), 43–63.
64. Adidas catalog, 1970, DC-339, 28.
65. Adidas catalog, 1973, DC-4211, 2.
66. Adidas catalog, 1972, DC-350, n.p.
67. Adidas-France brochure, 1989, Adidas archive, unnumbered item, 29.
68. Adidas catalog, 1968, DC-321.
69. Adidas catalog, 1969, DC-378.
70. Adidas catalog, 1977, DC-760, 15.

CHAPTER 10

Imagined Images, Surveyed Consumers: Market Research as a Means of Consumer Engineering, 1950s–1980s

Ingo Köhler

In the fictional advertising agency Sterling Cooper, advertisers and market researchers very soon know exactly where they stand with each other in the 1950s setting. Already in the first episode of the U.S. television series *Mad Men*, the charismatic ad executive Don Draper manages to secure the advertising budget of a tobacco corporation by throwing the analysis of the agency's market research department into the trash and instead trusting his gut on how to allure customers into enjoying the client's cigarettes. With this scene, the show subtly alludes to the self-perception of advertising experts in the mid-twentieth century. They regarded themselves as creative professionals and artists of persuasion who possessed an instinctive command of the marketing repertoire.[1] They were, as most academic marketing professionals would criticize later, convinced that they were able to mark products or brands with emotional connotations "in the way Pavlov's dog identified food with the tinkling of a bell." This self-image "free[d] them from any mundane constraints of reality."[2]

Certainly, the TV series in this case was merely reproducing stereotypes from the 1950s. If, however, we examine the current state of research on the genesis of marketing, market research seems to be a topic that has disappeared into the bottom drawer of the historian's desk. So far, we hardly know anything about the information on which commercial advertising companies and corporate advertising departments decided their sales strategies.

I. Köhler (✉)
Institute for Economic and Social History, University of Göttingen, Göttingen, Germany,

J. Logemann et al. (eds.), *Consumer Engineering, 1920s–1970s*,
Worlds of Consumption, https://doi.org/10.1007/978-3-030-14564-4_10

What techniques did they use to explore the market? How did they generate knowledge about the behavior and purchasing motives of consumers? And how did they manage to fashion useful target groups at a time when consumption was growing increasingly differentiated and pluralistic, more and more independent of behavior patterns once shaped by income and stratum? It seems that intuitive approaches ceased to promise success at the latest in the 1960s, when society underwent a massive transformation. The era of marketing gurus was coming to an end in the United States and Europe. Nevertheless, we know little about the innovations in market research that were a precondition for the professionalization of marketing.[3]

According to the standard historical narrative, market research emerged alongside modern marketing science as an auxiliary subfield. Beginning in the United States in the 1920s and in West Germany during the 1950s, marketing came to mean more than simply sales and advertising. In practice, it referred to a model of management that was moving beyond a company-centered, product-oriented way of doing business toward a more holistic, "consumer-driven" approach. Richard Tedlow's influential historical stage model links the gradual rise of marketing to market-induced adaptation processes.[4] From this macro perspective, the transition from homogenous to differentiated consumer markets forced companies to learn more about the behavior of competitors and consumers. This simple stage model, however, has been contradicted by recent company histories. These demonstrate that companies in similar markets varied greatly in the manner and timing of their introducing marketing approaches and market research tools into their management repertoires.[5]

Studies that discuss the rise of market research not as a dependent variable but as an autonomous force driving business strategies are entirely absent from the literature. This lacuna seems all the more surprising as New Institutional Economics teaches us that information management touches on core questions regarding economic practice. Standard economics textbooks define market research as any "systematic research intended to gain or improve information about the state of markets."[6] Gathering and analyzing data about relevant economic, political, and social processes seek to provide a basis for strategic decisions within companies. The simple fact that active market exploration is perceived as a necessity by economic actors calls into question such basic neoclassical assumptions as the complete transparency of markets or actors in possession of perfect information. Instead, the emergence of professional market research and the idea that one's level of information can (and should) be improved implies an original state of limited information. In order to come closer to understanding corporate decision-making, this chapter analyzes the accessibility of information. It asks what kind of information about consumers or other market factors was obtained in different historical contexts to counteract the uncertainties of less than transparent markets.[7] What kinds of research methods and instruments did companies use to select, interpret, and operationalize market information in order to adjust their marketing strategies to complex changes in their business environment?

The most important question, therefore, is whether the redoubling of efforts in marketing research actually represented a seismic shift toward consumer-sensitive management strategies. Examinations of marketing practices in the second third of the twentieth century cast doubt on the idea of a "management revolution."[8] In fact, this chapter shows that the concept of well-informed, farseeing marketing management diffused only gradually from science into practice. Moreover, German capitalism experienced an intermediate stage between production-led management and its consumer-oriented successor, a transition period of "consumer engineering" from the 1930s to the 1960s.

This period was characterized by the emergence of new psychological strategies for consumer research. Marketing experts in both the United States and Germany were starting to get a handle on consumer behavior. They experimented with various innovative methods to elaborate consumer psychology, and the progress of consumer research was undeniably profound. In business practice, however, the notion of "reading" consumers' minds was strongly bound up with an expectation of being able to manipulate consumers. At this stage, companies were concerned with uncovering the secrets of consumers' desires rather than with designing products that met consumers' wishes. In this view, the "consumer engineering" approach to creating demand describes a transitional phase in the implementation process of new knowledge about marketing management. The question is when psychological consumer research became common practice in companies and how Europe and the United States might have differed in the timing and nature of business modernization. In the 1940s and 1950s, systematic motivational research became popular in business consulting on both sides of the Atlantic. How do we historically interpret the rise of a marketing approach that treated consumers as simple stimulus-and-response machines and tried to make them puppets on the strings of "hidden persuaders"? Did this work represent an advance or a setback in the modernization of marketing research? At the same time, when and why were the more overtly manipulative consumer engineers and gurus of motivational market research replaced by more reflective, consumer-sensitive marketing experts?

As recent studies have shown, the field of marketing research was characterized by a dualism of competing qualitative and quantitative methodologies from its infancy. In this chapter, I argue that a professionalization of market prognostics in Germany—paving the ways for an application-oriented marketing management in practice—was not effectively initiated until the 1960s, when psychological market exploration, statistical measurement of consumer behavior, and serious consumer sensibility merged into a holistic approach of monitoring markets.

In order to highlight the most important steps toward consumer-driven marketing, I explore the process of generating market research knowledge in three chronological sections. In each, I sketch out the extent to which the decision-making processes of German consumer goods producers were based on different forms of processed information about consumers, and I consider the kinds of prognostics tools they used, whether from internal market research departments or external consultants. In this way, the chapter returns to the central question of whether consumer engineering ideas supported operational market research. At first glance, it might seem obvious they did, but we also have to ask if consumer engineering actually hindered management modernization by fooling managers into believing they were capable of manipulating consumers' habits.

To get at these questions, I use case studies from the West German Automobile Industry—not only because the car was one of the most symbol-laden products of the emerging mass consumption society but also because we can find both German producers (Volkswagen, BMW, or Daimler) and affiliates of U.S. Multinationals (Ford and Opel/GM) in this sector. Such a comparative sample is ideally suited to reveal differences and similarities in the implementation of market research. Did U.S. carmakers adapt their management strategies to changing business environments more easily than their German counterparts, due to their greater experience in dealing with a differentiation of consumption patterns? In the following, I view economic and social transformations of the postwar era through the eyes of businessmen, tracing when they began to apprehend consumers and other stakeholders (such as media, politicians, motoring organizations, or environmental activists) as relevant market factors. It shows the nature and timing of the transition process from the self-serving and blinkered views of consumer engineering to modern, dialogical forms of marketing to consumers.

Acting on a Sellers' Market: Rudimentary Market Research Until the Mid-1960s

By the 1950s and early 1960s, major German carmakers were producing cars for an "anonymous" market. Due to pent-up demand and a backlog of motorization, they were acting in a sellers' market where demand exceeded supply. Moreover, patterns of consumption seemed to be transparent and quite ordinary.[9] Mass motorization was still in its early stages. Car ownership was limited to the upper and middle social strata. Only gradually did cars cease to be luxury items and become affordable for working-class families as well. This change showed in the demand structure. In 1950, only 12 percent of all cars were in the hands of private users. Not until 1960 were there more private cars than business cars registered. Then, however, demand boomed. Between 1955 and 1965, new car registrations tripled. The degree of motorization rose from 51 cars per 1000 residents in 1958 to 173 cars per 1000 residents in 1966.[10]

Under these circumstances, the car market in the initial phase of German mass motorization was structured almost entirely according to the incomes of potential buyers. Yet not only the financial wherewithal to own a car correlated with the social stratification of West Germany. So did consumption habits and buying motives. Although most prospective customers were first-time buyers, their expectations regarding the product remained quite low. The price had to be affordable, and the cars were supposed to ensure basic needs of individual mobility. Above all, customers wanted to stay dry while driving to work, a requirement that motorbikes and scooters, the most common vehicles of postwar motorization in Germany, could not meet.[11] Only at the upper social levels did the desire for social distinction and the display of economic advancement begin to influence consumers' behavior. Successful sales of the Volkswagen Beetle and lots of other quaintly styled econoboxes on the streets reflected the still only "modest prosperity"[12] of postwar West German society.

At the same time, small German cars saw considerable international success. Foremost among these was the VW Beetle, exported in high quantities to countries with higher levels of motorization. Especially in the United States, these foreign offerings met increasing demand for a second car, a market that simply did not yet exist in Germany. Based on predatory pricing and cultish advertising campaigns, the Volkswagen filled a gap in supplies that had long been intentionally ignored by U.S. carmakers operating overseas. Small cars and small profits were the guiding principle of the "Big Three" car manufacturers in Detroit.[13]

Market conditions were nearly paradisiacal for the major German car manufacturers. With excellent export opportunities and an infant domestic car market at hand, they only had to build up their production and distribution capacities to meet the strongly increasing demand. As the car market analysts Harald Jürgensen and Hartmut Berg put it, the companies partitioned the market "in peaceful coexistence" in order to avoid direct competition.[14] Whereas Volkswagen served the majority of first-time buyers, mainly with subcompacts, Ford and Opel sold compacts and intermediates to middle-class consumers looking to replace a car. Daimler, for its part, offered luxury-class cars to the wealthier segments of society.[15] This oligopolistic market segmentation curtailed consumers' freedom of choice. The small range of car types and offerings determined buying decisions. As long as demand exceeded supply, "the market power of the consumer remained stuck at a level equal to zero."[16]

Under these conditions, market research seemed to be an easy task for the firms' sales departments. They prepared market forecasts by counting sales and correlating them with the current trends of rising incomes. In retrospect, the BMW marketing division described common practice in its firm during the 1950s as follows:

> As long as the boom in demand continued, none of us needed to think about customer profiles. If a company was able to offer a product, literally everybody who had the money became a client. We focused only on predictions that promised an ongoing growth of incomes, and so we were sure sales would still increase in every market segment for years.[17]

In this optimistic and somewhat naive statement, we can find the main reason why market research capabilities of firms were practically non-existent.

Acting on a seller's market, companies just counted sales to adjust production levels. They knew nothing about who bought their cars or why consumers chose specific car models—there was simply no apparent need to gather such costly information. Even the systematic customer files compiled by retailers included only names and addresses, nothing about social and economic backgrounds. The manufacturers gleaned information about their customers' preferences only from sporadic "conversations with dealers." In particular, they asked individual sales units about customers' reactions after the introduction of new models. On the whole, however, the flow of information between retailers and sales departments remained haphazard and intuitive.[18] The car companies neglected to implement either quantitative or qualitative research on consumer behavior and motives. Surprisingly, neither the German nor the U.S. companies showed any ambition to observe the market development. Based on their experiences in mature commodity markets, especially the U.S. firms should have known that the "seller's paradise" in the long run would be doomed by trends toward saturation, differentiation, and increasing competition. But situational reasoning marginalized strategic thinking and hindered the implementation of forward-looking corporate information management.[19]

If market research was put to use at all in the 1950s, then only when a newly engineered model could not win over customers despite generally high demand. The cases of BMW and Ford illustrate that market research was initially perceived by management boards as a short-term tool for coping with an immediate crisis. Significantly, the least successful car manufacturers on the West German market were the first in the industry to become interested in new forms of market analysis.

BMW, in particular, felt the devastating effects of failing to connect its product strategy to customers' wishes. In 1953, the company introduced the BMW 501 as a full-sized car, but it hardly attracted customers because of its obsolete design, unsatisfying engine performance, and high price tag. This attempt to enter the luxury segment dominated by Mercedes failed and led the company into an existential crisis.[20] In 1957, BMW's new chairman of the board Heinrich Richter-Brohm identified deficits in market research and marketing as the causes of management mistakes: "Market observation and research must be conducted much more diligently."[21] Only so could BMW prevent the introduction of an unwanted new product. BMW became the first company in the Federal Republic to establish a specialized market research department. There, praise and criticism from retailers and customers were to be collected and passed on to the engineers in product development because the engineers should "only develop what could really be sold."[22]

Ford found itself in a similar situation in this period. In 1958, the sales of its compact Taunus faltered after the model received a face-lift. Wondering why the German consumers rejected the model, the Detroit headquarters engaged Ernest Dichter to prepare the first motivational research study about the emerging German car market. On the basis of a small survey of 200 interviews with potential buyers of a Ford, an Opel, or a Volkswagen,

Dichter undertook an in-depth psychological analysis of the overall "personal relationship between German car owners and their cars." The "personality of a car mirrors the identity of its owner," he argued.[23] According to this diagnosis, the consumer viewed the excessive chrome of the car's design as "too American." He advised the carmaker to revise the product design and, foremost, to refresh the company's advertising campaigns with some typical German elements in order to reduce the psychological distance between an American car and its potential German user. By offering individual accessories, such as dashboard labels with a pet name engraved, Ford could add a personal touch to its product. First and foremost, the Taunus had to be made "Your Ford Taunus" in every future ad campaign in order to intensify the consumer's identification with "his friend, the car."[24]

This example contained the usual promise that sales could be boosted with manipulative advertising strategies. Understood in this way, consumer engineering hindered management modernization more than it supported a genuinely consumer-oriented mind-set. Believing in traditional approaches to selling, firms saw no reason to inform themselves about their target consumers. Yet the question remains why only Ford and BMW took up the tempting offers of motivational research pioneered in the United States already in the 1940s.

Travel reports of German automobile managers draw a telling and nuanced picture of the development of market research in the automobile industry. Even in the United States, the sales departments of automobile corporations only began to establish systematic reporting on consumer behavior in the 1950s. And for the most part, this effort merely entailed counting purchases and doing statistical surveys of buyers' sociodemographic data. Psychological market analyses had hardly gained a foothold in the automobile industry yet. Although Ernest Dichter had examined the psychology of car purchases together with the advertising agency J. Stirling Getchell (which probably accounts for the similarity of the fictional agency's name in the TV series) already in 1939, and although this study for Chrysler/Plymouth received great attention in the industry, his new methods of market research were accepted only gradually.

There were four broad reasons for this slow embrace. First, the new surveys were laborious and costly. Sales departments were mostly small and did not possess the financial and staff capacities required to conduct customer surveys systematically.[25] External expertise was therefore brought in, but only at certain points during exceptional crises in sales. Second, motivational researchers regarded themselves more as advertising trailblazers than management rebels. Dichter himself admitted that the purpose of his study could only be to offer the Plymouth company "support for its advertising and merchandising problems." The subject matter of the study really was not the "discovery of the consumer" but merely the description of emotional stimuli that could serve to influence the customer.[26] Third was the problem of transferability. Dichter's observations were supposed to have universal validity, to describe fundamental rules, or, so to speak, natural laws of the social symbolism and psychological effects of car usage, which only had to be applied to particular product designs and advertising slogans.[27] Therefore, the new techniques, crafted in the context of the United States, were expected to be basically applicable to the German market without any problems as soon as the car became a common consumer good that the majority of Germans could afford. Ford's experience during the 1950s, however, cast doubt on the possibility of such a simple transfer. Finally, many experienced automobile managers had their doubts about qualitative market research particularly because, in their perception, motivational researchers and the advertisers they worked with thought of themselves as the better experts on the needs of the market.[28]

German firms paid close attention to the cooperation between Ford and Dichter in the 1950s, but they remained skeptical. Daimler, e.g., denigrated Dichter's work as a "confusing hodgepodge" of consumer beliefs. In any event, as an internal statement pointed out, using such unscientific and speculative experiments for strategic management purposes could not be justified.[29] Industry managers recognized weaknesses in the method, especially the often seemingly speculative interpretation techniques used for evaluating results. Frequently, the question arose whether the images elaborated in the motivational studies really represented the customers' images of products or if they were the result of free association by the market researchers.[30] Apparently, establishing market research in practice required not only increased market pressure but also more sophisticated scientific approaches.

Toward the Image Approach: Market Research at the Growth Stage of the Market, 1964–1973

In the second half of the 1960s, market research rapidly gained acceptance in the German Automobile Industry. Changing structures of demand, uncertainty about the limits of market growth, and the emergence of image approaches gave a boost to the methodological principles of market research. Since the mid-1960s, the car market was showing, slowly but steadily, trends toward saturation. Klaus Busch, the market analyst of the *Verband der Automobilindustrie* (VDA, Association of the German Automotive Industry) forewarned its members of the consumer appearing as the new central element in market uncertainty. It was merely a matter of time, he stated in 1966, "before we reach this new stage of a mature market, which will keep us busy with sales problems and sustainable changes in the structures of demand."[31] Likewise, Volkswagen's CEO Heinrich Nordhoff saw "the seller's market of the Golden Fifties at its last gasp. The good times when business was so easy will now be followed by the difficult challenges of a buyer's market."[32]

Figure 10.1 shows a remarkable shift in demand from first-time automobile acquisitions to replacement purchases. Consequently, strategies to secure customer loyalty by expanding the range of products gained in importance. In addition, the industry was becoming much more dependent on cyclical movements. Car owners purchased a new one every four or five years on

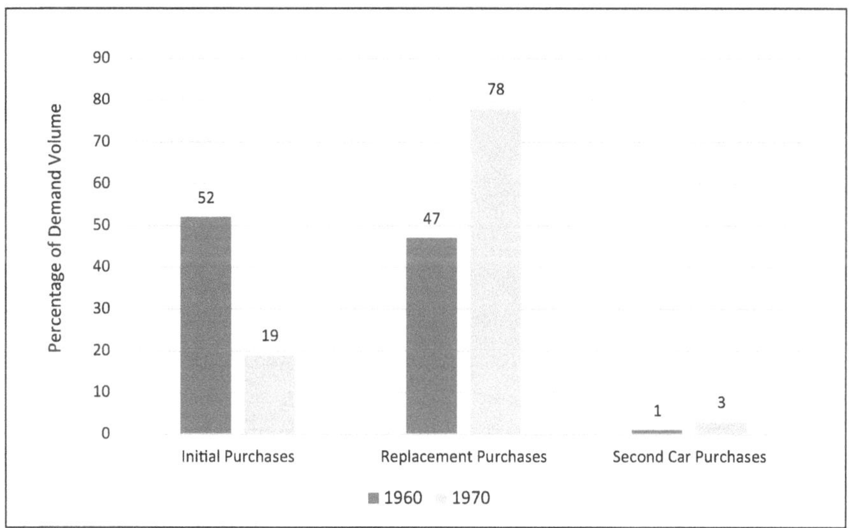

Fig. 10.1 Determinants of car demand, 1960 and 1980 (as percentage of sales). Source of data: W. Kater, "Struktur, Entwicklung und Bestimmungsgrößen des Marktes für gebrauchte PKW" (PhD diss., Technische Universität, Braunschweig, 1973), 1.

average, whereby they made their decisions for a subsequent car purchase with higher temporal and financial flexibility. If they perceived the signals of an economic crisis, for instance, they tended to delay such a major purchase. Such changes in the structure of demand forced the car manufacturers to face toughening conditions in an increasingly volatile and differentiated market. Manufacturers had to make much bigger efforts to encourage consumers to buy a new car and to opt for their particular make and models.[33]

Corresponding to an increase in the disposable income of potential buyers, cars still found a ready market, but consumers' preferences underwent a qualitative change. So-called trading up to more comfortable cars became the new general rule of car marketing and a major growth factor for the automobile industry. Cars had to do more than simply provide mobility. A growing number of buyers began to expect not only high quality and stylish design but also insisted on products that would give them a sense of social distinction and self-fulfillment.

Figure 10.2 shows overall car sales by different size classes. Minicars lost market share, and the sale of subcompacts like the VW Beetle stagnated, whereas compacts, intermediates and full-size cars gained market share during the mid-1960s. The carmakers adjusted their product lines to consumer preferences by offering a new range of upmarket cars, and they started competing with each other, especially in the middle sectors of the market.[34] In this new context, encouraging brand loyalty became a very important

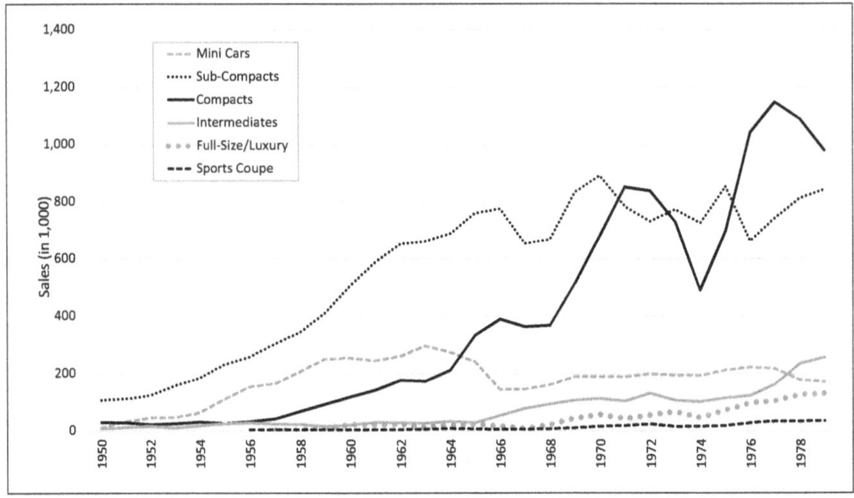

Fig. 10.2 Car sales by vehicle classes, 1950–1979 (in 1000s). Source of data: Verband der deutschen Automobilindustrie, *Tatsachen und Zahlen aus der Kraftverkehrswirtschaft* (Berlin: VDA-Verlag, 1965).

management objective; however, the carmakers now needed detailed information about their potential target groups.

Against this backdrop, new quantitative and qualitative approaches of market research began to receive the attention of managers. With the help of emerging commercial market research institutes like Allensbach, the companies' sales departments started to systematically gather information about consumers' sociodemographic characteristics: their income, profession, age, and marital status. Consumer surveys helped to create tremendous datasets that could then be evaluated using innovative consumer typologies.

Table 10.1 shows a consumer typology that BMW conceptualized in 1970 for its compact cars of the Series 3. Social profiling was the focus of the analyses. In addition, these reports were supposed to provide new statistical sketches of the way consumers behaved. They included segmentation studies, in which the car companies gathered information about the so-called *Käuferbewegung* (literally: consumer movement).[35] The manufacturers had previously deduced their relative market position rather intuitively from their sales numbers, but now all traces that consumers left in the market were to be collected and quantified meticulously. For how long, for instance, did customers own their old cars before they started thinking about buying a new one? Were they loyal to one brand or car make? Which sources of information did they use before they decided on which car to buy? BMW marketing experts sought to identify prospective buyers and catch their attention with

Table 10.1 Consumer typology, Model Series 3, BMW market research department, 1970

	Automobile make previously owned (%)							
Characteristics	*BMW*	*VW*	*Ford*	*Opel*	*Fiat*	*Another make*	*BMW 1970*	*BMW 1969*
Rate of prior possession	45	18	10	9	6	11	100	–
Period of ownership (years)	2.4	3.5	3.3	2.5	2.2	2.9	2.7	2.9
Average age of owner	38	37	35	36	34	38	37	35
Customers by profession								
Clerks	25	16	30	27	40	24	25	24
Technical employees	20	25	14	15	18	14	19	21
Civil servants	10	14	21	13	8	18	13	11
Blue-collar workers	15	16	21	10	8	14	15	14
Self-employed workers	13	9	4	25	10	12	12	12
Freelancer professions	13	13	7	6	8	9	11	12
Others	4	7	3	4	8	9	5	6
Household size								
1 Person	10	25	3	12	5	14	13	16
2 Persons	35	36	32	40	42	37	36	64
3 Persons	28	24	42	24	21	29	28	–
4 and more persons	27	15	23	24	32	20	23	20
Monthly net earnings (in DM)	2900	2700	2600	2600	2800	2900	2800	2600
Information sources used								
Own experiences	89	15	16	8	24	17	49	–
Experiences from friends	11	58	54	63	54	52	36	–
Test reviews	18	29	26	33	16	26	23	–
Prospects	10	29	46	35	38	26	23	–
Visit car dealer	9	33	37	33	24	29	22	–
Test drive	10	27	25	25	24	25	18	–
Advertising in magazines	2	2	–	2	19	–	2	–
Timing of decision in favor of BMW (weeks before purchase)	5.7	7	5.8	5	3.7	5.3	5.7	–

Source of data: BMW Classic, historical archive, UA 1464, purchaser typology (domestic), p. 10

sales campaigns in situations where they were thinking about buying a new car. Such reports were issued every six months, which lent them more scientific weight. The head of the BMW sales division claimed that his firm had "to develop [their] prospective selling strategy according to the motto 'planning—targeting—campaigning'" in 1970. Given the fierce competition on the German car market, he postulated an "intensified cooperation between the departments of market research, sales, and advertising ... to increase the efficiency of all our marketing activities."[36] Yet one flaw remained. Even repeatedly measuring all determinants of demand could only describe the current market situation, not explain why consumers acted as they did. Starting in the mid-1960s, qualitative image studies began to address that gap.

The concept of "image" built on earlier ideas developed by advertisers and motivational researchers, beginning in the 1920s. In essence, the image approach sought to comprehend existing conceptions of products in a new manner. Whereas the commodity, functional, and institutional schools of marketing classified products according to their physical characteristics, new cognitive approaches described them as complex manifestations of opinion. That is, the new approaches defined images of a product, brand, or company as a unique bundle of associations in the minds of target consumers.[37] In this view, the material quality or utilizable value of a product was much less important for market success than the product's symbolic significance. Using instruments like association tests, in-depth psychological interviews, and group discussions, image studies was trying to unpack consumer attitudes and expectations as they related to products and brands. And, as already mentioned above, motivational research experts understood consumer engineering in terms of making strategic image adjustments. From this point of view, however, "image" was a concept that somehow evaded precise definition or accurate measurement. Discursive analysis, psychological observation, and intuitive interpretation seemed to be the only methodological approaches available to make images visible.

By the mid-1960s, however, the theory and methodology of image-based market research had become more sophisticated. Consequently, German carmakers could discard their skepticism and begin to make practical use of qualitative market research techniques.[38] The vast improvement of market research occurred when concepts of social and cognitive psychology, both developed in the United States and Germany, could be combined with innovative approaches in behavioral economics. In particular, a 1961 pioneering work by Bernt Spiegel received a great deal of attention: *Die Struktur der Meinungsverteilung im sozialen Feld: Das psychologische Marktmodell*[39] (The Structure of Opinion Distribution in the Social Field: A Psychological Market Model). With his model, Spiegel sought to map the brand image of BMW cars within a socially determined field of consumer attitudes and perceptions. As a former professor of economic and social psychology in Göttingen and the founder of the Mannheim Institute of Market Psychology, Spiegel started measuring the connotations of objects with so-called semantic differentials. He asked test persons to rate how strongly they associated a given product or brand with certain semantic attributes and then he compiled the results into image profiles.

The great advantage of such "polarity profiles" was that they mapped and compared the "spatial" position of brand images within the range of existing opinions. These visualizations of psychological market positions were the main reason for the success of image profiles in business practice. They provided catchy new models of the market in terms of consumer perceptions, thus enabling managers to detect the relative strengths and weaknesses of their products and brands at a glance. Furthermore, these surveys could be repeated any time, which removed from marketing research the stigma of being more "speculative" than "scientific."[40] Finally, they offered car manufacturers a tool kit with which to segment markets on the basis of cognitive image criteria. Doing so facilitated the strategic placement of their products.

Figure 10.3 shows an original polarity profile comparing the brand images of Volkswagen, Audi, and BMW in 1970. The strengths and weaknesses of

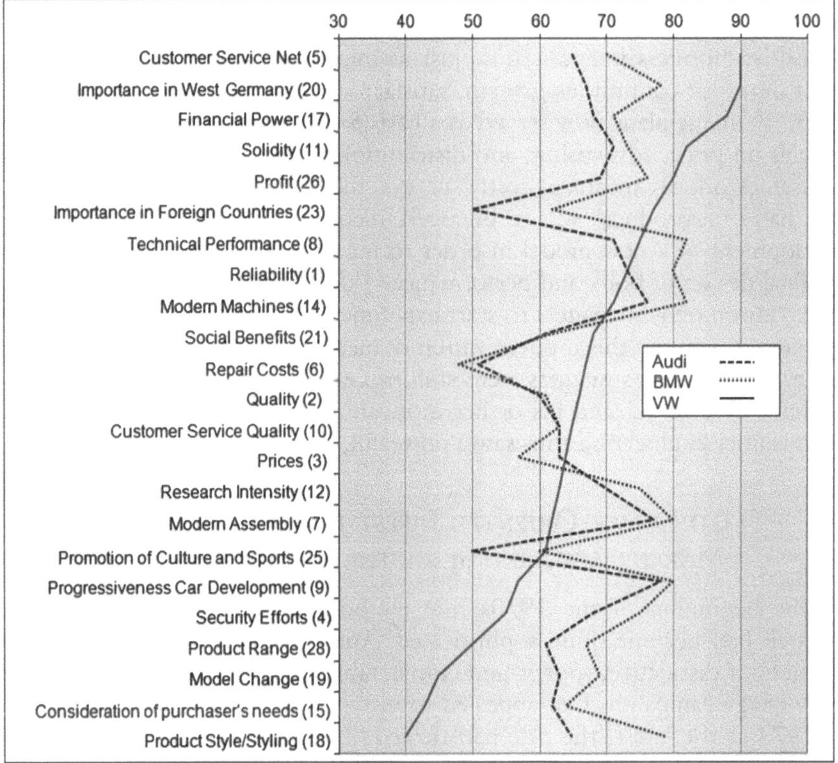

Fig. 10.3 Semantic differentials: brand images of VW, Audi, and BMW, 1970, with the relevance of buying motives in brackets. Source of data: Volkswagen Historical Communication Archive (VWA), 69/530/1, Image-Report of the Market Research Department, December 1971, chart 7.

each company are clearly evident. In particular, Volkswagen's image problems are conspicuous. Its competitors had tried to follow the trend of consumers toward trading up. Thus, they had expanded their product portfolios into the intermediate segment, for which demand was far greater. At the same time, they had modernized the design and performance of their models. "The German automobile designers pursue the trend toward the more expensive intermediate class with more displacement, more tinplate and prestige," observed *Der Spiegel* in 1970.[41] Volkswagen, however, had followed a different path, sticking with its once successful Beetle. Consumers punished this strategy with a relentlessly low approval rating.[42]

For the first time, however, there were qualitative research tools suitable for strategic marketing management purposes because they enabled companies to identify their respective market positions. With this new tool kit, marketing divisions started to occupy a more central position in corporate decision-making hierarchies. They became "keepers of the collected market knowledge" and the governing authorities for the formulation of customer-oriented business strategies. As a Volkswagen director put it in 1968, "Our primary management goal is to define and improve our brand image.... A positive business image is now just as important as the 'classic' management duties of continuous growth, satisfactory profitability, and full employment."[43] Image plans now served as a basis for product development, and for policies on price, advertising, and distribution within the famous 4P marketing framework. By means of costly surveys, the "impression a broad customer base had of a product" was to be ascertained as early as possible during the development of a new model in order to incorporate customers' wishes into the final design of body and performance.[44] Changing market conditions had forced automobile managers to start experimenting with new market research techniques. Despite this modernization of market research methods, however, the new marketing strategies were still informed by the idea that they could render the customer and his or her motivations transparent. Older "visions" of consumer engineering thus saw a powerful, if temporary revival.

Consumer-Oriented Lifestyle Segmentation: Market Research Since the Oil Price Crisis

By the beginning of the 1970s, the methods and instruments of market research had become quite sophisticated. Automobile manufacturers offered a variety of distinctive, sporty, and comfortable cars, and they launched elaborate image campaigns that appealed to buyers' emotions and ambitions. But by 1973 at the latest, the tide had turned. The effects of the oil price crisis meant companies had to cope with a 40 percent decline in sales. Car customers reacted to the massive price increase for petrol by postponing their purchase decisions several months or setting aside the purchase of a car in the first place. Now, the manufacturers' promising upmarket image strategies were threatened by failure. Moreover, in a situation of growing uncertainty, managers were losing their confidence in the idea of consumer engineering. At the peak of the crisis, market research departments were asked to present weekly supply figures in order to explore the depth of the slump.[45]

Even more alarming was that companies had to fear a change in consumer preferences. They could be quite certain that demand would turn up again. The problem, however, was whether customers would still demand the same cars after the oil price shock. New surveys and image studies all suggested that buyers now tended to spend less money for sporty vehicles, deemphasized matters of prestige, and harked back to fuel-efficient small cars. Moreover, studies provided strong indicators that consumer behavior had left the well-worn paths of sociodemographic segments. In 1975, after the external effects of the crisis diminished, the trend toward plural patterns of consumption continued.

Consumer behavior even began to seem arbitrary, almost unpredictable. Needing to find answers to explain such market changes, the companies discarded their self-centered, one-dimensional market views. Customers' reactions across all segments of the car market, a study by Daimler pointed out, could no longer be explained "by the facts alone." Indeed, according to the study, "we are presently experiencing a historically rare instance of the psychological crowding out the material on a significant scale."[46] Thus, the company began to consider overall social developments, which were well beyond the control of consumer engineering. Because of the diffuse signals from consumers, the automobile industry was fundamentally uncertain about the direction customer behavior would take.

By 1974, at the latest, it had become clear that the experience of the crisis would have a long-lasting effect on customers' attitudes toward the car. Volkswagen's market research discovered two fundamental structural processes, which partly overlapped. To start with, demand was expected to differentiate. The trend toward ever bigger and more powerful models seemed to have stopped. No car company could afford to put all its eggs in one basket by offering only models from the representative upper segments. At the same time, there was an increasing matter-of-fact attitude toward the automobile. High oil prices and a rising awareness of the environmental damage caused by mass traffic led to a deterioration in the car's sociopsychological significance. Depending on their individual attitudes, some customers now demanded "reasonable," that is, compact and economical vehicles.[47]

In order to grasp the complexity of this new market, all car manufacturers intensified their efforts to collect qualitative data about customer behavior. Continuous image observations and panel studies at regular intervals were established. The most important step toward professional, reflexive marketing, however, was marked by the inclusion of social scientists in the companies' market research concepts and practices.

First and foremost, commercial market research consultants turned their back on one-dimensional notions of consumer engineering. They started to describe market developments in terms of the deeply rooted social and cultural embeddedness of consumer behavior. Based on the experiences of the economic crisis, it seemed preposterous to assume that social change could be steered by simple corporate advertising and lobbying strategies. In this context, the target dimension of marketing received more than a sociopolitical expansion. The self-perception of companies and marketing experts changed; their role within the complex process of consumer communication reversed. Instead of setting and communicating trends, they now saw themselves having to adapt their market strategies to the requirements of modern consumer society. According to a study by the Heidelberg Sinus Institute, the fundamental problem of the car industry in the early 1970s was that its one-dimensional image strategies had put car sales into a position whose "stability depends to a large degree on the constancy of current socio-economic value orientations. However, one cannot exalt the car and make it the lodestar of our consumer society without anticipating that changes in the socio-cultural and socio-economic structures of perception [will] deeply affect the experiential significance of the car."[48]

The case of BMW illustrates that the effects of that change in perception were profound. As early as the summer of 1973, that is, even before the oil price crisis, the sales department demanded a modernization of the marketing framework so it could use changes in social values as a starting point for research into new motives behind purchasing decisions. The department regarded an approach as too rigid that continued to observe the development of demand purely as a function of rising consumption and increasing desire for such prestige purchases. In particular, the head of sales Robert Lutz made the case for a more dynamic and differentiating understanding of buyers' behavior. Because of the new ambivalence toward the automobile, Lutz argued, market research would have to account for "the social psychology of populations and individuals not staying the same."[49] As a solution to the industry's marketing problems, Lutz explicitly pointed out Maslow's theory of motivation and its assumption of a hierarchy of needs as an approach that "suits us very well in the here and now." Like the changing orientation of an individual consumer's behavior, which, depending on age and life situation, advanced in stages from the satisfaction of physiological needs to the fulfillment of psychological and emotional aims such as love, safety, esteem, and self-actualization, a long-lasting shift in the automobile needs of "whole markets" and "a whole nation" was occurring.[50]

The analytical depth attained by the automobile industry's managers' reflections on developments in Germany's automobile society is striking. Only two months after Inglehart had published his thesis on the silent revolution of social values, Lutz stated, "Maslow and Inglehart tell us that our society strives for individual self-fulfillment through consumption. In their search for identity, people ask themselves questions like 'Who am I?' or 'Why am I here?' The answers they find are never the same because consumers are individuals. In consequence, we have to face the fact that consumer expectations

Table 10.2 Psychological lifestyle typology, BMW/Compagnon (1977, excerpt)

	Description of driver types with below average share of BMW ownership		*Description of driver types with above average share of BMW ownership*	
Owner type	*1*	*2*	*3*	*4*
Above average use	Ford Taunus, Opel Ascona, Fiat 124-132	VW Passat, Opel Ascona, Citroen GS	DB 280-450 SLC, DB 280, S-450 SEL; Ford Consul; BMW 316-320	BMW 525, 520, 1502; Audi 80
Typical occupations	Craftsman, midlevel staff/satis-fied, powerless	Craftsman, blue-collar workers/enjoys occupation	Executive staff, self employed/ "served" at the top	Midlevel staff, executives, liberal professions/ achievers
Free time	Inactive, powerless	Wide interests	Inactive, domestic, shows financial wealth, and power	Contemplative recreation, but expects to have a say
Sports	No sporting activity	Swimming, cycling	Only for health reasons	Little sporting activities
Interests, hobbies	Yard work, TV	Versatile, but non intensive interests; literature, music	Yard work, watch-ing TV; literature and arts to take part to discussions	Literature, arts, music, antiques, photography, good food
Vacation	Convenient like at home	Exceptional destinations, usual comfort	Inactive, like at home but more costly	Convenient, costly, exceptional destinations
Social behavior	Introverted, domestic	Extroverted, many superficial friendships	Many friends, selection by same educational and financial status	Domestic, selects friends by educa-tion, money, and interests
Lifestyle	Petit bour-geois, norm	Enthusiastic, distinct, not extravagant	Status demonstra-tion of how "life capable" one is	Status-oriented individualist
Relationship to the automobile	No emotional relationship	Emotional rela-tionship that gets rationalized because of insufficient financial flexibility	Used to com-pensate for own deficiencies, spends a lot of money	Emotional rela-tionship, status demonstration
Driving style	Unaggressive, careful	Sporty driving style	Unsafe but fast, demonstrates superiority	Fast, but sees him/herself as cautious driver
Age	Emphasis: 40 to 49, highest share of 50- to 59-year-olds	Emphasis: 30 to 39, highest share of 33- to 39-year-olds	Emphasis: 40- to 49-year-olds	Emphasis: 30 to 39, highest share of 60-year-olds and above
Marital status	87% married	82% married	95% married	71% married
Characterization	"Norm oriented"	"Optimistic, spon-taneous, enthusi-astic master in the art of living"	"Conformist, look-ing for security, and status oriented"	"Sporty, active, sociable, or versatile optimist"

Source of data: BMW Classic, Historical Archive, UR 3022, Image Plan, September 1978, pp. 47–50 toward the car will be range between rational and emotional needs."[51] The car companies had begun to trace the differentiation of demand back to pluralized values and ways of life in modern society.

Accordingly, market research departments began to use innovative lifestyle concepts in order to identify consumer attitudes toward the car. Based on semantic descriptions, buyers were characterized in terms of their "activities" (in work and leisure), their "interests" (concerning family, education, and profession), and their "opinions" (cognitive orientations toward politics and economy). Such consumer-oriented lifestyle approaches quickly became very popular in corporate management practice, aiming to find new ways of market segmentation. BMW, e.g., engaged the market research institute Compagnon in 1977 to underpin their consumer-oriented product and marketing strategies. In the end, the lifestyle consumer typology—shown in a limited selection in Table 10.2—described nine types of car owner. The spectrum ranged from "the norm-oriented" owner with only minor social ambitions to the "optimistic enjoyer of life [*Lebenskünstler*]" and the extroverted lifestyle of "elitist conformists." With this new form of consumer segmentation at hand, the companies sought to adjust their products to consumer preferences. Ever since the second half of the 1970s, product policy, car design, and the style and vocabulary of ads were adjusted to these new "mental and social forms of [customer] expression." The car manufactures expanded their offerings by providing full product lines. These were established not only to give the consumers the opportunity to move up or down within the model range of one brand but to provide cars for every purpose, attitude, and budget.

Conclusion

The increasing use of market research by the automobile industry can be understood as a mechanism of crisis management. While German carmakers acted in a production-centered manner in the 1950s, they expanded their perspectives on the behavior of consumers in the more competitive market environment of the 1960s. Only under the pressure of the radical economic and social upheavals of the 1970s did they start to take the potential market effects of their changing external environment seriously. It is striking that the German affiliates of the major American car companies Ford and GM were not able to gain any clear strategic advantage from their greater experience in dealing with mass consumer markets in the United States. They made the same mistakes as their German competitors when they implemented modern academic marketing research quite late. Perhaps the historiography has so far adhered to an erroneous understanding of "Americanization" and of the extent and degree of transnational knowledge transfers. Another explanation might be that the "behavioral turn" of the mid-1960s was both a setback and a central driving force for the practical implementation of marketing and market research.

By examining how market research influenced business strategies on the micro-level, this chapter argues that the observable paradigm shift from producer-orientation to consumer orientation was less a "revolution" than an incremental process in which the ideas of consumer engineering hindered management modernization more than they supported a genuinely consumer-oriented mind-set. In this sense, modern marketing management, which understands markets as a communicative two-way street, stood very much in contrast to older notions of (manipulative) consumer engineering, which it began to supplant by the 1970s. Especially the former successful advocates of simple motivational approaches of consumer engineering lost their confidence in intuitive, not fully matured methods of prognosis as the economic crisis paved the way for a dynamic pluralization of buying habits in modern German consumer society. The engineers were trained by social changes to take consumers wishes and wants more seriously. The continuing professionalization of marketing research ended this period of consumer engineering in the 1970s at latest, even if the dream of steering the consumer still exists as a blatantly self-interested promise of consultants.

Notes

1. See also Ernest Dichter, *The Strategy of Desire* (Garden City, NY, 1960).
2. D. K. Scott and R. E. Ferner, "'The Strategy of Desire' and Rational Prescribing," *British Journal of Clinical Pharmacology* 37 (1994): 217.
3. Klaus Haupt, "Die Entwicklung der psychologischen Marktforschung in Deutschland," *Transfer—Werbeforschung und Praxis* 1 (2009): 24–33.
4. Richard S. Tedlow, "The Fourth Phase of Marketing: Marketing History and the Business World Today," in *The Rise and Fall of Mass Marketing*, ed. Richard S. Tedlow and Geoffrey Jones (London/New York, 1993), 8–35; *Hartmut* Berghoff, Philip Scranton, and Uwe Spiekermann, "The Origins of Marketing and Market Research: Information, Institutions, and Markets," in *The Rise of Marketing and Market Research*, ed. Hartmut Berghoff, Philip Scranton, and Uwe Spiekermann (New York, 2012), 1–26; and Harm G. Schröter, "Erfolgsfaktor Marketing: Der Strukturwandel von der Reklame zur Unternehmenssteuerung," in *Wirtschaft, Gesellschaft, Unternehmen: Festschrift für Hans Pohl zum 60. Geburtstag*, ed. Wilfried Feldenkirchen, Frauke Schönert-Röhlk, and Günther Schulz (Stuttgart, 1995), 1099–1127.
5. Ingo Köhler, *Auto-Identitäten: Marketing, Konsum und Produktbilder des Automobils nach dem Boom* (Göttingen, 2018); and Hartmut Berghoff, "Marketing im 20. Jahrhundert: Absatzinstrument—Managementphilosophie—Universelle Sozialtechnik," in *Marketinggeschichte: Die Genese einer modernen Sozialtechnik*, ed. Hartmut Berghoff (Frankfurt a.M., 2007), 11–58.
6. Josef Schnettler and Gero Wendt, *Marketing und Marktforschung: Lehr und Arbeitsbuch* (Berlin, 2003), 248; and Manfred Hüttner and Ulf Schwarting, *Grundzüge der Marktforschung*, 7th ed. (Munich, 2002).
7. Ronald H. Coase, "The Nature of the Firm," *Economica* 4, no. 16 (1937): 386–405; and Oliver E. Williamson, "Transaction Cost Economics: How It Works–Where It is Headed," *De Economist* 146, no. 1 (1998): 23–58.

8. Jagdish N. Sheth and Barbara L. Gross, "Parallel Development of Marketing and Consumer Behaviour: A Historical Perspective," in *Historical Perspectives in Marketing: Essays in Honor of Stanley C. Hollander*, ed. Ronald A. Fullerton and Terrence Nevert (Lexington, MA, 1988), 9–33; and Clemens Zimmermann, "Marktanalysen und Werbeforschung der frühen Bundesrepublik: Deutsche Traditionen und US-amerikanische Einflüsse, 1950–1965," in *Deutschland und USA in der internationalen Geschichte des 20. Jahrhunderts*, ed. Manfred Berg and Philipp Gassert (Stuttgart, 2004), 473–91.
9. Thomas Südbeck, *Motorisierung, Verkehrsentwicklung und Verkehrspolitik in der Bundesrepublik Deutschland der 1950er Jahre* (Stuttgart, 1994), 53.
10. Verband der Automobilindustrie, ed., *Zahlen aus der Kraftverkehrswirtschaft* (Frankfurt a.M., 1969/70), 32–36; and Hartmut Berg, "Automobilindustrie," in *Marktstruktur und Wettbewerb in der Bundesrepublik Deutschland: Branchenstudien zur deutschen Volkswirtschaft*, ed. Peter Oberender (Munich, 1984), 173.
11. Nils Beckmann, *Käfer, Goggos, Heckflossen: Eine retrospektive Studie über die westdeutschen Automobilmärkte in den Jahren der beginnenden Massenmotorisierung* (Vaihingen, 2006), 65–74; and "Das Ding aus Dingolfing," *Der Spiegel*, May 22, 1957, 46–47.
12. Michael Wildt, *Vom kleinen Wohlstand: Eine Konsumgeschichte der Fünfziger Jahre* (Frankfurt a.M., 1996).
13. Ingo Köhler, "'Small Car Blues': Die Produktpolitik US-amerikanischer und deutscher Automobilhersteller unter dem Einfluss umweltpolitischer Vorgaben, 1960–1980," *Jahrbuch für Wirtschaftsgeschichte/Economic History Yearbook* 2010, no. 1, 119.
14. Harald Jürgensen and Hartmut Berg, *Konzentration und Wettbewerb im gemeinsamen Markt: Das Beispiel der Automobilindustrie* (Göttingen, 1968), 135.
15. Köhler, *Auto-Identitäten*, 53–57.
16. Ibid.
17. BMW Historical Archive (hereafter: HABMW), UA 1344, "Marktstrategie eines Unternehmens" (typescript), May 15, 1968, 3–4.
18. Florian Triebel, "Marktforschung bei BMW 1957–1961," in *Marketing: Historische Aspekte der Wettbewerbs- und Absatzpolitik*, ed. Florian Triebel and Christian Kleinschmidt (Essen, 2004), 72.
19. Hagley Museum and Library (hereafter: HML), Ernest Dichter Papers, 2407, Box 37, 885.5A, Report of George Brown, March 28, 1957, 2.
20. Florian Triebel and Manfred Grunert, "Zur Typologie des Phänomens Unternehmenskrise," in *Jahrbuch für Wirtschaftsgeschichte* (2006), no. 2, 25; and Jürgen Seidl, *Die Bayerischen Motorenwerke (BMW) 1945–1969: Staatlicher Rahmen und unternehmerisches Handeln* (Munich, 2002), 33–36.
21. HABMW, UA 438/1, Minutes of the Meeting R&D and Sales, October 21, 1957, 15.
22. Ibid.
23. HML, Ernest Dichter Papers, 2407, Box 37, 885.5A, Report of George Brown, March 28, 1957, 2.
24. Ibid., 97.
25. Rolf Sigmund, "Marktforschung in der Automobilindustrie: Eine Untersuchung über die Möglichkeiten und Grenzen der Marktforschung in der deutschen Personenwagen-Industrie" (PhD diss., University of Stuttgart, 1957), 13.

26. Dichter, *Strategy of Desire*, 320.
27. HML, Ernest Dichter Papers, 2407, Box 37, 885.5A, Ford Motor Company, Report of Research Planning, March 28, 1957, 2.
28. Gerulf Hirt, *Verkannte Propheten? Zur "Expertenkultur" (west-)deutscher Werbekommunikatoren bis zur Rezession 1966/67* (Leipzig, 2013).
29. Hilger, Susanne, "*Amerikanisierung*" *deutscher Unternehmen: Wettbewerbsstrategien und Unternehmenspolitik bei Henkel, Siemens und Daimler-Benz, 1945/49–1975* (Stuttgart, 2004), 187.
30. Ursula Hansen and Matthias Bode, *Marketing und Konsum: Theorie und Praxis von der Industrialisierung bis ins 21. Jahrhundert* (Munich, 1999), 112.
31. Klaus Wilhelm Busch, *Strukturwandlungen der westdeutschen Automobilindustrie: Ein Beitrag zur Erfassung und Deutung einer industriellen Entwicklungsphase im Übergang vom produktionsorientierten zum marktorientierten Wachstum* (Berlin, 1966), 144.
32. Speech by Heinrich Nordhoff, London, 1966, quoted in Südbeck, *Motorisierung*, 37.
33. Statement by the Ford Europe CEO Peter Weiher, "Gegenwärtige Entwicklung und Zukunftsaussichten des Pkw-Bereichs," in *Die Automobilindustrie in der Bundesrepublik Deutschland*, ed. Theodor Eymüller and Horst Böcker (Frankfurt a.M., 1977), 14.
34. Köhler, "Small Car Blues," 119.
35. Köhler, *Auto-Identitäten*, 203–207.
36. HABMW, UA 1476, Consumer Survey, December 10th, 1970, 1.
37. Berghoff, Scranton, and Spiekermann, eds., "Origins of Marketing and Market Research," 3–5.
38. Ingo Köhler and Jan Logemann, "Toward Marketing Management: German Marketing in the 19th and 20th Centuries," in *The Routledge Companion to Marketing History*, ed. Brian D. G. Jones and Mark Tadajewski (Abingdon, UK, 2016), 381.
39. Bernt Spiegel, *Die Struktur der Meinungsverteilung im sozialen Feld: Das psychologische Marktmodell* (Bern, 1961).
40. Ursula Hansen and Matthias Bode, "Entwicklungsphasen der deutschen Marketingwissenschaft seit dem Zweiten Weltkrieg," in *Marketinggeschichte*, ed. Berghoff, 179–204.
41. "Sprung nach vorn," *Der Spiegel*, September 7, 1970, 66.
42. Ingo Köhler, "Overcoming Stagnation: Product Policy and Marketing in the German Automobile Industry of the 1970s," *Business History Review* 84 (2010): 64.
43. Volkswagen Historical Communication (herafter: HKVW), 250/2/1, Marketing Department, Marketing Plan 1968, 31.
44. Daimler Archive (hereafter: HAD), Fellbach, Press Department, Study trip USA 1964, quoted in Hilger, "Amerikanisierung," 187.
45. See HABMW, UA 852/1, Minutes of the Board Meeting, January 21, 1974, 2.
46. HAD, Zahn 292, Energy Crisis, Market Research Report 35/74, May 15, 1974, 62.
47. HKVW, Werkszeitung, "Der Marktforscher sagt: Ein 'goldrichtiges' Auto, zum 'goldrichtigen Zeitpunkt': Interview mit einem Marktforscher," in Autogramm 5/1975, Polo supplement, March 21, 1975, 2; and similar: HAD, Zahn 292, Energy Crisis, Market Research Report 35/74 (May 15, 1974), 72.

48. HABMW, UR 3021, Horst Nowak (Sinus): The Car Driver of the 1980s: Motives and Attitudes, ca. 1979/80.
49. HABMW, UA 1344, Robert A. Lutz, Viable Market Psychology, 1973, 6.
50. Ibid.
51. Ibid.

PART IV

Consumer Engineering and Consumer Movements

CHAPTER 11

Marketing a New Society or Engineering Kitchens? IKEA and the Swedish Consumer Agency

Orsi Husz and Karin Carlsson

In 1976, the Swedish edition of the IKEA catalog included a drawing of what was described as an ideally planned and equipped kitchen. The caption read, "This is how the Consumer Agency says that you best arrange your PAX modules" (Fig. 11.1). The following pages provided a more thorough presentation of "The Consumer Agency's ground rules for kitchens" and advised readers that the agency's handbook for kitchen planning and furnishing, along with its other informational brochures, could be ordered through IKEA or picked up in the furniture store itself.[1] This chapter seeks to understand how and why this drawing, along with the expertise and the social welfare policy ambitions it portrayed, came to be included in the IKEA catalog and subsequently went on to be used worldwide in IKEA's marketing communications. We analyze the contacts between the Swedish Consumer Agency (*Konsumentverket*), established by the Social Democratic state, and IKEA, a private company that had begun its international expansion. The discussion focuses on the 1970s, but the objective is to position "kitchen expertise" and its associated processes of knowledge circulation in a longer historical perspective.[2]

Historical research on consumption in Sweden has tended to concentrate either on societal values and normative policies or on the commercial

O. Husz (✉)
Department of Economic History, Uppsala University, Uppsala, Sweden

K. Carlsson (✉)
Department of History, Stockholm University, Stockholm, Sweden

J. Logemann et al. (eds.), *Consumer Engineering, 1920s–1970s*,
Worlds of Consumption, https://doi.org/10.1007/978-3-030-14564-4_11

PAX EFFEKT

Valmöjligheternas Pax! Hämta idéer hos IKEA!

Köksinredning och garderober. Inredning som, rätt utnyttjad, ger dig väsentliga förvaringsutrymmen precis där du behöver dem. Pax är de stora möjligheternas och den stora valfrihetens funktionsserie. Och den är prisbillig.
Man köper skåpstommar för sig. Och inredning för sig. Och man köper dörrar/lådförstycken för sig – Pax Opti (obehandlade som du målar själv), Pax Duett (furumönstrad laminat natur/brun) och Pax Effekt (furufaner i naturfärg).
Pax köks- och högskåpsstommar tillverkas av en välkänd svensk fabrik. Seriens enheter är måttanpassade till svensk standard med bygghöjd 210 cm. Monterbar konstruktion.
Pax levereras obehandlad för målning. Dörrar/lådförstycken Pax Duett och Pax Effekt är klara för användning.
Sidor, bottnar, hyllor och Pax Opti dörrar är tillverkade av dubbellimmade, hårda träfiberplattor på ram av furu, fyllning med Dufaylite. Samtliga högskåp och bänkskåp har fasta socklar, den främre sockelbrädan levereras lös. Sockelhöjd 15 cm.
Beslagsats, standardknopp/ar av plast samt magnetlås följer med skåpstommarna. Dörrar och luckor monteras valfritt för vänster- eller högerhängning.
Det är lätt att måla Pax, man behöver inte grundmåla. Pax levereras för enkel montering. Du behöver bara insexnyckel (den följer med), hammare och skruvmejsel.
Tre olika dörrar/lådförstycken! Dörrar, inredning och lådförstycken köper man alltså för sig, och här ligger mycket av valfriheten med Pax.
Pax Opti dörrar och lådförstycken är obehandlade för målning. Fritt fram för egna lösningar! Du kan t ex limma profillister på dörrarna, välja andra knoppar än dem du får i leveransen (se sidan 82) och måla i exakt den färg du vill ha.

Pax Duett. Furumönstrade laminatdörrar/lådförstycken – furu natur på ena sidan och furu brun på andra sidan. Vita kantlister. Montera önskad sida utåt, dörrarna är inte vändbara efter monteringen.
Pax Effekt. Dörrar med fris och liggande, spaltat furufaner i naturfärg. Klar plastlack. På 20 cm dörr och lådförstycken finns inte frisen.

Här på bilden ser du Pax med dörrar Pax Effekt och handtag Bygel (sidan 82). Tänk på att köket först och främst ska fungera bra som arbetsplats! Men glöm inte bort att köket också är en samlingsplats för familj och vänner. Skapa en trivsam, välkomnande köksmiljö – det är inte så svårt och inte så dyrt som du kanske tror!

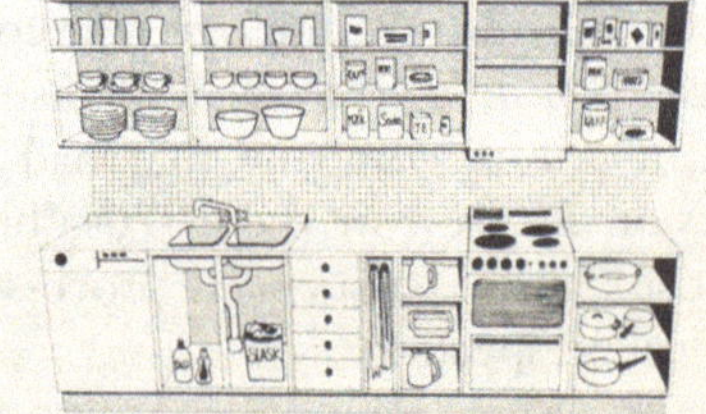

Så här anser Konsumentverket att man bäst utnyttjar sin Pax-inredning i köket. Du hittar fler tips på sidan 78!

77

Fig. 11.1 Page from the 1976 IKEA Catalog (Swedish) with the PAX kitchen solution, which followed the Consumer Agency's recommendations (© Copyright Inter IKEA Systems B.V., 2016).

practices of private enterprises. Some scholars have studied consumer education, consumer policies, and attempts to reform the domestic sphere, whereas others have focused on marketing innovations, advertising, and the promotion of new consumer goods and consumerist lifestyles. When these respective domains are considered in one and the same context, they tend to be portrayed as opposing forces.[3] This dichotomous view is not entirely misleading. The consumer policies of the welfare state in fact aimed to constrain and counterbalance commercial marketing. The dichotomous relation between these two forces can, however, be problematized, for example, by drawing attention to the constructive relationship between consumer policy makers and commercial actors.

European commercial consumer culture in the postwar era has often been described in terms of "Americanization."[4] In her extensive study, Victoria de Grazia argues that the United States had a hegemonic influence over mass consumption lifestyles in Europe. Other scholars criticize this thesis by identifying a broad range of national consumption patterns in Europe or pointing to European influences—often in the form of key individuals—on U.S. consumer culture.[5] In contrast, this chapter exemplifies a third type of argument against the idea of hegemonic Americanization within the field of mass consumption. We highlight how a global enterprise such as IKEA, with the power to influence the interior design of millions of homes across the world, was able to disseminate ideals rooted in a specific (non-American) national context. Furthermore, we show that these ideals, embodied in IKEA's kitchens, resulted from a longer Swedish history of explicit social welfare policy objectives. That said, what was considered specifically "Swedish" in the IKEA case, both in terms of commercial content and political ideology, was of course influenced by international predecessors and ideals.

Historians studying North American consumer culture have recently come to highlight the concept of "consumer engineering," coined in the United States in the interwar period to capture the advertising industry's aims. Marketing professionals did not just want to sell products. With product design and marketing techniques, they sought to create the "right" consumers.[6] By contrast, the concept of "social engineering," which is commonly used in histories of twentieth-century Sweden (and other countries), has different connotations. It concerns efforts to fundamentally reform society and its citizens through state-led, scientifically grounded planning and policy making as well as, especially in the case of Sweden, the creation of strong public institutions. The meticulous reform work of "social engineers," experts, and technocrats in Sweden was strongly supported by the Social Democratic state.[7] Our study maps the interaction and overlap of these two forces—social engineering by technocrats of the welfare state and consumer engineering by corporate marketing—in a specific case.

How the reformist ambitions of official Swedish consumer policies influenced IKEA's kitchens is of particular interest in hindsight because of the company's remarkably successful international expansion since the 1970s. IKEA was founded in 1943 in rural southern Sweden and started to sell furniture in the 1950s, initially by mail order. The first store was inaugurated in the small locality of Älmhult in 1958. The flagship store in Kungens Kurva, outside Stockholm, opened in 1965. After its national and Scandinavian expansion in the 1960s, IKEA turned to Europe and the rest of the world in the 1970s. Between 1974 and 1984, turnover grew tenfold and the number of department stores increased from 10 in five countries to 66 in 17 countries. Today, IKEA sells furniture in more than 300 stores worldwide. A basic principle of its business model is to market the same range of products in all its stores across the world, rather than seeking to cater to local trends and preferences. The IKEA catalog has more or less the same design in all countries and, since the 1970s, has emerged as one of the world's most widely distributed publications.[8] IKEA's marketing philosophy not only includes "educating" consumers to do some of the work themselves (by assembling flat packs) but also trains them to appreciate the products that the company has decided it can produce in large enough quantities.[9] This approach can aptly be described in terms of consumer engineering.

The design historian Sara Kristoffersson is the most recent scholar to have studied how IKEA uses narratives of Swedishness in its branding. She points to the company's references to an alleged Swedish affinity with nature and the parallels drawn to an egalitarian Swedish welfare society. Both Kristoffersson and the art historian Jeff Werner highlight the company's strategy—since the 1980s—of associating its furniture design with Swedish modernism.[10] In this study, we show that these connections began earlier and were more specific and partly different than this. We argue that IKEA's self-described mission to provide "democratic design" and its claim to represent the values of the welfare state were not just about clever marketing but steps toward making a virtue of necessity. This we conclude by tracing the interactions between IKEA and the Swedish Consumer Agency, focusing our attention on the initiatives of the latter and on the impact of Swedish consumer and social welfare policies on the marketing of IKEA's kitchens.

Our sources consist of printed materials from IKEA (1970s and 1980s) located in the National Library of Sweden's ephemera collection, kitchen-related volumes (1973–1976) in the Consumer Agency's archives, and the private archives of this agency's influential kitchen expert, Alice Thiberg. We have also studied two periodicals systematically: the Swedish Consumer Agency's *Råd och Rön* (Advice and Findings) and the furniture industry's trade journal *Snickeritidskriften/Träförädling* (The Carpentry Journal/Refining Wood), as well as select volumes or issues of other periodicals. Finally, we conducted interviews with key individuals from the fields of consumer policy and kitchen manufacturing.[11]

The article is organized as follows. We analyze the contacts between IKEA and the Swedish Consumer Agency as a sequence comprising three stages: conflict, resolution, and long-term effects. Sandwiched between these three stages, we contextualize the sequence of contacts. In the first of these intermediary sections, we present the setting in the 1970s by discussing official Swedish consumer policies. In the second, we introduce the historical background, namely the twentieth-century emergence and evolution in Sweden of the kitchen as an object of expert knowledge and as a field for social welfare policy ambitions. We conclude the chapter with a brief look at the 1990s and 2000s. We use the concept "social welfare policy" to denote the specific Swedish social policy ambitions of the emerging and mature Swedish welfare state. *Välfärdspolitik*, in Swedish, was a key concept for Social Democrats from the 1930s to at least the late 1970s; it designated general welfare reforms for the entire population rather than a social policy to help specific vulnerable groups.[12]

The Correct Kitchen

The Swedish Consumer Agency was formally established on January 1, 1973. In February, its appointed kitchen expert Alice Thiberg wrote a critical letter to IKEA. An architect by profession, Thiberg explained that she held a number of strong objections to how the latest IKEA catalog presented its kitchen designs. The kitchen layout was "in several respects very unfortunate." For instance, there was no workspace between the cooker and the sink. It was disappointing, she wrote, that a publication that reached so many people did not present correct kitchen solutions. Moreover, the catalog claimed that the cabinets and appliances were "adapted to European standards and are therefore produced according to completely modern measurements." Thiberg pointed out in her letter that "no such European standard exists! What we do have is a relatively decent consensus about measurements among most of the countries working within the ISO's [International Organization for Standardization] kitchen group."[13] With this, she indicated that the producers of the catalog were simply not knowledgeable enough in this matter.

Because the catalog for 1974–1975 included the same "faults" and even introduced some new ones, Thiberg wrote a new letter of protest dated September 2, 1974:

> We do not consider it worth our while in this letter to go into detailed criticism, but are open to discussing with IKEA how the next catalog might be able to improve people's kitchen environment rather than complicate it and even offer incorrect guidance.[14]

A few months later, *Vi*, the widely circulated magazine of the Swedish Consumer's Cooperative Union (*Kooperativa Förbundet*), published an article on Swedish kitchen manufacturers's catalogs. The piece was built entirely around extensive statements and material provided by Thiberg. It was a comprehensive piece of work with several illustrations, and the brunt of the criticism was directed at industry as a whole.[15] "They are selling eye candy.

Instead of providing realistic advice, kitchens are presented as living rooms or reception rooms." The worst part, however, was not the decorations or the kitchens "enshrouded in a mist of coziness" but all the glaring "faults in the plans." Here, again Thiberg referred to the example of the missing workspace between stove and sink. This section of the countertop was essential and could be neither too narrow nor too broad. Thiberg's critical eye also fixed on inset sinks, doors that were too wide on the overhead cabinets, and dishwashers mistakenly placed under the workspace. She also pointed out that drawers, for the sake of child safety, should not be located next to the oven, just as certain materials were simply not suitable for kitchen countertops.

> And all of this is so hopelessly unnecessary! Kitchens and kitchen work have been thoroughly researched, originally by the Home Research Institute [*Hemmens forskningsinstitut*], then by the Consumer Institute [aka the State Institute of Consumer Affairs or *Statens institut för konsumentfrågor*], and the Consumer Agency. Knowledge about kitchens is so easily accessible in various publications from the Consumer Agency and the Swedish Standards Institute [*Standardiseringskommissionen*]. There is no excuse for ignoring or forgetting to use such knowledge when presenting consumers with kitchens or kitchen drawings in brochures and magazines![16]

Thiberg adopted a similar tone in an article for *Form*, the magazine of the Swedish Society for Arts and Crafts (*Svenska Sljödföreningen*, today *Swedish Form*). She decried "bad planning," a meaningless variety of products, and "mendacious" kitchen environments with no connection to the requirements of everyday reality. The cause, she wrote, lay in ignorance and in a lack of meaningful communication in a market economy between consumers, on the one side, and retailers, manufacturers, and designers, on the other side. This was, she reckoned, basically an issue of power, but a shift of power toward the consumer could be achieved by means of consumer policy.[17]

Thiberg's letters, articles, and statements in the media are interesting for several reasons. First, they initiated what would become intense contacts between the Consumer Agency and kitchen manufacturers in the following years. Second, Thiberg's letters opened up a channel of communication between the Agency and IKEA in particular, which in the long run helped shape the kitchen interiors that IKEA displayed in its catalogs and stores.[18] Third, Thiberg now emerged as Sweden's most prominent kitchen expert, with the backing of the Consumer Agency. Not only that, she had also developed a vital network among Sweden's experts on home environment and standardization. Thiberg, dubbed "Mrs. Kitchen" in a retrospective interview, played a crucial role throughout the 1970s and 1980s in the design and development of kitchens. She even involved herself and the Consumer Agency in the commercial display and sales of kitchens.[19] She can be seen as a technocrat of the welfare state. She was an expert with the power to influence Swedish social welfare policy through knowledge production and to implement policy through her bureaucratic role at a public agency.[20] Thiberg's area of expertise had become all the more important in an era when welfare policy aimed to provide functional and modern housing to the population and when the "modern kitchen" was seen as emblematic for popular consumption across Europe and North America. Since the 1959 Cold War Kitchen Debate between Richard Nixon and Nikita Khrushchev, kitchen appliances, along with cars, seemed to symbolize domestic consumer modernity more than any other consumer goods.[21] In any case, kitchens affected the everyday lives of individuals in very direct ways.

The Consumer Agency and Consumer Policies of the 1970s

The Swedish welfare state was marked by strong public institutions, and the early 1970s was a high point of welfare state expansion. Until the first oil crisis, the country enjoyed an extended period of continuous economic growth, like most others in Western Europe. During the decades of Social Democratic governments, an extensive system of state-controlled social security had been rolled out. In this context, the state also took responsibility for people's housing conditions. The goal of the so-called Million Housing Program, a public housing endeavor begun in 1965 to build one million new homes (with built-in kitchens) within a ten-year period, had been achieved by the mid-1970s.[22]

Founded in 1973, the Consumer Agency's objective was to make the state's consumer policy more efficient and appropriate to contemporary needs. Much of the political discourse of the day was informed by strong criticism of market practices and commercial actors. The report from the public inquiry that had led to the establishment of the Consumer Agency included a warning about a new type of "intensive marketing" that was being combined with new (and implicitly unnecessary) products, "placing them on the market at a staggering pace."[23] In the face of this development, the Consumer Agency's mandate was to support consumers and strengthen their position in the market. This remit was only for citizens' interactions with private, commercial actors. The considerable consumption by council and state services was excluded from the Agency's area of responsibility.[24]

Previously, issues concerning consumer policy had been divided among a number of smaller public agencies, such as the above-mentioned Consumer Institute (est. 1957), the State Council of Consumers (*Statens Konsumentråd*, est. 1957), and other, only partly state-financed organizations, such as the Declaration Board (*Varudeklarationsnämnden*, est. 1951), the last responsible for the quality labeling of goods. These agencies had been charged with the responsibilities of quality control, researching the technical and economic conditions of private households, and consumer education. The Consumer Agency assumed responsibility for all these functions, albeit in new ways.[25] The most significant difference between the Consumer Agency and its predecessors was the Consumer Agency's remit to influence commercial producers of goods and services directly. Instead of merely educating and informing consumers about how to choose good products, the agency was now supposed to ensure that only such products were manufactured in the first place. Communicating with the producers—rather than consumers—was considered a novel and more efficient way of improving and simplifying market supply. Besides, so the reasoning went, if the producers followed the agency's guidelines, they could in fact function as intermediaries of consumer education.[26]

The Consumer Agency also used more conventional means of communication. They published the periodical *Råd & Rön* (Advice and Findings). This equivalent of the British publication *Which?* and the French *Que Choisir?* was founded in 1958 by the Consumer Institute. It provided both product tests and more extensive educational articles. The Consumer Agency also published brochures and informational leaflets as well as more substantial handbooks, such as *Kök: planering, inredning* (Kitchens: Planning and Interior Design), to which we will return. Although the Agency's explicit aim was to protect the weakest consumers, these publications were read above all by more educated and well-off citizens.[27] It was partly for this very reason that the main focus of consumer policy was redirected from educating and informing the public to attempting to influence the manufacturers themselves. The Consumer Agency was supposed to "scrutinize" market supplies, "monitor" marketing practices, and "intervene" when necessary. It was also supposed to actively "produce guidelines" for how companies developed their goods and even for how they marketed them.[28]

One Swedish observer at the time described this shift in consumer policy priorities as unique in the Western world.[29] Inevitably, debate over the policy ensued. Criticism from both the political opponents and the private sector was particularly intense by the end of the 1970s. The policy's detractors, on the one hand, argued that the Consumer Agency's mandate to influence producers treated consumers as if they were illiterate, thereby infantilizing them.[30] Because the Consumer Agency had assumed the role of "surrogate consumer," it was claimed, the consumer movement itself lost the impetus to become as lively as its counterparts in the United States and the United Kingdom. Admittedly, the consumer cooperative movement in Sweden had almost two million members in 1978 and had played an important role in Swedish society and politics since the early twentieth century. But, critics of the state's new consumer policy argued that the Cooperative Union, which had become increasingly engaged in the production of goods, resembled a major corporation in the 1970s and so had lost its identity as consumer representative.[31] Private companies, on the other hand, complained that the Consumer Agency was meddling excessively in their businesses and creating an administrative and financial burden. Some also argued that Swedish consumer policy regulations were harming exports.[32] The last point, however, does not seem to have been true in the case of IKEA.

The Consumer Agency and the Kitchen Manufacturers

The Consumer Agency used a number of strategies to influence the kitchen industry's product range. It presented current standards and new research findings in lectures, exhibitions, courses, and direct-mail campaigns. It conducted quality control tests on newly produced kitchen interiors, requesting components from manufacturers and testing them on site.[33] As we have seen for IKEA, the agency also monitored how producers marketed their kitchens. Another example involved Marbodal, one of the biggest kitchen manufacturers in Sweden. Thiberg noted in a critical *Råd & Rön* article how the company in its kitchen catalog from 1974 had "succeeded in violating all the well-tested principles of proper kitchen layouts" in its 1974 catalog despite the company's participation in the standardization process and despite the "exemplary fashion" with which it had introduced recommended standard measurements. Thiberg wondered whether the Consumer Agency could "count on the industry's cooperation." In a commentary on Thiberg's piece, Marbodal's chief executive assured her that yes, it could.[34]

Contact could also be taken up from the opposite direction. A number of kitchen manufacturers turned to the Consumer Agency to get their kitchens tested, or they asked for concrete advice as they developed their products, exhibited kitchens, or produced catalogs. Perhaps as a direct consequence of media reports about the agency's criticism of IKEA, the kitchen manufacturer Ballingslöv wrote to the agency asking for assistance in producing a catalog that "in terms of pictures is absolutely perfect."[35] Even if examples like this, taken from the agency's correspondence with manufacturers, indicate constructive cooperation, the relationship was not free from friction.

Already before the Consumer Agency's founding, there were skirmishes between proponents of standardization and rational kitchen expertise, represented by the Consumer Institute, and those focused on production processes and marketing strategies, the kitchen manufacturers. When the manufacturers gathered at the 1972 Idékök (Concept Kitchens) exhibition, the Consumer Institute instantly assumed a critical stance. It did not approve of the ostensibly impractical, if stylish "kitchen environments" at the exhibition, which were intended to create a "cozy" atmosphere, so it set about producing its own counterexhibit. The resulting *Kök med besked* (Kitchens for Real) sought to present the kitchen first and foremost as a functional space for rational work. In a panel debate arranged in connection with the two exhibitions, representatives of the kitchen manufacturers argued that fixed norms and standards left no room for individual preferences, alternative aesthetic ideals, or varying tastes. In response, the Consumer Institute's representative claimed such an attitude would lead to an "indefensible" abundance of colors and materials. Kitchen expertise, she argued, was being ignored for the sake of romantic, designer "dream kitchens."

One of the panel participants was Lennart Holm, Director of the National Board of Public Planning (*Planverket*). Trained as an architect, he was the leading expert on Swedish housing policy in the 1960s and 1970s, including the Million Housing Program. Holm was also one of the authors of the first (1952) edition of the Swedish handbook on kitchen planning and furnishing, a publication which was subsequently republished in revised versions by the Consumer Institute and the Consumer Agency. (IKEA later distributed the 1970s and 1980s editions of this book to its customers.) Holm lamented at the 1972 panel how novelty was consistently pitted against knowledge. Seeking to bridge the divide, he sought mutually beneficial cooperation between the industry's enthusiasm for innovation and the Institute of Consumer Affairs' amassed expertise.

Representatives of publicly owned construction companies such as Riksbyggen also participated in the panel. Raising the issue of class, they pointed out that "concept kitchens" were expensive, targeting a limited circle of individual consumers, whereas the majority of construction projects in Sweden were intended for large groups of "anonymous consumers." The Consumer Institute's representative insisted that practical kitchens did not have to be impersonal. Nevertheless, participants in the debate kept returning to a shared hope of reaching compromises.[36]

In a debate two years later, this time between the newly established Consumer Agency—represented by Alice Thiberg—and the kitchen manufacturers, the topic was the same, but the tone was decidedly sharper. The Agency had initiated the discussion because "producers persistently fail to live up to standards of quality and the industry is deviating from the most elementary rules of kitchen planning." It is clear that in comparison with the Consumer Institute, Thiberg was representing a public authority with a new mandate. The Consumer Agency was making its presence felt. Rather than offering manufacturers the ideal of compromise, it rebuked them. In her opening speech, Alice Thiberg made her view clear. New kitchens were often full of planning errors, that is, "nonsense and a lack of insight into the living conditions of ordinary people." These kitchens also fell short in terms of quality and durability, while most producers offered an endless array of "confusing variations in cabinet fronts." She reminded those present about the principle of offering a limited range of good products rather than too many and unnecessary choices. The general recommendation for layouts and standards should not be too difficult to respect, she argued, since it had "the character of common sense" and was supported by "proven experience from numerous practical and experimental studies."[37]

This particular debate continued in the media because the Consumer Agency chose to make its criticism public in a press release. The kitchen manufacturers reacted vigorously, likening the agency's actions to those of a crusade. They claimed the accusations were unfounded, pointing out that kitchen manufacturers had been involved in the standardization process since the 1930s while continuously balancing such requirements against the preferences of consumers.[38] In a letter addressed directly to the Consumer Agency, the manufacturers explained how its actions were helping to instill an attitude of "suspicion directed at cabinet producers, their product quality and marketing."[39] Refusing to retract her criticism, Thiberg responded that, in point of fact, the producers were making the Agency appear suspicious.

> This is a banal example of what you have to expect if consumer policy is to 'reach out,' [be] direct and open. The Agency's intentions and results will be misrepresented and discredited. But we also know that there are conscientious producers who comply, amending products and marketing that fail to meet the standards.[40]

These examples illustrate what was often a complicated relationship, where cooperation and conflict could develop simultaneously. They also reflect a more general criticism that had been heard since the end of the 1960s, one directed at the ongoing standardization attempts and intensified when consumer policy authorities were given more power in the 1970s. The architectural historian Eva Rudberg has shown how manufacturers at the time considered the codified norms outdated, awkward, and inhibiting.[41] As Thiberg herself put it, kitchen standards came to be seen as something "ugly," and the Consumer Agency's kitchens were described as "council gray" rooms that prevented individuals from "developing their personality."[42] Critics also claimed that standardization impeded flexibility in kitchen interior design. Thiberg, of course, did not agree. Not only did explicit norms ensure quality and protect consumers from the "kitchen cosmetics" cluttering up the market, but standardization was in fact a precondition for flexibility, making it much easier to combine different modules.[43]

IKEA does not appear to have been involved in these conflicts, however. With its own distribution chains and outlets, IKEA was a different type of company. The more traditional furniture producers in Sweden, including kitchen manufacturers, had for this reason excluded IKEA from their internal cooperation efforts, including their exhibitions.[44] Compared to the kitchen manufacturers like Ballingslöv (est. 1924) and Marbodal (est. 1929), IKEA was also a comparatively young actor on the market. It had only begun producing kitchen interiors in 1968.

IKEA and the Consumer Agency

IKEA only reacted to the Consumer Agency after Thiberg's second letter in 1974 and the subsequent media coverage of the issue. But then the company proved more than willing to accommodate Thiberg. It accepted the Consumer Agency's invitation to a meeting in its offices in Vällingby (a Stockholm suburb emblematic of Swedish welfare and planning), which gave its representatives a chance to go through the most recent IKEA catalog "picture by picture" with Alice Thiberg. The company found her "criticism to be well-founded" and assured the Consumer Agency that "mistakes" and "faults" in the kitchen arrangements both in the catalogs and in the stores would be "corrected."[45] In a survey conducted by the business scholar Olof Henell as part of his 1976 study on how firms viewed the state's consumer policy, representatives of IKEA stated that "the Consumer Agency needs us, just as much as we can make use of them." Billy Liljedahl, then responsible for advertising and information at IKEA, put it rather strikingly:

> The Consumer Agency cannot reach out on its own. We have embarked on the right course in our relationship with the Consumer Agency: they get their intentions across when we build them into our interiors. *It does not even have to be an intellectual process of choice for the consumer.*[46]

This was reminiscent of how earlier so-called social engineers in Sweden, such as Alva Myrdal, regarded consumers, who they believed had irrational or muddied ideas about their own needs. From this view, it followed that rather than focusing on consumer education, the state should ensure that people were offered "proper," fit-for-purpose products. This was especially the case when it came to the more important household goods—including the kitchen.[47] Liljedahl made a similar point. "Information" could easily become too advanced. Moreover, people could disregard reliable consumer information and "buy something completely ridiculous" all the same. For this reason, he favored a general system of basic requirements for the design and production of consumer goods.

The interviewed managers confirmed that IKEA did not have the in-house expertise and resources to develop "functional workspaces in the kitchens"; the company was happy to follow the Consumer Agency's recommendations.[48] Moreover, the IKEA managers emphasized, all standardization efforts ultimately benefitted the company because their business model centered on producing low-cost goods for a large market. They even welcomed the security regulations that the Consumer Agency produced: "[We have] no conflicts when it comes to functionality and security. We are pleased with the policy." Quality requirements were cast in positive terms: "We will do anything that diminishes the risk of customer returns and complaints." At the same time, they were careful to underscore IKEA's expertise in marketing kitchens from an "aesthetic" and "socio-psychological" perspective.[49]

One of the interviewees in Henell's study was Lennart Ekmark, at the time in charge of strategic marketing issues such as product range and exhibits. Now retired, he still displays a strong interest in IKEA's cooperation with public authorities, including how this work produced knowledge about furniture and functionality. In our own interview with him in February 2015, he explained that IKEA had had close contacts with the Consumer Agency, with Svensk Form (the former Swedish Society for Arts and Crafts), and with Stockholm's municipal household advisors (*hemkonsulenter*). "When we displayed new kitchen environments in Kungens Kurva, the ladies from the

Consumer Agency and Stockholm's municipal household advisors visited us," inspected the kitchen arrangements, and offered their advice. According to Ekmark, these public employees possessed extensive knowledge, "particularly [about] safety and functionality." Overall, Ekmark describes the relationship with the Consumer Agency as amicable, recalling several of its employees by name. Regarding Alice Thiberg and her husband, the professor of architecture Sven Thiberg, a leading expert on standardization and housing issues, Ekmark noted, "We had a hell of a [lot of] respect for them, they knew so much."[50]

The same picture emerged in our December 2014 interview with Morgan Lövgren, who was employed at Marbodal in the 1970s. During the process of introducing standard measurements in its product range, the company had continuous contact with the Consumer Agency. When Alice Thiberg's name came up in our interview, his spontaneous comment was "Damn, she pulled no punches!" Lövgren describes what he considered a close, constructive working relationship with the Agency, and recounts how Marbodal in turn passed on its acquired knowledge about kitchen planning to retailers by arranging "kitchen schools" of its own.[51]

Ekmark clearly also sees knowledge as a key resource because he repeatedly used the word and stressed its importance in the interview. According to him, IKEA realized it could implement the accumulating knowledge about kitchens, that is, "utilize it in order to create value." He also informed us that the employees in the stores "read the black and white, yellow-orange book about kitchen planning," obviously referring to the 1981 edition of the above-mentioned handbook by the Consumer Agency. According to Ekmark, whose view, of course, might be biased, IKEA was unique in this respect: No other company operating globally could claim such expertise in kitchen planning. He believes such expertise is gone now, as there is nowhere to access it.

We also interviewed Thiberg in May and November 2014. In those conversations and in the one with Ekmark, we explicitly asked about the contacts between the Consumer Agency and IKEA. Both confirm that there was a continuous dialog, but the difference is that the contacts appear to have had greater importance for the businessman Ekmark than they did for the public servant Thiberg. For Thiberg, IKEA was only one of many kitchen manufactures that had to be brought in line. Ekmark on the other hand repeatedly emphasized the value of his company's relationship with the Consumer Agency.

***

So far, we have explored the circulation of knowledge between the experts of a state agency and those in business (producers and retailers). The ultimate ambition of these state and business actors was to influence consumers, whether to improve their living conditions and thereby society, generate profits, or do both at the same time. Their kitchen knowledge circulated by means of regulations, publications, debates, and other dialogs. Most importantly, this knowledge was embodied in products and product displays. In the following, we look first at the historical origins of this knowledge and then at its wider dispersion abroad via IKEA catalogs, stores, and products.

The Genealogy of Kitchen Knowledge

The kitchen expertise that the Consumer Agency passed on to IKEA and the other manufacturers can be traced back decades, deeply rooted as it was in the history of the Swedish welfare state and the ideals and practices of the Social Democratic "people's home."[52] Such kitchen knowledge was closely related to the functionalist precept that designing rational housing and consumer goods would help "design" or shape the citizens of an improved society.[53]

Two entwined historical trajectories fed into the kitchen expertise of the 1970s. One, more relevant from a producer perspective, was the emergence and development of the standardization movement from the 1920s on. This movement was never led by the state, although it did evolve through contacts between private actors and public authorities. Its purpose was to enhance efficiency and flexibility in (among other areas) construction and interior design. The first standards for kitchen fittings were issued in 1950 by the Swedish Standards Institute. This minimum standard was expanded and revised in the early 1970s based on detailed research into the optimal dimensions for kitchen work when accounting for the human body's dimensions and movements.[54] The kitchen standard was integrated into the general quality criteria for housing construction (*God Bostad*) that the official Housing Board (*Kungliga Bostadsstyrelsen*) published in several editions.[55]

The other trajectory involved uses of the kitchen rather than its production. Especially important for the present study was how the kitchen in Sweden emerged as a site for the implementation of social welfare policy. As such, it became a subject of expertise and so had to be researched and rationalized according to scientific principles. When the Consumer Agency provided IKEA with guidelines in 1974, its immediate source was the knowledge base compiled in the revised 1972 edition of its kitchen handbook, *Kök: planering, inredning*. This book, in turn, was based on earlier editions but was supplemented with the results of a thorough kitchen study conducted in the late 1960s. With the help of the Royal Institute of Technology (KTH) and its division for Building Function Analysis (where Alice Thiberg's husband Sven Thiberg was a professor), the Consumer Institute (1957–1972) constructed a number of test kitchens to systematically analyze how kitchens were used in practice. The aim was to produce kitchen layouts that were practical and functional. In contrast to the older ideal of a lone housewife working in the kitchen, and following the new ideals of gender equality and the two-breadwinner model, kitchens were to be arranged for two adults to use simultaneously. The studies aimed to identify "situations of conflict," which could then be prevented with the right kitchen design. For instance, limited space could cause people to collide with open cabinet doors and extended drawers. All the movements in the test kitchens were recorded from a TV camera hung from the ceiling (Fig. 11.2).[56]

The technology and method were new, as was the ideal of gender equality in the kitchen, but in most other respects the experimental approach followed in the footsteps of studies conducted by the predecessor of the Consumer Institute, the Home Research Institute (1944–1957). Originally only partially supported by government funding, the Home Research Institute sprung from a collaboration between voluntary womens' and consumer organizations, private companies, and the state. Over the years, public funding became increasingly important. The aim was to work for "a systematic rationalization of the working conditions in Swedish homes."[57] Surveys around 1940 revealed that Swedes were living in housing that was overcrowded and substandard. When this problem was linked to the issue of low nativity, which had become a political issue already in the 1930s, the question of poor housing conditions attained broad political relevance. One proposed solution to low nativity rates was to improve conditions for women, that is, for potential mothers in their everyday domestic lives.[58] Consequently, official social policy also came to include the kitchen. The Home Research Institute closely examined different aspects of domestic chores—cleaning, cooking, and sewing—with the help of scientific methods inspired by Tayloristic time and motion studies. One of the goals, built on functionalist ideas, was to create logically planned, simple but efficient kitchens.[59] These rationalization efforts of the 1940s and 1950s were also influenced by international ideals. The U.S. home economist Christine Frederick had used time studies in the early 1900s to design optimal kitchens. The Frankfurt kitchen, designed by the Austrian architect Margarete Schütte-Lihotzky in the 1920s, had an even more direct influence in Sweden. But from the 1940s, research shows that representatives from other countries—above all the Nordic ones—were turning to Sweden to acquire knowledge about how kitchens ought to be designed and built.[60]

The expertise was efficiently summed up in the kitchen handbooks mentioned above, which IKEA also began distributing in 1976. The first edition of the book with the title *Kök: planering, inredning* was published already in 1952 by the Home Research Institute. The same publication was reissued in a series of updated editions during the 1960s and early 1970s. The Consumer Institute was responsible for producing it after the demise of the Home Research Institute, and the Consumer Agency in turn took over in 1973, republishing and revising it in varying degrees until 1994.[61]

The various editions of the handbook evince a strong continuity. The kitchen expertise that the Home Research Institute and its successors presented did not undergo radical changes, especially not since the 1960s, although the publication was continuously developed. There were

Fig. 11.2 Recording kitchen experiments on camera at the Royal Institute of Technology (KTH), Stockholm. Photos by Håkan Pettersson, in *Kök: planering, inredning* (1981), 9; and Studio Granath, in *Kök: planering inredning* (1972), cover, respectively.

Fig. 11.2 (continued)

adjustments: Standard measurements were revised, the recommended height of the work surface was slightly increased, "reserve spaces" for future appliances were added, and the larder was replaced by "artificially cooled storage." The late 1960s saw efforts to ensure a more flexible use of the kitchen modules, and in the following decade, as discussed above, the kitchen was adapted to a more gender-equal family norm. The 1981 edition included solutions for the disabled. Despite these additions, the recommendations for what constituted the "correct" kitchen remained more or less unaltered.[62] It was this kitchen, sprung from the work of Swedish social engineers and welfare state experts, which IKEA subsequently exported into the everyday lives of people around the world.

IKEA's "Basic Kitchen"

Almost all the evidence we have presented for IKEA's adaptation of the Consumer Agency's kitchen recommendations comes from what IKEA's representatives have said—then and now. The late 1970s kitchen displays in IKEAs stores are difficult to reconstruct, but the company's catalogs can be compared with the published recommendations of the Consumer Agency.

Alice Thiberg wrote about "building blocks" that had to be not only produced according to standardized measurements but also arranged correctly.[63] A number of different kitchens (all consisting of parts made according to the same standard) were therefore tested in the experimental kitchen surveys at the Royal Institute of Technology. The resulting alternative options were then depicted in the Consumer Institute's and Consumer Agency's handbooks. One core layout solution offered a base for several different kitchen interiors and was repeatedly used during the 1970s and 1980s with minor variations to demonstrate rational kitchen planning.[64] This representative layout of the Swedish kitchen included a row of cabinets 360 centimeters long (sometimes 340), planned in every detail according to the ground rules of functionality and safety. The countertop between the sink and the cooker afforded a workspace 80–100 centimeters wide, no more, no less. The drawers under the counter were near the sink, not the cooker. There were three wall cabinet units, each 80 centimeters wide (allowing more storage space than the 60 centimeter ones and pairs of smaller doors that were easier to open without having to take a step back); one fan unit above the cooker; and next to it a narrower cupboard, 40–60 centimeters, which was often depicted with food in it. This layout was often shown as part of a so-called parallel kitchen (two rows opposite each other) or as a single "straight kitchen," frequently flanked by a high storage unit.

The Consumer Agency reproduced and circulated this emblematic basic kitchen solution in many ways. The Consumer Institute had already used it to illustrate an advertisement for the 1972 Counter Exhibition. It appeared in different formats (photographs, drawings, and blueprints) on and between the covers of the different editions of kitchen handbooks and illustrated articles by Alice Thiberg.[65] The images often not only portrayed the optimal position of the various units but also suggested their ideal use.

The details and recurring circulation of this elementary kitchen solution through the Consumer Agency's own channels are interesting because the image, which IKEA published in its 1976 catalog (Fig. 11.1), depicted the exact same layout. Indeed, the picture—in different variations—and the Consumer Agency's rules for kitchen planning became a regular feature in the firm's catalogs during the following years. In a 1977 catalog specifically dedicated to the kitchen, a number of details were added to the image, and IKEA named it the Basic Kitchen [*Basköket*].[66] An informative text offering "Good advice on how to plan a kitchen" once again explained the basic principles, referring to the Consumer Agency's handbooks and brochures. Similar information appeared in the catalogs produced throughout the rest of the decade.[67] Although not all IKEA kitchens depicted in the catalogs' photographs were faultlessly planned according to the official recommendations, they represented a definite "improvement" in this regard when compared to those of the 1973 catalog. More to the point, the Consumer Agency's ideas and norms about kitchens were now disseminated through commercial channels to large groups of consumers. This did not just occur in Sweden. During this period, IKEA expanded overseas, and its kitchen sales often accounted for an important segment of its international turnover.[68]

The Journey Abroad

The first IKEA store outside Scandinavia opened in 1973, near Zürich in Switzerland. The following year, a store opened in Germany, in Eching outside Munich. Over the coming years, IKEA expanded swiftly in Europe, and by the early 1980s, there were stores in the Netherlands, France, Belgium, and Austria. The company also established itself further afield: first in Australia and Canada and later in places like Hong Kong, Singapore, and Saudi Arabia. The first IKEA store in the United States was inaugurated in 1985.[69] IKEA's international catalogs were initially printed in Sweden and are therefore included in the Swedish National Library's collection of commercial ephemera. Already by 1977, catalogs were being produced in Danish, Norwegian, and German, and they were nearly identical to the Swedish original. The same kitchen image was used, alongside a similar text about "*Bas køkkenet*" (Danish), "*Grunnkjøkkenet*" (Norwegian), and "*Grundküche*" (German)[70] (Fig. 11.3).

In 1984, the circulation of the IKEA catalog reached 45 million.[71] Specific kitchen catalogs were printed in different languages since the late 1970s. As IKEA's overseas presence increased, the production of the non-Swedish catalogs was moved abroad. This means that the Swedish National Library's collection becomes decidedly patchier from then on.[72] Nevertheless, from the evidence gleaned, it is still safe to say that in the overseas catalogs of

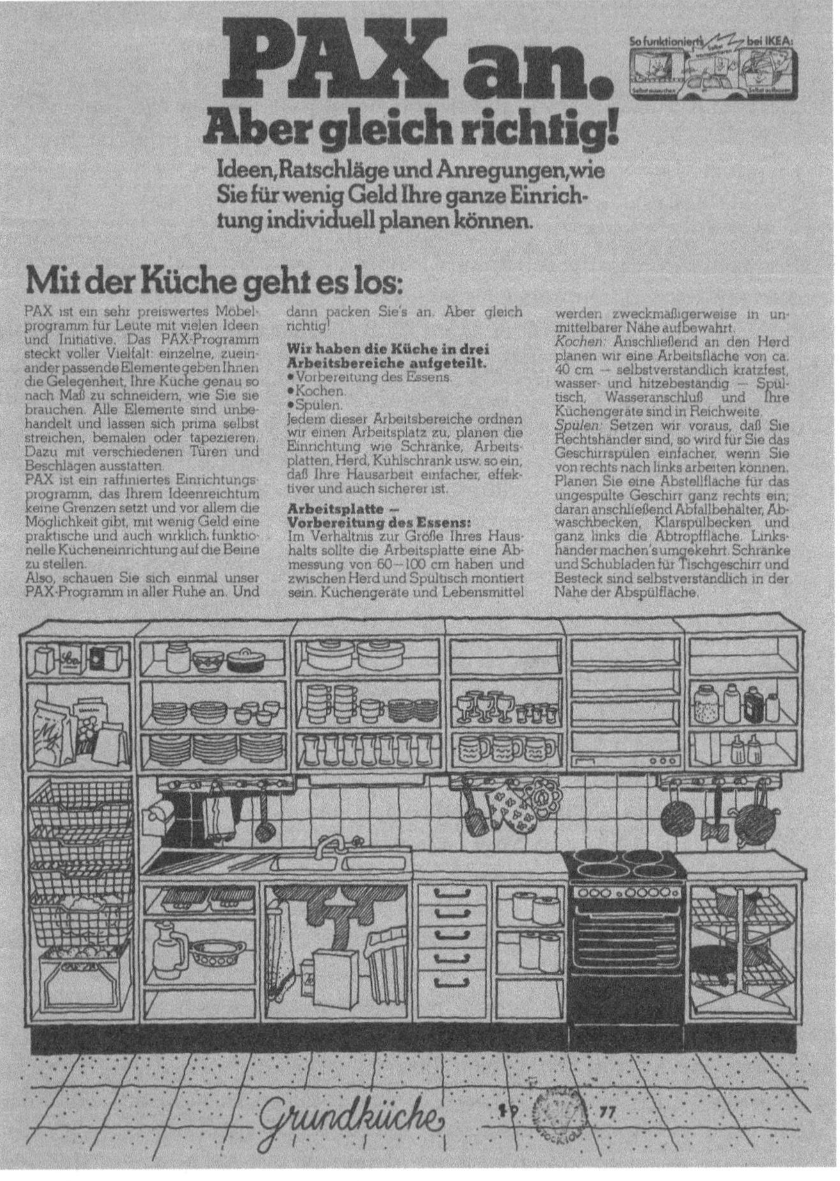

PAX an.

So funktioniert's bei IKEA:

Aber gleich richtig!

Ideen, Ratschläge und Anregungen, wie Sie für wenig Geld Ihre ganze Einrichtung individuell planen können.

Mit der Küche geht es los:

PAX ist ein sehr preiswertes Möbelprogramm für Leute mit vielen Ideen und Initiative. Das PAX-Programm steckt voller Vielfalt: einzelne, zueinander passende Elemente geben Ihnen die Gelegenheit, Ihre Küche genau so nach Maß zu schneidern, wie Sie sie brauchen. Alle Elemente sind unbehandelt und lassen sich prima selbst streichen, bemalen oder tapezieren. Dazu mit verschiedenen Türen und Beschlägen ausstatten.

PAX ist ein raffiniertes Einrichtungsprogramm, das Ihrem Ideenreichtum keine Grenzen setzt und vor allem die Möglichkeit gibt, mit wenig Geld eine praktische und auch wirklich funktionelle Kücheneinrichtung auf die Beine zu stellen.

Also, schauen Sie sich einmal unser PAX-Programm in aller Ruhe an. Und dann packen Sie's an. Aber gleich richtig!

Wir haben die Küche in drei Arbeitsbereiche aufgeteilt.

- Vorbereitung des Essens.
- Kochen.
- Spülen.

Jedem dieser Arbeitsbereiche ordnen wir einen Arbeitsplatz zu, planen die Einrichtung wie Schränke, Arbeitsplatten, Herd, Kühlschrank usw. so ein, daß Ihre Hausarbeit einfacher, effektiver und auch sicherer ist.

Arbeitsplatte – Vorbereitung des Essens:

Im Verhältnis zur Größe Ihres Haushalts sollte die Arbeitsplatte eine Abmessung von 60–100 cm haben und zwischen Herd und Spültisch montiert sein. Küchengeräte und Lebensmittel werden zweckmäßigerweise in unmittelbarer Nähe aufbewahrt.

Kochen: Anschließend an den Herd planen wir eine Arbeitsfläche von ca. 40 cm – selbstverständlich kratzfest, wasser- und hitzebeständig – Spültisch, Wasseranschluß und Ihre Küchengeräte sind in Reichweite.

Spülen: Setzen wir voraus, daß Sie Rechtshänder sind, so wird für Sie das Geschirrspülen einfacher, wenn Sie von rechts nach links arbeiten können. Planen Sie eine Abstellfläche für das ungespülte Geschirr ganz rechts ein; daran anschließend Abfallbehälter, Abwaschbecken, Klarspülbecken und ganz links die Abtropffläche. Linkshänder machen's umgekehrt. Schränke und Schubladen für Tischgeschirr und Besteck sind selbstverständlich in der Nähe der Abspülfläche.

Fig. 11.3 Basic Kitchen (*Gründküche*) from the German edition of IKEA's 1977 Kitchen Catalog (© Copyright Inter IKEA Systems B.V. 2016)

the 1980s, the classic pedagogical image of the basic kitchen, modeled after the Swedish Consumer Agency's recommendations, continued to be used, often in the form of a stylized photograph. For example, the German catalog from 1983 to 1984 demonstrated the ideal kitchen arrangement (including recommendations for the use of storage spaces) by showing the layout originally provided by Sweden's Consumer Agency. The Consumer Agency was not mentioned, but the illustration clearly reveals the connections. This educational kitchen display also appeared in other catalogs from the same year in English, French, and, of course, Swedish. In the catalogs produced over the following years, specifically those dedicated solely to kitchens, identical—or almost identical—images of the basic kitchen were a recurring feature. When comparing the price of an IKEA kitchen with those of other manufacturers or when explaining how the quality label *Möbelfakta* [Furniture Facts] was applied to kitchens, very similar layouts were used.[73]

Images of the basic kitchen were thus consistently displayed by IKEA for at least a decade. Even if the explanation for this has more to do with staying with a winning commercial concept than with any strong commitment to educate consumers or to satisfy the Consumer Agency, the finding remains significant. The image of the Consumer Agency's kitchen was circulated around the world to probably more than forty-five million readers.

Internal educational materials for IKEA's employees reinforce this impression. These publications reveal that the kitchen expertise offered by the Consumer Agency was used in the training of IKEA's international staff, certainly around 1980. A series of training booklets in different languages (Danish, Norwegian, German, French, and English) were produced in 1978, 1979, and 1980. Among them, *Kitchen—Function Booklet*, *Die Küche—Funktionsheft*, and *La cuisine—Cahier d'étude foncionelle* contained thorough presentations of the kitchen's various functions, including how it was to be planned and arranged. All this closely followed the same themes that the Consumer Agency's kitchen handbooks covered. The IKEA booklet dealt with the rational use of storage space and safety considerations, as well as information about the Swedish standards for kitchen interiors. Tests conducted by the Furniture Institute [*Möbelinstitutet*] and the quality label *Möbelfakta* were presented. This knowledge was then directly applied to IKEA's System 210 kitchen, successor to the PAX-series. The exposition was pedagogically designed, including study questions, practical exercises, and illustrations. The booklets concluded with an overview of kitchen expertise illustrated with IKEA's (and thus implicitly the Swedish Consumer Agency's) basic kitchen. Short explanatory notes next to the picture made the case for kitchen planning in general and this elementary kitchen layout in particular.

We do not know the extent to which IKEA employees and kitchen consumers around the world internalized this knowledge, but we do know that these materials enjoyed significant international circulation. In our interview, Lennart Ekmark notes that only in the United States did IKEA's consumer advice encounter certain resistance because it was seen as "patronizing." In Ekmark's opinion, U.S. consumers "did not want to base their purchases on knowledge but on emotions." Jeff Werner has shown that IKEA's central principle of selling the same products in all markets could not fully be implemented in the United States, but his explanation differs somewhat from Ekmark's. Aside from being accustomed to other standard measurements, Werner argues that Americans' tastes were more "conservative" and that U.S. consumers expected more customer service than IKEA usually offered.[74]

In practice, of course, virtually all purchasing decisions are based on both emotion and knowledge, and IKEA's marketing strategy was full of attempts to appeal emotively to their customer's reason. An internal educational booklet from 1985, for example, explained rather laboriously that the self-service setup in IKEA stores was designed to speak "both to the brain and the heart, as we make our choices with both sense and sensibility."[75] The showcase interiors (or "idea environments," as they were initially called) were intended to appeal to emotions, whereas the "compact," a display area for the full range of choices in every product category, was intended to appeal to reason.[76] What the Consumer Agency's representatives had tried to teach IKEA was that even its stores' showcase interiors had to be rationally planned. After all, next to their emotive appeal, they necessarily also conveyed a rational message.

In this sense, the Consumer Agency's intentions were indeed built into the kitchen environments on display in stores and catalogs, and in the layouts that IKEA staff promoted in their customer advice. Kitchen solutions developed on the basis of the knowledge amassed by experts in Sweden working for the Home Research Institute, the Institute of Consumer Affairs, and the Consumer Agency were thus ultimately disseminated to many millions of people far beyond Sweden. In this way, IKEA served as a powerful, international medium for Swedish social welfare policy and consumer policy. This conclusion stands despite Alice Thiberg's claim that IKEA was quick to proclaim its good intentions but often failed to act on them. This study has shown that to a significant extent IKEA did in fact integrate and disseminate the Agency's expertise. Whether the company could have done so more rigorously and to what extent IKEA's international consumers actually internalized the Agency's educational message are questions that lie beyond the scope of this chapter.

The Commodification of Swedish Social Engineering

We have shown that as an integrated part of its commercial operations, IKEA mediated the social welfare policy vision that had taken shape in the Swedish kitchen recommendations formulated by the Home Research Institute, the Consumer Institute, and the Consumer Agency. It seems that IKEA, perhaps more so than other Swedish kitchen manufacturers, was willing to internalize the knowledge on offer from the Consumer Agency. This conclusion is based on findings from a decade of testimony, beginning in the mid-1970s. We have not attempted to discern the company's underlying motives. It could have been a way of gaining legitimacy through quality control, for instance, or part of a marketing strategy, or a means to reinforce the demands it made on its subcontractors. Instead, we have focused on describing and contextualizing how kitchen expertise was transferred between different actors. In this process, both institutions (such as the newly founded Consumer Agency) and individuals (such as Alice Thiberg) played crucial roles.

Because IKEA and other manufacturers integrated the solutions recommended by experts at the Consumer Agency into their model kitchens, the Consumer Agency reached far broader circles than the educated Swedish consumers that read its publications. In this sense, adhering to the Consumer Agency's advice when buying a kitchen did "not have to be an intellectual process of choice for consumers," as one of our above-quoted sources put it.[77] Thus, it was a clear example of social engineering. Historians and historical actors alike have tended to see consumer engineering and social engineering as opposites. A case in point, the Consumer Agency was charged with protecting consumers from "manipulative" corporate marketing practices. Our study shows that these forces were intertwined, and that the dichotomous narratives therefore must be reconsidered and nuanced. After all, the 1970s also saw severe criticism in Sweden not only of the unwavering faith in economic growth propagated by industrialists and marketing professionals but also of the technocratic optimism of social planners.[78]

Scholars such as Sara Kristoffersson have shown how IKEA has utilized welfare state rhetoric and images of Swedishness in its branding since the 1980s.[79] We have examined the company's kitchen manufacturing in the 1970s as an example of a concrete point of contact between IKEA and Swedish social welfare policy makers. Because the outcome of these encounters went on to be displayed and sold on the international market, an element of "Swedishness" rooted in politics and history—beyond the rhetoric of branding strategies—was embedded in IKEA's exports. Other scholars have argued that the hegemonic American consumption regime was particularly salient for the European kitchen market.[80] Because our example deals with the global company IKEA, we are able to challenge this thesis in a novel way, going beyond pointing out distinct national or European variations. The American dream kitchen of the 1950s was certainly influential in many European countries, including Sweden. But if we look at the following decades and direct our focus away from electrical appliances toward kitchen interiors, an alternative point can be made. Integrating elements of rational Swedish kitchen expertise, the IKEA kitchen by the 1970s can be described as a specific alternative to its American counterpart. Not only that, but its global diffusion suggests it was indeed a genuine, and successful, alternative.

The Consumer Agency's kitchen (and consequently also IKEA's basic kitchen) was intended to de-emphasize class and promote gender equality. It focused more on the design and layout of the built-in interior than on the latest kitchen appliances. Although fridges, cookers, and ovens were integrated into the standard design, they were secondary to the layout of the cabinets, drawers, and countertops. A central design concern was practicality, which the "correctly" planned Swedish kitchen doubtlessly achieved in many respects. Yet the recommendations lacked any explicit reflections concerning how narrowly adapted the design was to a Northern European lifestyle and cooking culture. It did not, for instance, take any account of other possible habits, appliances, or utensils—despite the fact that immigration to Sweden at this point was increasing. This regionally specific approach makes its global journey by means of IKEA even more intriguing.

***

Official Swedish consumer policy has changed since the 1970s. It has become more decentralized, more market-friendly, and it is based on a rather different view of the consumer. No longer considered to be in need of protection from "unnecessary" choices, the Swede today is instead encouraged to act as an active consumer in all aspects of life, including the welfare sector. The Swedish kitchen standard and its recommendations remained in place until 1997, at which point a less detailed European standard was introduced. The long trajectory of developing and codifying Swedish kitchen expertise thereby came to an end, and its continued dissemination among architects, consumers, and producers was markedly diminished. Around the same time, new kitchen ideals were being popularized. The kitchen as a site of work was toned down, and its character as a space for social gatherings or lifestyle consumption was emphasized.

Nevertheless, in its catalogs and on its Web site, IKEA retained a focus on practical kitchen planning into the 2000s. What expertise this draws on today is not clear. In a 2001 newspaper interview, a now retired Alice Thiberg criticized IKEA's catalogs for calling the kitchens "work-friendly," practical, and safe, despite a number of details that proved the contrary. The measures and planning recommendations provided for a functional layout were also "faulty," claimed Thiberg, and she lamented that consumers were now completely in the hands of kitchen manufacturers. "There is no longer a counterforce." When the newspaper confronted IKEA with this criticism, the interviewed sales manager asserted the company's kitchen interiors were still being designed ("as far as possible") on the basis of the "old Swedish standard," and promised (once again) that IKEA would "do better."[81] Some fading traces of the Swedish welfare state's "kitchen expertise" were thus still detectable in a new era of lifestyle consumption.

Acknowledgements Our research was supported by grants from Riksbankens Jubileumsfond (RJ), The Magnus Bergwall Foundation, and The Åke Wiberg Foundation.

Notes

1. 1976 IKEA catalog (Swedish ed.), 77. The catalog referred to two Consumer Agency publications: *Kök: planering, inredning*, rev. ed. (Stockholm, 1972); and *Fakta från KOV*, June 1974.

2. On the concept of knowledge circulation, see, for example, Johan Östling et al., eds., *Circulation of Knowledge: Explorations in the History of Knowledge* (Lund, 2018).
3. Peder Aléx, *Konsumera rätt—ett svenskt ideal: Behov, hushållning och konsumtion* (Lund, 2003); Sophie Elsässer, *Att skapa en konsument: Råd & Rön och den statliga konsumentupplysningen* (Göteborg, 2012); Britta Lövgren, *Hemarbete som politik: Diskussioner om hemarbete, Sverige 1930-40-talen, och tillkomsten av Hemmens forskningsinstitut* (Stockholm, 1993); Orsi Husz, *Drömmars värde: Varuhus och lotterispel i svensk konsumtionskultur 1899–1939* (Hedemora, 2004); Cecilia Fredriksson, *Ett paradis för alla: EPA mellan folkhem och förförelse* (Stockholm, 1998); and Kenth Hermansson, *I persuadörernas verkstad: Marknadsföring i Sverige 1920–1965* (Stockholm, 2002).
4. Victoria De Grazia, *Irresistible Empire: America's Advance Through Twentieth-Century Europe* (Cambridge, MA, 2005). On Americanization and kitchens, see Ruth Oldenziel and Karin Zachmann, eds., *Cold War Kitchen: Americanization, Technology, and European Users* (Cambridge, MA, 2009); Gro Hagemann, "Kjøkkenet som samfundsprojekt," *Tidskrift för kjønnsforkning* 4 (2010): 307. On Americanization in Sweden, see Amanda Lagerkvist, *Amerikafantasier: Kön, medier och visualitet i svenska reseskildringar från USA 1945–63* (Stockholm, 2005); Tom O'Dell, *Culture Unbound: Americanization and Everyday Life in Sweden* (Lund, 1997); and Per Lundin, "Confronting Class: The American Motel in Early Post-War Sweden," *Journal of Tourism History* 5 (2013), 305–24.
5. Per Lundin and Thomas Kaiserfeld, *The Making of European Consumption: Facing the American Challenge* (New York, 2015); Martin Wiklund, *I det modernas landskap: Historisk orientering och kritiska berättelser om det moderna Sverige mellan 1960 och 1990* (Eslöv, 2006); Oldenziel and Zachmann, *Cold War Kitchen*; Daniel Horowitz, "The Emigré as Celebrant of American Consumer Culture," in *Getting and Spending: European and American Consumer Societies in the Twentieth Century*, ed. Susan Strasser et al. (Cambridge, 1998), 149–66; and Chapter 1 of the present volume.
6. Roy Sheldon and Egmont Arens, *Consumer Engineering: A New Technique for Prosperity* (New York, 1932). See Chapters 1–2 in the present volume.
7. Karl Popper, *The Open Society and Its Enemies*, 5th ed. (London, 2002); Hirdman, *Att lägga livet tillrätta*, 11–12. See also Yvonne Hirdman and Urban Lundberg, eds., *Sveriges historia 1920–1965* (Stockholm, 2012), 209–10; and Carl Marklund, "Bridging Politics and Science: The Concept of Social Engineering in Sweden and the USA" (PhD diss., European University Institute, 2008).
8. The circulation of the IKEA catalog increased from 13 million to 45 million between 1974 and 1984. Today about 217 million copies are published annually. See *IKEA facts 85/86* (1985), in The Collection of Ephemera in Kungliga Biblioteket (The Royal Library) (hereafter: KB, Ephemera), IKEA 1985–1986. See also "About the IKEA group," http://www.ikea.com/ms/en_GB/this-is-ikea/about-the-ikea-group/index.html.
9. Stellan Björk, *IKEA: Entreprenören, affärsidén, kulturen* (Stockholm, 1998), 120–21. See also "IKEA Systemet: IKEAs sortiment" (internal training leaflet), KB, Ephemera, IKEA 1985–1986.
10. Sara Kristoffersson, *Design by IKEA: A Cultural History* (London, 2014), esp. 70; and Jeff Werner, *Medelvägens estetik: Sverigebilder i USA. D. 2* (Hedemora, 2008).

11. We are greatly indebted to Alice Thiberg (The Swedish Consumer Agency) and the late Sven Thiberg (Professor of Building Function Analysis at the Royal Institute of Technology and, among other engagements, former chairman of the prestigious Swedish Society for Arts and Crafts and of the Swedish Furniture Research Institute); they shared some of their insights and memories with us during two long interviews on May 2 and November 21, 2014. Alice Thiberg also provided materials from her extensive collection of printed matter on kitchen planning. We also thank Lennart Ekmark (former Vice President Creative Manager for IKEA of Sweden, interviewed on February 18, 2015) and Morgan Lövgren (former executive at Marbodal, interviewed on December 1, 2014).
12. The Swedish language does not distinguish between politics and policy, so that the terms are sometimes conflated in English-language historiography. Nils Edling, "The Primacy of Welfare Politics," in *Multi-Layered Historicity of the Present: Approaches to Social Science History*, ed. Heidi Haggren, Johanna Raino-Niemi, and Jussi Vauhonen (Helsinki, 2013), 125–50.
13. Riksarkivet (The National Archives, hereafter RA), the Archives of Konsumentverket (hereafter KV), volume F1a:10, record number (Diarienummer, Dnr) 502/73-41. Citations to the archival material will thus be shortened as follows: RA, KV, FIa:10, Dnr 502/73-41.
14. RA, KV, F1a: 56, Dnr 1367/74-41.
15. *Vi*, no. 18, May 3, 1975.
16. Ibid.
17. *Form*, no. 1 (1975).
18. The Agency's criticism of IKEA was observed by economist Olof Henell, who wrote a report on the company's reaction. See Olof Henell, *Företagens reaktioner på konsumentpolitiken: Med sju praktikfall* (Stockholm, 1976). Aléx (*Konsumera rätt*, 151) and Elssässer (*Att skapa en konsument*, 202) both briefly note the Consumer Agency's criticism of IKEA, drawing on Henell.
19. For an insight into these areas of expertise, see the 1985 edition of *Bostadsboken*, edited by Alice Thiberg's husband Sven Thiberg. It was also published in many other languages (Spanish, Japanese, English, etc.), e.g., Sven Thiberg, ed., *Housing Research and Design in Sweden: 22 Researchers on Housing Design* (Stockholm: Swedish Council for Building Research [Statens råd för byggnadsforskning], 1990); For "Mrs Kitchen", see Inger Sundelin, "Fru Kök vet var skåpet ska stå," *Dagens Nyheter*, March 3, 2002.
20. Per Lundin and Niklas Stenlås, "The Reform Technocrats: Strategists of the Swedish Welfare State 1930–1960," in *Scientists' Expertise as a Performance: Between State and Society, 1860–1960*, ed. Joris Vandendriesche et al. (London, 2015). See also Edling, "The Primacy of Welfare Politics."
21. See Oldenziel and Zachmann, "Kitchens as Technology and Politics: An Introduction," in *Cold War Kitchen*, 1–10.
22. Carina Gråbacke and Jan Jörnmark, "The Political Construction of the Million Housing Programme," *Science for Welfare and Warfare: Technology and State Initiative in Cold War Sweden*, ed. Per Lundin and Niklas Stenlås (Sagamore Beach, MA, 2010).
23. *Konsumentpolitik: riktlinjer och organisation*. Statens offentliga utredningar (Swedish Government Official Reports, hereafter SOU) 1971:37 (Stockholm, 1971), 54. See also Gary Cross's chapter on "fast capitalism" in the present volume.

24. Svensk författningssamling (SFS) 1972:739 and 1976:429; Gunnar Eliasson, "Politikerna och konsumenternas problem," in *I konsumentens intresse?* ed. Solveig Wikström (Stockholm, 1979), 158.
25. The Consumer Ombudsman, in existence since 1971, was fused with the Consumer Agency in 1976. The Ombudsman then also became the Agency's director. SFS 1976:429. See also: SOU 1971:37, 35–37, 46.
26. *Konsumentverket KO: Uppgifter, organisation, verksamhet* (Vällingby, 1977), 1; and *Perspektiv på en verksamhet* (Vällingby, 1982), 11, 48.
27. Elsässer, *Att skapa en konsument*, 186, 201–3.
28. *Konsumentverket KO: Uppgifter, organisation, verksamhet* (Vällingby, 1977).
29. Kersti Gylling, "Riktlinjer som producentpåverkan—ett samhällsintresse?," in *Måste konsumenten gå till Verket?* ed. Fride Antoni and Ann-Charlotte Plogner (Stockholm, 1978), 69.
30. Göran Bystedt, "Konsumentpolitiken från ett företags perspektiv," in *Måste konsumenten gå till verket?* 66; and Gylling, "Riktlinjer som producentpåverkan," 69.
31. Ibid., 69 and Olle Wästberg, "Ämbetsverk konsumenthot," in *Svenska Dagbladet* (hereafter *SvD*), March 16, 1978; see also the article by Consumer Ombudsman Sven Heurgren "Privata konsumentgrupper behövs ej," *SvD*, February 14, 1978.
32. Göran Bystedt, "Konsumentpolitiken från ett företags perspektiv," 66.
33. RA, KV, FIa:170, Dnr 749/76-43, 760409; RA, KV FIa:10, Dnr 557/73-41, 730306; RA, KV, FIa:140, Dnr 70-719 1975; and *Råd & Rön*, no. 1 (1973).
34. *Råd & Rön*, no. 9 (1974): 12.
35. RA, KV, FIa: 118, Dnr 1020/75-422; see also FIa:119, Dnr 282/75-43; FIa:57, Dnr 342/74-422; FIa:118, Dnr 292/75-422 and Dnr 641/75-422; and FIa:170, Dnr 151/76-422.
36. "Två utmanande utställningar gav upphov till klargörande köksdebatt," *Råd & Rön*, no. 1 (1973): 19–23; and "Köket en glad arbetsplats trots standardisering," *Råd & Rön*, no. 9 (1972): 26.
37. *Svensk Snickeritidskrift Träförädlingen*, no. 19–20 (1974): 987, 988, 993.
38. Ibid., 973.
39. RA, KV, FIa:57. Dnr 1882/74-422.
40. RA, KV, FIa:118. Dnr 565/75-422. See also: RA, KV, FIa:57. Dnr 1882/74-422 and FIa:118. Dnr 565/75-422.
41. Eva Rudberg, "'Stäng in arkitekten i kokvrån!' Kvinnorna och bostadsplaneringen," in *Den okända vardagen: Om arbetet i hemmen*, ed. Brita Åkerman (Stockholm, 1983), 214.
42. *Form*, no. 4–5 (1973): 154, 158; and *Svenska kök i konsumentpolitiken, i forskningen i verkligheten* (Vällingby, 1992).
43. *Form*, no. 4–5 (1973): 158.
44. Erik Berglund, *Tala om kvalitet: Om möbelmarknaden och brukarorienterad produktutveckling* (Västerljung, 1997), 63.
45. Henell, *Företagens reaktioner*, 63.
46. Ibid.; italics added.
47. Yvonne Hirdman, *Att lägga livet till rätta. Studier i svensk folkhemspolitik* (Stockholm, 1989), 186 and 198. Orsi Husz, "The Morality of Quality: Assimilating Material Mass Culture in Twentieth-Century Sweden," *Journal of Modern European History* 10 (2012), 168. See also: *Arbetarrörelsens efterkrigsprogram. De 27 punkterna med motivering* (Stockholm, 1944), § 5 and 26;

Familjeliv och hemarbete, SOU 1947:46 (Stockholm, 1947), 26–29; and Alva Myrdal, "Folkvaror—kvalitetsvaror," *Vi*, no. 32 (1945): 9–11, 24–26.
48. Henell, *Företagens reaktioner*, 65.
49. Henell, *Företagens reaktioner*, quotes in order from 64, 67 and 62.
50. Telephone interview with Lennart Ekmark, February 18, 2015.
51. Telephone interview with Morgan Lövgren, December 1, 2014.
52. The notion "people's home" [*folkhemmet*] was, since late 1928, a widely used political metaphor referring mainly to the Social Democratic welfare society, first as a vision, later as a description of the actual society. See, for example, Hirdman and Lundberg, *Sveriges historia 1920–1965*.
53. Helena Mattsson, "Designing the Reasonable Consumer: Standardization and Personalization in Swedish Functionalism," in *Swedish Modernism: Architecture, Consumption and the Welfare State*, ed. Helena Mattsson and Sven-Olov Wallenstein (London, 2010), 74; Husz, "The Morality of Quality," 158–69, especially 166–69; and Lucy Creagh, "An Introduction to Acceptera," in *Modern Swedish Design: Three Founding Texts*, ed. Idem et al. (New York, 2008), 127–39.
54. Not only measurements but also quality aspects were standardized. On the Standards Institute and its various incarnations, see Alice Thiberg, "Standard för valfrihet," *Form*, no. 4–5 (1973): 154; Kerstin Wickman, "När kvinnorna rätade på ryggen," *Form*, no. 4–5 (1973): 153; and *Kök med standard: Anvisningar till svensk standard för inredning i bostäder* (Stockholm, 1972).
55. Kungl. Bostadsstyrelsen, *God Bostad* (Stockholm, 1954), 2, 8. See also later editions, 1960, 1964.
56. *Form*, no. 4–5 (1973): 155–156; and *Råd & Rön*, no. 5 (1971): 19.
57. Statutes for the Home Research Institute 1944. Quoted in Lövgren, *Hemarbete som politik*, 146.
58. SOU 1947:46, 242–244; Alva Myrdal and Gunnar Myrdal, *Kris i befolkningsfrågan* (Stockholm, 1934); Yvonne Hirdman, *Att lägga livet till rätta: Studier i svensk folkhemspolitik* (Stockholm, 1989), 96–97, 154–56.
59. Brita Åkerman, *Kunskap för vår vardag—forskning och utbildning för hemmen* (Stockholm, 1984); Hirdman, *Lägga livet till rätta*, 205–7; Lövgren, *Hemarbete som politik*, 148–49; and Rudberg, *Kvinnorna och bostadsplaneringen*, 210.
60. "'Drømmekjøkkenet': Ettertanker om kjønn og modernitet," in *På kant med historien: Studier i køn, videnskab og lidenskab*, ed. Karin Lützen and Annette K. Nielsen (Köpenhamn, 2008), 78; Kirsi Saarikangas, "Whats New? Women Pioneers and the Finnish State Meet the American Kitchen," in *Cold War Kitchen: Americanization, Technology, and European Users*, ed. Ruth Oldenziel and Karin Zachmann (Cambridge, MA, 2009), 288; Karin Zachmann, "Managing Choice: Constructing the Socialist Consumption Junction in the German Democratic Republic" in ibid., 267, 273; and Martina Hessler, "The Frankfurt Kitchen: The Model of Modernity and the 'Madness' of Traditional Users, 1926 to 1933," in ibid., 179.
61. Ing-Marie Berg, Lennart Holm, and Carin Boalt, *Kök: planering, inredning* (Stockholm: Hemmens forskningsinst, 1952, 1954); Ing-Marie Berg, Lennart Holm and Carin Boalt, *Kök: planering, inredning*, Statens institut för konsumentfrågor (Stockholm, 1960, 1962, 1964); *Kök: planering, inredning*, rev. ed. (Stockholm: Statens institut för konsumentfrågor, 1972); *Kök: planering, inredning*, Konsumentverket (Vällingby, 1974, 1977, 1981); and *Kök: en bok för den som planerar, bygger eller bygger om*, Konsumentverket (Vällingby, 1994).

62. See in addition to *Kök: planering, inredning* also HFI's and KI's other publications, such as *Kost och kök 1 & 2* (1947, 1950) or the series *Köksstudier* 1968–1972. See also Rudberg, *Kvinnorna och bostadsplaneringen*, 229. The quote "artificially cooled storage" ("konstkylda utrymmen") is from *God bostad i idag och imorgon* (Stockholm, 1964), 19–20.
63. *Kök: planering, inredning* (1981), 16; and Thiberg, "Standard för valfrihet," *Form*, no. 4–5 (1973): 154.
64. *Kök: planering, inredning* (1972), 43–60; and *Kök: planering, inredning* (1981), 9.
65. For example *Kök: planering inredning* (1972); 1981; *Råd och Rön*, no. 9 (1972): 3; and *Vi*, no. 18 (1975): 17.
66. The concept "basic kitchen" is reminiscent of the production line ("basic wardrobe" and later also "basic furniture") that was being introduced by the Cooperative Union (KF) at the time. In both cases, the idea was to offer reasonable, simple and fashion-insensitive products.
67. IKEA Köket 1977, KB, Ephemera, 1977–1980 and IKEA. Catalog 1979, 208 and 213.
68. According to information IKEA's archives in Älmhult (e-mail, August 14, 2015, from Cia Eriksson, Creative Project Leader & Content Responsible, IKEA Museum, Inter IKEA Culture Center AB). The archives are not open to research.
69. Leaflet "IKEAS värld" in KB, Ephemera, IKEA 1985.
70. Catalogs in KB, Ephemera, IKEA 1977–1980.
71. Leaflet "IKEAS värld" in KB, Ephemera, IKEA 1985.
72. See, for example, international catalogs from the early 1980s printed in Italy, in KB, Ephemera, IKEA, 1981–1984.
73. IKEA Kitchen 1986; IKEA köket 1986, 18–21; and "Kvalitet och funktion präglar IKEA-kökets inredning," ibid. 30–31; all in: KB, Ephemera, IKEA, 1985–1986. *Möbelfakta* was a quality control system introduced in 1972 that tested the durability and quality of furniture. It was controlled by the *Möbelinstitutet* ("The Furniture Institute," 1967–1995), which grew out of the increased concern displayed by policy makers and civil society actors for improved housing conditions in the wake of a number of public surveys in the 1940s. One of the initiators, Brita Åkerman, had previously been in charge of the Home Research Institute. IKEA built its own testing laboratory in order to apply *Möbelinstitutet*'s quality control procedures on its own products. Berglund, *Tala om kvalitet*, 20–21, 50–51, 63–67, 82–83.
74. Werner, *Medelvägens estetik*, 249–69, esp. 253. See also Björk, *IKEA*, 148.
75. "IKEA varuhuset. 5. Självbetjäning är IKEAs livsluft," 6 in KB, Ephemera, IKEA, 1985–1986.
76. "IKEA varuhuset. IKEA varuhusets planering," 20 in KB, Ephemera, IKEA, 1985–1986.
77. Liljedahl quoted in Henell, *Företagens reaktioner*, 63.
78. Wiklund, *I det modernas landskap*; See also Chap. 1 of the present volume.
79. Kristoffersson, *Design by IKEA*.
80. Oldenziel and Zachmann, *Cold War Kitchen*.
81. "Satsa rätt när du gör om köket," *Uppsala Nya Tidning*, November 19, 2001.

CHAPTER 12

"The Consumer Crusader"—Hugo Schui and the German Consumers Association

Kevin Rick

In 1964, the West German weekly *Die Zeit* published several articles dealing with Hugo Schui, a self-proclaimed "Crusader for Consumers" and former employee of the Federal Ministry for Nutrition, Agriculture, and Forestry. One of these articles described Schui as "problematic, not an easy person, hard to put in a certain category, opaque, naive, and slick at once, always dressed as neat as a pin, tall and lean, round-eyed, maybe indeed driven only by noble-mindedness."[1] Born in the Ruhr region in 1913, the educated advertising expert was characterized as a "new type of person, fitting very well into our social system, a pragmatical idealist," but also "desperately craving power." While representatives of trade associations called him esoteric and a dreamer, a ministry official even called him a "sectary" because his engagement in consumer politics manifested the fervor of a cult member.[2]

In recent research, Shui's kind of commitment has been called an outstanding example of a "more activist approach" to West German consumer politics in the 1960s.[3] For Gunnar Trumbull, "Schui's early success suggests that a grass-roots consumer movement of the kind that emerged in France might have been possible in Germany."[4] However, in contrast to well-known consumer advocates like the American Ralph Nader, Schui's early success was only short-lived. By the end of the decade, he had not only lost his job at the ministry but also his faith in consumer sovereignty and the power of the people. But the fierce opposition and bitter rejection Schui encountered was not just because of his personality. In this chapter, I argue that a great part of his efforts and failure was closely linked to the predominant concepts of political

K. Rick (✉)
EWE AG, Oldenburg, Germany

J. Logemann et al. (eds.), *Consumer Engineering, 1920s–1970s*,
Worlds of Consumption, https://doi.org/10.1007/978-3-030-14564-4_12

consumer engineering at that time. That is, state policy tried to cultivate specific consumer behaviors that, contrary to commercial efforts, were based in large part on the normative idea of economic rationality. Political efforts tried to arm consumers against the often "overtly manipulative bent" of modern marketing.[5]

Through education and information, consumers were to attain "enlightenment" so they could "emancipate" themselves from the "hidden persuaders." Instead of falling for persuasive advertising, consumers ought to support the domestic economy by choosing only useful, high-quality products, which in the long run would force corporations to produce rationally themselves and eventually lead to a "clean" functioning market. Rational consumption by responsible consumers (*mündige Verbraucher*) was emphasized as crucial to sustaining competition in the market economy. Rational consumption was not just stressed as a precondition for freedom of choice in the marketplace. The free market economy and free consumption were emphasized as the essential qualities that distinguished the "free West," with all its wealth and prosperity, from the "unfree East," afflicted by planned economies and scarcities of consumer goods.[6]

Due to the social, economic, and political importance of consumer behavior, German state policy makers established a dense network of advice and information centers already in the 1950s, and they conducted campaigns to educate and enlighten the citizenry. Consumers as sovereigns on the free market were not to be patronized by strong regulations and laws. Political consumer engineers with their agenda of rational consumption worked for consumers, who would decide autonomously, based on objective and neutral information rather than emotions, feelings, and "irrational desires" evoked by their counterparts, the commercial consumer engineers and "hidden persuaders."

This chapter takes a closer look at the underlying ideas of this specific approach to consumer policy and at the central institutions of the West German consumption regime in the 1960s, drawing on the story of the political consumer engineer Hugo Schui and his attempts to establish a consumer organization as a counterweight to both politics and corporations.[7]

The Fight for Price Competition

Hugo Schui's career as a consumer activist began in 1957. Until then, he had been merely an eager and reliable employee of the Ministry for Nutrition, Agriculture, and Forestry. In the ministry's department of sales promotion, the advertising expert had been designing campaigns to boost agricultural sales for West German farmers. During several special missions and supported by millions of marks, he had successfully supported hops and dairy farmers, and he had coordinated international advertising measures for agricultural goods.[8]

By 1957, however, he felt that something was amiss. While an increasing number of Germans at that time were coming to enjoy the many pleasant advantages of the so-called economic miracle, Hugo Schui began to worry about the sustainability and the nature of the social market economy. Since the end of World War II, West Germany had lived through a rapid economic recovery. In 1948, the Reichsmark had been replaced by the Deutsche Mark as legal tender. At the same time, Ludwig Erhard, later Minister of Economics under Chancellor Konrad Adenauer, had begun to implement the social market economy as a third way between laissez-faire economic liberalism and socialist planned economies.[9] In Erhard's view, the state should actively implement regulations to sustain competitiveness and a functioning market, for example, by preventing the formation of trusts and monopolies. Additionally, social policies based on Christian ethics should provide citizens with the security of an extensive system of social welfare.

At the beginning of the 1950s, West German industry began to boom, boosted by increasing international demand for industrial goods following the Korean War. High unemployment nearly shifted to full employment in the middle of the decade, and with rising incomes, more and more people could afford nonessential consumer goods.[10] While Erhard credited the social market economy for the country's rapid economic growth, the term "economic miracle" provides a sense of how contemporaries perceived West Germany's rapid and extensive economic recovery from the devastations of World War II.

Consumption and consumers had been highly debated in public since the early postwar years, but interest in the topic increased in 1957.[11] A lot was happening at the time. The economics ministry came up with its first plans for a comparative product testing institute.[12] Pension reforms improved the living conditions of millions of people. With the Treaty of Rome, the European Economic Union and the Common Market were finally established. Meanwhile, West Germany was experiencing not only full employment but actual labor shortages. If the Sputnik crisis was unnerving, the Act Against Restraints on Competition ultimately secured a free market economy in the Federal Republic.[13] Yet Schui was primarily concerned about something else. For him, prices were the problem: In his perception, most German retailers defined their profit margins not according to their actual expenses, but instead exploited consumers with excessive prices.[14]

In general, prices were an important political issue ever since the currency reforms in 1948. After the inflation and hyperinflation crises in the 1920s and especially after World War II, their steadiness and stability was received as a sign of economic recovery and growth. Competitive price formation was generally seen as an important prerequisite to the free market economy, even if many prices were still regulated by the state in the 1950s and 1960s. In theory, at least, sovereign consumers would avoid products with unreasonable prices; however, many Germans apparently engaged in conspicuous consumption and even took high prices as a direct sign of quality.

In Schui's view, therefore, West German consumers were very likely falling prey to smart dealers who simply raised the prices for certain goods to stimulate sales.[15] As a citizen, he felt the urge to do something. In 1957, while he was still coordinating ministry advertising programs, he founded his first consumer organization, the Käufer-IG or Buyers' Interest Group (BIG).

At first, BIG comprised only ministry staff because Schui used ministry working committees to promote his project. In this sense, Schui's approach offered no real innovation. After a few weeks, however, word spread in the German capital that BIG members could access a whole range of consumer goods at significantly reduced rates. Schui had contracted with a large number of companies, which he guaranteed a certain purchase quantity in return for their offering BIG member products at reduced rates. For a small monthly fee, members received a newsletter with an order sheet, designed and printed by Schui himself, offering products such as vacuum cleaners, television sets, washing machines, and record players. Between 1957 and 1965, Schui together with his wife and his young daughter processed over 500,000 orders after work at the family's small house in Bonn, only receiving a small commission payment from the suppliers.[16]

As an advertising expert, Schui knew very well how to separate the BIG from other "price breaker" groups and similar predecessors of discount stores. From the beginning, he stressed his political ambitions, aiming to change the whole market.[17] His strategy was very simple, based on the assumption that a market failure could only be remedied by the market itself. In Schui's view, true market freedom not only forbade political interventions but also made them obsolete in the long run. While the state should guarantee a general framework for this freedom by dismantling cartels and monopolies, Schui believed consumer attitudes were crucial to the economy, especially their attitudes toward prices.

BIG's contracts were meant to show producers, retailers, and consumers that there was no justification for trading ranges above 20 or 30%.[18] Furthermore, Schui aimed to unite active consumers who, in his words, were "convinced of the uselessness of wordy protests against high prices" but instead would punish unfair traders and producers with contempt and avoidance.[19] Such behavior would lead to a profound change of the market to the benefit of the buying public. In a somewhat neoliberal sense, then, BIG was expected to function as a catalyst for the natural mechanisms of a free market economy.

Initially, Schui and BIG were widely celebrated by the press as successful "price breakers," fighting for consumer justice and wealth.[20] With success, however, criticism grew. Retailers and producers started insulting Schui, calling him "Hugo the Cheap"[21] and comparing him to Bruno Göring, a well-known ghost healer wandering through Germany and curing people with supernatural powers.[22] Schui's mostly exaggerated statements in the press angered merchants. Despite their scathing criticisms, however,

Schui continued to propagate his creed of "sustaining affluence by cutting prices" in the following years.[23] If Schui was highly skilled at building castles in the air, his "price-breaking" efforts remained largely fruitless. Most of his projects failed. His reputation worsened, and he was branded a dreamer and troublemaker with a general lack of economic expertise. Despite Schui's claims to the contrary, it is doubtful that BIG was even a true consumer association. Apart from its self-proclaimed consumerist agenda, it was not much more than a moderately successful one-man-agency for buying discount products without any options for members to participate in the group's governance. Nevertheless, Schui's BIG experience influenced his later consumer projects to a great extent.

Promoting "Rational" Consumers

Schui finally gave up BIG in 1965.[24] Since its founding in 1957, there had been important changes in retailing and consumption. Supermarkets and discount stores were steadily replacing old mom-and-pop shops. Prepackaged and frozen foods were becoming increasingly popular, and the prices of goods like refrigerators and television sets were steadily declining because industry was finally able to match demand.[25] At the same time, Chancellor Adenauer explicitly warned his cabinet in 1962 that the time of the "dizzying upswing" was finally over.[26] Politics would have to prepare the country for slower economic growth. To maintain stability and fight economic uncertainty, it would be crucial to promote thriftiness and rational shopping. Against this background, the cabinet voted to pursue a more countercyclical budgetary policy. It also approved the foundation of an initially state-funded institute for comparative product testing, which was realized as Stiftung Warentest in 1964.[27]

The primary idea behind comparative product testing was to independently produce objective information for consumers to help them make more rational decisions. This effort would support competition and keep supply and demand in check. The basic assumption was that, despite their theoretical sovereignty over the market, consumers lacked the skills necessary to assess products and therefore they could not exercise their true power.[28] Furthermore, it was commonly believed that most consumers did not have a proper understanding of their role and duties in the market. Additionally, consumers were perceived as falling prey too easily to slick advertising techniques, which seduced them into making irrational choices and pursuing useless consumption practices. Economic Minister Ludwig Erhard, who in the 1950s had put great efforts in promoting the "courage to consume," now tried to curtail consumer demand through "calls for restraint." He warned his fellow citizens of the dangers of affluent "self-indulgence."[29]

What united comparative product testing and calls for restraint had in common was each aimed to change consumers' attitudes and behaviors.

In general, consumer politics focused mostly on consumers as individuals, stressing their system-relevant market power. Even when the number of complaints by consumer organizations and disappointed citizens about market failure grew, politics mostly shifted the blame to consumers. This gap between theoretical power and practical weakness was in fact the basic justification for the state's paternalistic claim to protect consumers. Put differently, practical limits to consumer sovereignty prompted calls for consumer protection "not only through [the] self-help of vigilant consumers and their organizations but from the state itself."[30] This protection was expressed through various laws and regulations, but for the most part West German consumer policy focused on education, "enlightenment," and advice—in other words, on political consumer engineering. The state also had its own agenda in promoting specific consumer behaviors. It tried to fashion rational, emancipated consumers able to resist the influences of "hidden persuaders" and the purely emotional, desire-driven impulses to buy luxury goods or things that went beyond the usual needs of a humble household by generally accepted standards at the time.

Crucial to its success was the strict limitation of political consumer engineering to measures compliant with market mechanisms. While avoiding direct interventions in the market, the state sought to influence consumer choices by providing certain kinds of information and promoting specific patterns of choice. In this way, it could maintain economic growth. In the state's view, only "rational" consumer choices, although hard to define with precision, would promote prosperity and affluence for individuals and society. Against that background, "the consumer was meant to fit the nationally useful economic situation."[31] In simple terms, rational shopping was perceived as necessary to maintain a market economy and consequently a Western democracy. Only rational consumer choices would sustain a well-functioning market and push German producers to develop the ability to compete internationally. Only this would, in the long run, perpetuate the economic miracle and thus the general welfare, too.

The political importance of consumer issues grew tremendously in the early 1960s, and the number of consumer-related institutions rose simultaneously.[32] Since the early postwar years, two consumer committees and two departments for consumer issues had existed at the federal ministries for economics and for agriculture and nutrition, which now were enlarged. Furthermore, every state government in the Federal Republic had its own consumer departments in several ministries. They stayed in close contact with the federal government but also started pursuing their own consumption policies. In addition, since the late 1950s, eleven so-called Verbraucherzentralen, consumer advice centers, had been founded, one in every federal state, initiated and funded by both state and federal ministries. While these centers brought together most state-level consumer associations, the leading consumer organization at the time, the Arbeitsgemeinschaft der

Verbraucherverbände, or Association of Consumer Groups (ACG), unified such groups at the federal level.

Both the advice centers and the ACG eschewed individual memberships.[33] They only accepted organizations, conflicts of competence worsened when a number of states began to claim consumer policy as members because individual consumer interests seemed too various to be organized directly. Of course, this organizational strategy led to specific consumer policy approaches. Whereas the ACG was primarily a lobbying organization with a central executive board in Bonn, each of the eleven consumer centers acted autonomously. Originally founded to provide information, the centers quickly developed a political posture, being both able and willing to amplify and represent consumer interests on a regional, state, and federal level.[34] The centers engaged continuously in national and even international debates on the role and duties of consumers. By building dense personal and formal networks, they were in close contact with federal and state governments as well as other consumer groups. It is no surprise that in the early 1960s the centers became a preferred partner for politicians to disseminate their policy objectives.[35] This circumstance was mostly due to the centers' direct access to consumers but also because they were perceived as reliable and predictable partners.[36] Since they received state and federal funding, the centers had to regularly report on their activities. At the same time, they remained politically independent on the surface. Therefore, they could host consumer events like lectures and demonstrations of household appliances without being perceived as a state actor. They also organized activities like guided factory tours and roundtables, but mainly they advised consumers during regular consultation hours in person and through media, especially in magazines, journals, brochures, and radio broadcasts.

In the second half of the 1960s, however, these consumer centers were no longer backed by just economics and nutrition ministries. Now they received inputs from various other government offices. Prompted not least by debates on comparative product testing, more and more government offices started to engage in consumption policy. Since the field had not yet been strictly defined, certain conflicts emerged when the Ministries for Economics, for Nutrition, Agriculture and Forestry, for Labor, for Housing, for Health, and for Family Affairs at the federal and state levels all claimed responsibility for consumer issues.

In this context, the Economics Ministry founded an Interministerial Committee on Consumer Affairs in 1965 to establish consumer policy as an "integrating part of general policy." Nevertheless, conflicts over responsibilities worsened when a number of states began to claim consumer policy as their own. In particular, several states tried to gain more control over the consumer centers. The centers' growing importance, however, was a major problem for the ACG, the self-proclaimed leading consumer organization, which depended heavily on governmental subsidies.[37] Furthermore, the ACG experienced increasing difficulties in legitimizing itself as "the consumer's voice" because it accepted only organizations as members and was also involved in several failed comparative product testing attempts.[38]

Since 1953, this association had attempted to gain acceptance as a partner in the market, like the corporations on the supply side. Consequently, the ACG's actions were constrained to mainly cooperating measures, focusing foremost on delivering consumer information, advice, and education.[39] In this sense, the ACG's agenda was based on the same assumptions that government officials made. Both emphasized the importance of not intervening too directly in the market, stressing that consumers had both rights and duties rooted in freedom of choice and equality in the market economy. As market partners, the ACG saw cooperation, information, and communication with producers and retailers as the only acceptable approaches to consumer policy. Against this background, ACG executive members tried hard to gain access to decision-making committees and to gain a voice as consumer representatives within the federal government.

Schui and the West German Consumption Regime

Without getting into further details, one can say that the West German consumption regime in the 1960s was shaped by conflicts over jurisdiction, overly complex bureaucratic structures, and a heavy focus on economic rationality. Hugo Schui, however, did not think that enough was being done for the consumer. In 1965, he gave up the BIG and founded the Deutscher Verbraucherbund, or German Consumers Association (GCA). At the time, he was still working at the Ministry for Agriculture and Nutrition, although his field of work had changed. Due to his activities in the BIG, Schui had come to the attention of the Federal Chancellery. Using funds budgeted to the Federal Press Office, the Chancellery organized a project for consumer education on grocery prices and rational shopping using weekly TV shows.[40]

The main goal was to inform consumers that they were able to influence prices to the better by their shopping routines. Of course, this had been Schui's whole concern. His project, however, was supposed to focus especially on foods and agricultural products. Schui was supposed to spread the message that consumers had a significant influence on the agricultural market, even though the Common Market regulated and set a large number of prices, price margins, and quality norms.[41] Furthermore, Common Market states were required by law to buy overproduction and directly intervene in the market to maintain a balance in supply and demand.[42] Strictly speaking, Schui had to calm consumers who were too critical. Unsurprisingly, this contradiction between promoting ideas of sovereign consumers and protectionism at the same time, together with his BIG experiences, led Schui to found the GCA in the summer of 1965.

Unlike the ACG, Schui's GCA accepted no organizations, only individual members.[43] As with its funding, the GCA's political legitimation was to be based on as broad a membership base as possible. For Schui, the ACG was just an "agency without specific authorization," an agency nobody authorized to speak for consumers.[44] The GCA's organizational strategy also led to a specific consumer policy approach. Whereas the ACG primarily focused on lobbying and communication, and the consumer centers primarily advised and informed, Schui was convinced that only "true action" on the market would lead to improvements.[45] He advocated for a free market and for eliminating all market regulations, believing that only unlimited free competition would lead to economic growth and prosperity for all.

Whereas the BIG had fought only against retailers and producers, the GCA's biggest opponent was the government. To Schui, it was clear that a true consumer organization had to be independent from both supply side and state or political party interests. Independence from government primarily separated the GCA from the consumer centers and from the ACG, both of which cooperated with federal and state governments. Schui instead proclaimed, "we are a power—stronger than all associations of the other side!"[46]

By "the other side," Schui meant the supply-side organizations that had been opposing him since the BIG days. However, his choice of words indicated a specific view on the modern market economy. This view was inspired by Harvard economist John Kenneth Galbraith and his 1952 work *American Capitalism: The Concept of Countervailing Power*, which criticized the notion that free markets would automatically provide socially optimal solutions. Galbraith compared worker unions' struggles against exploitation with the need for consumers to organize. Consumers could only fight exaggerated prices and stand up for a competitive market if they were united.[47] While consumers in the United States had formed a collective countervailing power in the 1920s, Schui criticized German consumer groups as lazy, illegitimate, and state controlled. However, in Galbraith's analysis, consumers like workers needed to exercise their power on the market through organized boycotts and strikes. In that sense, Schui defined the use of consumer boycotts as the main principle of the GCA's work.[48] For him, it was not enough to educate consumers on confidence and awareness. Although common consumer policy had that precise aim, Schui tried to unify consumers to attack the supply side. He criticized the state's paternalistic approach to consumer issues. Instead, he was convinced that only amplifying their individual buying power in a consumer grassroots movement could correct market failures.

Besides its organizational structure, this focus on confrontation over cooperation was the main difference between the GCA and other consumer groups. While the ACG wanted to be the "third partner on the market," Schui and the GCA wanted to be a countervailing force, stronger than all other associations.[49] Against this background, it is natural that Gunnar Trumbull calls the GCA's strategy a "more activist approach." Hugo Schui indeed preferred true action to wordy protests.

Although Schui stressed the idea of general civic responsibility to consume rationally, he also believed it was critical to create a system of exclusive benefits for GCA members.[50] These selective incentives seemed essential to acquiring and maintaining a broad GCA membership base, which would be needed for effective consumer boycotts. By paying a monthly fee, members did not just receive "The Alarm Clock *(Der Wecker)*," the GCA's monthly journal, but could also book very cheap flights to the United States. Officially, these flights were planned as opportunities for Germans to connect with American consumer advocates. Indeed, Schui himself stayed in close contact with American consumer advocates and strove to copy their concepts.[51] But since most GCA members used the flights for cheap vacations instead of political education, the events were usually poorly attended. In general, member engagement was a problem for the GCA. The initial rapid growth in membership declined steadily after peaking in 1966. Unfortunately, there are no confirmed figures; however, according to Schui's official statements, the GCA gained about 10,000 members in the first weeks after its founding in 1965.[52] In the following year, membership apparently grew to 70,000. Yet given Schui's poor administrative capabilities at his small house in Bonn, which functioned as the GCA's head office, these numbers are highly doubtful. Contemporary journalists agreed, however, that significantly more men than women enrolled in the organization.[53] Since Schui explicitly claimed that consumer policy should not be limited to housewives and often used war-like, aggressive speech, this certainly was no surprise. But even when Schui offered members legal protection insurance for consumption-related issues, their number declined steadily. In the meantime, his public temperament became increasingly more low key.[54]

Yet GCA's problems were not restricted to declining membership. Because Schui wanted the GCA to be as powerful and flexible as possible, he opposed the development of regional or local subdivisions. Instead, the whole organization centered on him personally.[55] He was the only individual who ultimately could decide to call a boycott. He also published the GCA magazine and wrote every article himself. At the same time, he was the association's press officer, president, and managing director. Due to Schui's remarkable self-confidence, there was no way members could participate in building and shaping the GCA. The organization had no democratic structure at all. Against this background, it is no surprise that off record ministry officials called Schui a "sectary."[56] To them, it was clear that Schui was acting as an eccentric loner who craved power and whose political actions had no broader societal or economic impact.

Boycotts and consumer education were not the only strategies Schui pursued. He was convinced that to successfully change consumer attitudes, it was crucial to offer proper shopping alternatives; otherwise, consumers would just fall back into old habits. Thus, with the GCA, he founded the so-called PILOT community, a group of about 60 retail stores that contractually committed themselves not to charge prices higher than 35% above wholesale cost.[57] Among other things, the stores also agreed to make public their financial records, which were checked by Schui himself on the weekends. Unsurprisingly, the cooperative group fell apart after only a few months. Store owners were naturally opposed to Schui monitoring their businesses.[58]

This was not the only setback Schui experienced shortly after founding the GCA, however. In 1966, he was finally forced to leave the Ministry for Agriculture and Nutrition, where he had worked for more than fifteen years.[59] Members of parliament had criticized Minister Hermann Höcherl in public because of Schui's engagement and his public attacks on the government.[60] His criticism had become too radical and aggressive. Furthermore, Schui had exploited his position at the ministry to gather price statistics and data for his GCA work.[61] His cooperation with business owners was seen as inappropriate for someone who focused on consumer issues.[62] Given this situation, it is understandable that state and federal agencies ended their cooperation with Schui. His former duties were simply delegated to the consumer centers, which seemed more reliable and usually eschewed antagonizing politics and business.[63]

After leaving the ministry, the GCA's success became even more important for Schui. According to internal ministry files, he could cover his living costs at that time more or less with commission payments of the PILOT-stores and GCA membership fees. Unfortunately, the few announced GCA strikes and boycotts failed completely. Nobody wanted to rally in the streets for lower butter prices, and it was a total disaster. Even if people had vociferously complained about agricultural protectionism, they were not willing to do without milk or butter. People obviously liked to listen to this eccentric, charismatic man, but their situation was not as bad as in the early 1950s, when every Deutschmark had counted. In sum, consumers in the 1960s were primarily focused on quality and health, but not on prices.[64] Schui had come too late.

The Limits of Grassroots Rebellion

Despite this failure, Schui kept trying. Eventually, he intensified cooperation with American consumer advocates and together with his son Michael founded a minor consumer organization in the United States similar to the GCA.[65] Overall, however, Schui faded from a position of significance in the 1970s. His last interview appeared in the German newspaper *Die Zeit* in 1972 on the occasion of successful consumer boycotts in Sweden. There was not much left of the former idealistic consumer advocate, who now said, "It is extremely hard to persuade the affluent German citizen to fight against exaggerated prices.... Only a dreamer would imagine a German housewife protesting in the streets."[66] For Schui, the German mentality was the crux of the GCA's failure, together with the state- and business-induced consumption patterns he had tried to fight. Discounting his personal shortcomings, Schui described his calls for strikes as mere education campaigns and insulted German consumers as too lazy and unconcerned to unify as a countervailing power.

It is questionable, however, if this assessment sufficiently explains GCA's failure. Obviously, Schui's character played a certain role, too, and the GCA did not offer any opportunities for members to participate in any meaningful way. This starkly diminished its chances for success as a grassroots movement. Also, Schui's pipe dreams, his reputation, and his stubbornness made it unbearable for state actors and other consumer groups to cooperate with him. Whereas the ACG had worked hard to engage in discussions and to provide a certain kind of expert knowledge for political and economic committees, Schui stuck to his creed, "I will cause trouble!" ("*Ich bringe Unruhe!*"), preferring confrontation over conversation.[67]

At the same time, German consumer mentalities were closely linked to a specific political environment, the West German consumption regime.[68] But while historians can hardly examine the contemporary thinking of every single consumer, it is important to remember how dense and powerful the network of governmental and non-governmental consumer institutions was at the beginning 1960s. This consumption regime primarily comprised state and federal agencies, various state-funded consumer groups, and a large number of more or less technical committees dealing with issues like labeling, standardization, and norms. As there was a strong tendency to depoliticize consumer issues, there was no place for strikes. Consumer policy was not to be pursued in the streets.

German consumers obviously did not feel the urge to demonstrate against state consumption policy. They appreciated the state-led foundation of the *Stiftung Warentest* and were content with the consumer centers' work, which provided them with practical advice and knowledge. The state-funded comparative product testing institute, in particular, was perceived as an important contribution to transparency on the market and as a stronghold against the persuasions and manipulations of commercial consumer engineers. This organization, *Stiftung Warentest*, stands out as an important example or political consumer engineering by the state, as its agenda was and still is to exclusively produce and distribute objective and neutral information but not to intervene directly in the consumers' behavior as commercial consumer engineers would normally do. Pure information was supposed to function as a basis for rational consumer choices from which not only personal affluence but, in the long run, also national economy would benefit through enhanced competitiveness and higher standards in quality, prices, and innovation.

Contrary to that approach, Schui had demanded that consumers make sacrifices in their daily lives for the greater good, that they invest time, energy, and money, while governmental funding for consumer organizations and state actions remained negligible. So even if consumers at that time had had a real chance to participate in a true consumer grassroots movement at the federal level, it most likely would not have been very attractive from a simple cost–benefit point of view. Instead, consumers mostly depended on the state. Stressing that fact in particular, a German news magazine stated in 1965 that "moral philosophers are taken aback and grumpy because plain old politics—whatever one may think of it—has done far more for consumers than they have in all their years of noble work!"[69]

In sum, Hugo Schui was certainly one of these moral philosophers. His agenda shifted from criticizing merchants for exaggerated prices to fighting economic state intervention in general. The solutions he had in mind for "healing" the market evolved from the idea that only organized consumers had the right and power to change the economy. His emphasis on consumer countervailing power and boycotts evolved in a distinctly different way from leading consumer policies and consumer organizations at that time. In this way, his failure sheds light not only on a single eccentric consumer advocate but also on the West German consumption regime as a whole. Already in the 1960s, this regime was shaped and fostered primarily by the state. GCA's agenda was a direct reaction to how both government and business viewed consumers: not as political activists, but as consuming economic actors.

Notes

1. Ingeborg Zaunitzer-Haase, "Enfant terrible unter den Verbrauchern," *Die Zeit*, October 1, 1964, 36.
2. Letter from Britsch to Dohnanyi, "IMA, Bezug auf Vorlage vom 10.05.1968," May 31, 1968, Bundesarchiv Koblenz (hereafter BAK) B102/168507.
3. Gunnar Trumbull, "Contested Ideas of the Consumer: National Strategies of Product Market Regulation in France and Germany," European University Institute Working Papers, RSC No. 2000/01, 14; and Matthew Hilton, *Prosperity for All: Consumer Activism in an Era of Globalization* (Ithaca, NY, 2009), 40.
4. Gunnar Trumbull, *Consumer Capitalism: Politics, Product Markets, and Firm Strategy in France and Germany* (Ithaca, NY, 2006), 58–59.
5. See Chapter 2 in this book by Jan Logemann.
6. This theme was mirrored, for example, in the famous 1958 "Kitchen Debate" between Nikita Krushchev and Richard Nixon. See Ruth Oldenziel and Karin Zachmann, eds., *Cold War Kitchen: Americanization, Technology, and European Users* (Cambridge, MA, 2009).
7. For a general overview, see Hartmut Berghoff, "Konsumregulierung im Deutschland des 20. Jahrhunderts: Forschungsansätze und Leitfragen," in *Konsumpolitik: Die Regulierung des privaten Verbrauchs im 20. Jahrhundert*, ed. Hartmut Berghoff (Göttingen, 1999), 7–21; Harm G. Schröter, "Konsumpolitik und 'Soziale Marktwirtschaft': Die Koexistenz liberalisierter und regulierter Verbrauchsgütermärkte in der Bundesrepublik der 1950er Jahre," in *Konsumpolitik*, ed. Berghoff, 113–33; Katherine Pence, "From Rations to Fashions: The Gendered Politics of East and West German Consumption, 1945–1961" (PhD diss., University of Michigan, 1999); Gunnar Trumbull, "Strategies of Consumer-Group Mobilization: France and Germany in the 1970s," in *The Politics of Consumption: Material Culture and*

Citizenship in Europe and America (Leisure, Consumption and Culture), ed. Martin Daunton et al. (Oxford, UK, 2001), 261–82; Christian Kleinschmidt, "Konsumgesellschaft: Verbraucherschutz und Soziale Marktwirtschaft: Verbraucherpolitische Aspekte des 'Modell Deutschland' (1947–1975)," *Jahrbuch für Wirtschaftsgeschichte/Economic History Yearbook* 1 (2006): 13–28; Christian Kleinschmidt, "Massenkonsum: 'Rheinischer Kapitalismus' und Verbraucherschutz," in *Gibt es einen deutschen Kapitalismus? Tradition und globale Perspektiven der sozialen Marktwirtschaft*, ed. Volker R. Berghahn (Frankfurt a. M., 2006), 143–53; Matthew Hilton, "Consumers and the State Since the Second World War," *The Annals of the American Academy of Political and Social Science* 611 (2007): 66–81; and Nepomuk Gasteiger, *Der Konsument: Verbraucherbilder in Werbung, Konsumkritik und Verbraucherschutz 1945–1989* (Frankfurt a.M., 2010).

8. Zaunitzer-Haase, "Enfant Terrible," 36; "Stumme Milchverkäufer," *Frankfurter Allgemeine Zeitung*, February 21, 1961, 17; and "Deutsche Handelszentren geplant," *Frankfurter Allgemeine Zeitung*, February 6, 1963, 18.
9. Werner Abelshauser, *Die Langen Fünfziger Jahre: Wirtschaft und Gesellschaft der Bundesrepublik Deutschland 1949–1966* (Düsseldorf, 1987), 31–33.
10. Arne Andersen, *Der Traum vom guten Leben* (Frankfurt a.M., 1999), 41–42 and 55–90; and Christian Kleinschmidt, *Konsumgesellschaft* (Göttingen, 2008), 131–62.
11. Schröter, "Konsumpolitik"; Kleinschmidt, "Konsumgesellschaft"; Kleinschmidt, "Massenkonsum."
12. Kevin Rick, "Die Gründung der Stiftung Warentest als 'zweitbeste Lösung'? Verbraucherpolitik zwischen Verbraucherverbänden und Staat in den 1960er Jahren," *Historische Zeitschrift* 303, no. 2 (October 2016): 428–56.
13. Kleinschmidt, "Konsumgesellschaft," 23–24.
14. "Kampf den überhöhten Gewinnspannen," *Bonner General-Anzeiger*, August 11, 1965; "Wer streikt mit?" *Abendecho*, August 28, 1965, 15; "Bonner Kaufleute: 'Schui will den Handel diskriminieren!'" *Rundschau am Rhein*, October 16, 1965, 242; and Wolfgang Hoffmann, "Schui macht die Händler scheu," *Stern*, November 24, 1966, 162–63.
15. As Jan Logemann points, the overreaching concern with quality was one thing that separated West German from U.S. consumers at the time. This emphasis also impacted German marketing strategies. Nevertheless, I have found no sources that show Schui was systematically trying to change German consumer habits in order to make them more amenable to American consumer engineering efforts. See Jan L. Logemann, *Trams or Tailfins? Public and Private Prosperity in Postwar West Germany and the United States* (Chicago, IL, 2012).
16. "Initialzündung 'Jedermann'? Bonner 'Käufer-IG' fördert den Direktbezug aus dem Ausland," *Die ZEIT*, November 14, 1957; "Billige Jedermann-Einfuhr," *Frankfurter Allgemeine Zeitung*, November 9, 1957, 7; "Umgang mit Außenseitern," *Frankfurter Allgemeine Zeitung*, December 12, 1957, 15; and "Herr Schui als Preisbrecher: Ein Angestellter des Bonner Ministeriums gründet die Käufer-Interessengemeinschaft," *Frankfurter Allgemeine Zeitung*, July, 3, 1958, 5.

17. "Aktion gegen Waschmaschinen-Spannen," *Frankfurter Allgemeine Zeitung*, May 25, 1960, 17; Peter Stehle, "Der Bonner Preis-Pilot," *Die ZEIT*, October 16, 1964, 46; and "Herr Schui als Preisbrecher. Ein Angestellter des Bonner Ministeriums gründet die Käufer-Interessengemeinschaft," *Frankfurter Allgemeine Zeitung*, July, 3, 1958, 5.
18. "Jedermann-Einfuhren durch Käufer-IG," *Passauer Neue Presse*, November 29, 1957, 8.
19. "Initialzündung 'Jedermann'?"
20. "Billige Jedermann-Einfuhr," 7; and "Umgang mit Außenseitern," 15.
21. "Umgang mit Außenseitern," 15.
22. Andreas Plagge, "Bruno Gröning," in *Biographisch-Bibliographisches Kirchenlexikon* (Nordhausen, 2005), 736–39.
23. Stehle, "Der Bonner Preis-Pilot," 46.
24. Reply by Ministry for Nutrition, Agriculture, and Forestry (hereafter BMELF) to query by members of parliament, Funck et al., "Verbraucheraufklärung" (Bundestag Drucksache V/109), December 22, 1965 (Bundestag Drucksache V/143).
25. Michael Wildt, "Die Kunst der Wahl. Zur Entwicklung des Konsums in Westdeutschland in den 1950er Jahren," in *Europäische Konsumgeschichte. Zur Gesellschafts- und Kulturgeschichte des Konsums, 18. bis 20. Jahrhundert*, ed. Hannes Siegrist et al. (Frankfurt a.M., 1997), 307–25.
26. "49. Kabinettssitzung am 08.10.1962, TOP 1: Regierungserklärung" ('Kabinettsprotokolle der Bundesregierung' online), Das Bundesarchiv, http://www.bundesarchiv.de/cocoon/barch/0100/k/k1962k/kap1_2/kap2_48/para3_2.html.
27. Kevin Rick, "Die Gründung der Stiftung Warentest als 'zweitbeste Lösung'?"
28. Günter Silberer, "Fünf Jahrzehnte Stiftung Warentest – Entwicklung einer Testinstitution im Lichte ökonomischer Zwänge und ordnungspolitischer Vorstellungen," *Zeitschrift für Unternehmensgeschichte* 2 (2014): 220–44.
29. Logemann, *Trams or Tailfins*, 41–42.
30. Pence, "From Rations to Fashions," 379.
31. Ibid.
32. Here and in the following see for further details: Kevin Rick, "Landesgeschichte und Verbraucherpolitik," *Hessisches Jahrbuch für Landesgeschichte* (2014): 103–28; and Kevin Rick, "Verbraucherpolitik als Gegenmacht? Das Scheitern einer westdeutschen Konsumentenbewegung 'von unten'in den 1960er Jahren," *Vierteljahresschrift für Sozial- und Wirtschaftsgeschichte* (2015): 161–81.
33. Frank Janning, *Die Spätgeburt eines Politikfeldes: Die Institutionalisierung der Verbraucherschutzpolitik in Deutschland und im internationalen Vergleich* (Baden-Baden, 2011), 152–53.
34. Note by Voigt, "ACG," July 11, 1961, BAK B102/168669.
35. Ibid.; "Stand der derzeitigen Lage," February 8, 1965, BAK B102/168670; see also Martens to Bayerische Verbrauchergemeinschaft e.V. – Verbraucherzentrale, "Verbraucheraufklärung": "Markt- und Preisbericht," July 28, 1966, BAK B116/24254; and Baetzgen to Neef, "Interministerieller Ausschuß für Verbraucherfragen," April 12, 1966, BAK B102/168504.

36. Note by Voigt concerning ACG and "Stand der derzeitigen Lage," February 8, 1965, BAK B102/168670.
37. Directors of ACG to Timmermann (Verbraucherzentrale Baden-Württemberg) "Wettbewerbsvereinbarungen durch den Kohleneinzelhandel," December 1, 1959, BAK B102/35987; Hessischer Minister für Arbeit, Wirtschaft und Verkehr to Bundesminister für Wirtschaft, Bundeskartellamt und die Minister für Wirtschaft der Länder, "Anhörung der Verbraucher nach §§ 2, 3 und 5 Abs. 1 GWB," October 20, 1959, BAK B102/140361.
38. Voigt to Baetzgen, "Vergleichende Warentests," June 18, 1962, BAK B102/168587; Martens to Bayerische Verbrauchergemeinschaft e.V. – Verbraucherzentrale, "Verbraucheraufklärung,": "Markt- und Preisbericht," July 28, 1966, BAK B116/24254; and Baetzgen to Neef, "Interministerieller Ausschuß für Verbraucherfragen," April 12, 1966, BAK B102/168504.
39. Janning, *Die Spätgeburt eines Politikfeldes*, 152–53.
40. Note III B 1 (BMELF), "Einsatz von Schui," July 7, 1965, BAK B116/24254; Rogge to Amt für öffentliche Ordnung Bayreuth, August 9, 1965, BAK B116/24254; Preisamt Berlin to BMELF, "Preisermittlungen für Herrn Hugo Schui," March 11, 1966, BAK B116/24254; Bayerisches Staatsministerium für Wirtschaft und Verkehr to BMWi and BMELF, "Preisermittlungen für Herrn Hugo Schui," February 8, 1966, BAK B116/24254; and Letter by Gnam (Bayerisches Staatsministerium für Wirtschaft und Verkehr) to BMWi, "Preisermittlungen für Herrn Hugo Schui mit Bezug auf Schreiben vom 13.04.1966," April 25, 1966, BAK B116/24254.
41. Presse- und Informationsamt der Bundesregierung to Martens, "Hugo Schui," September 3, 1965, BAK B116/24254.
42. Kiran Klaus Patel, *Europäisierung wider Willen: Die Bundesrepublik Deutschland in der Agrarintegration der EWG 1955–1973* (Munich, 2009), 312–33 and 380–81; Mark Spoerer, "'Fortress Europe' in Long-Term Perspective: Agricultural Protection in the European Community, 1957–2003," *Journal of European Integration History* (2010): 143–62, especially: 143–48; for contemporary reports, see: "Am Butterberg," *Die ZEIT*, April 29, 1966, 34; "Butter – Dampf in der Pfanne," *Der Spiegel*, August 14, 1967, 26; "Butter im Trog," *Der Spiegel*, July 29, 1968, 23; Sybil Gräfin Schönfeldt, "Keine Gramm-Bagatelle: Manipulation mit Milch," *Die ZEIT*, November 15, 1968, 62; and Hermann Bohle, "Hohe Preise—unruhige Bauern," *Die ZEIT*, October 31, 1969, 40.
43. Trumbull, *Consumer Capitalism*, 51.
44. Hugo Schui, "Werben Sie neue Mitglieder!" *Der Wecker*, December 1967/ January 1968, 10.
45. "Gegen überhöhte Verbraucherpreise und 'Wohlstandstick'," *VWD Landwirtschaft und Ernährung*, June 29, 1965, 9–10.
46. Schui, "Werben Sie neue Mitglieder!" 10.
47. John Kenneth Galbraith, Der amerikanische Kapitalismus im Gleichgewicht der Wirtschaftskräfte (Stuttgart, 1956), 126–27.
48. Note III B 1 (BMELF) "Einsatz von Schui," July 7, 1965, BAK B116/24254; and Wolfgang Hoffmann, "Schui macht die Händler scheu," *Stern*, 47/1966, 162–63.

49. Britsch to Dohnanyi "IMA, Bezug auf Vorlage vom 10.05.1968," May 31, 1968, BA, B102/168507.
50. Hugo Schui, "Flugplan PILOT-Reisen USA," *Der Wecker*, November 1967, 7; Wolfgang Hoffmann, "Die Anwälte der Konsumenten. Viele Verbraucherverbände – wenig Erfolg," *Die ZEIT*, March 26, 1971, 29; Hugo Schui, "Liebes Mitglied!" *Der Wecker*, September 1968, 2; and "Vorschuß von Schui," *Die ZEIT*, May 8, 1970, 35.
51. "Asoziale im Frack," *Der Spiegel*, September 21, 1970, 61–62.
52. "Wer streikt mit?" *Abendecho*, August 28, 1965, 15; "Bonner Kaufleute: 'Schui will den Handel diskriminieren!'" *Rundschau am Rhein*, October 16, 1965, 242; and Hoffmann, "Schui macht die Händler scheu," 162–63.
53. Stehle, "Der Bonner Preis-Pilot," 46.
54. "Vorschuß von Schui," *Die ZEIT*, May 8, 1970, 35.
55. Note III B 1 (BMELF), "Einsatz von Schui," July 7, 1965, BA, B116/24254.
56. Britsch to Dohnanyi, "IMA, Bezug auf Vorlage vom 10.05.1968," May 31, 1968, BA, B102/168507.
57. "Pilotgemeinschaft will Preisklarheit schaffen," *Frankfurter Allgemeine Zeitung*, May 22, 1964, 26; and Hugo Schui, "Was sind Pilotfirmen?" *Der Wecker*, November 1967, 5.
58. "Asoziale im Frack."
59. VI B 1 (BMELF) to Diskussionskreis Mittelstand der CDU/CSU-Fraktion des Deutschen Bundestages, "Deutscher Verbraucherbund," November 18, 1966, BAK B116/24254.
60. Request ("Kleine Anfrage") by members of parliament, Funck et al., to Bundesregierung "Verbraucheraufklärung," December 8, 1965, Bundestag Drucksache V/109.
61. Preisamt Berlin to BMELF, "Preisermittlungen für Herrn Hugo Schui," March 11, 1966, BAK B116/24254; Gnam (Bayerisches Staatsministerium für Wirtschaft und Verkehr), to BMWi, "Preisermittlungen für Herrn Hugo Schui mit Bezug auf Schreiben vom 13.04.1966," April 25, 1966, BAK B116/24254; Gnam to Preisreferate der Regierungen Oberbayern, Niederbayern, Oberpfalz, Oberfranken, Mittelfranken, Unterfranken, Schwaben, "Preisermittlungen für Herrn Hugo Schui," June 28, 1966, BAK B116/24254; Martens to Bayerische Verbrauchergemeinschaft e.V. – Verbraucherzentrale, "Verbraucheraufklärung,": "Markt- und Preisbericht," July 28, 1966, BAK B116/24254; and VI B 1 (BMELF) to Diskussionskreis Mittelstand der CDU/CSU-Fraktion des Deutschen Bundestages, "Deutscher Verbraucherbund," November 18, 1966, BAK B116/24254.
62. Hessischer Rundfunk to Hessischer Minister für Wirtschaft und Verkehr, "Hugo Schui," July 29, 1966, Hessisches Hauptstaatsarchiv Wiesbaden (HHStAW) Abt. 507, Nr. 8060.
63. Martens to Bayerische Verbrauchergemeinschaft e.V. – Verbraucherzentrale, "Verbraucheraufklärung,": "Markt- und Preisbericht," July 28, 1966, BAK B116/24254; Baetzgen to Neef, "IMA," April 12, 1966, BAK B102/168504.
64. Irmgard Zündorf, "Der Preis der Marktwirtschaft. Staatliche Preispolitik und Lebensstandard in Westdeutschland 1948 bis 1963" (*Vierteljahrschrift für Sozial- und Wirtschaftsgeschichte* Beihefte Nr. 186) (2006), 303–5.

65. "Asoziale im Frack."
66. Ingeborg Zaunitzer-Haase, "Streik der Hausfrauen? Fragen an Hugo Schui zum Käufer-Boykott," *Die ZEIT*, March 10, 1972, 34.
67. "Asoziale im Frack," 61–62.
68. For further details, see my recently published dissertation: Kevin Rick, *Verbraucherpolitik in der Bundesrepublik Deutschland: Eine Geschichte des westdeutschen Konsumtionsregimes* (Baden-Baden, 2018).
69. Norbert Harlinghausen, "Er blieb der Individualist am Markt," *Mann in der Zeit*, June 1965, BA, B102/168670.

CHAPTER 13

Consumer Engineering by Belgian Consumer Movements: From Modern Marketing with a Transnational Touch to Late-Modern Insecurities, 1957–2000

Giselle Nath

As marketers learned to effectively conjure up dreams and engineers designed new, more streamlined consumer worlds, how did the conscious and engaged consumer respond? Was there a backlash from organized consumers who based their purchases on autonomous reason, rather than skillful persuasion by advertisers? We know of course that the postwar period gave rise to a transnational consumer movement that took many nationally distinct forms. We might assume that these movements, as activist groups and political representatives of the consumer, would have delivered the most sustained criticisms of consumer engineering as wasteful manipulation. That would be jumping to conclusions, however. Just like products, consumer action and consumer agency were themselves increasingly promoted and commodified. The comparative testing organizations that emerged in Western Europe from the 1950s are a good illustration of this counterintuitive development.

If their purpose was to aid consumers in their consumption decision-making, these organizations actually betrayed ambivalent attitudes toward mass consumer society in general and modern advertising in particular. In this, they were children of their time and social environment. Consumer activist groups relied on the very notions that had kick-started consumer engineering—more rational compromise between demand and supply, for example, material prosperity as a valuable social goal. Some of the

G. Nath (✉)
De Standaard, Groot-Bijgaarden, Belgium

J. Logemann et al. (eds.), *Consumer Engineering, 1920s–1970s*,
Worlds of Consumption, https://doi.org/10.1007/978-3-030-14564-4_13

movements even had more in common with the disciplines of design and marketing than with traditions of social protest. In fact, they shared a common and remarkable transatlantic history with these disciplines.

The Belgian case is instructive. Two consumer organizations with distinct political profiles coexisted in Belgium, beginning in 1957 and 1959 respectively, until one of them collapsed in 1984. Each published its own periodical with the results of product comparison tests and other consumer advice. One of them was produced by an advertising professional, the other by less educated, working-class women. The Belgian consumer organizations were no marginal players. During the sixties, about one in three Belgian households had a subscription to a consumer advice periodical.[1] At its height during the seventies, the higher brow Test-Achats had 300,000 subscribers, which arguably made it the largest middle-class movement in Belgian history. Per capita, Belgium was in the top seven of subscriptions to comparative testing magazines in 1969, behind the Netherlands and the Scandinavian countries, but ahead of the United States, West Germany, and France.[2]

Consumer organizations railed against deceptive advertising practices, making consumers more conscious of price–quality ratios or pointing out structural injustices in the market. Yet these selfsame organizations, hybrids of social movement and commercial publishing house, relied on similar marketing techniques to get their messages across. Their shifting attitudes toward marketing and commercial survival allow us to observe a form of consumer engineering that spilled into the social, political, and cultural fields.

Interestingly, one Belgian movement initially rejected "scientific" methods of promotion, whereas the other thrived with the use of direct mailings, surveys, enticing advertising campaigns, and even the mobilization of peer pressure. While competing in the same market under the same social conditions, one movement streamlined its entire product, both visually and politically, for an audience aspiring to affluence and an easy lifestyle. This movement owned much of its success to a subtle, almost subliminal psychological theme, that to be a distinctive and distinguished consumer, one had to read rather than pursue collective action.

Yet the methods for recruiting subscribers that Belgian consumer movements employed during the mid-century "modern planning" frenzy ultimately proved insufficient to entice consumers in so-called late modernity, the phase starting after the seventies, which represented not necessarily a total rupture with the early years of the Cold War, but rather an intensification of factors associated with modernity.[3] The countercultural and often environmentally inspired critiques of the late sixties and early seventies harmed the image of progressiveness that consumer movements had long esteemed. In an age of attacks on the conformity and wastefulness of mass consumer society, consumer activists were no longer assumed to be valuable agents of social reform. Consequently, consumer magazines suddenly found their precarious business model at the mercy of a fickle readership and a fast-changing publishing market. They had to look for new strategies to "sell" consumer activism. By assessing these strategies, this chapter engages with far-reaching changes in the political economy and social fabric of mature consumer societies. At the same time, analyzing these strategies helps to historicize "consumer engineering" as a very broad trend, something even pursued by a rather unusual suspect: critical consumer activists themselves.

Organizing Consumers Across the Atlantic: The Transfer of a Challenge

Consumer activist confidence in the viability, even superiority of testing the technical properties of goods, of evaluating products comparatively, and of then selling that information through periodicals originated in the United States. It was first put into practice just before the Great Depression. Consumer Research Inc (CR), founded in 1929, was the answer of intellectuals and technocratic engineers to a perceived "waste of the consumer's dollar."[4] But there were other, more radical forms of consumer social mobilization in the United States, including the left-leaning League of Women Shoppers and the older National League of Consumers. None of these organizations relied on testing as heavily as CR did. The fact that CR originated among consumer engineers who had taken their testing work for corporations into the field of activism highlights the extent to which comparative testing and consumer engineering shared a family history.[5]

During the 1930s, the intellectual call for reform of the economy led to a polarization of the U.S. debate on consumer rights. Some attributed the Great Depression to "underconsumption" and advocated an expanded definition of the consumer interest. This line of thinking led to the foundation of the socially progressive Consumers Union (CU) in 1936. Others—most notably the management of CR—believed that defending the consumer interest had nothing to do with broader social or welfare policies. They defined consumer education as merely a technical, nonpartisan, and nonpolitical activity. This point of view was already apparent when one of CR's leaders went on a crusade against unions in the company and even actively joined Congressman Martin Dies in the prosecution of so-called subversive consumerist organizations with an alleged "communist bias."[6] These efforts culminated in the establishment of the House Committee on Un-American Activities, which had CU (not coincidentally CR's biggest competitor) on its list until 1954. CR ultimately rejected the incorporation of sustained critique of American consumer capitalism in its evaluation of consumer goods. Although this attitude could be defended (whether one defines consumer society in terms of goods rather than social relations is a matter of opinion), it is much harder to appreciate CR's technocratic liberalism as truly nonpolitical, which they claimed it was.[7] Despite being blacklisted, CU eventually overtook CR in subscriber numbers. For a few crucial years during the late 1930s,

CU's predominantly liberal management of lawyers, doctors, and social workers from the New York area tried to channel the interests of workers and "underprivileged" consumers. In the end, however, political pressure and a pervasive climate of anti-Communism drove them to accept a more cautious, supposedly nonpolitical agenda during and after World War II.[8] Yet CU still broke new ground abroad. Backed by American Cold War diplomacy, which wanted to reconstruct European economies in a more demand-driven direction, CU leader Colston Warne started to spread a so-called Anglo-Saxon model of organized consumerism to Western Europe during the early 1950s.[9] This resulted in the founding of the Dutch Consumentenbond (1953), the British Consumers' Association (1957), the Belgian Test-Achats (1957), and others.

The crux of the whole endeavor was that such consumer organizations were essentially commercial publishing houses. For instance, Test-Achats published the eponymous monthly and bilingual magazine *Test-Achats*, which depended on the subscription revenues of their consumer–members instead of advertising by businesses.[10] In this Anglo-Saxon model of independent, ostensibly nonpolitical consumerism, there was also little room for coalitions with trade unions, working-class cooperative movements, or (a more obvious starting point at the time) women's organizations, all of which had traditionally taken up consumer and household issues. The tenets of modernization theory were never absent from the Anglo-Saxon consumer organizers. They believed that the ideal model of organized consumerism was to be found in the United States and had to spread in a uniform fashion to other countries. They also posited that "modern" consumer movements sold "objective" information to rational-minded men (a predominantly female readership was not preferred). In practice, the early verbose technical reports could only appeal to a minority of highly educated, technically literate men.

This framework immediately saddled the newly founded European consumer associations with large problems, particularly because the Americans never really understood the particularities of their own pluralist and relatively wealthy society. Outside of the United States, cooperatives, trade unions, and women's groups had a claim to social legitimacy and prominence that the editors of testing magazines could only dream of. Meanwhile, consumer start-ups faced huge costs. Producing a marketable periodical required trained staff and a laboratory infrastructure, whereas in the other type of social movement, mobilizing members was a cheaper, grassroots activity. The social movements Europeans were accustomed to did not sell a product, they united people. Finally, unlike for instance the Norwegian, Swedish, and Danish public consumer institutions, some of those following the Anglo-Saxon ideal were not even interested in policy making or public interventions in the market. They took inspiration from a rather implicit market-liberalism and preferred making a private effort at educating what they called the "intelligent" individual.[11] Certain class and gender prejudices were never absent, as when a Belgian consumer magazine published a satirical "Buyer's Column" on the experiences of the down-to-earth breadwinner who buys a new kitchen and finds himself dismayed at his "incapable and distracted" wife, not to mention the fat and lazy blue-collar workers who come to install it. Frequently, test results were narrowly technical research reports on high-brow goods such as whiskeys, deep fryers, and kitchen scales and available only through an expensive yearly subscription fee.

In most European societies, a completely independent social movement built on individual membership and magazine sales faced grim prospects. Markets were small (as many workers still lacked significant disposable income). Civil society was geared toward party politics and public intervention, not providing information. Moreover, companies tended to intimidate the consumer testers by taking them to court. Even in the well-developed American consumer society, CU did not start operating from scratch, as it naively exhorted Europeans to. CU could always rely on influential partners in government, media, and civil society. There was also a tradition of charities giving grants to liberal causes, not to mention the groundbreaking work by CR, the predecessor of CU. Tellingly, the British Consumers' Association could not have survived its early years without a large grant from the American Elmhurst Foundation.[12]

Belgian Test-Achats (TA) was founded in 1957 by the advertiser Louis Darms following close contacts with Colston Warne of CU. TA became one of the most ardent continental defenders of what it called the "scientific," "modern," independent Anglo-Saxon model of consumerism. But it, too, could not have survived without repeated bailouts and loans from its American colleagues at CU and the British Consumers' Association, which valued the Anglo-Saxon model too much to allow its symbolic defeat. Nonetheless, unwilling to admit the need for significant outside investment in its start-up phase, TA consistently claimed that it derived its income only from paying members, while publicly denying allegation of American support. However, the organization only reached financial equilibrium in the second half of the sixties.[13] So this mystifying use of the label "Anglo-Saxon" indicates that there was more at stake than simply classifying products with objective, scientific arguments. By focusing on the private aspect of the movement, certain comparative testing organizations hoped to make further government interventions obsolete. TA was one of the most vocal defenders of individual empowerment in a free consumer market (and Darms' mind-set showed eerily close similarities to that of Hugo Schui, discussed by Kevin Rick in this book). TA prioritized the creation of a more perfect, a more rational and explicitly globalized market over collective action on behalf of the consumer-citizen. In TA's view, the creation of such a market ultimately depended not on adequate regulation but on smarter individual choices. In fact, TA even dismissed the idea of a vulnerable consumer. TA's form of education was not geared toward working class; it assumed instead that the consumer problems of the working class (most notably: lack of purchasing power and quality in basic necessities) were already a thing of the past (they were not). TA valued cheaper free trade over concerns about decent wages or safety regulations. Additionally, it frequently referred to its "American" or Anglo-Saxon approach to lend itself a strong rhetorical marker of modernity without openly discussing its more ambiguous implicit political message (Fig. 13.1).

This somewhat veiled Cold War vision on the political economy was not always shared by the Americans of CU themselves, who initially championed the "progressiveness" of Social-Democratic (and explicitly political) consumer initiatives in the Scandinavian countries.[14] But Belgian TA, and to a lesser extent the Dutch Consumentenbond, the British Consumer Association, and the consumer-minded bureaucrats flocking to Adenauer in West Germany all favored a more technocratic, even moralizing approach. They framed social problems caused by corporate negligence (or, in cases like medicines and cigarettes, corporate crime) into the responsibility of the individual, who was said to buy frivolously and possess insufficient knowledge. Even more important, none of these groups favored the more interventionist policies to shape the market that Social Democrats advocated. When Warne surveyed the young consumer movements in Europe and reported back to CU, he noted that the West German model for organized consumerism was an attempt to forestall "labour encroachment."[15] As for Belgium, TA's leading managers were closely connected to the Catholic political establishment. Their faith in self-improvement under the (patronizing) wings of enlightened experts and their repeated insistence that governments should not intervene directly but merely create the conditions under which civil society organized itself were consistent with a longer tradition in Belgian political Catholicism.[16] Given the massive popular support for trade unions, Social Democrats, and welfare policies in the 1950s, political Catholicism was looking for a way to strengthen its message. Transatlantic connections, forged in the context of U.S. Cold War diplomacy, provided a means. After all, Colston Warne received a significant degree of support and facilitation by the State Department.[17] While he himself did not favor political Catholicism per se (indeed, he struggled to understand it), he tended to consider consumer organizations linked to the male, upper-class establishment as more "professional" than other competitors.

Nonetheless, competitors to TA were on the rise. TA's highly political and somewhat elitist appropriation of comparative testing soon encountered opposition. In 1959, two women's associations within the Belgian Social-Democratic movement founded the Union Fémine pour l'Information et la Défense du Consommateurs (UFIDEC). One of these founding groups was the Cooperative Women's Guild; all funding (indirectly) came from Social-Democratic civil society groups such as the Social-Democratic trade union, the cooperative movement, and the Social-Democratic bank. The most noticeable difference between TA and UFIDEC was that UFIDEC explicitly wanted to be an inclusive social movement for political consumer defense rather than a company that provided information. UFIDEC's commitment

Fig. 13.1 Cover of October 1965 issue of *Test Aankoop* (the Flemish version of *Test Achats*), which contained test results for "electric water kettles" and "caviar and false caviar." Emphasizing household technology and luxury products, the cover's layout shows the intention to appeal to the "modern consumer." "*Wij lazen voor*": We read for you. The organization represented by this magazine positioned itself as a service provider for Belgian shoppers, offering, for example, questions and answers about product guarantees and after-sales services.

to the working class and to social reform resulted in different priorities (for instance, proposals for food safety laws), a more popularizing editing style, more modest international ambitions (unlike TA, UFIDEC did not join the International Organization of Consumers Unions), as well as a cheaper subscription fee. UFIDEC could maintain this cheaper fee only because the compounded rank-and-file base of several Social-Democratic groups initially gave it a much larger membership than TA had.

Consumer activists found from early on that forging an activist consumer subjectivity among the masses was not an easy job, however. The challenge did not just entail getting Europeans to adopt rational buying habits in the face of so many new products for sale. It also involved targeting citizens as consumers and convincing them that this new, social movement was worth contributing to. In Belgium, for instance, unemployment was a far bigger concern to average consumers than getting a guide to rationally navigating affluent society's consumer choices. Moreover, during the fifties and early sixties, the highly educated consumers targeted by testing publications formed only a small minority of the consumer population at large. For the others, such a purchase was an unnecessary luxury. Women's neighborhood networks and household teachers had until then been the quintessential consumer educators. People had to get used to this new, more commercial form of consumer education.

Even if export-geared Belgium shared in the European postwar boom, affluence for all remained a problematic and contentious ideal rather than a reality. Employers kept stressing wage moderation. After disappointingly low growth levels in the fifties, economic expansion only really took off during the sixties. Some cars entered everyday life in the fifties, homeownership was increasing, and the 1958 Brussels World Fair symbolized the commercial dream worlds of mass consumption. Yet the middle-class consumer standard long remained a rather thin veneer on a society with significant inequalities. Belgian mass consumer society excluded some social groups. Outsiders included working-class Belgians in the fifties; single mothers, pensioners, and blue-collar workers in the late sixties; and migrant laborers and welfare recipients in the seventies and eighties. The "consumer" problems faced by such groups sparked continual debates on the shortcomings of the welfare state.

The consumer movements played a rather marginal role in these core debates on welfare and the role of the state. This was partly because the political arena was already crowded with more established interest groups. Additionally, consumer movements had a hard time convincing their rank-and-file that they belonged in that scene. The political goals of a would-be nonpolitical social movement remained ill-defined. Could the often ambitious, technocratic movement "entrepreneurs" claiming to represent everybody be taken seriously?[18] Would women be allowed to discuss macroeconomic policy? During the entire Cold War, political leaders, trade unions, and academic experts in social policy remained the primary participants in debates about welfare, wages, and the market. In the early postwar decades, the consumer movements had more modest tasks to deal with: ensuring the survival of their organization and producing content for their publications.

To accomplish these goals, ironically, they themselves increasingly needed to communicate their market value and brand to consumers. As a project of female, working-class social activists, UFIDEC had distinct disadvantages compared to TA. The latter was founded by a trained and experienced advertiser who could count on a wide circle of academic acquaintances and establishment groups. As time passed, these very different attitudes to marketing and resource mobilization made for very different trajectories.

Recruiting Rank-and-File in the Fifties and Sixties

One of the most conspicuous elements of TA's "marketing mix" was a product with a glamorous look and feel, especially compared to UFIDEC. TA offered a magazine printed on glossy paper, with witty features and lots of pictures that tapped into the optimistic zeitgeist of the golden sixties. UFIDEC, by contrast, used simple drawings and the occasional picture of a housewife. Nonetheless, Gilbert Castelain, lifelong director of TA, suggested in hindsight that "when you look at our first issues, they were not fun at all… If one took a subscription to that horrible thing, it was based on conviction."[19] Notwithstanding its pretty packaging, TA's content was below standard during its first years due to a lack of members and correspondingly low funds. The first issues did not even offer a "best buy" recommendation but instead went into detailed technical explanations.[20]

To promote its organization, TA pioneered a number of marketing approaches that were somewhat alien to working-class strategies for social mobilization. It combined large-scale direct mailing with elite recruitment, and it convinced readers to recruit their peers by offering material incentives ("buy a subscription, get a gift"). But unlike the consumer cooperative tradition, which was very strong in Belgium, membership in TA conferred no sense of ownership. The incentives were based on immediate gratification and material profit, which UFIDEC objected to on principle.

Direct mailing, at the time a rather novel way to target customers based on sociographic segmentation and psychological profiling, was something TA picked up through seminars in Canada and the United States, and from the British editor of Readers Digest. But even if this "innovative" strategy seemed like an instant winner, the first attempts yielded embarrassing results. A campaign aimed at 3000 architects resulted in thirty-five new subscriptions; one that targeted 1022 pharmacists brought in eight. Such results could not cover the investment, and TA actually lost money on these new members.[21] What made the difference in the long term was not the use of novel transnational techniques per se but the alliance TA made with the Christian-Democratic trade union and women's associations. With a large database of addresses gathered on the basis of political loyalty instead of market value, promotional mailings really started to pay off for TA. Because the Catholic and Christian-Democratic movement dominated Belgian civil society and politics numerically (especially in the northern part of the country), this coalition amplified TA's reach tremendously. TA also adapted its message to the new audience. Unlike in its first promotional campaigns, TA's message to Christian-Democratic popular associations stressed not its usefulness in helping consumers save money (as in the more elitist message to the architects) but instead focused on the consumer cause as a valuable form of social activism. TA argued for the first time that organizing consumers was a matter of social justice.[22]

Through their networks, the professionals and academics in TA's management had more favorable opportunities for elite recruitment than UFIDEC did. High-ranking influential professionals (most notably the Association of Female Journalists, household education teachers, and even officials in government and the army) assured favorable exposure among the audiences that really mattered. TA was furthermore promoted in Rotary Clubs, at YMCAs, and at the high-brow club Touring Assistance for car owners.[23] Elite recruitment offered strategic, rather than numerical advantages. Elites could be hired to do further promotion in what advertiser and founder Louis Darms of TA called an autonomous or even "contagious" fashion. For instance, if TA made itself known among female journalists, these could spread the news and multiply readership without TA having to make further efforts. People or institutions with money further alleviated the costs of promotion. In 1961, TA reached an agreement with the Kredietbank to offer TA's magazine to its male and married staff at a reduced price. The bank effectively compensated TA for the discount.[24] Finally, TA created a high-brow and desirable image. To read TA was to aspire to no longer be working class, to no longer worry about bread-and-butter issues.

A final strategy was peer-to-peer recruitment. TA repeatedly launched campaigns with imaginative names such as Opération 1-2-3 (a 1962 campaign that urged readers to recruit one friend, one colleague, and one family member), Objective 64 (1964) and Tache d'huile (literally, Oil Stain, 1966).[25] The Objective 64 campaign urged readers to convince one new member every month; it led to an exasperated readers' letters from a member who felt pressured by these demands. Such campaigns, modern though they looked, in fact mirrored the quasi-artisanal, community-based efforts made by UFIDEC militants. The latter lectured at workplaces, mobilized women's or Social-Democratic neighborhood clubs, hosted plays, and even set up raffles during community events. What distinguished TA from UFIDEC was that it gradually began to award its members for these efforts with rather expensive material gifts for high-brow tertiary workers, such as leather pocket calendars and watches.[26]

Even in distribution and price-setting, TA demonstrated that it had paid attention to the latest insights into what it considered to be modern consumer engineering (as opposed to what it saw as vulgar, old-fashioned collective action by "*les classes populaires*"). The leisure-oriented, middle-class character of TA was underscored by a first promotional campaign near the office of tourism at the Belgian coast.[27] And by the time UFIDEC lowered its subscription fee even further to 20 Belgian Francs a year, TA reacted to this potential death blow by "risking everything"; it raised its own subscription fee to 150 (later 200) Belgian Francs. Castelain recounted,

> this perhaps astonishing reaction was based on two realities. First of all the reality of marketing, because the public is a priori more favorable towards expensive products, which it tacitly considers to be superior. Secondly the logic of numbers [of subscriptions]. TA did not have the means to follow UFIDEC in a price battle. They were subsidized by the socialist cooperative movement, we were subsidized by nobody![28]

Underpinning these different approaches to recruitment were convictions about the identity and agency of consumers. TA needed as many subscribers as possible so it quickly became an interest group run like a business. Transatlantic exchanges played an interesting role in this respect. Castelain claimed that he traveled to the United States "every three or four years" and learned there to manage TA like a company (although CU's way of operating differed significantly from that of TA and CU's records show only one attempted visit by Castelain).[29] Interestingly, TA's initial underdog position entrenched a zero-sum game mentality. For instance, it "hijacked" Ralph Nader for an exclusive press conference, whereas the original plan had been for all Belgian consumer-minded organizations to join forces in hosting the famous American consumer activist.[30] TA's main goal was of course to enhance its reputation among potential subscribers.

UFIDEC meanwhile believed its readers should and could balance their private consumer demands with their social responsibilities as Social-Democratic citizens. It spoke to prospective activists and financially badly pinched housewives rather than anonymous buyers intent on saving money. Although UFIDEC considered the work of CU and the British Consumers Association valuable, its management was much less inclined to adopt everything "American" as modern or superior. Its board suggested that the so-called Anglo-Saxon organizations had reduced publishing to an end in itself instead of a means to an end.[31] UFIDEC also opposed slick advertising on principle. That TA capitalized on the same attitudes it tried to dissuade its audience from following blindly (think of the gifts, the psychologically targeted messages, and the visual communication) was considered bad practice by UFIDEC. With the moralizing social policies of Catholic origin still in its memory, the Social-Democratic UFIDEC also stressed that consumers needed to learn to think for themselves. A critical consumer attitude was worth more than any buying recommendation. In contrast to TA's designation of an ultimate best deal, or *Maître-Achat*, among the products tested, UFIDEC stressed individual differentiation (because not every consumer valued the same criteria) and critical consumer awareness:

"[TA's] ready-made opinions on consumer problems disempower the consumer and take away their responsibilities."[32] Although the UFIDEC anticipated market segmentation in theory, it did not use these insights into brand itself better. It just stubbornly and steadily continued its work of testing products, suggesting legislation, and answering reader complaints. UFIDEC's self-proclaimed goal was not selling as much as possible (although important in practice) but informing critical consumers about strategies for a safer marketplace.

To characterize TA's approach as the more professional one or to classify UFIDEC as traditional and drab would ignore important structural factors relating to class, gender, and identity construction. The two Belgian consumer movements were actually operating in different social universes, which led them to employ different cultural codes. From the perspective of UFIDEC, TA had sold out to commercialism and its behavior was unworthy of a true consumer movement. TA's reliance on gadgets for subscribers allegedly made it too docile toward the companies whom it needed to obtain such gadgets. UFIDEC consistently claimed to be the more ethical, credible alternative: "How can a consumer organization use tactics which it opposes on principle?"[33] UFIDEC furthermore objected to TA's sensationalism and its aggressive, one-dimensional framing of complex social problems. Seen from a business perspective, however, media scoops were essential. TA got in the habit of not openly referring to or criticizing its "competitor," although it clearly felt more comfortable with the laws of the commercial jungle. It channeled its profits into expanding the organization, hiring trained specialists, and setting up new activities. By the early seventies, TA could call itself the bigger and more dynamic consumer movement.

Nonetheless, the success of TA's form of consumer engineering owed just as much to the changing social fabric of the emerging mass consumer society as it did to marketing skills. TA exploited obvious desires for social distinction. Its focus on rationality and social status (exemplified by their subscribers' ability to obtain state-of-the-art products without loosening the purse strings too much) attracted those who wished to distinguish themselves from the "political" or "militant" attitudes of working-class politics, while clearly also not really belonging to the most prosperous social groups.[34] TA's magazine reflected the spending patterns and even the moderate-to-conservative political opinions of an expanding middle class.[35] Its concerns also fitted a society that was rethinking its very foundations after two painful occupations during the world wars. Both occupations had seen steep rises in inequality, material deprivation for broad segments of the population, and fears of destabilization and chaos among the elites. The interwar years only saw further erosion of savings as well as the intensification of social conflicts. After World War II, the Keynesian-Fordist compromise for regulation promised higher wages but at the same time called for efficient spending of these wages to avoid the "excessive" pay increases that employers still vigorously objected to. So the things that TA communicated about (status, security through material possessions, mass consumers with considerable discretionary income and individual strategies of improvement) were topical to say the least.

The Belgian welfare state also further institutionalized a model of male breadwinners and female housekeepers.[36] This development implied both formal and emotional recognition of domesticity as a desirable social goal for both sexes, not just one. Whereas consumer education during the first half of the twentieth century was entirely focused on women and scarcity, post-1945 consumer magazines attracted men with articles on "luxuries" and consumer durables such as lawn mowers, cars, and television sets. They used not the language of housekeeping but that of technical expertise.

Considering Vance Packard's perspective on "waste making," it is noteworthy that more exacting standards for private domesticity silently accompanied this trend. During the 1950s, working-class organizations in France advocated obtaining a shared washing machine. In the following decades, consumer needs became increasingly privatized and possession—not use—became the standard solution. The products of cooperatives were seen as low-brow, while colorful labels and new products consistently referred to consumers' unconscious desires and fears. One suddenly had to fashion an identity through products and procure every good for oneself. As one "scientific" consumer advice piece stated in Belgium, "a sandbox in the backyard is better for children than a crowded beach."[37] The mid-century prestige of technocracy, especially the authority of the exact sciences, played a decisive role here too. The gaze of the engineer trumped the perspective of the socially concerned housewife.

Consumer organizations surely responded to a genuine need for information on new products, technologies, and services that the mass of European consumers was unaccustomed to. But the boom of consumer organizations also owed a lot to political and business attempts to restore and stabilize "everyday" life after the chaotic first half of the twentieth century. Both Belgian consumer movements—both organizations and their subscribers—were in a sense direct, complementary responses by civil society to consumer engineering as mid-century social engineering. But they did not agree on the extent to which a consumer protection organization could itself use consumer engineering, meaning a set of methods for marketing and advertising. As for the critique of planned obsolescence and corporate manipulation, there was actually surprisingly little difference between the market liberal and Social-Democratic Belgian consumer movements. UFIDEC might have been more on guard ideologically, more willing to criticize consumer society, but TA needed scoops and spectacular findings. Neither movement was afraid to tell companies some hard truths about low-quality products.

Limits to Growth (1973–2000): Late-Modern Insecurities

With the indispensable support of foreign partners, Christian-Democratic organizations, and social elites, TA's strategic advantage in terms of marketing ensured it a critical number of subscribers. From the late sixties, this set a self-sustaining cycle in motion, as new members provided additional revenues, which could in turn be used to advertise TA to potential members. At its peak in the seventies, TA had a dazzling 300,000 subscriptions. Despite structural underfinancing, UFIDEC peaked at about 200,000 members. But UFIDEC's membership began to dwindle earlier than TA's did.[38] Compared to mass movements like the Christian-Democratic and Social-Democratic trade unions (both with almost a million members in 1971), consumer movements were of course still midgets. But considering that the average circulation of a Belgian newspaper in 1980 was 87,300 copies and that the political scientist Paul Claeys estimated that one in three household units in Belgium received some consumer advice periodical in the seventies, consumer periodicals were indeed popular.[39]

If the spectacular growth of consumer organizations owed much to a mid-century belief in technocracy and modernity as self-evident categories, this growth was seriously undermined by a number of social contradictions and tensions during the period of late modernity. The energy crises of 1973 and 1979 are often taken as the symbolic starting points of this period, which can be differentiated from "organized" or "high" modernity by increased individualization, globalization, and complexity, not to mention fundamental changes in the Belgian economy (most notably, abandoning full-employment policies, instead focusing on inflation and budgetary orthodoxy). The consumer movements, products of the Keynesian-Fordist compromise, now faced a difficult situation. Their sales started collapsing dramatically after the energy crisis and the ensuing period of austerity and unemployment in Belgium, part of a structural phenomenon that threatened all private consumer movements in the West.[40] Between 1981 and 1984, TA lost nearly 15% of its members. Alarmed by the signs, but unwilling to make more investments, Belgian Social Democracy abruptly sacrificed UFIDEC in 1984, halting its funding.[41]

At first, this crisis led movements of the Anglo-Saxon type to invest in even more sophisticated branding. But by the nineties, more fundamental analyses were made with regard to private, independent comparative testing as a sound business model.[42] The test itself lost its legitimacy even among those most convinced of its value. Consumer activists also noticed that public efforts for consumer protection were becoming more prevalent. Whereas during the fifties the British, Dutch, and Belgian consumer organizations exhorted each other to start testing even the most insignificant objects (the example of matches was given) as quickly as possible, TA admitted by the late nineties that "a test of ballpoint pens seems completely nonsensical nowadays."[43] The typical techniques of marketing (one) affluent lifestyle to the general public—techniques that had guaranteed success during the sixties and early seventies—no longer seemed to work as segmentation became the name of the game. Readership declined, and the magazines came to seem old-fashioned. What were the causes and how did the consumer activists involved in them reflect on what happened?

Consumer movements had built their success on a generational cohort that was disappearing. Lifelong, loyal subscribers of UFIDEC and TA passed away in the eighties. In the case of UFIDEC, the inability to rejuvenate was especially marked, not just among rank-and-file members but even in the leadership of the organization itself. The second wave of feminism had severed the a priori connection between women and the household, thereby rerouting women's activism toward other goals. To a lesser extent, the countercultural reaction against mass consumer society made it difficult for traditional consumer movements to connect with younger generations. As fair trade activism, small-scale organic production, the squatter movement, boycotts of South African oranges (supported from early on by Social-Democratic women), and other forms of protest gained momentum, regarding product quality as the alpha and omega of consumer awareness became an anachronism.

Yet looking at generations is a somewhat tautological explanation for change. Down to the present day, the countercultural consumer movements form a niche—they are merely a sliver of the mass market on which comparative testing organizations built their success. Countercultural consciousness affected TA's growth potential somewhat, but not its growth per se. Were there in fact more inherent factors that undermined the sale and distribution of comparative testing results?

Organized consumerism offered information. And by the eighties, their product was in fact unattractive on a number of levels. Test results from a laboratory were often less conclusive than they were made to appear. The interpretation of results was complex and often entailed more normative values than management wished to admit. Methods of analysis were not always up to date—as innovation speeds up, today's technical knowledge is surpassed tomorrow.[44] More complicated and relevant analyses (for example, on the long-term effects of certain additives) required longitudinal scientific studies, which consumer movements—even the mighty American CU—could not afford.[45] Consumer organizations also did very little research on durability and sustainable production, especially compared to more obvious or superficial parameters.[46] Additionally, their format was not particularly user-friendly. Before the Internet allowed consumer movements to set up database-like Web sites, readers who truly wanted to make informed everyday purchases had to collect all issues and hope that the editor's selections would cater to their needs. Testing projects sometimes took over a year to complete.[47] With fast changes in product lines, TA's subscribers sometimes felt embarrassed for demanding outdated products in the shop.[48] It should thus not surprise us that few bought into a luxury item that often did not give them much practical advice, especially in times of austerity.

Economic factors also contributed to the decline of product testing. The market for the industrial, mass-produced consumables upon which comparative testing had been founded had reached some degree of maturity. During the eighties, many products had been subjected to qualitative standardization or had been made safe—in many cases due to (international) legislation—to the extent that repeated testing cycles became redundant.[49] In a few other cases, the mass market in fact offered nothing but substandard quality. In these latter cases, consumer magazines of the Anglo-Saxon type had little constructive advice to give since they did not advocate any control over production. They were simply dealing with the market as it was, not as it could or should have been. Because the magazines catered to a general mass audience, referring to more expensive niche markets was not an easy option either.[50]

Moreover, service sector spending (ranging from doctors to insurance and plumbers) began to form a more significant expenditure item, while comparative testing organizations claimed that these were more difficult to test. A final economic difficulty was increasingly intense competition in the information market. Consumer advice had become a successful template, offered by the general media, on television, in specialized outlets (for instance, professional wine catalogs), and later through peer groups on the Internet, "advertorials" and so on. Consumer magazines no longer had a monopoly on their core activity.

The social factors that private comparative testing organizations identified as working to their detriment are even more revealing. During the nineties, TA and the Dutch Consumentenbond suggested privately that postmodern shoppers were suffering from information overload and time pressure. Modern-day consumers had allegedly become less prepared to invest time in the shopping process than their predecessors had been.[51] This seems to indicate that domesticity and informed spending (especially when simple products are involved) had lost much of their social legitimacy. One obvious contributing factor was the rise of the two-income household, with rising time pressure. Additionally, it might be the case that many former luxuries had become simple basics to which consumers give little thought. Do we want to read about vacuum cleaners, or should we spent time finding a fitting retirement plan? Another tentative possibility is that advertisers restored their image of corporate reliability, which had been contested more intensively during the radical seventies.

Interestingly, as the state let go of Keynesian or Fordist economic planning policies in the seventies and beyond, individuals seem to have let go of the ideal of an organized household as well.[52] They increasingly began to expect hard action and legal victories from consumer movements. The global popularity of Ralph Nader (who was much more combative than the comparative testing movement) is a case in point. Consumer movements found that their (often depressing) media scoops earned them less loyalty than fighting for a convincing regulatory framework. During the seventies, Belgian consumers actually began to complain that the producers of consumer information "did nothing for them, except lie and manipulate."[53]

At the same time, consumers showed less tolerance for the somewhat patronizing tone adopted in the fifties and sixties by the technocrats engaged in comparative testing. One of TA's lifelong staff members claimed that prominent technological disasters of the era such as Bhopal (an industrial accident in India that caused massive chemical pollution in 1984) and Chernobyl (the nuclear accident in Ukraine that was labeled a level seven event on the International Nuclear and Radiological Event Scale) had undercut the ideological prestige of the exact sciences.

On a more basic level, Belgian comparative testers began to ask themselves during the nineties how they could sell consumer advice to a "generation of potentially unemployed." As labor became increasingly precarious and full-employment policies were sacrificed for monetarist ones, consumer movements felt the consequences. According to Jacques Neirynck of TA, people no longer looked to consumer periodicals to tell them how to spend their money (which they like to do for themselves), but rather for how to participate most efficiently in a "savings society." This explains the relative and continuing success of one of TA's side businesses, magazines offering financial and legal advice.[54] Additionally, some pointed out that "one-parent families, migrant families and a growing group of pensioners" meant less uniform, even contradictory demands for information.[55] The surprising conclusion might be that postwar advice for the mass consumer, including even the selection of products and their appraisal, thrived on uniformity rather than on the far-reaching individualization of late modernity.

But the issue was not consumer spending per se, which still enjoys higher levels today than in the seventies. Rather, consumers value different things now, and consumer movements operate in a different kind of society. While income has risen since the seventies and eighties, in some ways consumers now live more precarious lives. Consider, for instance, that during the nineties divorce rates rose sharply along with the prices of property. The fact that policies of the Belgian government in the late eighties stimulated shareholdership and participation in pension funds explain why TA's laboratory equipment for dishwashers became less essential than its unit on financial investments. The model of commercial comparative testing was now operating in a very different institutional setting.

Saving Consumer-Owned Comparative Testing?

Some of those involved in comparative testing have admitted privately that perhaps the testing format itself could or should be abandoned. But few organizations liquidate themselves voluntarily. Representatives of what used to be called the "independent" Anglo-Saxon model of consumerism are now effectively private organizations who identify as nonprofits but which need to survive commercially to keep up their non-profitable activities. These activities, mainly advocacy and lobbying, are the ones that their audience really expects from them. The magazine publishers had to reinvent themselves as they could no longer rely on their status-enhancing image.[56] To compensate for a more fickle audience, TA tried to optimize its existing marketing strategies already during the early eighties. Rather than asking for a full yearly fee, TA invited its members to make automatic monthly payments. Such interventions aimed at lessening the psychological resistance of consumers to spending their money on subscriptions.[57] Some consumer movements started selling issues at newspaper stands too.

A better or more enticing version of the same, however, could not change the tide. In the context of the late-modern insecurities discussed, the capital-intensive model of comparative testing did not seem to offer enough value for money to sustain itself through member revenue only. Consumer movements in the West reacted to this development in different ways, and their efforts continue to be innovative and interesting. From the perspective of this volume, their most interesting strategy was the shift from doing "consumer engineering" in the name of consumer defense to becoming more all-round service providers. During the nineties, the Belgian consumer movement considered providing services to other businesses (B2B), a valuable form of additional income. Such activities would have been seen as a complete betrayal during the fifties, sixties, and seventies. Nonetheless, TA proposed to produce content for other publishers or to participate in small public research projects.[58]

Even more remarkably, some consumer organizations have increasingly invested in loyalty schemes, through which they offer consumers not just information but also sustained material advantages and discounts. TA has had a call center and legal advice service since the late eighties, but during the nineties it actually planned to offer a versatile TA credit card, much like the British CA had done before them. Because of the sensitivity of the matter (consumer defense and stimulating indebtedness do not rhyme), the credit card scheme was eventually abandoned. But members of TA could until fairly recently still access a host of advantages, cheaper rates, and even accounts with beneficial interest rates that ordinary consumers could not earn.[59] Because this shift toward becoming a "service club" amounts to a cooperation with business that gives TA a stake in a commercial partnership, it has been criticized by insiders and outsiders alike. Tellingly, the idea of cooperatives, which have recently been rediscovered as an inclusive, valuable tool for social change, had been completely discarded by TA's founders, who consistently favored the high-brow idea of a commercial "service club."[60]

Although the available documents suggest that the Belgian consumer movements protected the balance in favor of consumer interests (for instance by selecting only the most consumer-friendly business partners), this strategy has significantly blurred the social movement dimension that consumer unions have historically always manifested. In 1980, TA even went to trial over the matter and claimed that certain of its marketing practices could not be condemned by the law on commercial practices since "the objective [of TA] is not to sell subscriptions, it is to unify and defend consumers."[61] This was in clear contrast to decades of earlier statements, which had claimed that TA was not a political movement like the Social-Democratic UFIDEC. In other words, when it came to marketing, TA claimed it was not an impartial company but an activist social movement. When it came to politics, however, it claimed the reverse.

This mix of interest group and company has historically lain at the core of postwar organized consumerism. TA's strategies to replace the old forms of "consumer engineering" made for a more confused, less secure situation because it laid itself open to charges that it was in the pocket of producers.

Conclusion

This chapter outlines the historical conditions under which a technocratic, commodified version of consumer activism arose in postwar Belgium. It also traces how these consumer movements have used consumer tests to engineer—or anticipate—consumer preferences for their own institutional survival. Yet comparative testing was not just a scientific project that harnessed engineering and "objectivity" to guide the masses. Instead, the Anglo-Saxon approach to consumer activism was based on partisan political motivations. Moreover, consumer organizations like TA dismissed any ethical objections to new marketing practices such as direct mailing, subscriptions with premiums, and psychological approaches to advertising its "product." Its competitor UFIDEC, on the other hand, protected the balance between pursuing sales and stimulating social mobilization more rigidly. Their less aggressive marketing stance and a lack of investments made UFIDEC the more vulnerable consumer movement, leading to its liquidation in 1984. But these outcomes should not just be analyzed in terms of professionalization. What appears at first sight as the result of professionalization and dynamism in fact owed much to certain cultural codes bounded by class and gender and embedded within transnational networks of knowledge exchange. Moreover, TA's approach to consumer engineering only worked so well because of a specific configuration of social and political forces. There was, for instance, the buildup of a welfare state in a Keynesian-Fordist political economy, the importance of social distinction through domesticity, the breadwinner–housekeeper model, and the belief that the exact sciences provided the most objective criteria for good ways of consuming. The technocrats of TA actively claimed to be the sole consumer experts in Belgium, using their "American-style" model to reinforce their authority.

When comparative testing organizations faced challenges during the eighties and nineties, it turned out that their market value was essentially related to social and historical forces more than any intrinsic value of their "product." It became clear that a social movement for consumers could not simply be reduced to a product, even if it relied on some of the established corporate recipes to survive. TA's ambivalent attitude toward its own goals was often criticized, and the 1980 court trial shows that the organization relied on some degree of doublespeak. Today, TA has to compete with NGOs and interest groups that do not sell but rather rally enthusiasm for social causes.

The transition toward a more changeable or fluid society undermined the conditions under which comparative testing had thrived. A host of economic and social factors made testing magazines (the technocratic, objective, and "modern" approach for consumer protection) seemingly obsolete for younger generations. Organizing consumers today requires more social efforts and political expertise than during the sixties, when it was seemingly a matter of hiring an engineer and testing six cars. Yet if Belgian-organized consumerism adopted new strategies during the nineties, this was not because of ideological or reflective discussion about its goals and future. Rather, the organization was not able to conceptualize a place for organized consumerism outside of the market.

Combining social reform with commodification hence entailed some risks because it endangered the activism as soon as sales dropped. One could also criticize how only a specific, well-off audience could truly participate in this form of activism. Most consumer associations were able to walk a reasonable middle ground as long as their membership was on the rise. But as the economy began to globalize, so did consumer risks. Here again, the transformation into a commercialized service provider presented risks. Interest groups that defended something of a public (or general) interest had their own specific appeal. But the new strategy of offering individual premiums and discounts could strip consumerism even more of *ideological* richness and an inclusive social message. How a general publication like that of TA could compete with ever faster flows of (free) information without reminding readers of its postwar ideals and its potential for social change remains unclear. The days of organized consumerism as a mass movement and as a countervailing political force were, if not numbered, then at least uncertain.

Finally, the Belgian case illustrates that consumer engineering was not a straightforward game of easy manipulation. The supply side (in this case TA) was caught in an intense fight for an ever elusive demand side (the Belgian population). Rather than creating consumers, comparative testing organizations had to investigate the everyday lives of their readers and guess the extent to which their product matched the wishes of this audience. There were failures (such as TA's first efforts at direct mailing) and alternative approaches (like the social movement perspective adopted by UFIDEC). During the sixties, TA used social status and conformity, whereas UFIDEC stressed social commitment. During the late eighties, things were no longer as clear-cut.

An organization like TA has in fact created an important, even performative reality. TA's perennial focus on value for money for the individual shopper was not at all a widespread concern in Belgian society when the organization first started publishing in the late fifties. TA was able to produce a more critical consumer (for instance when it asked local governments to extend their opening hours[62]), even if it sometimes divorced production too rigidly from the overall political system (for instance, when Gilbert Castelain claimed that TA would never dissuade people from investing in South African gold mines despite Apartheid[63]). But as TA had to convince the so-called Gen Xers and millennials of its value, its own conceptualization of the consumer interest backfired somewhat. From that perspective, as well, TA's version of consumer engineering was only a transitory phenomenon.

Notes

1. Paul Claeys, *Groupes de pression en Belgique: les groupes intermédiaires socio-économiques. Contribution à l'analyse comparative* (Brussels, 1973), 259. This figure was a combination of subscribers to TA, UFIDEC, and the Family League (a group set up in 1921 to represent large families, which redefined its mission after 1958 to focus more on consumer education).
2. Matthew Hilton, *Prosperity for All: Consumer Activism in an Era of Globalization* (London, 2009), 25.
3. Sociologists such as Anthony Giddens and Zygmunt Bauman contrast late modernity with the notion of postmodernity. The latter term implies a total rupture with the project of modernity and the tendencies associated with it. By contrast, sociologists of late modernity argue that changes that began in the late seventies, changes that are now coming to full fruition, represent an intensification of modernity rather than a break with it.
4. Stuart Chase, *Your Money's Worth: A Study in the Waste of the Consumer's Dollar* (New York, 1927), 285.
5. See Jacqueline Dirks, "Righteous Goods: Women's Production, Reform Publicity and the National Consumers' League, 1891–1919" (Ph.D. diss., Yale University, 1996); and Lizabeth Cohen, *A Consumers' Republic: The Politics of Mass Consumption in Postwar America* (New York, 2003), 22.
6. Quoted from Inger Stole, *Advertising on Trial: Consumer Activism and Corporate Public Relations in the 1930s* (Chicago, IL, 2006), 94.
7. Lawrence Glickman, "The Strike in the Temple of Consumption: Consumer Activism and Twentieth-Century American Political Culture," *Journal of American History* 88, no. 1 (June 2001): 109; and Lawrence Glickman, *Buying Power: A History of Consumer Activism in America* (Chicago, IL, 2009), 194 and 207.
8. Consumer Union Archives, New York (hereafter CU), Colston Warne Papers, 119/3 Lecture series on consumerism for the Kansas State University, 1977.
9. This is explored in more detail in part two of Giselle Nath, "Shaping Consumer Interests: Belgian Consumer Movements between Technocracy, Social-Democracy and Cold War Internationalization" (Ph.D. diss., University of Ghent, 2016).

10. I am not adopting Mancur Olson's a priori assumptions about the presumed weak mobilization of consumers or the inevitability of free-rider behaviour. On this issue, see Gunnar Trumbull, *Strength in Numbers: The Organization of Weak Interests* (Cambridge, MA, 2012).
11. See, for instance, Letter Reich to Mason, August 25, 1961, Colston Warne Papers 27/1, CU and Political charter of the union Belge des Consommateurs (s.d.), Fund Willy Van Rijckeghem (hereafter Ughent, WVR) 111, University of Ghent Archives.
12. Kansas State University, Thomas Brooks Collection, Box 1 Administrative Files, folder 6, C. Warne, Proceedings of the 2nd Institute on consumer problems of the University of Minnesota, September 10–11, 1956 (unpublished research paper on consumer problems in Europe), p. 22 (hereafter C. Warne, *Proceedings of the 2nd Institute…*) Many thanks to Anthony Crawford of the Consumer Movement Archives at Kansas University.
13. "Financiële steun?" *Test-Achats*, no. 42, May 1965, and again in no. 50, March 1966.
14. C. Warne, *Proceedings of the 2nd Institute* 28: "On all of this, I think Europe has a very real lesson for us because of the progressiveness of some of these undertakings. We will have to look to Europe for leadership. I think we [in the United States] have exported a little and we can import quite a little too."
15. Ibid., 23.
16. In the Belgian context, this is known as subsidiary liberty. See, for instance, *Test-Achats*, no. 53, June 1966.
17. For a detailed overview, see Nath, "Shaping Consumer Interests," 224–57.
18. See, for instance, "De verbruikers en de macht," *De bediende*, May 1962.
19. Ughent, WVR, 44, transcript of interview with Gilbert Castelain of TA by J. Blavier, 1992, 24.
20. *Test-Achats*, no. 5, June 1960.
21. Ughent, WVR, 114, Situation des effectifs de [TA], October 3, 1961.
22. "On leur écrivait un mot: "vous êtes militante, les consommateurs doivent s'organiser, etc.," Gilbert Castelain interview, 27.
23. Ughent, WVR, 113, Bulletin de Liaison (for executive members), 1e trimester 1962.
24. Ughent, WVR, 114, Van Rijckeghem to Delfosse (Kredietbank), November 13, 1961.
25. "Hoe zullen wij het aanpakken?" *Test-Aankoop*, no. 15, December 1952; "Herinnering aan operatie 1…2…3," *Test-Aankoop*, no. 18, March 1963; and "Aktie 64," *Test-Aankoop*, no. 28, February 1964.
26. C. Matton, *La défense des consommateurs en Belgique de 1957 à 1984: UFIDEC et Test-Achats* (Unpublished Masters' Thesis, Université Libre de Bruxelles, 2005), 121.
27. Ughent, WVR, 113, minutes of the board meeting of January 9, 1962.
28. Gilbert Castelain interview, 42.
29. Ibid., 56.
30. W. Van Rijckeghem, *L'histoire de Test-Achats: d'une revue de consommateurs à une multinationale* (Brussels, 2005), 88 and 93; and "Le célèbre Ralph Nader a été accaparé par Test-Achats?" *Le Peuple*, April 25, 1973.

31. M. Driessen, "De Vrouwenbond voor Informatie en Verdediging van de Consument (VIVEC), 1959–1984" (Ph.D. diss., Free University of Brussels, 2014), 84 and 91.
32. "Défense et représentation des consommateurs," *Rapports du Centre de Recherches* et d'information socio-politiques (hereafter CRISP reports), no. 699, October 1975; and M. Driessen, *De Vrouwenbond voor Informatie*, 102.
33. "Schipperen is onze regel niet," UFIDEC no. 175 (1981); and C. Matton, *La défense des consommateurs en Belgique*, 102.
34. L. Van Outrive, "De differentiatie in de arbeidersklasse," *De Gids op maatschappelijk gebied*, no. 9, September 1961, 749; and *Test-Achats*, July 1959, 8.
35. For this middle-class bias of TA's membership, see the graph in J. Bohets, ed., *Het land waarin wij werken: Een doorlichting van het Belgisch economisch systeem* (Antwerpen, 1975), 168. For an example of such conservative beliefs, see "Dagboek van een consument," *Test-Achats*, no. 54, January 1966.
36. E. Vanhaute, "Het kostwinnersmodel als historische fictie: Arbeid en inkomen van gezinnen in langeterijnperspectief," in *Het kostwinnersmodel voorbij? Naar een nieuw basismodel voor de arbeidsverdeling binnen de gezinnen*, ed. W. Van Dongen et al. (Leuven, 1998), 62.
37. Rebecca J. Pulju, *Women and Mass Consumer Society in Postwar France* (Cambridge, UK, 2011), 168n; and *Koop zo het best*, no. 3, 1980, 12–13.
38. Interview with Armand De Wasch of TA in *Trends: Financieel-economisch magazine*, November 7, 1966, 36.
39. Val Lorwin, "Labor Unions and Political Parties in Belgium," *Industrial and Labor Relations Review* 28, no. 2 (1975): 250; Paul Claeys, *Groupes de pression en Belgique: Les groupes intermédiaires socio-économiques: Contribution à l'analyse comparative* (Brussels, 1973), 295; and Sylvie De Schryvere, "De evolutie van de oplage van de Belgische dagbladpers: 1960–1990" (Ph.D. diss., University of Ghent, 1992), 39. This average refers to the papers in the Dutch-speaking market, at the time the largest. The Belgian press in the French language had an average circulation of 43,200 copies per title, but there were more titles available.
40. Ughent, WVR, 66, *Consumer information in developed countries* (note for the 15th IOCU congress in Chile), 1997.
41. Van Rijckeghem, *L'histoire de Test-Achats*, 154.
42. Public institutions for testing face, of course, other challenges.
43. Ughent, WVR, board meeting of Conseur, 1997 (Milan).
44. "Les consommateurs en Belgique," *CRISP Reports*, no. 12 (1978): 7.
45. Conversations with CU employees by the author, February 2015.
46. Ughent, WVR, 27, Ecologie et consumérisme: réflexions sur l'Association des Consommateurs, sa politique, ses choix et ses champs d'actions," 2002.
47. Ughent, WVR, 66, "The future of consumer magazines in Holland" (note for the 15th IOCU Congress in Chile), 1997.
48. Gilbert Castelain interview, 69.
49. Ughent, WVR, 121, board meeting Euro-Labo, April 15, 1980.
50. Ughent, WVR, 72, Quel futur pour le test comparative? (note by Jacques Neirynck), 1997.
51. Ughent, WVR, 66, Consumer information in developed countries (note for the 15th IOCU Congress in Chile), 1997.

52. Additional, the idea of consumers as a necessary countervailing power has also been undercut by neoliberal tendencies. While in the Dutch case this decoupling of consumer self-organizing and public policy resulted in fewer public subsidies for consumer organizations, the Belgian TA did not rely on government funding and was thus not affected by cuts or new policy visions. Ughent, WVR, 66, The future of consumer magazines in Holland (note for the 15th IOCU Congress in Chile), 1997.
53. *Koop zo het best* 11, no. 2 (1973); *Test-Achats*, no. 110, September 1971; and Ughent, WVR, 54, interview of Gilbert Castelain by Jean Blavier, 1992.
54. Ughent, WVR, 72, Quel futur pour le test comparative? (note by Jacques Neirynck), 1997 and 66, The future of consumer magazines in Holland (note for the 15th IOCU congress in Chile), 1997.
55. Ughent, WVR, 66, the future of consumer magazines in Holland (note for the 15th IOCU congress in Chile), 1997.
56. Quel futur pour le test comparative? (note by Jacques Neirynck), 1997.
57. Gilbert Castelain, interview, 72; and E. Van Vooren, *Direct marketing praktijkboek: tips, cases en adviezen* (Leuven, 2006), 13.
58. Ughent, WVR 87, business plan 2001.
59. See Ughent, WVR, board meeting Conseur, January 30, 1998; "Test-Aankoop mikt op ledenkorting." *De Standaard*, August 24, 2006; and "Special offer for members of Test-Achats," https://www.fortuneo.be/nl/partners/test-aankoop, last consulted September 2015.
60. Ughent, WVR, 73, board meeting Conseur, March 1998, 8: "Certain of the proposed activities represent a return to the spirit of the cooperative, an old-fashioned idea abandoned two centuries ago. We hesitate to see our organization engage with it."
61. Ughent, WVR, 121 Press statement April 28, 1980 ("Test-Achats n'est pas un produit").
62. *Test-Achats*, no. 99, September 1970.
63. Gilbert Castelain interview, 99.

Index

J. Logemann et al. (eds.), *Consumer Engineering, 1920s–1970s*, Worlds of Consumption, https://doi.org/10.1007/978-3-030-14564-4

Zeitfracht Medien GmbH
Ferdinand-Jühlke-Straße 7
99095 Erfurt, Deutschland
produktsicherheit@kolibri360.de